INTERNATIONAL URBAN PLANNING SETTINGS: LESSONS OF SUCCESS

INTERNATIONAL REVIEW OF COMPARATIVE PUBLIC POLICY

Series Editors: Nicholas Mercuro
Michigan State University, USA

Philip R. Smith
Michigan State University, USA

INTERNATIONAL REVIEW OF COMPARATIVE
PUBLIC POLICY   VOLUME 12

INTERNATIONAL URBAN PLANNING SETTINGS: LESSONS OF SUCCESS

EDITED BY

JACK F. WILLIAMS

*Department of Geography, Michigan State University
East Lansing, MI 48824, USA*

ROBERT J. STIMSON

*School of Geography, Planning and Architecture,
University of Queensland, Sst. Lucia, Brisbane, QLD 4072 Australia*

2001

JAI
An Imprint of Elsevier Science

Amsterdam – London – New York – Oxford – Paris – Shannon – Tokyo

ELSEVIER SCIENCE Ltd
The Boulevard, Langford Lane
Kidlington, Oxford OX5 1GB, UK

First edition 2001

Library of Congress Cataloging in Publication Data
A catalog record from the Library of Congress has been applied for.

British Library Cataloguing in Publication Data
A catalogue record from the British Library has been applied for.

ISBN: 0-7623-0695-5

⊚ The paper used in this publication meets the requirements of ANSI/NISO Z39.48-1992 (Permanence of Paper).
Printed in The Netherlands.

CONTENTS

LIST OF CONTRIBUTORS

Kenneth E. Corey	Office of the Vice President for Research & Graduate Studies, Michigan State University, USA
John Dean	Cairns Region Economic Development Corporation, Cairns, Queensland, Australia
Chi Wing Ho	Department of Architecture, University of Hong Kong, Hong Kong
Laura Huntoon	School of Planning, College of Architecture, Planning, and Landscape Architecture, University of Arizona, Tucson, Arizona, USA
Andrew J. Jacobs	School of Planning, University of Cincinnati, Cincinnati, Ohio, USA
Mitsuhiko Kawakami	Department of Civil Engineering, University of Kanazawa, Japan
Rajendra Kulkarni	The School of Public Policy, George Mason University, Fairfax, Virginia, USA
Guicai Li	Land & Planning Bureau of Futian District, Shenzhen, China
Tatsuo Masuta	Department of Architecture and Planning, Kanazawa Institute of Technology, Ishikawaken, Japan
Gina Meng	Department of Urban & Environmental Science, Peking University, China

Breada J. Moscove   Department of Finance School of Business &
                         Public Administration, California State
                         University, Bakersfield, California, USA

Peter Newman   Institute for Sustainability and Technology
                         Policy, Murdoch University, Perth, Western
                         Australia, Australia

Manuel Perez   Urban Art Design & Development
                         Consultants, California, USA

Cboon Piew Pow   Department of Geography, National
                         University of Singapore, Singapore

Trevor Reddacliff   Brisbane City Council Urban Renewal Task
                         Force, Brisbane, Australia

Brian Roberts   Queensland University of Technology,
                         Brisbane, Queensland, Australia

Victor Savage   Department of Geography, National
                         University of Singapore, Singapore

Robert Stimson   School of Geography, Planning and
                         Architecture, University of Queensland,
                         Brisbane, Queensland, Australia

Roger Stough   The Center for Regional Analysis and
                         Transport Policy, George Mason University,
                         Fairfax, Virginia, USA

Akahito Tani   Department of Architecture and Planning,
                         Kanazawa Institute of Technology,
                         Ishikawaken, Japan

Bruce Taylor   The Open University of Hong Kong,
                         Hong Kong

Mark Yaolin Wang   Department of Geography & Environmental
                         Studies, University of Melbourne,
                         Melbourne, Australia

Richard Watson   Richard Watson & Associates, LLC, Mission Viejo, California, USA

Jack F. Williams   Department of Geography, Michigan State University, East Lansing, Michigan, USA

Mark I. Wilson   Urban & Regional Planning Program, Michigan State University, East Lansing, USA

Elwyn Wyeth   Elwyn Wyeth Management, Spring Hill, Queensland, Australia

STATEMENT OF SCOPE

The *International Review of Comparative Public Policy* is an interdisciplinary series dedicated to publishing original scholarly contributions that systematically analyze international public policy issues. It is a nationally refereed annual, sponsored by the Center for Advanced Study of International Development, Michigan State University. Each yearly edition is devoted to a different public policy issue that can benefit from comparative political, legal, economic, and social scientific examination. The topic, together with the volume editor(s), is selected through a competitive prospectus-selection process.

An individual who is interested in editing a future volume of the *International Review of Comparative Public Policy* should submit three copies of a 5-page, double-spaced prospectus to either of the Series Editors. Each prospectus must include: (1) identification of the issue / topic and a prospective title of the volume; (2) a detailed description of the international dimensions of the particular policy issue; (3) a statement as to why and how the chosen issue can benefit from a comparative political, legal, economic, and social scientific examination, and most important, (4) a list of potential contributors along with tentative titles of their contributions. Each edition is expected to contain contributions from both the United States and abroad.

Please note that the Series Editors do not accept individual manuscripts for publication consideration.

Send prospectus to either:

Nicholas Mercuro, *Series Editor*
E-mail: mercuro@msu.edu

or

Philip R. Smith, *Series Editor*
E-mail: phlsmith@msu.edu

Center for Advanced Study of International Development,
Michigan State University, 306 Berkey Hall, East Lansing, MI 48824

1. INTERNATIONAL URBAN SETTINGS: INNOVATION IN PLANNING APPROACHES

Jack F. Williams and Robert J. Stimson

INTRODUCTION

The literature on urban development around the world is replete with the stories of failures and the multitude of problems facing urban centers everywhere, but especially in the less developed countries. This is not surprising, in that scholars and practitioners in urban development/urban planning tend to seek out problems that need analyzing and solutions. Such literature, however, can easily convey a sense of frustration and hopelessness, an attitude that the world's urban problems defy real resolution.

A desire to provide some balance to negativist literature was the foundation for development of this volume of contributions, by a variety of scholars and practitioners from a number of countries, especially those situated around the Pacific Rim. While never intending to underestimate the magnitude and variety of problems facing urban centers everywhere, nonetheless, in this volume we deliberately chose to highlight innovative approaches to planning and urban development through what might be termed "urban success stories." By this expression, we are referring to cities and regions in various places that have managed to develop urban planning policies or strategies for development that have been successful or at least hold great promise of success. The variety of cultural and geographic settings represented in the chapters in this book provide what we hope will be a useful collection of case studies of

International Urban Planning Settings: Lessons of Success, Volume 12, pages 1–17.
2001 by Elsevier Science Ltd.
ISBN: 0-7623-0695-5

contemporary innovative approaches to urban and regional planning, policy and development.

SHIFTS IN PLANNING APPROACHES

Not all that long ago, planning, and public policy associated with it, tended to be quite narrowly focused on: (a) the allocation of land to accommodate projected future urban and regional population growth; (b) the zoning of land for commercial, industrial, residential and open space users; and (c) the provision of hard infrastructure, including transport networks.

However, during the last three to four decades, urban and regional planning has changed dramatically, to embrace issues having to do with: (a) social justice and equity in the provision of access to human services; (b) economic development and employment; and (c) environmental quality. The planning process also has evolved, moving away from "top-down" planning to more "bottom-up" approaches incorporating consultative mechanisms and community participation. In addition, planning has evolved to become more concerned with processes and mechanisms of urban and regional governance and management, and a focus began to be placed on integrating planning with broader strategic frameworks for the development and management of cities, towns, and regions.

But also during the 1980s, and especially into the 1990s, there was an increasing concern with issues to do with the environment, and in particular new planning paradigms emerged incorporating principles of "sustainability" in the development of cities and regions. This led to the development of frameworks to guide local and regional planning which have integrated economic, social, and environmental concerns.

More recently we have seen the emergence of considerable community concern over the paradoxical uneven distributional outcomes, across both people and places, in the impacts of processes of "globalization", creating increasing tensions between the concepts of globalism and localism. This is presenting significant new challenges for governments at all levels in terms of what are the appropriate planning responses to a situation where local and regional divides seem to be increasing.

We also need to recognize that dramatic changes have emerged in the nature and structure of households and families, that there have been major shifts in gender roles, that in many places communities are becoming much more diverse in terms of their multiculturalism. An incredibly dynamic set of social processes have emerged that are generating widely diverse lifestyles with profound implications for the nature of demand for different types of housing, goods and services in human settlements.

Finally, rapidly changing technologies, particularly in telecommunications with its attendant innovations in the way production processes operate and how business is transacted-as seen, for example, in the emergence of e-commerce-present even more complex challenges for planners and policy makers.

CASE STUDIES OF INNOVATION AND SUCCESS IN URBAN AND REGIONAL PLANNING AND DEVELOPMENT

In describing and evaluating case studies which represent a range of different approaches to urban and regional planning and development, we need to be aware of the macro societal and the micro local level processes of change in which plans and projects are conceived and implemented.

What we have sought to do is to select a range of case studies which represent both innovative approaches to planning formulation and implementation and the public policy philosophies underlying them, and which have demonstrated, by and large, successful development outcomes.

The case studies have been organized into three broad groupings:

(1) The six case studies in Part 1 (Chapters 2 through 7) represent a range of approaches at the macro level of city-wide or regional planning and policy development and implementation.
(2) The five case studies in Part 2 (Chapters 8 through 12) focus on more micro level planning projects and policies which incorporate and emphasize participation and partnership approaches in the context of urban renewal or historic preservation.
(3) The three case studies in Part 3 (Chapters 13 through 15) address either the impacts of a major event or of new technology and new industry development and the planning initiatives or responses that are or could be occurring.

City and Regional Planning Strategy

The six chapters in Part 1 reflect many of the contemporary planning issues referred to above as the authors look at the overall process of effective master or strategic planning in four existing cities (Nagoya, Japan; Cairns, Australia; Singapore; Long Beach, California; and the Brisbane-South East Queensland region in Australia) and one completely new city (Shenzhen, China). Six very different cities, in six very different geographical and cultural environments, yet all sharing commonalities in the relative success of the planners in developing viable and vibrant urban places that residents are glad to call "home".

However, these case studies differ also in both the time scale of planning and policy formulation and the development implementation being considered and in the scope of focus, some having a broad comprehensive concern about the overall development of a city or region, and some having a more specific concern such as regional economic development.

In Chapter 2 Andrew Jacobs brings a fresh outsider's analysis of Japan's third largest city, Nagoya, and shows how, in the face of global restructuring and many other factors pushing population and employment to the suburbs, Nagoya City has remained the locus of activity in the Chukyo Region, adding population and jobs. Nagoya thus has seen far less of its share of population and economic activity shift to the suburbs than most other cities in Japan, especially its two largest rivals, Tokyo and Osaka. A combination of national statutes, capacity building prefectural policies, and progressive city planning have been the keys to Nagoya's success. Nagoya's city government has put to best advantage prefectural and national policies and programs that can best serve the needs of Nagoya and help maintain a healthy and vibrant city. Thus, Nagoya suffers much less than other cities in Japan from congestion, cramped housing conditions, air and water pollution, and a lack of open space.

Brian Roberts and John Dean, in their presentation in Chapter 3 of Cairns' economic development strategy, show how and why Cairns, along with its contiguous northern part of the State of Queensland, is one of Australia's fastest growing and most internationalized regional economies. Through the initiatives and enterprise of the local community and government, the region built an international airport, developed international tourism, fishing, mining and tropical agriculture industries, and substantially diversified its service industry base. The various government bodies and business groups involved were committed to integrated economic and regional planning which emphasized the development of strategic infrastructure, industry clusters, public and sector investment and partnerships, sustainable development, and the development of human and natural capital.

Victor Savage and C. P. Pow in Chapter 4 provide a detailed and comprehensive analysis of a city that is widely praised as a model of urban development for today's world, that is, Singapore. Of course, in reality Singapore is a city state, rather than a city in a larger country, and with unique geographical, cultural, economic, and political characteristics that have definitely given the city some considerable advantages in its development approach since the city state became a completely independent country in 1965. Nonetheless, Savage does show clearly that Singapore's success is due far more to hard work and wise policies than just to luck. He distills the primary explanation for Singapore's success into three overarching factors: (a) The government recognized early the importance of, and took a long-term commitment towards, key urban provisions, especially housing, education, and health care. Without doing everything possible to support Singapore's most important asset, its human resources, all the rest would have been impossible. (b) The government focused on long-term strategic planning, rather than rely on fortuitous circumstances. Planners adopted pragmatic yet flexible approaches. This is evident, for example, in the decision in the last decade to shift toward an information technology economy and society, to make Singapore a regional and world leader in the area of IT. (c) Underlying Singapore's management strategy has been strong adherence to a meritocracy which enables the civil administration to tap into a wide array of talents, regardless of race, family background or any other social characteristics. This approach has ensured the government's ability to recruit the best and the brightest into Singapore's civil service.

In Chapter 5 Richard Watson and Manuel Perez focus on a city that is probably the least familiar to readers of this volume, because of its more modest size and far less widely known reputation, especially as a "successful" city; that is, Long Beach, California. Yet, the story of Long Beach, a coastal port on the southern flank of the Los Angeles metropolitan area, is a remarkable one in the annals of American cities, a true comeback story that many thought never possible. As a "secondary" city, existing in the shadow of its far larger neighbor, Long Beach originally served as a resort suburb of Los Angeles. Then the city had the reputation for over 50 years before and after World War II as primarily a naval port, servicing ships and sailors, with the grimy and tacky imagery frequently associated with naval ports. Oil drilling and aircraft manufacturing provided other support to the economic base. During those years, earthquakes, land subsidence (from oil drilling), profound transportation changes, changing migration patterns, all brought severe ups and downs to the population and economy of Long Beach. The post-Vietnam War era, from the mid-1970s on, however, led to base closures and collapse of defense contractors, and Long Beach had to reinvent itself once more. This is the principal "success" part of the story, which shows how dedicated municipal leadership, with close involvement of the community and its people, have started a process (still incomplete) of strategic planning that is transforming Long Beach into a very different and very appealing new city. Long Beach is now capitalizing on its comparative advantage in tourism, conventions, health care, a revitalized and expanded deep water port, a redeveloped and formerly rundown city center, and development of high-tech industry. Long Beach is a remarkable, and encouraging, lesson in how cities can indeed save themselves and reverse urban decline.

Mark Wang, Xiaochen Meng, and Guicai Li present in Chapter 6 the case of one of the world's most successful new cities, Shenzhen in southern China. Once merely a small farming town on the border crossing between Guangdong province and the British colony of Hong Kong, Shenzhen has been built virtually from scratch in the space of just 20 years to become one of China's largest and most thriving cities, currently holding the title of having the highest per capita income of any city in China, ahead even of Shanghai. Shenzhen is one of the most dramatic and visible products of China's reform era, that started in the late 1970s with the opening of the country to foreign investment, trade, and real engagement with the global economic system. Shenzhen rapidly became the largest and most successful of the Special Economic Zones that China set up as transition zones in which to concentrate foreign capital and China's initial efforts at modern industrialization. Shenzhen was built just next to Hong Kong expressly to tap into the rich capital resources and entrepreneurial talent of Hong Kong. Shenzhen thus benefited greatly from Hong Kong, but the then British colony also prospered because of ready access to the much cheaper labor and infrastructure found in Shenzhen. Nonetheless, the success of Shenzhen was not due just to Hong Kong's proximity.

Now with some four million people in the urban area, Shenzhen was developed under the government's objective of trying to duplicate "Singapore's city environment and Hong Kong's city efficiency." The glittering high-rise metropolis that now greets visitors is testament to that policy's relative success. Shenzhen shares the same objectives with the other SEZs in China; i.e. attract foreign investment, develop export-oriented manufacturing, serve as social and economic laboratories for China's reform program. Shenzhen differs most importantly from the other SEZs in the fact that it has become one of the most livable cities in China, including having a very good ecological record and clear air, definitely an "environmentally friendly city." Thus, there are lessons to be learned here by other cities in China, as well as outside of China.

In Chapter 7 Elwyn Wyeth presents another very different overview of the recent new regional planning process in South East Queensland (SEQ), Australia, in an analysis of what he calls "the virtual organization." Growth management became a political priority in SEQ by the late 1980s due to rapidly increasing population, failing air and water quality, increasing traffic conges-tion, and misalignment of the aims and ambitions of planners and politicians of adjoining municipalities through the region. These are problems familiar to almost any urbanizing region in the world. The SEQ2001 Growth Strategy Project thus came into being. The project team, or "virtual organization", was a complex mix of representatives from various levels of government, the private and institutional sectors, the business/industry/unions group, the professionals/ academics group, and the social/cultural/environmental group. The intent was to give all parties involved in the objective of planning (that is, a better SEQ) a real say in the planning for that future. Very careful procedures, methods of communication and consultation, and division of responsibilities were worked out to minimize inefficiencies and maximize effectiveness of the outcome. Careful monitoring of the various actor groups involved revealed where weaknesses existed in the process, so that corrective measures could be taken. The experience of SEQ has broader lessons for other regions involved in planning.

Urban Renewal, Preservation and Participation

The chapters in Part 2 illustrate especially well the role of citizenry in urban development and the importance of incorporating bottom-up planning into the whole process. This can involve a mixture of individuals, resident groups, activists, business and professional groups, and public agencies. Often public-private-community partnerships are involved. In all cases the planning issue or project was more area specific, involving redevelopment or preservation.

In Chapter 8 Chi Wing Ho analyzes the case of harbor reclamation in Hong Kong to show how effective citizen involvement can not only stop bad urban development policies but also play a directly constructive role in helping authorities to formulate good urban development policies. Since the 19th century, Hong Kong has been gradually filling in its harbor in order to provide more land for urban expansion in a desperately land-short geographical setting. The economic success of Hong Kong since its founding in the early 1840s, but especially its phenomenal growth from the 1950s onward, steadily pushed real estate values higher and higher, forcing city planners and private developers to go up (up the steep hills and up in numbers of storeys to buildings) and out (outward into the harbor). Many cities and countries in Asia, most notably in Japan, have done likewise. But in Hong Kong, the limits were pushed too far in the eyes of many local citizens and critics. By the 1980s, the magnificent natural harbor between Victoria on Hong Kong Island and Kowloon on the mainland had been reduced by fully one third, and new reclamation plans called for further narrowing of the harbor to half its original 19th century width. Critics warned that planners were destroying one of Hong Kong's most precious assets, its harbor, which is so important to the economy and to visitors and residents alike. Thus, by the mid-1990s, many groups and organizations began to protest, to develop petitions and position papers to show the government exactly where it was wrong, and to offer well-reasoned and rational alternatives. Initially resisting these citizenry efforts, the government finally changed course in mid-1999, a dramatic success for advocacy planning and community actions in a place renowned in the past for its laissez-faire economic policy and community apathy. Hong Kong's experience shows that if advocacy planning can work there, it can work just about anywhere

Trevor Reddacliff and Robert Stimson in Chapter 9 look at urban renewal in Brisbane, Australia's third largest city. They show how an effective public-private-community partnership approach has facilitated very significant levels of private sector investment in redevelopment projects in a planned way, and in so doing, avoiding market flooding and massive public sector spending. Urban renewal in inner city areas is a problem facing countless cities around the world. Brisbane, the capital of Queensland state, experienced inner city population decline and associated inner city problems, especially its inner north-eastern suburbs during the period of the 1960s, 70s and 80s, at the same time that rapid growth was occurring, especially toward the Gold Coast tourist belt not far away (the South East Queensland, or SEQ, region). Thus, in the early 1990s an Urban Renewal Task Force, involving government as well as community and private groups, was organized, with the task of developing an urban renewal program that would accomplish specific, detailed objectives. Close consultation with the community has been a hallmark of the process. By the end of the decade, the urban renewal process has resulted in notable successes. The approach taken in Brisbane has been widely recognized for its success in managing the urban renewal process in a transparent manner, with a dynamic macro-planning framework, and through collaborative and facilitative partnership with the business sector and the community. So far, the process, the program, and its projects have been remarkably devoid of media and interest group criticism; it is not perceived as a blatant political exercise; it has not produced white-elephant icon projects; nor has it flooded the market with oversupply. The program is well on track to achieve its 20-year development and investment targets.

In Chapter 10 Peter Newman provides an analysis of how changes to urban public policy away from car dependency through the renaissance of railways have been used to enhance the urban renewal process in Perth, the capital city of Western Australia. He traces how, since the OPEC oil shocks of the 1970s, as social changes such as the increasing entry of women into the labor force and an ageing population, and as we have progressed from an industrial to a knowledge-based economy, community attitudes towards, and involvement in, planning have changed dramatically. In particular, increasing concerns over environmental issues have gradually led both communities and governments to seek new planning approaches to better integrate transport and land use patterns. Newman looks at the roles of various actors, including community activists, local citizens, and elected representatives, as well as the State Government, in the revitalization of rail transit infrastructure in Perth and its links with broader planning initiatives that embraced urban revitalization in the old port city of Fremantle and the renewal of the old inner city suburbs of East Perth and Subiaco. He focuses on what he calls the creation of "livable communities". This chapter provides an important discussion of the planning conflicts and challenges in stemming urban development through continuing suburban development by refocusing on reurbanization.

The final two chapters in Part 2 address the increasingly important issue of historic preservation. Long ignored, or at best given lip service by most cities and planners, historic preservation has taken on both a new image and new respectability as an important component of the process of urban planning in recent decades, even in developing countries.

In Chapter 11, Akihiko Tani, Mitsuhiko Kawakami, and Tatsuo Masuta look at the issue within the context of Kanazawa, Japan. Once the fourth largest city in Japan (at the time of the Meiji Restoration in 1868), Kanazawa got left behind in terms of growth as the great cities on the "front" (Pacific) side of Japan catapulted to dominance during the following century or more of Japan's emergence as a great industrial power. Fortunately, this fact saved Kanazawa from allied bombing during World War II (the city had no military significance whatever), and gave the city a head start, in effect, in terms of post-war opportunities to save historically important buildings and districts. Japan as a whole had a poor record in terms of historical preservation after the war, in part because of the extreme devastation of most cities of any economic consequence and far more pressing needs during the rebuilding years of the 1950s and 60s, and the single-minded determination of the country's leaders to make Japan No. 1 in the world in economic growth.

Historic preservation took a decidedly backseat position in national as well as prefectural priorities. Nonetheless, by the late 1960s some interest in historical preservation was beginning to arise in both government and public circles, and definitely in Kanazawa. Various preservation and restoration laws and ordinances were passed over succeeding years, designed to preserve Kanazawa's precious Meiji-era structures, and especially whole districts in the inner city, that evoked that long-ago period of Japan's history. In the process, Kanazawa has become a kind of model of how the old castle towns of Japan can go about the task of saving important parts of Japan's cultural heritage.

Thus, Kanazawa today, with its some 600,000 population in the total urbanized area, is widely regarded as one of the most livable medium-sized cities in Japan.

Bruce Taylor in Chapter 12 takes readers to a vastly different city in a quite different geographical and cultural environment, the former Portuguese colony of Macau, located on the opposite side of the Pearl River estuary from Hong Kong. As the first foreign colony on the China coast, and one of the first in all of Asia, Macau's real golden age was in the period leading up to the Opium War of 1840, when Macau was the main center of Western colonial traders trying to deal with China.

Once Hong Kong was established soon after that war, Macau went into a downward slide as it fell increasingly under the shadow of the much more powerful Hong Kong trading economy. That decline accelerated with the emergence of Hong Kong as the dominant port on the China coast after the People's Republic of China was established in 1949. Macau became renowned (or infamous, depending on one's perspective) as a rather dilapidated and eccentric mix of Portuguese and Chinese architecture and lifestyles in a terribly overcrowded urban site. About the only thing that brought visitors to Macau was the gambling and the somewhat seedy environment vaguely reminiscent of Hong Kong in the 1950s and 60s before it began emulating Manhattan. Yet, as Taylor points out, one planner's idea of "successful" urban development policies is another's idea of failure. Thus, Macau's efforts at preserving elements of its colonial architectural heritage can be viewed as a triumph of incrementalism, rather than as a victory for a comprehensively-designed preservation policy. In an effort to encourage "heritage" tourism as a counterfoil to what some see as distasteful casino-related tourism, the Macau government initiated a wide range of policies and programs with the common aim of encouraging the retention and, where appropriate, the active use of historic buildings, and enhancing the visual appeal of those districts that retain much of their historic character. Given that Hong Kong has obliterated almost all traces of its rich colonial architecture, with just a few notable exceptions, Macau really did not have to do that much to provide visitors a taste of what these former colonial centers once looked like. For example, a stroll through the carefully maintained Protestant Cemetery in Macau is to step back more than a hundred years into East Asian history. While much was lost in Macau, especially during the years of 1965–1980 when some notable economic growth did occur, the government has struggled to save much that remains. As Taylor notes, to have merely retained any part of the pre-existing built environment in the face of such pressure for change should be counted as a success for Macau's Portuguese administrators. To equally successfully build on that legacy is a challenge that the now Macau Special Administrative Region's leaders face in the years ahead.

Special Events and New Technologies

External events and processes have always had a profound impact on planning and policy in cities and regions. In Part 3 we present three case studies which provide interesting perspectives on this notion.

In Chapter 13 Mark Wilson and Laura Huntoon examine a very different but very important issue of the impact or catalytic effect a major event of world significance can have on the development of a city, and in particular how this may be used to focus redevelopment of parts of the urban fabric that have degenerated through the transition from one form of production technology to another. They look at world fairs, events which have long been sought by cities to "showcase" themselves to the world. They do so in a case study of Lisbon, Portugal, and its EXPO98. World fairs date back all the way to the Crystal Palace exposition in London in 1851, but they have become key instruments of urban renewal primarily in the past 50 years. The purpose of such fairs has changed greatly over the past century and a half, but in recent decades have been designed especially to showcase scientific and technological progress while promoting the economy, culture and image of the host city and country. Part carnival, part educational exposition, world fairs also benefit the host city typically by being built in a rundown area targeted for urban renewal, often in the inner city or harbor front. Such fairs often leave behind notable pieces of architecture or other developments that transform a city and its image, such as the Eiffel Tower in Paris, the Space Needle in Seattle, Golden Gate Park in San Francisco, the lakefront parks and museums in Chicago. Unfortunately, not all world fairs have been financially successful; some have left their host city with a huge debt.

Wilson and Huntoon focus primarily on the Lisbon EXPO98 as an example of how to plan and mount a successful world's fair. Lisbon's success can be attributed to several factors: (a) Having a clear theme that is relevant to the host city. In Lisbon's case, the dominant theme was the world's oceans and broader environmental issues that tied in both with Lisbon's past and its future ambitions. (b) Using the world's fair as a vehicle to emphasize national identity. In Lisbon's case, this meant establishing Portugal's identity in the rapidly changing economic and political environment of Europe. (c) Having a clear plan for urban renewal directly linked to the fair and its aftermath. In Lisbon's case, the fair was built on a brownfield site east of the center of Lisbon on the Tagus River, an old, deteriorating industrial area. (d) Closely linked to the factors above is using the world's fair as a vehicle to proclaim the ability of the city to host and manage a major international event. While participants and visitors alike praised the quality of Lisbon's EXPO98, and Lisbon was left with a handsomely redeveloped area, it may be too soon to fully discern the long-lasting impact of the fair.

Certainly Lisbon's fair was more successful, financially as well as in attendance, compared to some other fairs of recent decades. But in general, world fairs seem to be a vanishing species of decreasing appeal to cities and countries around the world. In their place, the international Olympics, now held every two years alternating between the summer games and winter games, have evolved into the successor to world fairs as vehicles for showcasing the host city and country while simultaneously leading to the renewal of a depressed urban area. Even though far more expensive than most world fairs, the Olympics are eagerly competed for by contending cities.

The final chapters in this volume delve into various aspects of the impact of technology on urban and regional planning.

In Chapter 14 Roger Stough and Rajendra Kulkarni examine the recent development history of the U.S. National Capital Region as an example of technology-induced development and the so-called "New Economy." The case is unique in many ways because the region has developed in the past 30 years one of the largest information technology (IT) industrial sectors in the country, creating for the first time an entrepreneurial commercial industry component. And, this has occurred in spite of minimal strategic leadership and planning, commonly regarded as essential in today's world for sustained economic development. Technology and the pace of technological changes are two of the most important distinguishing characteristics of the new economy. After reviewing the issue of technology-led economic growth in general across regions, the authors focus specifically on the capital region.

Historically, the capital region's primary economic base has centered around government and related public/private services, plus tourism. But in recent decades, technology employment has mushroomed, especially in IT, drawing upon the region's natural strengths: the center of national government, educational institutions, and organizations of all kinds, a highly educated labor force, and geographical location. Yet, this growth occurred in a multi-state, federal district metropolitan region of different geographic parts with different histories and cultures, each going its own way. The authors conclude that the region's success is due, in addition to the natural strengths noted above, to unanticipated and unintended consequences of federal government policy changes. Thus, the region has not really needed cohesive strategic leadership, or a carefully designed strategic plan and broad based cooperation across the local and state jurisdictions. This may not be permanently true, however, in light of such problems as the region's extremely congested transportation systems.

Robert Fletcher, Brenda Moscove, and Kenneth Corey in Chapter 15 bring readers to the very edge of the technological revolution with their examination of the role that electronic commerce (e-commerce) can have on urban and regional development. The authors first present a summary of this rapidly evolving frontier of Information Technology (IT) and how its many permutations are spreading into virtually all aspects of life, especially in the more developed countries. The main thrust of this chapter, however, is presentation of what the authors call a "primer" designed to help planners in successfully integrating e-commerce into the planning of urban areas and regions, for developed as well as developing countries. Ten planning elements are distilled in this primer: vision and leadership, modern infrastructure, regulatory environment, human resources and training, organizational dynamics, culture and political economy, timing, spatial organization, research and evaluation, and e-commerce primer electronic resources. Since e-commerce is certain to become increasingly popular and important, it behooves planners to become well versed in the nature of e-commerce and how it is to be integrated into the planning process. The spatial implications of e-commerce, for example, are enormous. E-commerce may demand different models and different ways of thinking about location, distance, and agglomeration, in the way business is conducted, where it is conducted, and when it is conducted.

LESSONS FROM SUCCESS

The purpose of this volume is to present, through case studies drawn from around the world, a range of innovative and successful approaches to planning and policy that address a range of issues facing urban areas in contemporary times. This diverse set of studies has more divergent than uniform characteristics, both in terms of cultural and geographic settings, scale, focus and intent. It is thus difficult to generalize from the outcomes represented in these case studies. Nonetheless, what we can do is to identify a number of key issues that seem to be evident from these case studies which might have broad relevance in helping guide planners, policy-makers and the broader community in addressing macro and micro level concerns in urban development, planning and management.

The Global, National and Local Context

It should be self-evident that urban planning and policy needs to be driven by considerations of the cultural context of place and society. This is clearly the message from the Shenzhen case study by Wang, Meng and Li (Chapter 6). However, processes such as globalisation and its implications for cities and regions to be competitive in a rapidly changing world also are important, as shown in the Cairns-Far North Queensland economic development strategy by Roberts and Dean (Chapter 3). The Shenzhen case study also demonstrates the significance of this global context for planning and development strategy.

Reconciling conflicts and harnessing complementarities between policy directions and objectives at different levels of government is a further consideration in this scale context. This is clearly evident, for example, in the case study of Nagoya by Jacobs (Chapter 2).

Reactive and Proactive Action

Paradoxically, urban planning and policy is a complex mixture of reactive and proactive action and response to both exogenous and endogenous forces. Many of our case studies demonstrate the rapidity and magnitude of change over time in the character, performance and fortunes of cities and regions, as is very evident in the work by Watson and Perez on Long Beach (Chapter 5).

All too often planning and policy interventions are undertaken in the context of "playing catch-up" in response to a situation that is out of control or where it is perceived that a region is facing difficulties. This is evident in the case study by Wyeth on the South East Queensland region (Chapter 7). In a way it is also evident in the Hong Kong case study by Ho (Chapter 8), where the citizenry reacts against a perceived over-kill approach occurring in the execution of an existing policy.

However, many of the case studies presented here show that it is not uncommon for cities and regions, either through public, business or community action, or combinations of these, to be proactive in setting the agenda for their future development. This is evident in the Shenzhen case study, but also in the case of Singapore's strategy for development presented by Savage and Pow (Chapter 4).

Top-Down and Bottom-Up Initiatives

The case studies in this volume illustrate that considerable planning and policy success can derive from both "top-down" and "bottom-up" approaches. For example, the Shenzhen and Singapore case studies (Chapters 6 and 4) demonstrate that strong action by central government can be effective.

But increasingly there is evidence that planning strategies at the regional and area/project levels of scale are being shaped more strongly through broad participatory processes, and indeed by community activism. This is evident in the Hong Kong case study (Chapter 8), and also in the South East Queensland regional planning case study (Chapter 7), as well as in Newman's piece on Perth (Chapter 10).

One of the interesting aspects that emerges from the increasing levels of participation and broad consultation, however, is that it can act to slow down the planning process and potentially dilute the effectiveness of outcomes. This is referred to by Wyeth in Chapter 7 and by Roberts and Dean in Chapter 3.

Public, Private and Partnerships

While it is most common for the public sector to be the initiator or implementer of planning and policy (all too often in reactive rather than proactive mode), nonetheless increasingly we see private sector initiative and involvement. Clearly it has been entrepreneurship that has played a key role in the emergence of the North Virginia component of the Washington region as discussed by Stough and Kulkarni in Chapter 14.

However, in many of these case studies we see how partnership approaches are now commonplace and powerful instruments of both process and implementation for urban and regional planning and policy. This is demonstrated in the work by Reddacliff and Stimson on Brisbane's urban renewal initiative (Chapter 9), in Newman's Perth case study (Chapter 10), and in the work by Watson and Perez on Long Beach (Chapter 5). Further, the historic preservation case studies by Tani, Kawakami and Masuta on Kanazawa in Japan (Chapter 11) and by Taylor on Macau (Chapter 12), demonstrate the need for partnerships.

Image Building

An important and longstanding aspect of city development in particular has been the great efforts by city administrations, and especially mayors, to promote city image through signature/icon projects and by competing for international events, such as the Olympics and Expos. These high profile projects require substantial funding of infrastructure, and often provide an opportunity to focus attention on the rejuvenation of redundant spaces. The case study of Lisbon and Expo 98 by Wilson and Huntoon (Chapter 13) focuses on this aspect of urban planning and policy. The issue is revealed also in the case of the Queen Mary ship that Long Beach purchased some years ago in order to create a new image for that city (Chapter 5).

But "image" building is also evident for other purposes, such as in the Shenzhen case study (Chapter 6) which shows how special economic zones are used by national governments to provide a "showcase window" to the outside world.

Sustainable Development

Sustainability issues certainly are becoming increasingly important in reshaping planning strategy paradigms, and this is occurring through a realization of this imperative on the part of community, government and even business. The driving force of sustainability criteria is evident in many of the case studies presented in this volume, and in particular in Reddacliff and Stimson's piece on urban renewal in Brisbane (Chapter 9), and in Newman's work on Perth (Chapter 10), as well as in the regional plans for SEQ in Wyeth's Chapter 7, and in Roberts and Dean's work on Cairns (Chapter 3). The theme is also a strong undercurrent in a number of papers from other geographical locations, including Nagoya (Jacobs, Chapter 2), Singapore (Savage and Pow, Chapter 4), Hong Kong (Ho, Chapter 8), Kanazawa (Tani, Kawakami and Masuta, Chapter 11).

Harness New Technologies

In the modern era of globalisation, rapidly changing technology and how cities and regions tap into them is crucial in shaping their competitiveness, affecting quality of life and sustainability from an economic perspective at best.

Our case studies are replete with examples, both historic, contemporary and futuristic, as to how technology change affects city and regional development and performance, including how it might in the future.

For example, the Nagoya case study by Jacobs (Chapter 2), the Singapore study by Savage and Pow (Chapter 4), the Long Beach study by Watson and Perez (Chapter 5), and the Washington region case study by Stough and Kulkarni (Chapter 14), all show the crucial roles of changing technology as it affects urban and regional economies, and infrastructure requirements and investments. Chapter 15 by Fletcher, Moscrove and Corey places this issue of technology change in its immediate future context in a discussion on the implications of e-commerce in planning for successful regional development.

Concerted Commitment and Leadership

A final general issue to emerge from the case studies presented in this volume is the importance of concerted, sustained commitment to the process of planning and policy, and of consistency in strategy implementation. Here leadership, and the institutional context in which it is exercised, is a key issue. This is made explicit, for example, in the Wang, Meng and Li case study of Shenzhen (Chapter 6), as well as in the Jacobs work on Nagoya (Chapter 2), and in the Singapore case study by Savage and Pow (Chapter 4). It is also considered in the slightly different context of quality criteria in managing the regional planning process in Wyeth's work on Brisbane (Chapter 7).

CONCLUSION

In conclusion, we feel that these 15 case studies, while hardly comprehensive either in geographical locations or in topics, do provide some room for optimism regarding the world's increasingly urbanized environment. With the right mix of actors (public and private), the right goals, the right strategies that stress communication and consultation between all concerned parties, hard work and much patience, and undoubtedly sometimes plain good luck, urban and regional development problems can be overcome to create the kind of livable urban environments that all reasonable people want, regardless of where they live in the world.

NOTE

A number of the contributors to this volume are members of the Pacific Rim Council on Urban Development (PRCUD), an organization founded in 1989 for the purpose of bringing together urban practitioners from the academic, private, and public sectors to enhance development of linkages between cities in the Pacific Rim region. PRCUD maintains a website and serves as a clearinghouse to facilitate this process. An Annual Forum and Professional Visit are held each year in a different Pacific Rim city to bring members together, with an emphasis on group interaction and dialogue between members and the host city's counterparts, culminating in publication of an annual report. For further information about PRCUD, contact: (email) prcud@mizar.usc.edu, or (webpage) http://www-rcf.usc.edu/ ~ prcud.

PART I

CITY AND REGIONAL PLANNING STRATEGIES

2. PLANNING FOR A VIBRANT CENTRAL CITY: THE CASE OF NAGOYA, JAPAN

Andrew J. Jacobs

ABSTRACT

While many large U.S. central cities have suffered population and employment declines over the past three decades, the City of Nagoya, Japan has continued to flourish. A city of two million inhabitants in 1970, Nagoya's population has grown by only 126,000 over the past 30 years. However, this growth was a relatively healthy increase when compared to other older, large industrial cities of the U.S. and Japan. Further demonstrating Nagoya's continued vitality is the fact that employment in the city expanded by more than 400,000 new jobs between 1969 and 1996. Utilizing historical literature, descriptive data, and in-depth interviews with land use and development planners in Japan's Chubu Region, this chapter chronicles how national policies, prefectural facilitated inter-municipal cooperation, and progressive local planning have combined to maintain Nagoya as a vibrant center for commercial and residential life.

INTRODUCTION

Although many large cities of the world have suffered population and employment declines as a result of suburbanization and changes in the global economy over the past 30 years, Nagoya has continued to flourish. Add the fact

International Urban Planning Settings: Lessons of Success, Volume 12, pages 21–59.
Copyright © 2001 by Elsevier Science Ltd.
All rights of reproduction in any form reserved.
ISBN: 0-7623-0695-5

that the city was severely damaged during World War II, the City of Nagoya is clearly a success story worth documenting.

Like most large cities in Japan, Nagoya suffers from high land prices, traffic congestion, cramped housing, and a scarcity of open space due to the country's rapid growth in the 1950s and 1960s. However, these problems seem to be less severe than many of Japan's other large cities, especially, Tōkyō and Ōsaka. This chapter chronicles how national policies, prefectural facilitated inter-municipal cooperation, and progressive local planning, have combined to create a vibrant, livable central city in Nagoya.

HISTORICAL DEVELOPMENT

A Castle Town is Built

Located in the central part of the Japanese archipelago, Nagoya City is the political, economic, and cultural heart of Japan's Chūbu Region, a five prefecture region with nearly 17 million residents and roughly 8.8 million jobs.[1] More specifically, the capital of Aichi Prefecture lies west of the Chūbu mountains and north of the Bay of Ise, on the southeastern corner of the Nobi Plain, the largest lowland area between Tōkyō and Ōsaka (see Fig. 1). As of January 1999, with 2.16 million residents and 1.58 in employment in its 326.37 square kilometers (or 127.5 square miles), Nagoya was Japan's fourth largest city, and its third largest employer.

The city's name was derived from a famous 12th century estate which was called *Nagono*. Although the manor was abolished in the 14th century, the name remained, though the pronunciation was changed: the Chinese characters used to write Nagono can also be read as *Nagoya*, which was adopted as the area's name in the 16th century (Nagoya City, 1998).

The first settlement is said to have occurred near the Atsuta Shrine, currently in the southern most portion of the city. The shrine, which serves as an important center of Japanese Shintoism, is said to have been established approximately 1,900 years ago (Nagoya City, 1998), although some studies claim it was originally inhabited sometime between the 13th and 16th centuries (Kodansha, 1993).

Most scholars concur, however, that Nagoya did not truly begin to prosper until around 1610. It was at this time that the entire Town of Kiyosu, then the locus of politics in central Japan, was transplanted to an area known as "Nagoya Hill." Kiyosu had suffered from frequent flooding, which prompted Japan's Shogun at the time, Ieyasu Tokugawa, to instruct his subjects to

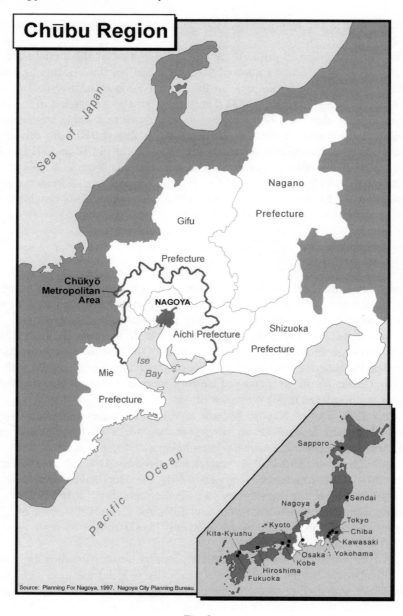

Fig. 1.

relocate southeast to Nagoya Hill, to build a new castle for his son, Yoshinao (Nishio, 1989).

Nagoya Castle served primarily as the military base of the feudal state of Owari.[2] Its central location allowed Tokugawa and his descendants to better control the feudal lords *(daimyo)* in the Kansai Plain (Ósaka-Kyōto) of the western part of Kyōto (Eyre, 1982). Thus, the original development of the city, and its current high level of development, owe much to it being strategically situated at the center of the Tōkaidō Region, an almost 350 mile stretch of continuous urbanization that currently extends along the old Tōkaidō Highway, between Japan's traditional eastern and western capitals, from Edō (Tōkyō) to Kyōto (Eyre, 1982). As a result, Metropolitan Nagoya is also known as the Chūkyō, or the Middle Capital, a metropolitan area which hosts roughly 8.65 million inhabitants and 4.73 million workers.

The Beginnings of a City

During the 17th century, Nagoya functioned primarily as a castle town, comprised mainly of *samurai* and the artisans and merchants who served their needs. However, as the city's non-military population grew, large expansions occurred to the west and to the south of the castle. In the west, the Hori River, which had been excavated to transport materials for the castle's construction, served as the base for a burgeoning lumber industry. Five or so miles south of Nagoya Castle, on the west coast of Ise Bay, tourism and small shipping/ferry enterprises flourished in the port town of Atsuta.

In the 18th century, Nagoya became a regional commercial center, whose influence spread beyond Owari. Improvements made to the Tōkaidō and Nakasendō Highway trails, with the latter being a northern route from Kyōto to Edō through Owari, attracted new merchants and artisans to the area. Thanks to its flourishing commercial activities along the Hori River, and Atsuta's booming amusement quarters, Nagoya gained a reputation for being the most thriving community between Kyōto and Edō. As a result, by the mid-18th century, its population had grown to about 75,000 residents, with another 15,000 in Atsuta (Eyre, 1982: 22).

However, during the early and mid-19th century, serious flooding and other natural calamities in the Nobi Plain dramatically reduced the local rice crop. This, along with civil unrest, (i.e. the unraveling of Shogunate rule), and new foreign conflicts, (Admiral Perry's black ships landing in 1853), fostered depressed local economic conditions in Nagoya.

Imperial Rule and Modernization

At the time political power was restored to the Meiji Emperor in 1868, and Japan was opened to western trade, Nagoya's population had surpassed 100,000 (Eyre, 1982: 22), and the Owari State had grown to nearly 700,000 (Hanley & Yamamura, 1977: 52). During the restoration period, the new central government vigorously imported foreign technology and knowledge to the country, in an effort to rebuild Japan's economic, political, and military systems, and to "catch up" with the West (Morishima, 1982).

Among the first efforts towards modernization was the abolishment in 1869 of the feudal states (*kuni*), and their smaller domains (*han*), and the creation of a civil government system. During this process, after a series of territorial consolidations, Aichi Prefecture, with Nagoya as its seed, was established in 1872. Over the next twenty years, several laws were introduced by the national government in order to institute a modern civil local government system. This included the Municipalities Formation Law in 1878, and the Municipal Government Act in 1888. The latter granted local property owners, for the first time, the right to elect their own municipal assemblies.[3] The former divided prefectures into *Gun* (districts or counties) and *Shi* (cities). Under this act, Nagoya was granted city status in 1889.

At the same time the local government system was being established, the national government took a leadership role in the building and the promoting of new industries. During the 1870s and 1880s, the Meiji government constructed railroads, ports, and telegraph lines in the city, as well as jails, schools, and public offices, though many of the latter were destroyed during the Great Nobi earthquake of 1891.

In spite of this investment, one major problem persisted for Nagoya and other former castle towns; how would the city assimilate and employ its many de-classed ex-samurai? The Aichi Prefectural Government played a major role ·in helping to solve this dilemma. In 1877, the prefecture established a cotton weaving factory which employed almost exclusively the wives of ex-samurai (Eyre, 1982). It also subsidized numerous private samurai-run textile mills. Workshops were also opened in the 1880s to train samurai in the trades of cotton reeling and lacquer. As a result, Nagoya became an important center of textiles manufacturing.

However, it was not until 1889, when Nagoya Station was completed as a part of Japan National Railways' (JNR) Tōkaidō Line, providing a link from the city to the port facilities in Tōkyō-Yokohama and Ósaka-Kōbe, that substantial industrial and commercial development began to occur in the area

(Eyre, 1982). By July of that year, Nagoya (pop. 157,000), was officially designated the first city in Aichi Prefecture (Nagoya City, 1997: 8).

In 1898, the construction of an electric streetcar line, from Nagoya Station to the Prefectural Government offices, only the second such system in Japan, after Kyōto, further attracted enterprises to the city (Meitetsu, 2000; Nagoya City, 1998). Operated by Nagoya Denki *Tetsudō* (Nagoya Electric Railway Company), the original route extended from the Sasashima neighborhood of the city's current Nakamura ward (*ku*), just a few blocks south of the current site of Nagoya Station, to the Aichi Prefectural Hall, in Naka-ku (see Fig. 2).[4]

In the same year, a young inventor, Sakichi Toyoda, started a small business in Nagoya City, built around his newly invented steam-powered looms. A year later, the large conglomerate, Mitsui Corporation, agreed to sell his looms from a new factory in the city. Toyoda's looms became so successful that in 1907, he opened his own Nagoya plant, Toyoda's Loom Works. Twenty-six years later, Toyoda's group of companies would spawn Toyota Motor Company, the driving force behind Central Japan's post-World War II economic boom (Toyota, 1988).

A Military City Again: War Spurs Industrialization

While the roots of Toyota Motor were being planted, industrial growth in Nagoya during the late 19th century was greatly stymied by the lack of adequate port facilities to handle bulk shipments of coal. Due to its shallow water depth, Nagoya's port was unable to handle large sea going ships (Nishio, 1989; Eyre, 1982). Additionally, being further removed from Japan's supplies of coal in northern Kyūshū and Hokkaidō than either Ōsaka or Tōkyō, the city suffered from higher than normal energy costs, which severely inhibited the growth of heavy industry (Eyre, 1982; Edgington, 1996).

This situation was rectified when, in 1907, the prefectural government constructed a new seaport in Atsuta, in support of the munitions plants built there during the Russo-Japanese War of 1904–1905 (see Fig. 2). Also in 1907, coinciding with the port's completion, the city annexed a significant stretch of land south from its borders to Ise Bay, including Atsuta and its port. Further improvements to waterways, such as the dredging of canals, the improving of bridges, and the widening of rivers, allowed for the shipping of goods between the new port and the city center (Nagoya City, 1998).

The local development of hydro-electric power, made possible by the construction of dams along the main rivers of the Chūbū mountains, helped bolster the city's industrial capacity. Increased energy resources also enabled

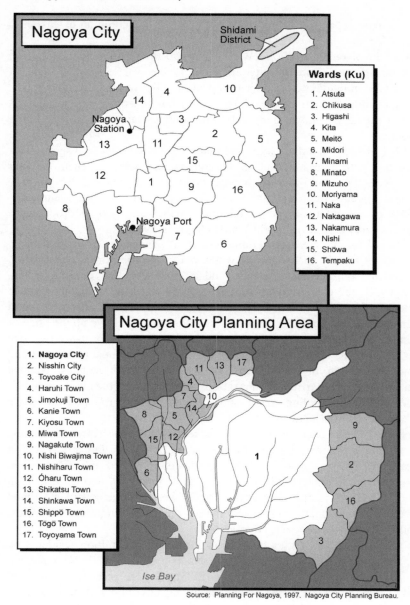

Source: Planning For Nagoya, 1997. Nagoya City Planning Bureau.

Fig. 2.

the wide-scale expansion of the city's rail network, including an extension to new port facilities in 1909 (Eyre, 1982).

Japan's involvement in World War I, spawned the development of aircraft engine manufacturing in the city. In addition, the war temporarily cut off Southeast Asian markets from their European supplies of manufactured goods. Nagoya factories which produced ferrous metals, castings and machinery, industrial chemicals, and rubber goods, were able to play a large role in filling this void.

In 1921, the region's first large steel plant was constructed in Nagoya. This plant, along with a large Mitsubishi Aircraft factory, which opened one year earlier, were built in order to handle the post-war demand for military equipment. Twenty years later, the latter plant was responsible for manufacturing 60% of the infamous Zero Fighters, which were used to drop planes carrying *kamikaze* pilots in World War II (Nagoya, 1998).

By the 1920s, the city had definite locational advantages as a result of an abundance of factory space, ground water, hydro-electric power, cheap labor, an excellent transportation system, and a relatively low cost of living. Consequently, the city's employment soared, which pushed its population to just under 430,000 in 1920 (1970 Census of Population). However, rapid growth also spurred land speculation, which dramatically drove up the price of land in the city (Eyre, 1982). This, along with the expansion of the rail service to the small towns north and northeast of the city, fueled new residential and commercial growth in the suburbs. In step with these changes, Nagoya completed a series of territorial annexations. In 1921 alone, the city annexed all or part of 16 surrounding towns and villages, which propelled the city's population to 617,000 (Nagoya, 1998).

A couple of years later, when an earthquake devastated the Tōkyō-Yokohama Area, the city's economy became further focused on heavy industry. Then, in the early 1930s, as Japan's military expansion marched into Manchuria, Nagoya was completely transformed into an arsenal city, acting as a main supplier of military aircraft. Rapid growth followed, as large new plants, many financed by the national government, churned out steel, aluminum, chemicals, and other war related products (Eyre, 1982).

As a result, Nagoya City's population surpassed one million residents by 1932, and peaked at 1.38 million in 1941 (Nagoya City, 1998: 1; Nagoya City, 1997: 8). However, the final years of World War II were perhaps the worst in the city's history. As the Allied Forces cut off Japan's supply of raw materials from the Western Pacific, industrial activity rapidly declined. Then, two severe earthquakes hit the city, the first of which occurred on December 7, 1944.

These disasters were followed almost a week later by the beginning of regular allied bombings.

During this period, over 500,000 local citizens were either injured or killed, and many more were evacuated. By the end of the war, the city's population had dropped below 600,000 (Nagoya City, 1998: 2). Nagoya, the industrial powerhouse that was at the forefront of the military's territorial expansion lay in ruins; whatever factories that remained standing were now dormant.

Golden Dolphins Rise From the Ashes

In spite of the great destruction suffered during the War, Nagoya was not down for long. Propelled again by munitions contracts, especially Allied orders during the Korean War, and foreign demand for Japanese products, such as machinery, airplanes, and steel, Nagoya grew into a modern industrial city in the 1950s (Nagoya City, 1997). An additional catalyst was the construction of a regional airport just north of the city, which became a hub for both commuter and military air service (Miyakawa, 1990).

As a result of employment growth in and around the city, Nagoya rapidly repopulated after World War II. With the help of returning evacuees and other new migrants, its population returned to over one million by 1950, and surpassed its pre-war peak by 1956 (Nagoya, 1997). In that same year, under Japan's post-war Local Autonomy Law (*Chihō Jichi Hō*), Nagoya was authorized special status by the central government as a *Seirei Shitei Toshi* or "Designated City". According to Local Autonomy Law, to be classified as a Designated City a municipality's population must be greater than 500,000, with an expectation that it will reach one million in the near future (Alden & Abe, 1994).[5] Upon this designation, Nagoya City was granted land use planning powers and responsibilities which were similar to those that prefectures have in other areas. In 1959, in celebration of the city's 350th anniversary, the reconstruction of Nagoya Castle, destroyed during the war, was completed, and its *Kinshachi* (Golden Dolphins) restored.

The emergence of the automobile industry, especially in Toyota City, to Nagoya's southeast, local investment in plant modernization and new technology, and the creation of a huge iron and steel complex south of the city's main port in Tōkai City, fueled further growth in Nagoya during the 1960s (Eyre, 1982; Miyakawa, 1990). As a result, by 1969 the city had more than two million residents and over 1.14 million non-governmental jobs (Nagoya City, 1997: 8; 1969 Establishment Census). However, while employment growth continued to forge ahead full steam after 1969, expanding by more than 402,000 non-governmental jobs, population growth slowed. Between 1970 and

1999, Nagoya gained only 126,774 residents. As in many central cities in Japan, extremely high land prices and a booming economy have favored the development of more lucrative, office and commercial uses in Nagoya, rather than the construction of housing. This has pushed most new residential development into Nagoya's suburbs, in particular, Aichi Prefecture's Owari and Nishi Mikawa Sub-Regions, where land and the cost of living have been lower (see Table 1).

Nevertheless, the fact that the city did indeed grow by more than 126,000 people, rather than decline, is impressive in comparison to older, large industrial cities of the United States, such as Chicago, Detroit, Philadelphia, and New York, which each have lost close to half-a-million people since 1970. This figure also represents a relatively healthy increase when compared to Tōkyō and Ósaka, traditionally Japan's two largest cities, whose populations have declined by more than 873,000 and 378,000, respectively, between 1970 and 1995 (See Table 2).

There have been several key ingredients to Nagoya's success. The most telling of these factors, which will be discussed in the sections to follow, include: (a) national development policies which have mandated integrated development planning and have supported healthy central cities; (b) prefectural coordinated metropolitan planning which promotes inter-local cooperation; and (c) progressive land use, transportation, and economic development planning by the City of Nagoya.

NATIONAL POLICIES WHICH HAVE SUPPORTED NAGOYA

Integrated Development Planning

In accordance with the Comprehensive National Land Development Act, originally authorized in 1950, the Government of Japan is required to periodically formulate a National Development Plan. Drafted by the National Land Agency, and adopted by the Prime Minister's Cabinet on March 31, 1998, *The Grand Design for the 21st Century,* is Japan's fifth and current National Plan. Among its many objectives, the current plan stresses the need to redevelop, rehabilitate, and preserve the economic and social vitality of central cities. It also calls for the equitable geographic distribution of industries and public investment, among and within these regions, as well as the efficient use of the country's land.

To further these goals, the country has been divided into ten multi-prefecture regions. National Development Law also mandates that each of these regions

Table 1. Population Change: Nagoya City, its Region, and Japan, 1970–1995.

	1970	1995	Change 1970–1995	% Change 1970–1995
Japan	104,665,171	125,570,246	20,905,075	19.97
Chūbu Region	13,735,012	16,741,682	3,006,670	21.89
Nagano Prefecture	1,956,917	2,193,984	237,067	12.11
Gifu Prefecture	1,758,954	2,100,315	341,361	19.41
Shizuoka Prefecture	3,089,895	3,737,689	647,794	20.96
Mie Prefecture	1,543,083	1,841,358	298,275	19.33
Aichi Prefecture	5,386,163	6,868,336	1,482,173	27.52
Owari Sub-Region	3,844,976	4,741,233	896,257	23.31
Nishi Mikawa Sub-Region	931,919	1,380,279	448,360	48.11
Higashi Mikawa Sub-Region	609,268	746,824	137,556	22.58
Chūkyō Major Metropolitan Area	6,759,584	8,652,486	1,892,902	28.00
Nagoya City	2,036,053	2,152,184	116,131	5.70
Nagoya City's Metropolitan Share	30.12%	24.87%	-5.25 points	

Sources: 1970 and 1995 Population Census of Japan.

Notes:

1. Chūbu, Chūkyō, and Aichi's Sub-regions were calculated from Census data. Nagoya city is included in the Owari Sub-Region total.

2. Chūkyō comprises all of Aichi's Owari Sub-Region, the eastern half of its Higashi Mikawa Sub-Region, as well as the urbanized portions of Nishi Mikawa, southern Gifu Prefecture, and northern Mie Prefecture.

Table 2. Population Change: Nagoya and Selected Japanese and U.S. Cities, 1970–1995.

City	Population 1970	Population 1995	Change 1970–95	% Change 1970–95
Tōkyō, Japan	8,840,942	7,967,614	–873,328	–9.88
Ōsaka, Japan	2,980,487	2,602,421	–378,066	–12.68
Nagoya, Japan	2,036,053	2,152,184	116,131	5.70
New York, USA	7,894,862	7,347,275	–547,587	–6.94
Chicago, USA	3,366,957	2,801,014	–565,943	–16.81
Philadelphia, USA	1,948,609	1,496,013	–452,596	–23.23
Detroit, USA	1,511,482	1,005,283	–506,199	–33.49

Sources: 1970 and 1995 Population Census of Japan, U.S. Census Bureau, 1970 Census of Population, and Annual Time Series of Population Estimates, 1991 to 1998.

Notes:

1. Tōkyō represents the sum of the 23 wards of Tōkyō.

adopt their own development law and policy plan which are vertically consistent with the goals and objectives set forth in the national plan. Nagoya City, and the other communities within its five prefecture region, are governed by the Chūbu Region Development and Improvement Law and the Basic Chūbu Region Development and Improvement Plan.

While the national and regional plans set the general policy course and the framework for development, it is the municipalities and prefectures which create the more specific comprehensive master plans which guide economic and land use development in Japan. (Nagoya City, 1997). Prefectures devise long-term comprehensive plans which identify development goals for administrative planning areas within the prefecture. Prefectural plans then serve as a guide for municipalities in the adoption of their own plans (Sano et al., 1998).

In addition to two National Development Laws, a variety of other national statutes have also greatly influenced land development in Japan and have promoted an integrated planning system (i.e. planning consistency among levels of government). The City Planning Law (*Toshi Keikaku Hō*) and the Building Standards Act (*Kenchiku Kijun Hō*), provide city governments with most of their tools for land use planning. Both of these laws were first enacted in 1919, and at the time were only enforced in cities.

Modeled partially after the Prussian system of building controls, the original Urban Building Act was the country's first legislation regulating the construction of buildings in cities, zoning, setbacks, height limitations, and the demolition of dilapidated structures (Nakamura, 1986a). When the Act was revised and renamed in 1950, in concert with the adoption of National Development Law, it was applied to all municipalities.

The City Planning Act established Japan's first legal framework for urban land use controls, including the creation of a land classification system (that is, the designation of land for residential, commercial, industrial, institutional, port, and recreational uses), and guidelines for the provision of urban infrastructure and public facilities, such as roads, parks, sewers, and housing (Edgington, 1994). Under the auspices of these two laws, the urbanized portion of Nagoya was delineated as a city planning area in 1920, and a zoning system was introduced. Urban facilities were greatly improved and numerous urban development projects, helped tremendously by an aggressive local land readjustment program, greatly contributed to the orderly planning and development of the city after 1925 (Nagoya City, 1997).

However, rapid re-urbanization and growth after World War II produced problems in many of Japan's cities during the 1950s and 1960s, such as cramped housing, rising land prices, environmental degradation, and sprawling development. In an effort to address these issues, a new and more comprehensive "New" City Planning Law (*Shin Toshi Keikaku Hō*), was passed in 1968. Under the new law, municipal comprehensive plans became compulsory, and urban growth boundaries were introduced to guide and phase growth more efficiently within each municipality, multi-municipal city planning area, and prefecture (Nagoya City, 1997; Callies, 1997). In addition, citizen participation in the process was greatly expanded, and a development permit system was instituted to ensure greater concurrency between infrastructure capacity and new land development. The Act also reduced central control by delegating city planning powers to prefectures and municipalities (Alden & Abe, 1994; Edgington, 1994; Callies, 1997).

To oversee these activities, each prefecture established a City Planning Council. Under the council's direction, municipalities located within prefectural delineated city planning areas were required to designate Urbanization Promotion (*Shigaika Kuiki*) and Urbanization Control Areas (*Shigaika Chōsei Kuiki*). Urbanization Promotion Areas were defined as lands which had already been urbanized, and those adjacent areas which were expected to develop within the next ten years. Within these areas, land was divided into use-specific zoning districts, in accordance with the Building Standards Act. Unlike in Promotion Areas, where development is preferred, in the Control Areas it is restricted, in principle (Nagoya City, 1997). City Planning Law also dictated that any grouping of farmland of 20 hectares (50 acres) or more, and woodland areas of 100 hectares (250 acres) or more, were to be designated as an Urbanization Control Area (Hanayama, 1986). In addition, only those developments or "transactions of land that fulfill approved purposes," were to be allowed in the control area (Nakamura, 1986a: 26).

Under City Planning Law, each prefecture's City Planning Council is responsible for reviewing municipal Urbanization Promotion and Control Areas for their consistency with the prefectural master development plans. A prefectural urban development map is then forwarded to the respective regional Bureau of the Ministry of Construction (MOC) for approval. The MOC only approves prefectural maps if they are consistent with national plans for development in that specific region (Callies, 1997).

The delineation of Urbanization Promotion and Control Zones was first decided in Nagoya City in November 1970. These areas were slightly revised in 1979, 1984, and 1991, corresponding to changes in urban development patterns (Nagoya City, 1997). A new zoning system, which more specifically defined permissible uses in each zone, was instituted in the city in 1972. Nagoya has twelve different zonal use districts: one exclusively for industrial, four exclusively residential, with the remaining zones allowing a variety of uses.[6] Like all municipalities in Japan, Nagoya has a pyramid-style zoning system.

Nagoya differs from most cities in Japan, including all other cities in the Chūbu Region, in that it has a great deal of autonomy to regulate development within its own boundaries. As a Designated City, the central government has authorized Nagoya with land use planning powers and responsibilities which are similar to those granted to prefectures. For example, under City Planning Law, in most municipalities, development projects require a permit from the prefectural governor. For particularly large projects, a development license may be required from the Ministry of Construction. However, since Nagoya has been granted Designated City status, its Mayor has authority to grant development permission for those projects normally under the jurisdiction of the Aichi Governor. In the year 2000, Nagoya was also given authority to regulate some retail developments which were formerly under the jurisdiction of the national government.

In addition to monitoring urban growth boundaries, the Prefecture's City Planning Council is also charged by City Planning Law to ensure that all local comprehensive master plans, as well as their urban development and urban facilities projects, are consistent with the prefecture's long range plans (Nagoya City, 1997). Comprehensive master plans describe each local government's future and present policies, and implementation strategies regarding land use, economic development, transportation, parks and recreation, as well as any other urban or social services a municipality decides to provide. Aichi Prefecture works closely with its cities, towns, and villages during the master planning process. According to municipal officials in Aichi, however, Nagoya, like other Designated Cities, has a great deal of influence over Aichi's master plans. Some local officials suggest that Nagoya first drafts its plan, then presents it to the prefecture, which amends its plan accordingly (Jacobs, 1999).

The City of Nagoya formulated its first Master Plan in 1980, then drafted a new plan in 1988, and is currently in the process of revising it, yet again. The goals of the most recent plan are to improve the quality of life of Nagoya citizens by improving administrative efficiency, and by making the city a base for international exchange, high technology, and environmentally sensitive development (Nagoya City, 1997).

Japan's integrated development planning system has been a key element to Nagoya remaining the focal point of employment in its region, as well as preserving the integrity of the city as a place for residential life. By encouraging compact, dense development in cities, the designation of

Urbanization Promotion and Urbanization Control Areas has helped to promote orderly development and more efficient urban service delivery.

National Urban Redevelopment Policies

In contrast to the United States and the United Kingdom, where cities have had to address the problems provoked by de-urbanization, one of the greatest concerns of major cities in Japan, since the 1960s, has been the over-concentration of activities. As mentioned, rapid re-urbanization and growth in cities following World War II produced severe urban problems in many Japanese cities. However, national policies concerning urban redevelopment have greatly aided the City of Nagoya in its efforts to lessen these problems and remain a vibrant central city. Two policies, Land Readjustment (*Tochi Kukaku Seiri Hō*), and the Urban Redevelopment Law (*Toshi Sai-Kaihatsu Hō*), particularly merit attention.

Japan's first national law particularly regulating land readjustment was the Arable Land Readjustment Law (*Kōchi Seiri Hō*). Enacted in 1899, this law and its successor, the Agricultural Consolidation Act of 1909, aimed to re-plot paddyfields in order to provide better irrigation and drainage to farmland (Hanayama, 1986). However, the concept of land readjustment was first recognized as a legal urban development tool with the enactment of the Tōkyō Urban Renewal Ordinance in 1888 (Dawson, 1984; Nakamura, 1986a). This ordinance, Japan's first written law regarding urban planning, focused primarily on the construction of urban and industrial infrastructure (Hanayama, 1986; Nakamura, 1986a; Edgington, 1994). In 1918 the law was broadened to include five additional large cities, among them, Nagoya. A year later, urban land readjustment became general policy under the City Planning Act of 1919, which was created based on the principles outlined in the Tōkyō Ordinance (Hanayama, 1986).

Similar to Adickes Law, enacted in 1902 by the Prussian government in the rapidly growing, newly annexed German Province of Frankfurt, land readjustment in Japan has attempted to improve infrastructure, public facilities, service delivery, and land utilization in urban areas, by the purchasing, consolidating, and then replotting, of small and irregularly shaped parcels of land (Dawson, 1984; Minerbi et al., 1986; Nagoya City, 1997; Sakamoto, 1998). Following these tenets, the Japanese government enacted a Special City Planning Act in September 1946, to guide the rebuilding of cities severely damaged during World War II. However, while urbanized land was covered by this law, agricultural areas within cities were not. This omission, along with the agricultural land reform programs implemented by the Allied Occupation after the war, including the abolition of the Agricultural Land Consolidation Act in 1949, left much of the non-urban land in and near Japan's major cities more highly fragmented than ever before.

The combination of these policies and land tax laws, which discouraged the sale of agricultural land, made the large-scale conversion of agricultural land into urban uses extremely difficult in the 1950s. In a period of rapid growth, the consequences were haphazard development patterns in major metropolitan areas, with housing shortages, overburdened infrastructure, and rapid increases in land prices in major cities. Recognizing the urgent need for a new policy to address this situation, the Japanese Government enacted a new Land Readjustment Law in 1954 (Nakamura, 1986a).

After the new national Land Readjustment Law went into effect in 1955, Nagoya accelerated its efforts in order to develop new residential areas and industrial sites. From the implementation of the first project in 1955, through 1996, almost 13,000 hectares (32,000 acres) of land in Nagoya had been improved under the Land Readjustment Law (Nagoya City, 1997: 51–52). Public-private partnerships were key to this process, especially in the providing of infrastructure for housing sites (Nakamura, 1986a; Nagoya City, 1997). Public-private ventures were responsible for the construction of major extensions to the Higashiyama and Tsurumai subway lines and have contributed land for station plazas, bus terminals, train garages, and station shopping malls throughout the city. They have also helped support the urbanization of the city's two newest wards, Meitō and Tempaku (See Fig. 2).

In the city's Moriyama-ku, land readjustment has aided in the development of the Shidami Human Science Town, "where housing, research and development, manufacturing, and recreation functions all exist in harmony" (Nagoya City, 1997: 56). A special land readjustment project nearby has been instrumental in preparing land for the introduction of Japan's first Guideway Bus System, which is scheduled to begin operation sometime in the year 2000. A Guideway Bus is a special transit vehicle which can travel both on ordinary pavement and on a specially dedicated elevated expressway. When riding on this dedicated right-of-way, the bus is automatically guided along the road, allowing it to run as fast as the train.

While many policies of the 1940s and early 1950s helped to rebuild a war damaged Nagoya, land readjustment has been perhaps the city's most vital redevelopment tool since the late 1960s. According to Nakamura, this is because land readjustment has been "predicated upon the contribution of equitable portions of private lands for the construction of public facilities and the creation of reserve lands for sale to cover the project costs. While landowners lose a portion of land through construction, the value of [their] property is enhanced by improvements realized by the project's completion" (Nakamura, 1986b: 43). It has been the lure of increased property values that has encouraged both the public and private sectors to become willing partners in the process.

The National Urban Redevelopment Law of 1969 has also supported Nagoya's continued vibrancy. Set up to facilitate urban renewal, particularly in large cities, this Act paved the way for the integrated development/ rehabilitation of urban infrastructure and buildings in designated target areas (Edgington, 1994; Karan, 1997). The 1980 revised version of the law required all major cities in Japan to draft an Urban Redevelopment Master Plan (Karan, 1997).

Redevelopment under this system has primarily consisted of the construction of residences and retail stores; however, building uses vary from project to project (Sakamoto, 1998). Renewal Projects are supervised by local governments, but are carried out in cooperation with the private sector and local residents. They are funded via a combination of municipal public subsidies, private sector funds, and local resident land contributions. Local residents contribute their land in exchange for equal compensation in the form of either cash, a new plot of land, and/or occupancy rights in a redeveloped residential structure.

Similarly, the objectives of Nagoya's Urban Redevelopment Project are to implement effective land use by the rejuvenation of urban land, through the collective improvement of buildings, sites, and public facilities in an area (Nagoya City, 1997). Under this program, the Nagoya International Center was constructed. The Center functions as an important nucleus for international exchange in Japan.

Several other projects have built mixed-use office and commercial developments, while others have constructed housing, as well as commercial and cultural facilities, in connection with the renovation of city rail stations. Approximately 1,700 housing units have been built in Nagoya under the Urban Redevelopment Project, and another 2,700 units under the auspices of other city redevelopment programs (Nagoya City, 1997).

Combined with timely local actions, land readjustment and urban redevelopment have greatly improved the quality of life of Nagoya's residents. The Agricultural Promotion Arrangement Law, the Large-Scale Retail Stores Law, and Local Government Laws in general, have also supported central cities in Japan.

Other Complementary National Policies

Agricultural Laws

Contrary to conventional accounts, a sizeable supply of habitable land still exists in Japan (Hanayama, 1986; Calder, 1988; Noguchi, 1992; Yamamura, 1992). Rather, land for urban development has been restricted/made scarce in practice, by agricultural price supports, tax laws, and other national policies geared toward preserving farmland, in order to protect domestic agricultural production. As a result there is a much higher proportion of urban land in Japan which is reserved for agricultural activities than there is in most other industrialized countries (Dawson, 1984; Calder, 1988). In fact in some urbanized areas acreage designated for agricultural uses is greater than the actual land that is utilized for housing (Calder, 1988; Noguchi, 1992).

The Agricultural Promotion Arrangement Law of 1969 (APA) has been a main mechanism in supporting these practices. Through its tightly controlled permitting process, APA has served to not only protect agriculture, but has also furthered the implementation of the Urbanization Promotion and Control areas by preventing the disorderly and unplanned conversion of farmland into urban uses (Dawson, 1984). For example, if a private development project includes agricultural land of greater than two hectares (five acres), the developer must receive permission from the Ministry of Agriculture, Forestry, and Fisheries (MOA), both to build on a site, and to receive sewer services. The MOA has been very cautious about extending sewers to developments that might reduce the agricultural productivity of rural areas. Since the passage of the APA, in most cases where a developer wanted to build on land which was both in an Urbanization Control district and a designated Agricultural Promotion Area, the developer has had to omit that portion from the project (Alden & Abe, 1994). This has greatly reduced the number of large scale developments which have been built in rural areas on Nagoya's urban fringe.

Agricultural land has even been heavily protected within Nagoya, itself a city of two million people. Over 2,600 hectares (6,600 acres) in the city are designated as Urbanization Control Areas (Nagoya City, 1997: 16). In addition, the city has classified approximately 436 hectares (1,100 acres) as specially protected Agricultural Promotion Areas, in accordance with the Productive Green Field Law of 1992. These areas are "designed to conserve farm land and other green tracts within urban areas to prevent pollution and provide protection against disasters" (Nagoya City, 1997: 36). Much of the impetus for the latter comes from the Post-Quake Reconstruction Scheme adopted for Tōkyō, after the Great Kantō Earthquake of 1923. The lack of open space was blamed for the great number of deaths in the disaster, as citizens had few open areas to flee the fires which accompanied the earthquake (See Calder, 1988).

National agricultural policies, such as APA, MOA tight control of sewers in rural areas, agricultural price supports, and taxation policies, which have provided strong incentives to farmers to hold onto agricultural land, rather than sell it for urban uses, have preserved farmland, by tightly restricting the supply of suburban rural land which could be converted into urban uses. This has helped to protect Nagoya from the massive out-migration of people and commerce which has stricken many central cities in the U.S. Nagoya's vitality has also been maintained by the Large-Scale Retail Stores Law, a national statute that has regulated the location of large retail developments.

Large-Scale Retail Stores Law
The traditional downtown retail districts of cities in the Chūkyō Region were primarily built around commuter rail stations or historic castles. Officials in the region believe that the success of such retail districts has been, and will be, crucial to the continued vibrancy of central cities in Japan. The central government has generally shared this belief. As a result, large retail developments have been among the most highly regulated land uses in Japan. Proposed retail developments have been evaluated for their compatibility with current land use patterns, and for their potential impacts on existing local businesses in their city planning area. When projects have been deemed inappropriate, they have been delayed, downsized, or in some cases even stopped by the central government (Upham, 1993). This has served to reduce the number of shopping malls that have been located in suburban greenfields in the Nagoya Region, which has helped to maintain the economic vitality of Nagoya's downtown retail districts.

Regulation of large retail developments began in 1937, with the passage of the Department Store Law (*Hyakkaten Hō*). This law regulated the construction or expansion of single retail stores of greater than 1,500 square meters (16,000 square feet) floor space. The Department Store Law was repealed in 1947, as part of the Allied Occupation's efforts to break up monopolies. Nevertheless, political pressure from small retail associations led to the enactment of a new Department Store Law in 1956. Similar to the first law, the 1956 Act required all single retail units of more than 1,500m^2 to secure a permit from the Ministry of International Trade and Industry (MITI). This has served to both limit entrants into the department store market, as well as to protect small retailers (Upham, 1993).

However, the law's definition of large stores as single retail units allowed for construction of numerous large chain "superstores," without MITI permits. In other words, in contrast to single unit department stores, a superstore is a large retail complex, consisting of legally separated entities, each less than 1,500m² in size, but operating "under a common corporate identity on different floors of the same building" (Upham, 1993: 270). In response to the lobbying efforts of department stores and small retailers, this loophole was closed in 1973, with the authorization of the Large-Scale Retail Stores Law (*Daikibo Kouritenpo Hō*).

There were three significant changes in the new law. First, it provided a greater voice for local consumers. Second, it replaced the MITI permit with a notification and adjustment system. Third, it reclassified retail space within the same building as one retail unit, regardless of legal status (Upham, 1993). The notification process also gave MITI, chambers of commerce, as well as local retail and consumer groups, four months to comment on any proposed projects of greater than 1,500m². After the feedback period, if MITI felt the project was not in the public's best interest, it could ask that it be delayed, downsized, or not built at all.

Despite these changes, chain retailers still were able to circumvent the law by adjusting the size of their new developments under the permit threshold. Within a year the number of chain stores had doubled (Upham, 1993). In response, local governments passed their own ordinances to oversee retail developments under 1,500m². Calls for tighter restrictions prompted the Japanese Diet to amend the law, in 1978, to cover all stores of more than 500m² (about 5,400ft.²). Stores above 1,500m² remained under the direction of MITI, but stores between 500 and 1,500m² were placed under the jurisdiction of prefectures and municipalities.

Foreign pressure to deregulate the retail industry led to the relaxation of the Large-Scale Retail Stores Law in 1991 (and then again in 1998, effective June 1, 2000). Partially as a result of the law changes made in 1991, and other global forces, many traditional downtown commercial districts have seen their shares of retail sales decline since the early 1980s (Upham, 1993). Nagoya has been an exception to this generalization.

While many of the reasons for Nagoya's continued retail success can be gleaned from the commentary in the remainder of this chapter, three factors are worth highlighting here. First, Nagoya is much less densely developed than Tōkyō and Ōsaka. Nagoya's population density in 1995 was roughly half that of either Tōkyō or Ōsaka, and its employment density in 1996, was but a third of the two other cities (see Table 3). Nineteen of Tōkyō's 23 wards, and 18 of Ōsaka's 24 wards, have population densities of greater than 10,000 persons per square kilometer. However, Nagoya's most dense ward, Kita-ku, has a residential density of less than 10,000. As a result, there has been a larger

Table 3. Population and Employment Density: Japanese Cities with Populations of Two Million or More.

City	Population 1995	Employment 1996	Land Area (sq. km)	Population Density (pop./km)	Employment Density (emp./km)
23 wards of Tōkyō	7,967,614	7,476,744	621.0	12,830.3	12,039.8
Yokohama	3,307,136	1,388,493	435.9	7,567.1	3,185.4
Ōsaka	2,602,421	2,728,539	220.7	11,793.8	12,365.4
Nagoya	2,152,184	1,580,201	326.4	6,594.3	4,841.7

Sources: 1995 Population Census of Japan; 1996 Establishment Census of Japan.
Notes:
1. Employment is by Place of Work and includes Government Sector Employees.

supply of available land for new retail developments in Nagoya than the other two cities.

Second, as the largest and most prestigious city in its metropolitan area, Nagoya has remained the most attractive place for commercial establishments wishing to expand into the region. Since 1969 the city has added more than 125,000 retail jobs, and 48,000 since 1981, (including 6,300 in Naka-ku, the city's traditional downtown). All of its wards have increased their retail employment since 1969, and only one, Mizuho-ku, southeast of the city center, has suffered a retail decline since 1981 (a mere 55 jobs). On the other hand, despite being much less densely developed than Nagoya, no other city in the Chūkyō Major Metropolitan Area has experienced an increase of even 25,000 retail jobs since 1969 (See Table 4).

Finally, national policies which have encouraged compact development (i.e. the previously described urbanization zones) and have discouraged metropolitan fragmentation, have also been key factors. The latter, which has to do with national laws concerning local governments in Japan, will be discussed in the next section.

Nevertheless, while other national policies and spatial factors have been important, if not for the continued existence of the Large-Scale Retail Stores Law, Nagoya might not have been able to remain the dominant locus of commercial activity in its metropolitan area, over the past 30 years.

National Laws Concerning Local Government
Japan's local government laws have also been key to Nagoya's continued vitality. For example, since achieving city status brings prestige and greater local autonomy in Japan, an area's population must be at least 50,000 before the central government will authorize it as a city. Greater autonomy and status, along with Japan's Town and Village Merger Promotion Law (*Shi-Chō-Son Gappei Tokurei Hō*), have encouraged municipal consolidations and annexations, in the name of urban service efficiency, and discouraged jurisdictional fragmentation (Kitazaki & Ogawa, 1997). Since the introduction of the merger law in 1953, the number of municipalities in Nagoya's region has dropped to about one-third of its 1950 total, as Nagoya and other cities in the region have regularly annexed entire adjacent municipalities, and new cities have often been created through the consolidation of several towns and villages (1950 and 1995 Population Census of Japan).

Local government law has also promoted urban financial stability and equity. On average, municipal governments in Japan collect only about one-third of their revenues through local taxes, as compared to about two-thirds in the United States (Jacobs, 1999). This signifies that most municipalities rely

Table 4. Density and Private Retail Employment Growth: Chūkyō's Cities with 300,000 or more Inhabitants.

City	Population 1995	Employment 1996	Land Area	Population Density (pop./km)	Employment Density (pop./km)	Retail Employment Change 1969–96
Nagoya City, Aichi Prefecture	2,152,184	1,580,201	326.4	6,594.3	4,841.7	125,798
Gifu City, Gifu Prefecture	407,134	226,776	196.1	2,076.3	1,156.5	17,468
Toyohashi City, Aichi Prefecture	352,982	172,965	260.9	1,352.8	662.9	16,173
Toyota City, Aichi Prefecture	341,079	200,058	290.1	1,175.7	689.6	24,826
Okazaki City, Aichi Prefecture	322,621	153,180	227.0	1,421.4	674.9	20,487

Sources: 1995 Population Census of Japan; 1969 & 1996 Establishment Census of Japan.
Notes:
1. Employment is by Place of Work and includes Government Sector Employees.
2. Retail Employment Change is for privately owned establishments only.

heavily on the central and prefectural governments for funds to provide urban services. A large share of this comes in the form of a Local Allocation Tax Grant (LAT). The LAT is an equalization grant, provided by the Ministry of Home Affairs (MOHA), to municipalities and prefectures if their "basic financial revenue" falls below their "basic financial need" for a standard level of public services (Tsuji, 1984). The LAT has thus lessened fiscal distress by ensuring that all local governments have quality urban services.

The MOHA's fiscal capacity index, (i.e. basic financial revenue divided by basic financial need), also provides a demonstration of how strong economically Nagoya remains. The city regularly has an index of well over 1.0 and thus, annually, does not qualify for a LAT grant. In both Fiscal Years 1998 and 1999, Nagoya was one of only 119 municipalities in Japan, among 3,233, which did not receive a LAT grant (Asahi Shimbun, 1999). A fair amount of this success can be attributed to the special status it has been accorded by Local Autonomy Law.

As mentioned earlier, Nagoya was given special regulatory authority when it was classified by the MOHA as a "Designated City" in 1956. In a society where companies, universities, and cities are granted prestige based upon their ranking against similar organizations, this status has made Nagoya especially attractive to new and existing businesses. It has also encouraged other municipalities in the region to cooperate rather than compete with Nagoya on development planning.

Nagoya's continued growth has been further supported by fairly uniform local tax rates. Unlike in the United States, where local governments have a great deal of freedom to set their own tax rates, and higher tax burdens are common in the urban core, as compared with the suburbs, in Japan municipal property, income, and enterprise tax rates are determined by the MOHA. As a result, tax rates are very similar in central cities and suburbs. This has reduced some of the capital flight from Nagoya which might have left the city for lower taxes in the suburbs.

In sum, through policies which discourage fragmentation, encourage inter-municipal equity, and grant special importance to large central cities, Japan's local government laws have helped to promote a strong City of Nagoya.

PREFECTURAL FACILITATED INTER-MUNICIPAL COOPERATION

Although not often mentioned, prefectures in Japan have been actively involved in the development process (Reed, 1986). As mentioned previously, each prefecture's City Planning Council is charged to ensure that municipal master plans are crafted both vertically consistent with superior government plans, and horizontally consistent with adjacent local governments. This means that prefectures have been actively involved in both local and national development activities. Aichi Prefecture's Municipal Affairs Department and the Land Use Planning Division have taken leadership roles in this process, as staff support to the City Planning Council.

To help coordinate comprehensive planning at the prefectural level, and within administrative planning areas, Aichi has divided its 88 municipalities into three administrative sub-regions, 14 broader administrative metropolises, and 20 city planning areas.[7] Nagoya is within Aichi's Owari Sub-Region, as well as the Nagoya Metropolis. While most city planning areas have two to five communities, Nagoya, due to its special Designated City status, is the lead city in the Nagoya City Planning Area, which contains a total of 17 Owari municipalities (see Fig. 2). According to local officials, Nagoya has worked closely with these communities in the planning of urban facilities, urban development projects, and in the delineation of Urbanization Promotion and Control Areas. Such joint metropolitan planning has helped these communities to develop a sense of regionalism, or a feeling that if the region does well, then each municipality will do well (Jacobs, 1999). This mind-set has supported a strong Nagoya.

Many area officials felt that this inter-municipal cooperation had been fostered by the coordination and capacity building efforts of Aichi Prefecture, which has worked closely with its localities to guide development in the best interest of all communities in the prefecture. In other words, they have transferred knowledge about the planning process, and have built local commitment to prefectural policies (Burby & May, 1997). Cooperation has been enhanced by the prefecture's decision to organize its administrative planning areas, based upon historical ties among municipalities, some of which date back to Japan's feudal period. Inter-local cooperation has then helped lessen the negative impacts that outside forces, such as inter-regional and international competition, have had on the prefecture and the City of Nagoya. Thus, prefectural facilitated cooperation has helped to maintain a vibrant Nagoya.

PROGRESSIVE CITY PLANNING IN NAGOYA

According to Calder (1988) and Hebbert (1994) there has been substantially less adherence to land use development planning in Japan as compared with the most densely developed nations of Europe. Calder stated that Nagoya City was a major exception to this generalization. He claimed that interest groups and politicians have been less able to emasculate local development planning in Nagoya than they have in Tōkyō and other large cities in Japan. However, Nagoya City has been long known for its progressive planning policies.

In addition to its outstanding land readjustment/urban redevelopment efforts discussed earlier, key elements of Nagoya's progressive approach have been: (a) pro-active land use and transportation planning, including a multimodal transportation system, and the transforming of transit stations into centers for commercial and residential activity; and (b) strategic development planning, in order to build a diverse economic base for the city, such as the continued expansion of Nagoya Port.

Pro-Active Land Use and Transportation Planning

Nagoya has been actively planning land use and transportation since the early 1920s, when the city's first comprehensive plan was drafted. This plan was the first step toward functional zoning, and the creation of the city's present administrative core, just east of Nagoya Castle and the historic feudal area, via the construction of a new city hall and prefectural offices in the 1930s (Eyre, 1982).

The comprehensive plan also guided the city administration in its improvement of urban infrastructure. In the twenty years leading up to World War II, Nagoya became well known, in Japan, for the improvements it made to the city's water, sewer, road, and park systems, through its aggressive land readjustment programs (Nishio, 1989). By 1945, more than half of the city's land had been subjected to some form of land adjustment (Nagoya City, 1997). The city was also especially well known for its wide boulevards.

The city's progressive approach to land use planning also stood out in the early post-war period. Calder (1988) stated that Nagoya was among the select few local governments which developed rather farsighted land use planning programs during this period. He wrote that these policies had helped to minimize the problems of overcrowding and poor urban amenities, as well as to contain the sprawl which had emerged elsewhere in Japan, due to the rapid growth of the 1950s and 1960s.

One explanation might have been that the city received huge grants from the national government to rebuild the city after World War II. After all, almost one-third of the city was destroyed during the war, including roughly 118,000 buildings, Nagoya Castle, and most of the city's historic downtown. However, in this case, Nagoya officials chose not to wait for national legislation to act. While the central government did not enact its Special City Planning Act until September 1946, the City Assembly took just 45 days from the end of the war to establish its own War Rehabilitation Land Readjustment Project to reconstruct the city (Nagoya City, 1998). "This plan included everything needed for a modern city such as city streets, subways, parks, and greenways" (Nagoya City, 1998: 7), and played a major role in shaping the present layout of the city (Nagoya City, 1997).

As had been the case in the 1920s, progressive transportation planning was an integral part of this plan. The plan called for the construction of two 100 meter-wide boulevards, Hisaya Ódóri and Wakamiya Ódóri, and nine 50 meter-wide roads. Rare to Japan, these avenues provide citizens with large public spaces at the city center, and continue to serve as the main routes for automobile transportation in the city (Nagoya City, 1998). Again, these planning efforts outdid the national standard in Japan; the Special City Planning Act only mandated that arterial roadways in major cities be a minimum of 50 meters wide (Nakamura, 1986a).

While three national expressways provide excellent access to the city, it is, however, the Nagoya City Expressway, and the City's Inner Loop or Ring Highway, "which form the backbone of the Nagoya Metropolitan Region road network" (Nagoya City, 1997: 28). Four more freeways (two national and two city), including a city outer loop, are presently under construction or are planned for the next few years. When the national expressways are completed there will be even better access to the city from the inside and outside the region. However, it will be the two city freeways that enhance the quality of life of Nagoya residents and workers by greatly improving traffic circulation within the city.

In terms of public transportation, in 1957 the city opened its first 2.6 kilometers of subway line, only the third such system in Japan at the time (Eyre, 1982). This line linked Nagoya Station to the city's traditional central business district, Sakae. Since that time, the subway system has been continuously expanded. The city now has five subway lines (*Chikatetsu*), providing 76.5 km of track (47.8 miles) to over 1.13 million riders a day (Nagoya City, 1997: 31). A sixth line, currently under construction, and other planned extensions, will add another 20.7 km (13 miles) of service. When these scheduled improvements are completed, subway access to many parts of the city will be greatly improved, as Nagoya will be the first city in Japan to have a subway line which forms a complete loop (Nagoya City, 1997).

Nagoya is also served by an extensive railway network. Three private railroad companies, Meitetsu, JR Tōkai, and Kintetsu (Kinki Nippon Railroad), provide 12 rail routes, and *Shinkansen* bullet train service, to over 1.65 million riders per day (Nagoya City, 1997: 25, 30).[8] Although carrying a much lower proportion of all travel than in Tōkyō and Ósaka, railways in Nagoya still capture a significant number of commuter trips. However, realizing the growing demand for, and importance of mass transit, Nagoya's present master plan recommends several rail extensions and the establishment of a comprehensive transportation system that gives greater priority to public transit improvements.

Bus service is another important element of this policy. City operated routes carry roughly 540,000 passengers per day, and other private companies another 90,000 (Nagoya City, 1997: 25). However, the city feels the future of urban bus service lies in a Guideway Bus System. As mentioned earlier, a Guideway Bus is a special vehicle which can travel both on an ordinary road surface and on a high speed, automated track.

The system's first application, scheduled to open in the Year 2000, will run northeast along an elevated road from Ōzone Station in Higashi-ku, to Obata Green Park in Moriyama-ku. It will then travel along surface streets to Moriyama's Shidami District at the northeastern edge of the city. During the morning rush hour, it currently takes 42 minutes for a bus to travel from Ōzone to Obata Green Park. However, once the Shidami Guideway line is in place, the time for this trip will be cut to only 13 minutes. In addition to easing traffic congestion in the city center, Guideway buses will cost much less than subway extensions and will improve access to the Shidami District, where the city has a planned new town development project (Nagoya City, 1997; 1999a).

The City of Nagoya has also made other efforts to incorporate transit facilities in planned land use developments. With the help of national urban development grants, private sector funds, and citizen involvement, urban redevelopment projects have been completed, or are underway, adjacent to seven major transit stations (Nagoya City, 1997). Several more projects are in the planning stages, including the redevelopment of the Sasashima District, the original site of Nagoya Station, into a regional nucleus for international information and communication activities. In these projects, the city has creatively integrated new office, retail, and multi-family housing units with the restoration of historic properties, to transform existing transit stations into new centers of commercial and residential activity.

Of course a mention of such activities in Nagoya would be incomplete without a reference to the role Nagoya Station has played in the city's continued vitality. Serving as central Japan's transportation hub, Nagoya Station is a massive multi-modal complex, which houses a multi-line subway depot, a regional and city bus center, countless taxi stands, a multi-track Shinkansen station, and the main or regional terminal for several commuter rail companies. Passenger rail travel between most of the Chūkyō Region's largest cities, as well as most of Japan's largest regions, requires passage through

Nagoya Station. The station is also a main cog in the area's commercial activities, hosting three regional department stores and an underground mall. Planned expansions to the building will make it the tallest building in the city.

In sum, progressive land use and transportation planning have been major factors in understanding why Nagoya has remained the locus of employment in the Chūkyō Region. They have also improved the quality of life of city residents by providing almost everyone, regardless of age and income, with full access to residential and employment opportunities.[9]

Strategic Planning and a Diverse Economic Base[10]

The economic growth policies set out by the national government in the 1950s and 1960s fostered the over-concentration of population and employment in three metropolitan areas, Tōkyō, Ósaka, and Nagoya. In addition to migrating to these regions, people in search of employment left their farming villages for the growing opportunities in the region's central cities (Alden et al., 1994). As a result, by 1969, in addition to having two million residents, Nagoya City had 1.14 million non-governmental jobs. Since that time, non-governmental employment in the city has increased by more than 402,000 workers to almost 1.55 million in 1996. Nagoya's employment gain during this period represented almost 30% of all the employment growth in Aichi Prefecture, and almost one-quarter of the increase in the Chūkyō Major Metropolitan Area (See Table 5).

One of the reasons for this is the fact that the city's manufacturing industries are quite diverse. Of the city's more than 237,000 industrial jobs in 1996, six sectors had roughly 20,000 workers, including almost 26,000 in transport equipment, the third largest total in the Chūkyō Region.[11] Nearly 78% of these jobs were in Motor Vehicle, Parts and Accessories, including Mitsubishi, Nissan, and Toyota Motor related factories.

However, since 1969 the city has lost roughly 130,000 manufacturing jobs or 35.5%. As a result, unlike in 1969, manufacturing no longer holds the greatest proportion of the city's employment. Most of this decline occurred between 1969 and 1981 (99,000). Similar to other cities in the region, which have suffered manufacturing declines since 1969, a significant number of these jobs were in the textiles and ceramics sectors. The city lost 83.43% (22,498) of its textile mill employment between 1969 and 1996, its largest sectoral decline, and 69.67% (15,821) of its ceramics employment. Almost 16,000 of its decline in textiles, and over 13,000 of its loss in ceramics, were between 1969 and 1981. Most of these jobs were transferred to developing markets in East and Southeast Asia, where labor costs were much lower (Edgington, 1996).

Table 5. Non-Governmental Employment: Japan, Nagoya City and its Region, 1969–1996.

	1969	1996	Change 1969–1996	% Change 1969–1996
Japan	38,177,026	60,931,256	22,754,230	59.60
Chūbu	5,532,406	8,582,875	3,050,469	55.14
Nagano Prefecture	748,250	1,077,068	328,818	43.94
Gifu Prefecture	653,260	982,028	328,768	50.33
Shizuoka Prefecture	1,220,969	1,889,258	668,289	54.73
Mie Prefecture	549,538	861,972	312,434	56.85
Aichi Prefecture	2,360,389	3,772,549	1,412,160	59.83
Owari Sub-Region	1,748,874	2,679,942	931,068	53.24
Nishi Mikawa Sub-Region	384,816	741,148	356,332	92.60
Higashi Mikawa Sub-Region	226,699	351,459	124,760	55.03
Chūkyō Major Metropolitan Area	2,928,234	4,635,393	1,707,159	58.30
Nagoya City	1,144,969	1,547,156	402,187	35.13
Nagoya City's Share of Chūkyō	39.10%	33.38%	−5.72 points	

Sources: 1969 & 1996 Establishment Census of Japan.
Notes:
1. All employment is by Place of Work and includes Government Sector Employees.
2. The Chūbu Region, and the Aichi Sub-regions were calculated from source data. Nagoya city is included in the Owari Sub-Region total.

Nevertheless, Nagoya more than replaced its manufacturing loss with employment growth in Wholesale-Retail (a combined 203,000) and Services (up 233,000). As a result, the city now has more employment in Retail and Services than it does manufacturing (See Table 6). These sectors are primarily responsible for the city's continued vibrancy over the past 30 years. This is somewhat ironic, since commerce and services were also responsible for Nagoya's growth from a castle town to a modern city.

In addition to the national statutes mentioned earlier in the chapter, the Large-Scale Retail Stores Law in particular has been a major reason for Nagoya's continued growth has been city policies to create a more diverse economic base. For example, various strategic initiatives, such as the creation of special assessment districts for small and medium size firms, have helped attract business to the city (Edgington, 1996). Joint ventures between city and private development associations have also been important. The previously mentioned Shidami New Town Project in Moriyama-ku is the city's most dynamic effort.

Due to its steep slopes, the Shidami District remains the city's largest section of undeveloped land. Covering approximately 758 hectares (1,900 acres), the city's plan for the area calls for the creation of a "Human Science Town, where housing, research and development, [high-tech] manufacturing, and recreation functions [are to] exist in harmony" (Nagoya City, 1997: 56). The city government has sponsored several international conferences to attract aerospace, biotechnology, robotics, and other advanced technology firms to locate in the Shidami area.

Nagoya has also facilitated the development of a diversified economy, through the creation of the Japan Fine Ceramics Institute, an International Design Center, the Nagoya Software Center, two Industrial Research Institutes, business incubators, and high-tech industrial parks, as well as through the offering of subsidies to promote new industries (Edgington, 1996). Opened in 1987, the Ceramics Institute works closely with both small and large businesses in the area. A joint public-private venture, it is staffed by more than sixty researchers, half of whom are employed by the center, and half representing the more than twenty companies which have invested in the Institute, including Toyota, Toshiba, Nippon Steel, and Chūbu Electric Power (Miyakawa, 1993). The Institute's activities have helped to make Nagoya a center of high-tech fine ceramics. However, perhaps the main local economic development strategy behind Nagoya's recent employment growth has been the continuous expansion of Nagoya's port facilities.

As mentioned earlier, the Port of Nagoya was originally a landing place for small ferries. It was not until 1907 that a modern port was completed. A year

Table 6. Non-Governmental Employment Change by Industry Sector: Nagoya City, 1969–1996.

	1969	1996	Change 1969–1996	% Change 1969–1996
Total Non-Governmental Employment	1,144,969	1,547,156	402,187	35.13
Agriculture, Forestry, & Fishing	1,444	512	–932	–64.54
Mining	103	31	–72	–69.90
Construction	76,298	131,749	55,451	72.68
Utilities	9,291	11,156	1,865	20.07
Transportation & Communication	100,822	116,348	15,526	15.40
Manufacturing	367,995	237,349	–130,646	–35.50
Wholesale trade	181,984	258,923	76,939	42.28
Retail trade & eating establishments	189,854	315,652	125,798	66.26
Finance and Insurance	45,692	56,614	10,922	23.90
Real Estate	10,907	25,197	14,290	131.02
Services	160,579	393,625	233,046	145.13

Sources: 1969 & 1996 Establishment Census of Japan.
Notes:
1. All employment is by Place of Work.
2. Includes non-governmental employment at publicly owned companies, but not government sector employment.

later the port was designated as an international trading port under the name "Port of Nagoya" (Nagoya Port Authority, 1995).

In 1951, a year after the national government enacted the Laws and Regulations regarding Ports and Harbors, Aichi Prefecture and the City of Nagoya jointly established the Nagoya Port Authority. A Basic Concept Plan for the port was adopted in 1955, and has been revised several times, most recently in 1990. Since that time, the city and the Port Authority have continued to improve its port facilities by actively planning for its future. A special port development district was designated in 1965, and land around the wharf was rezoned to further encourage the port's development (Nagoya City, 1997).

A Port Authority Basic Plan Roundtable Conference was convened in 1986, and several of its recommendations were adopted in 1988. The project concepts forwarded at this conference stressed the need to improve the port facilities in order to keep pace with changes in the global economy over the next 30 years. Among the adopted proposals, the roundtable called for the development of an advanced integrated distribution base, an international trade and information center, an aerospace park, a waterfront residential community, and a waterfront park and promenade (Nagoya City, 1997: 74).

As a result of such pro-active planning, today 'the Port of Nagoya has grown to encompass a vast land and water area which falls within the cities of Nagoya, Tōkai, Chita, along with the Town of Yatomi and the Village of Tobishima' (Nagoya City, 1997: 72). Consistently one of Japan's busiest harbor, and among the top ten in the world (Nagoya Port Authority, 1995), Nagoya Port accommodated over 9,500 foreign and 32,900 cargo vessels in 1997 (Nagoya City, 1998: 8). Since 1977, the port has annually handled more than 100 million tons of cargo, including in 1996 when its volume exceeded 137 million tons, the most of any port in Japan in that year (Nagoya City, 1997: 72).

The growth of Nagoya Port has well complemented the city's goals for creating a more diverse economic base. An example of this, and of how the city and the region's economy continues to diversify, can be found in the port's cargo handling statistics. In Fiscal Year 1996, transportation equipment accounted for 62.4% of the port's exports. While this figure remains high, it represents an over eight percentage point drop from 1991 (Nagoya City, 1992: 73, 1997: 73). The port also handles the exporting of general machinery, basic metals, and rubber and chemical products, to North and South America, Europe, East and Southeast Asia, and Oceania. Much of its advances can be attributed to the actions of the Nagoya Port Authority, whose opening of a public aquarium in 1992, and other recreational facilities have also brought an improved quality of life to city residents.

Located just 30 minutes from the city center by car or subway, Nagoya Port, like many of the city's other economic development strategies, has played an important role in maintaining a vibrant Nagoya.

CONCLUSION

In the face of global restructuring and many other factors pushing population and employment to the suburbs, such as cheaper land and the growth of Toyota Motor, Nagoya City has remained the locus of activity in the Chūkyō Region. Since 1969 it has added over 126,000 people and more than 400,000 jobs. As a result, its proportion of metropolitan population and employment have declined by only five percentage points over the past 30 years (See Tables 1 and 5). These drops are quite small when compared with the fall in regional share suffered by many other central cities in Japan and in the United States.

A combination of national statutes, capacity building prefectural policies, and progressive city planning have been the keys to Nagoya's success. National statutes have facilitated integrated development planning and central city revitalization through: (a) the requiring of vertically and horizontally consistent development planning; (b) the protecting of agricultural lands and downtown retail from the unplanned conversion of suburban land to urban uses; and (c) local government laws which have promoted inter-municipal equity and administrative and urban service efficiency.

Aichi Prefecture has taken a leadership role in the coordinating of vertical and horizontal consistency through its administrative planning areas, built upon historical ties. These efforts have fostered inter-municipal cooperation between Nagoya and its adjacent municipalities, and have built a sense of mutual interdependence (i.e. regionalism) among communities.

While national and prefectural guidance have taken precedent in many cases, Nagoya's Designated City status has allowed it to play a major role in the planning process. Nagoya has then taken full advantage of its authority, taking a progressive approach to land use, economic, and transportation planning. The city's strategic development planning, centered around the Port of Nagoya and Nagoya Station, has nicely complemented national and prefectural policies. The combination of planning at all three levels of government has helped to build a high enough quality of life and diverse enough economic base to combat the forces of global restructuring and suburbanization, which have plagued other large cities of the world. The result also has been, from this author's perspective, that Nagoya suffers less from congestion, cramped housing conditions, air and water pollution, and a lack of open space, than do many of Japan's other large cities. In other words, the national, prefectural, and city governments have together planned for, and created, a vibrant, livable central city in Nagoya.

NOTES

1. According to the National Land Agency in the *Grand Design for the 21st Century: Comprehensive National Development Plan,* Japan's Chūbu or Central Region encompasses Nagano, Gifu, Shizuoka, Aichi, and Mie Prefectures (or *Ken* in Japanese).

2. The feudal State of Owari or *Owari no kuni* in Japanese, covered primarily the Shōnai and Kiso River areas (Aichi-ken, 1997).

3. It was also during this year that Japan's prefectures were basically reorganized into their present form. The Ryūkyū Islands (Okinawa), became the country's 47th prefecture in 1972.

4. Formerly Aichi *Bashatetsudō,* or Carriage Company, Nagoya *Denki Testudō* became Nagoya *Tetsudō* (Nagoya City Railway Company) or *Meitetsu* in 1921 (Meitetsu 2000).

5. Japan currently has one Metropolitan Government, Tōkyō, and 12 Designated Cities. In addition to Nagoya, there are: Chiba, Fukuoka, Hiroshima, Kawasaki, Kitakyūshū, Kōbe, Kyōto, Ósaka, Sapporo, Sendai, Yokohama. Saitama City, which will be created in May 2001 by the merger of three cities, Urawa, Ómiya, and Yono, will become the thirteenth, in 2002 or 2003.

6. The Building Construction Standards Act provides for up to 12 use districts, including one locally specified special district. Therefore, municipalities may have less than, but not more than, 12 use districts.

7. These names were translated from the Japanese, *chiiki* (administrative regions), *kōiki gyōsei ken* (broader administrative metropolises), and *toshi keikaku kuiki* (city planning areas).

8. Japan National Railways or *Kokutetsu*, was broken up and privatized in 1987. Central Japan Railway Company, or JR Tōkai, now serves the Nagoya area.

9. Physically disabled residents, however, are not well served by the public transit system.

10. Employment data in this section comes from 1969, 1981, and 1996 Establishment Censuses of Japan.

11. In descending order these six were: general machinery, printing and publishing, foodstuffs, motor vehicle equipment, fabricated metals, and electric machinery.

ACKNOWLEDGMENTS

The author would like to thank Jennifer Jacobs and Shuko Kimura Jacobs for their comments on this chapter.

REFERENCES

Aichi Prefecture (April 2000). Linear Chūō Shinkasen. Online. HTTP: http://www.pref.aichi.jp/ linear/.

Aichi Prefecture (1994). Some Strengths and Weaknesses of Japanese Urban Planning. In: P. Shapira, I. Masser & D. Edgington (Eds), *Planning for Cities and Regions in Japan* (pp. 12–24). Liverpool: Liverpool University Press.

Alden, J., Hirohara, M., & Abe, H. (1994). The Impact of Recent Urbanisation on Inner City Development in Japan. In: P. Shapira, I. Masser & D. Edgington (Eds), *Planning for Cities and Regions in Japan* (pp. 33–58). Liverpool: Liverpool University Press.

Asahi Shimbun Yūkan (July 24, 1998). Aichi to Mie wa Kōfu Zei Gengaku ni. [*Asahi Newspaper*, Evening Edition. Aichi and Mie Getting Less Allocation Tax than Last Time.]: 2. In Japanese.

Browne, W., & VerBurg, K. (1995). *Michigan Politics and Government: Facing Change in a Complex State*. Lincoln, NE: University of Nebraska Press.

Burby, R., & May, P. (1997). *Making Governments Plan: State Experiments in Managing Land Use*. Baltimore: Johns Hopkins.

Calder, K. (1988). *Crisis and Compensation: Public Policy and Political Stability in Japan*. Princeton, NJ: Princeton University Press.

Callies, D. L. (1997). Urban Land Use and Control in the Japanese City: A Case Study of Hiroshima, Osaka, and Kyōto, In: P. Karan & K. Stapleton (Eds), *The Japanese City* (pp. 135–155). Lexington, KY: University of Kentucky Press.

Dawson, A. (1984). *The Land Problem in the Developed Economy*. Totowa, NJ: Barnes & Noble Books.

Edgington, D. (1994). A Chronology of Major Urban and Regional Planning Legislation in Japan. In: P. Shapira, I. Masser & D. Edgington (Eds), *Planning for Cities and Regions in Japan* (pp. 184–189). Liverpool: Liverpool University Press.

Edgington, D. (1996). *Firms, Governments and Innovation in the Chūkyō Region*, Paper Presented at the Association of American Geographers annual meeting. North Charlotte, NC.

Eyre, J. (1982). *Nagoya: The Changing Geography of a Japanese Regional Metropolis: Studies in Geography No. 17*. Chapel Hill: University of North Carolina.

Hanayama, Y. (1986). *Land Markets and Land Policy in a Metropolitan Areas: A Case of Tōkyō*. Boston, MA: Oelgeschlager, Gunn & Hain.

Hanley, S., & Yamamura, K. (1977). *Economic and Demographic Change in Preindustrial Japan: 1600–1868*. Princeton, NJ: Princeton University Press.

Hebbert, M. (1994). 'Sen-biki' amidst 'Desakota': Urban Sprawl and Urban Planning in Japan. In: P. Shapira, I. Masser & D. Edgington (Eds), *Planning for Cities and Regions in Japan* (pp. 70–91). Liverpool: Liverpool University Press.

Jacobs, A. (1999). *Intergovernmental Relations and Uneven Development in the Detroit and Nagoya Auto Regions*, Unpublished Dissertation. Michigan State University.

Karan, P. (1997). Introduction. In: P. Karan & K. Stapleton (Eds), *The Japanese City* (pp. 1–11). Lexington, KY: University of Kentucky Press.

Kitazaki, S., & Ogawa, Y. (1997). Local Government. In: Y. Isozaki (Ed.), *The Local Administration in Japan* (pp. 1–115). Tōkyō: Local Autonomy College.

Kodansha Limited (1993). *Japan: An Illustrated Encyclopedia*. Tōkyō: Kodansha, Ltd.

Management and Coordination Agency, Government of Japan, Statistics Bureau (1992). *Establishment Census of Japan, 1991, Volume 2 – Results For Prefectures, Parts 21–24: Gifu, Shizuoka, Aichi, and Mie*. Tōkyō: Statistics Bureau.

Management and Coordination Agency, Government of Japan, Statistics Bureau (1997). *1995 Population Census of Japan, Volume 1-Total Population*. Tōkyō: Statistics Bureau.

Management and Coordination Agency, Government of Japan, Statistics Bureau (1998a). *Establishment Census of Japan, 1996, Volume 1–5, Result of Establishments for Japan, Establishments for Municipalities.* Tōkyō: Statistics Bureau.

Management and Coordination Agency, Government of Japan, Statistics Bureau (1998b). *Establishment Census of Japan, 1996, Volume 2 – Results of Establishments for Prefectures, Parts 21–24: Gifu, Shizuoka, Aichi, and Mie.* Tōkyō: Statistics Bureau.

Meitetsu Company (2000). Meitetsu Virtual Town Home Page, Train and Bus. Online. HTTP: http://www.meitetsu.co.jp/kensaku/start.html [15 March 2000].

Minerbi, L., Nakamura, P., Nitz, K., & Yanai, J. (Eds) (1986). *Land Readjustment: The Japanese System – A Reconnaissance and a Digest.* Boston, MA: Oelgeschlager, Gunn & Hain.

Miyakawa, Y. (1990). Japan: Towards a World Megalopolis and Metamorphosis of International Relations. *Ekistics, 57*(340/341), 48–75.

Miyakawa, Y. (1993). The Core of Japan's Global Manufacturing Industries. In: K. Fujita & R. Hill (Eds), *Japanese Cities in the World Economy* (pp. 159–174). Philadelphia: Temple University Press.

Morishima, M. (1982). *Why Has Japan Succeeded? Western Technology and the Japanese Ethos.* Cambridge: Cambridge University Press.

Nagoya City (1992). *Planning for Nagoya.* City of Nagoya City Planning Bureau.

Nagoya City (1997). *Planning for Nagoya.* City of Nagoya City Planning Bureau.

Nagoya City (1998). *Nagoya: Sketch of A City.* Nagoya City's International Relations Division.

Nagoya City (1999a). Welcome to Nagoya: Hot News, Road and River, New Urban Traffic System, Guideway Bus. Online. Available HTTP: http://www.city.nagoya.jp/indexe.htm [1 June 1999].

Nagoya City (1999b).Welcome to Nagoya: Introducing Nagoya, Statistical Sketch of Nagoya, Population. Online. Available HTTP: http:/www.city.nagoya.jp/indexe.htm [1 June 1999].

Nagoya Port Authority (1995). Nagoya Port Information, History in Brief, Nagoya, Japan.

Nakamura, H. (1993). Urban Growth in Prewar Japan. In: K. Fujita & R. Hill (Eds), *Japanese Cities in the World Economy* (pp. 26–49). Philadelphia: Temple University Press.

Nakamura, P. (1986a). A Legislative History of Land Readjustment. In: L. Minerbi, P. Nakamura, K. Nitz & J. Yanai (Eds), *Land Readjustment: The Japanese System – A Reconnaissance and a Digest* (pp. 17–31). Boston, MA: Oelgeschlager, Gunn & Hain.

Nakamura, P. (1986b). Foundations of Land Readjustment. In: L. Minerbi, P. Nakamura, K. Nitz & J. Yanai (Eds), *Land Readjustment: The Japanese System – A Reconnaissance and a Digest* (pp. 43–46). Boston, MA: Oelgeschlager, Gunn & Hain.

National Land Agency, Government of Japan (1998). *Grand Design for the 21st Century: Comprehensive National Development Plan.* Tokyo: National Land Agency.

Nishio, T. (1989). Metropolitan Development in the Great Turning Age of Socioeconomic Factors. In: *United Nations Center for Regional Development Meeting Report Series, 37* (pp. 18–24). Nagoya, Japan: United Nations Center for Regional Development.

Nitz, K. (1986). A Brief Thought on Land Readjustment. In: L. Minerbi, P. Nakamura, K. Nitz & J. Yanai (Eds), *Land Readjustment: The Japanese System – A Reconnaissance and a Digest* (pp. 15–16). Boston, MA: Oelgeschlager, Gunn & Hain.

Noguchi, Y. (1992). Land Problems and Policies in Japan: Structural Aspects. In: J. Haley & K. Yamamura (Eds), *Land Issues in Japan: A Policy Failure* (pp. 11–32). Seattle, WA: Society for Japanese Studies.

Office of the Prime Minister of Japan, Bureau of Statistics (1952). *1950 Population Census of Japan, Volume 1 – Total Population.* Tōkyō: Statistics Bureau.

Office of the Prime Minister of Japan, Bureau of Statistics (1970a). *1969 Establishment Census of Japan, Volume 1 – Results for Japan*. Tōkyō: Bureau of Statistics.
Office of the Prime Minister of Japan, Bureau of Statistics (1970b). *1969 Establishment Census of Japan, Volume 2 – Results for Prefectures, Parts 21–24: Gifu, Shizuoka, Aichi, Mie*. Tōkyō: Bureau of Statistics.
Office of the Prime Minister of Japan, Bureau of Statistics (1971). *1969 Establishment Census of Japan, Volume 3 – Results for Cities*. Tōkyō: Bureau of Statistics.
Office of the Prime Minister of Japan, Bureau of Statistics (1972). *1970 Population Census of Japan, Volume 1 – Total Population*. Tōkyō: Statistics Bureau.
Office of the Prime Minister of Japan, Bureau of Statistics (1982). *1981 Establishment Census of Japan, Volume 2 – Results for Prefectures, Parts 21–24: Gifu, Shizuoka, Aichi, Mie*. Tōkyō: Bureau of Statistics.
Sakamoto, S. (1998). Urban Redevelopment Methods in Japan. In: G. Golany, K. Hanaki & O. Koide (Eds), *Japanese Urban Environment* (pp. 303–323). New York: Pergamon.
Sano, Y., Tsubouchi, F., & Uenomachi, T. (1998). National and Land Development Plans in Japan. In: G. Golany, K. Hanaki & O. Koide (Eds), *Japanese Urban Environment* (pp. 262–282). New York: Pergamon.
Toyota Motor Corporation (1988). *Toyota: A History of the First 50 Years*. Toyota City, Japan: Toyota Motor Corporation.
Tsuji, K. (1984). *Public Administration in Japan*. Tōkyō: University of Tōkyō Press.
U.S. Department of Commerce, Bureau of the Census (1973). *1970 Census of Population, Volume 1, Characteristics of the Population*. Washington, DC: Government Printing Office.
U.S. Department of Commerce, Bureau of the Census (June 30, 1999). Annual Time Series of Population Estimates, 1991 to 1998, and 1990 Census Population for Places, Online. Available HTTP: http://www.census.gov/ population/www/ estimates/cityplace.html
Upham, F. (1993). Privatizing Regulation: The Implementation of the Large-Scale Retail Law. In: G. Allinson & Y. Sone (Eds), *Political Dynamics in Contemporary Japan* (pp. 264–294). Ithaca, NY: Cornell University Press.
Yamamura, K. (1992). LDP Dominance and High Land Price in Japan: A Study in Positive Political Economy. In: J. Haley & K. Yamamura (Eds), *Land Issues in Japan: A Policy Failure* (pp. 33–75). Seattle, WA: Society for Japanese Studies.

3. AN ECONOMIC DEVELOPMENT STRATEGY FOR CAIRNS

Brian Roberts and John Dean

ABSTRACT

Cairns, in the northern part of the State of Queensland, is one of Australia's fastest growing and internationalized regional economies. In the 1970s, the Cairns Region was a branch line economy growing sugar and tobacco. Through the initiatives and enterprise of the local community and government, the region built an international airport, developed international tourism, fishing, mining and tropical agriculture industries and substantially diversified its service industry base. This was the result of a commitment and focus by the region to economic and integrated regional planning which emphasised the development of strategic infrastructure, industry clusters, public and private sector investment and partnerships, sustainable development and the development of human and natural capital. This chapter describes the way the community and government have worked together to develop and transform the economy of the region.

INTRODUCTION

Cairns is one of Australia's most popular tourism destinations. Located in the northern part of the State of Queensland (see Fig. 1), the region was once a small backward economy producing mainly sugar, timber, tobacco and beef. In the early 1980s, the Cairns and Far North Queensland region experienced a

International Urban Planning Settings: Lessons of Success, Volume 12, pages 61–85.
2001 by Elsevier Science Ltd.
ISBN: 0-7623-0695-5

remarkable transformation, which was brought about by the influence of national economic reforms, environmental policies, and the vision of a few community leaders to build an international airport. The opening of the Cairns International Airport in 1984 started a development process that has led to Cairns becoming one of the most internationalized and rapidly growing regional economies in Australia.

Like many regions of the world that have experienced rapid development, the initial bubble of success faded in the early 1990s. Between 1985 and 1991 over A$1 billion in foreign investment poured into the local economy, mainly into tourism and residential property development. Much of this was from Japanese sources. In 1991, the Japanese economy entered a prolonged recession and foreign investment in the Cairns region dried up. At the same time, the global recession, high foreign exchange rates and a disastrous airline pilot's strike resulted in a significant contraction to the region's economy. Unemployment

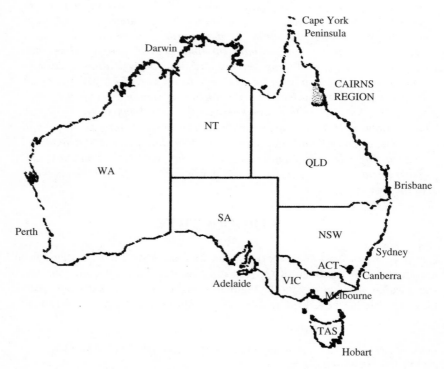

Fig. 1. Map Showing Location of Cairns Region.

bankruptcies rose sharply and social issues related to rapid growth began to emerge (Duke, 1993). Much of the development that had occurred in the region during the 1980s had not been well planned and was having an impact upon the region's fragile natural environment. The economic base of the region had become distorted, with a high dependence upon tourism that had left the economy very exposed to cyclical features and fluctuations synonymous with this industry (Stimson et al., 1996).

In 1992, the Queensland State Government, in response to concerns about the economy and the environment, began a series of initiatives designed to improve the future management and development of the region. A partnership between government, local business and the community was established to prepare an Integrated Regional Development Plan to guide the growth of the region to the year 2010 and beyond. One of the key initiatives of the plan was the Cairns Regional Economic Development Strategy and the establishment of the Cairns Regional Economic Development Corporation (CREDC) which provides the mechanism for implementation of the strategy.

This chapter describes the remarkable success story of a region that has learned to understand globalization and to mobilize its community to benefit from it. It has done this by meticulous attention to research, community consultation and planning. The region is aware of the factors that make it competitive, and has set about to leverage and develop these for competitive advantage. This region has adopted a very open and consultative approach to the economic development, with a strong emphasis on encouraging innovation, partnerships, alliances and clustering. At the same time, the region has adopted sustainable approaches to the management of social and environmental issues that are a consequence of rapid development.

The chapter begins with a brief profile of the economic geography and development of the Cairns region. This leads on to a discussion of issues that led to a crisis in the region's development in the early 1990s. One of the responses to the crisis was the preparation of an Integrated Regional Development Plan. The plan involves a partnership between government, business, the community and other stakeholders to collaborate on the management of regional growth and development. This is followed by a discussion on the development of the Cairns Regional Economic Development Strategy, including the strategies that focus on innovation, import substitution and industry clustering, and the role of the Cairns Regional Economic Development Corporation as a catalyst in implementing the strategy and in facilitating new ideas and initiatives for economic development in the region. The chapter also discusses the lessons learned from the implementation of the

Economic Development Strategy and suggests directions for the future development of the economy.

ECONOMIC GEOGRAPHY OF THE REGION

The Cairns and Far North Queensland (FNQ) Region covers an area of approximately 50,000 sq km and has a population of approximately 210,000. The population of the region has grown at over 3.4% since 1991. At any time there are over 25,000 visitors in the region. The region incorporates eight local governments, of which the City of Cairns, population 125,000, is the largest urban centre.

Geographic Features

The region has four distinct geographic features:

(1) The coastal zone consists of a 5–15 km stretch of coastal lowlands and valleys nestled between the coastal ranges and a steep rainforest escarpment that runs 300km along the length of the region. The lowlands are very fertile and are used for intensive sugar and tropical agriculture. Most urban settlement in the region occurs in this zone.

(2) The rainforest escarpment forms part of the northern end of Australia's Great Dividing Range. The escarpment has some of the highest rainfall in Australia. Most of the range is included in the World Heritage listed Wet Tropics Rainforest and contains some of the most ancient forests on earth.

(3) The Tablelands are a series of plateaus 500–600m above sea level to the west of the escarpment. The plateaus slope gently to the channel country of the Gulf of Carpentaria several hundred kilometres west. The Tablelands have high quality soils and lower rainfall and are an important horticulture, tropical fruit and tobacco growing area.

(4) To the east of Cairns lies the Coral Sea and the World Heritage listed Great Barrier Reef. The reef comes closest to the Australian mainland at Cook Town 160km north of Cairns. The Wet Tropics Rainforest and Great Barrier Reef are major attractions for over one million visitors each year.

The Old Economy

The old economy of the Cairns region was based on forestry, fishing, sugar, bananas and tobacco. Fishing, sugar and tropical fruit are still important industries; however, tourism and mining represent more than 45% of regional exports. In 1986, the Gross Regional Product (GRP) of the economy was estimated at A$1.84 billion. In 1998 it was estimated at A$4.3 billion (NIEIR, 1998). The economy has been growing at more than 5.5% per annum since 1985. In some years in the late 1980s its growth rate exceeded 8% (Roberts, 1996).

Table 1 indicates the estimated contribution to GRP by 18 industry sectors and household consumption in the region's economy for 1986, 1990, 1994 and 1998. Finance, tourism/recreation services, retail trade, mining, food processing and community services are the dominant sectors of the economy. Tourism contributes an estimated 25% to the GRP (Horwarth and Horwarth, 1993). Building construction and transport services grew significantly during the 1980s, but slumped during the early 1990s as foreign investment in the region declined (Stimson et al., 1996) and the recession slowed the growth of the economy. The construction industry began to recover in 1996 as visitors and new investment to the region increased.

Table 1. Estimated Percentage Industry Contribution to GRP (1986, 1990, 1994, 1998).

	1986	1990	1994	1998*
Animal	2.0	1.9	1.5	1.3
Other Agriculture	5.0	6.3	6.6	6.7
Forest/Fish	2.7	1.9	1.6	1.6
Mining	4.9	8.7	7.6	7.4
Food Processing	4.2	3.9	4.6	5.1
Wood & Paper Man	1.6	1.2	1.2	1.1
Machinery Man	1.7	1.8	1.5	1.3
Metals	2.6	0.8	1.1	1.1
Non Metals	0.5	0.6	0.5	0.4
Other Man	0.3	0.4	0.5	0.4
Elect/Gas/Water	1.6	1.8	1.5	1.4
Build/Construction	9.9	7.6	5.6	6.2
Trade	13.8	11.3	11.7	12.0
Transport (Trans)	10.6	8.0	7.4	7.1
Finance	14.2	11.7	10.1	9.5
Public Administration	2.9	3.2	5.4	5.2
Community Services	12.1	11.7	12.7	12.7
Tourism/Personal Services	8.9	7.9	11.1	11.4
H-Hold Consumption	0.5	9.2	7.8	8.1
GRP	100.0	100.0	100.0	100.0

Source: AHURI 1995   * NIEIR Regional Report Estimate

The 1980s Boom Times

The tourism potential of the Cairns Region was recognized in 1947 in a report on *The Tourism Potential of the State* presented to the Queensland Premier (Ferguson et al., 1947). It would be over 20 years before the visions of this report were realized. In 1967, the World War II aerodrome at Cairns was upgraded to enable domestic jet aircraft to land. In 1981, the Great Barrier Reef was listed as a World Heritage area. The closeness of the Reef to Cairns is a factor that draws an increasing number of international and domestic visitors to the region.

In 1981, the members of the Cairns Port Authority recognized that there was strategic advantage to be gained by the region developing an international airport in Cairns. The Port Authority acquired the airport from the Commonwealth government. Raising capital through a government loan, the Authority constructed and opened the Cairns International Airport in March 1984. A new international terminal was opened in 1990 adjacent to the domestic terminal. The airport is now the fifth largest airport in Australia with over 160 weekly international flights to and from Asia and the Pacific.

The Cairns International Airport was a significant initiative for the region, given the Federal Airports Corporation (which controlled Australia's major airports at the time) had selected Townsville, 350km to the south, as the second international airport for the State. Townsville, which is larger than Cairns (but not growing nearly as fast), is the major government center for the north. However, the rivalry that existed between the two cities, and in particular the preference for public sector invesment and for government functions to be located in Townsville, meant Cairns and the FNQ region were continually disadvantaged in terms of public sector investment to support economic development. The FNQ region had very little choice but to take a more private sector approach to its future development. The airport provided the catalyst that was to result in the Cairns region easily out performing its southern rival.

However, the State Government during the 1980s did help pave the way for accelerated domestic and international investment in tourism facilities and infrastructure in resort destinations at Port Douglas, Green Island, Dunk Island, Palm Cove, Central Cairns and Mission Beach. Between 1985 and 1990 over A$1 billion was invested in major tourism facilities. But most of this was private sector investment and often highly speculative. The Japanese company Daikyo was a very substantial investor in the region owning at one stage 10 major tourism facilities and land holdings in the region (Stimson et al., 1998). During the late 1980s, there was substantial investment in new mining activities in the region and in Papua New Guinea and West Irian Jaya (Indonesia), most of which were serviced from Cairns. The impact of these developments gave rise to new investment in retail, residential, commercial and business services (Daly & Stimson, 1993).

The Crisis of 1989–1991

The October 1987 stock market crash was the first setback to the region's booming tourism industry. Quintex, a major domestic tourism resort developer collapsed, followed by several other resort developers. The rapid devaluation of the Australian dollar against the yen following the stock market crash led to an increase of Japanese and Asian investment in the region. Japanese investors began cashing in on the fire sale prices of domestic tourism ventures that had failed and were being held by national banks and other financial creditors anxious to remove bad debts and poorly performing assets from their investment portfolios. The rise in foreign investment continued until late 1991, when the first signs of a recession in the Japanese economy emerged. The sudden withdrawal of foreign investment led to a rapid downturn in the construction industry and the slowing of other economic activities.

In August 1989, a national pilot's strike occurred. The strike was expected to last a few days but it dragged on for more than eight months. The airforce and international carriers were mobilized by the Federal Government to provide a makeshift national airline service. The impact of the strike on the region's economy and community was severe. The rise in domestic interest rates began to impact on the residential and commercial construction industry. Regional imports for the first time began to exceed regional exports, leading to deepening regional trade imbalance (Roberts, 1996). The prospects for the economy looked less than optimistic.

Two saving features for the region at the time were the weak Australian dollar and the start up of a discount airline, Compass Airlines, which was offering cheap national fares to the region and other state capital cities. These two features made the Cairns region a favourable tourism destination for international and domestic visitors. International visitor numbers grew by 18% per annum between 1989 and 1992, with domestic numbers increasing by 9% (NCSTT, 1993; Premier's Department, 1994).

The boom in tourism was important in offsetting the slump in other sectors of the economy such as mining, sugar and agriculture, which were in recession. Many other regions of Australia, including the metropolitan regions, were in deep recession. Cairns with a more diversified, open and export-orientated economy continued to maintain strong regional growth. There was the realization, however, that the drastic fall off in foreign and domestic investment would eventually have an impact upon the region, and that the slowing of economic growth was a good opportunity to take stock of the past and consider strategic directions for the future.

In 1991, the Queensland Government commissioned a report to examine critical development issues affecting the economic growth of Far North Queensland (FNQ) (Blurton Russell & Associates, 1991). The report identified numerous infrastructure problems, planning and environmental issues requiring attention if the region was to prosper.

In 1992, the State Government initiated a regional planning process referred to as Far North Queensland (FNQ) 2010. Its aim was to prepare an integrated regional development plan. This process took seven years to complete, but it laid down one of the most comprehensive planning and decision-making frameworks for the sustainable development of a region ever attempted in Australia. The plan outlined principles for ecologically sustainable development, economic development, resource management, community development, urban development and infrastructure, and native title. Without proper management of future development, there was the strong likelihood that the region would not be able to provide the economic and social infrastructure needed to support its growth (Blurton Russell & Associates, 1991). There was concern also that the continuation of poorly planned development was not sustainable and would have a detrimental impact on the region's natural environment.

The integrated development plan involves government, industry and the community working collaboratively to develop new initiatives for the sustainable development of the region. The Economic Development Strategy for the Cairns Region forms a key element of the regional plan.

FNQ 2010 REGIONAL PLANNING PROJECT

The first step in the FNQ 2010 process began in 1992 with the establishment of the State Government Regional Planning Advisory Committee (RPAC). The RPAC was given the responsibility to investigate the impacts of development on the region, and to prepare the Integrated Regional Development Plan. The process was modelled on the earlier project SEQ 2001 being prepared for the Brisbane Metropolitan region in the south-east corner of the state (Abbot, 1995), and which is discussed by Wyeth in Chapter 7 of this volume. The RPAC was comprised of representatives from the three levels of government, community organizations and industry.

The aim of the Integrated Regional Development Plan was to provide a broad planning and policy framework within which decisions could be made with greater confidence, certainty and community support. The planning process adopted was to ensure growth and development were planned and managed in a way that enhanced the positive benefits to the region's community whilst minimizing or avoiding potential negative impacts, especially on the environment. The Regional Plan was to ensure the key environmental, social and economic values were not degraded but enhanced wherever possible, and that infrastructure services were delivered in a timely, cost-effective manner to support the community and economic development.

There was considerable debate in the community and the RPAC about how to prepare the regional plan. It was agreed the plan should not be a statutory document and should not add a new layer of bureaucracy between the state and local government planning systems (FNQ2010, 1998). The plan was to be used as a framework for all three levels of government and the community to aid cooperative decision making and to ensure planning and development were undertaken on a consultative, responsive, collaborative and integrated basis.

Planning Process

A three stage process was established to develop the regional plan. Stage 1 involved the preparation of a *Far North Queensland Regional Growth Management Framework* (RGMF) report (RPAC, 1996). This report identified the key growth management issues facing the region and presented a broad planning framework to guide the preparation of detailed regional strategies for the plan. The RGMF comprized three key elements: a regional vision statement; a set of integrated regional goals to guide the development of detailed strategies; and a regional structure plan (broad based land-use plan) which establishes the broad physical arrangements and preferred settlement pattern for the region until 2016.

Stage 2 of the process involved the preparation of an integrated set of detailed regional strategies. The regional strategies incorporated a comprehensive set of objectives and strategy statements and provided the mechanisms by which the regional vision, goals and structure plan were to be achieved. Two key reports were produced as part of the Stage 2 process. The first, the *Strategic Directions and Regional Priorities for Far North Queensland* report (RPAC, 1998a), outlined the key issues facing the region and the strategic initiatives proposed to deal with these. The report also identified key implementation actions that needed to be undertaken in the short-term to alleviate existing or potential problems or to take advantage of regional opportunities. These included: incorporation of regional planning outcomes into capital works programs and policy making processes of federal, state and local government;

and the incorporation of regional planning outcomes into local government land use policy plan making processes, in particular, local government planning schemes.

Implementation will also involve a wide range of community and industry groups and individuals, particularly at the sub-regional and local levels. The second report titled *Draft Integrated Regional Strategy* (RPAC, 1998b) outlined nine key strategies to support the implementation of the Regional Growth Management Framework. These are shown in Fig. 2. The Tourism Strategy (Office of the Coordinator General, 1994) was undertaken as a separate process to FNQ 2010 and was completed well in advance of the other strategies. The Tourism Strategy was incorporated into the draft integrated plan with some changes in 1998. The FNQ Regional Economic Development Strategy (DTSBI, 1996), which forms a key element of the Integrated Regional Development Plan, was also undertaken as a separate planning process and will be described in more detail below.

Regional Development Plan

The Regional Plan for Far North Queensland was released in 1999 and contained a range of documents that integrate the different strategies with the planning and policy parameters contained in the RGMF. The plan establishes a broad policy and decision-making framework to guide the management and development of Far North Queensland well into the 21st century. The implementation mechanisms involve a series of multi-disciplinary task forces, committees or organizations responsible for overseeing the implementation of regional strategies. These task forces have considerable autonomy, and are encouraged to collaborate and leverage resources between responsible agencies whenever possible. A representative from each task force sits on the Regional Planning Advisory Committee, which has overall responsibility for plan implementation and monitoring.

Importance of Community Input

The success of the regional planning process has been due largely to involvement from the outset by the community. The community maintains a strong presence in the implementation of the plan and the regional strategies. Community organizations maintain representation on the RPAC, and are called upon for advice and consultations on different issues related to the implementation of the regional strategies. The incorporation of community representation, targeted consultation and the opportunity for broad public

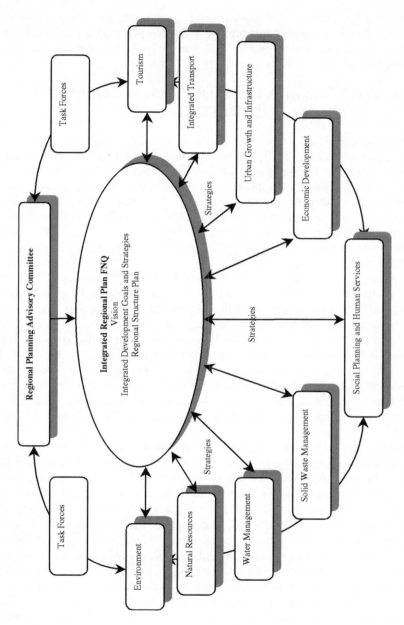

Fig. 2. Integrated Regional Plan for FNQ 2010.

involvement has ensured community values and needs have been properly considered and integrated into the regional plan. The planning process has been transparent and accountable, and this has helped to build community confidence and support for the plan.

CAIRNS REGION ECONOMIC DEVELOPMENT STRATEGY

The Cairns Region Economic Development Strategy began as a separate planning process to FNQ 2010. The first detailed economic development study of the region was undertaken in 1986 (Cameron McNamara, 1986). This report placed a strong emphasis on the development of physical infrastructure and promotion of FNQ comparative advantages. The report presented a very optimistic view of the future of the economy. The Blurton Russell (1991) report on development issues reinforced the need to improve infrastructure, but raised a wide range of other issues, including issues related to regional economic development.

With the rapid downturn in foreign investment in 1991, and a slowing in Asian visitor numbers two years later, there was a realization by government and by business that further diversification of the economy was necessary. There was acknowledgment by the business sector that the region needed to focus on factors that would improve its competitiveness, such as quality of services, and to embark upon initiatives that would make it more attractive for investment (Hassell & Associates, 1992). In October 1993, the state government took the first step to establish a Regional Economic Development Committee to formulate a regional economic development strategy (CREDS) for the Cairns region. The CREDS planning process was to be linked to FNQ 2010.

In 1994, the Federal government had initiated a regional development program following the publication of the Kelty (1994) and McKinsey (1994) Reports. These reports produced for the Federal Department of Housing and Regional Development involved surveys of 44 regions in Australia and led to the setting up of a series of Regional Development Organizations throughout the country. The Federal Government supported the establishment of the Cairns Regional Economic Development Organization (CREDO) and provided funds to prepare regional economic development strategies. The FNQ REDS strategy commenced in 1995 with the REDO commissioning a series of background studies on the region's economy. One of the most important studies was on the Internationalization of the FNQ Regional Economy (Roberts & Daly, 1995). This research identified key factors that were responsible for the region's competitiveness, including core competencies, strategic infrastructure and market orientation (Roberts & Stimson, 1998).

Other studies commissioned by the REDO included: a *Baseline Economic Profile – Growth Factors Analysis* (CERU, 1994); *Import Replacement Strategy* (Roberts & Lanarch, 1996) and *The Tradeable Services Strategy* (Daly et al., 1996). There were a further 25 industry position and discussion papers prepared as background material for the Strategy (FNQREDS, 1997).

In 1996, the Federal Coalition Government withdrew support for the regional development program. Custodianship of the FNQREDS was transferred to the Department of Tourism Small Business and Industry (DTSBI) in Cairns to complete the work on the strategy and report to the Regional Planning Advisory Committee. A draft FNQ Economic Development Strategy (DTSBI, 1996) was prepared in consultation with local business, industry and government sectors and the final strategy released in 1988. The Cairns Regional Economic Development Strategy incorporates a comprehensive set of aims, objectives and strategy statements and provided the mechanisms by which the strategy is being implemented (www.credc.com).

Aim of the Economic Strategy

The aim of the Far North Queensland Regional Economic Development Strategy is to: "achieve a regional economy in Far North Queensland" which will foster appropriate economic development and preserve the quality of life and the region's unique environment and enhance community lifestyle and well-being, now and for future generations. It is intended that future economic development in the region should be viable, ecologically sustainable, diverse, dynamic and competitive. The focus of economic activity is intended to be based on local, domestic and international markets and will be driven by key industries such as primary production, tourism and knowledge-based industry supported by a broad range of secondary and tertiary industries.

Priority Issues for Economic Development

The strategy recognizes the prime importance of developing a secure, diverse regional economy and strong export orientated service industries. The FNQREDS acknowledges there are some critical issues that need to be addressed if regional economic growth is to become more sustainable in future. These issues primarily relate to the growing regional trade imbalance, stemming the leakage of capital out-flows and ensuring greater retention and reinvestment of profits in the region. An important issue facing the region was its lack of corporate identity as a business center. Reversing the decline in foreign investment was affected by all of the above.

FNQREDS recognized the need to capitalize on the benefits that tourism had introduced to the region. This was to be achieved by developing and collaborating between the tourism sector and other industry sectors. Additionally, the region needed to increase business co-operation and networking, improve resource management and identify changing international trading structures, particularly in Asia, to enhance the region's export potential. While the FNQ economy showed every sign of prospering, these key development issues needed to be addressed if the region was to realize its potential and maintain its standing as a highly competitive international trading economy.

To capitalize on long-term economic opportunities the strategy identified a number of objectives. These are listed in Table 2 below. A series of initiatives in the form of projects and programs were formulated and costed in support of the strategy objectives.

Key Initiatives

The FNQREDS strategy put forward three important strategies to drive the economic development of the region. These were a focus on: (a) industry clusters; (b) development of trade and producer services; and (c) import substitution.

Industry Clusters
The economic strategy recognized the significant benefits to be gained through encouraging industry clusters, in the belief that this would encourage greater collaboration, cooperation and co-existence of competitive industries in the

Table 2. FNQ 2000 Strategy Objectives.

Develop and promote a corporate image for the region.
Enhance value added export performance.
Encourage import replacement industries.
Improve the availability and adoption of new information technologies.
Identify critical infrastructure requirements and address infrastructure constraints.
Encourage the capability of the region to self-fund and attract investment.
Ensure labour force skills meet employment and future industry requirements.
Enhance the quality of life by managing the impacts of economic development on the environment.
Encourage indigenous enterprise development.

---

region. Fifteen industry clusters were identified using location quotients and input-output analysis. While some of these were very weak clusters, they were considered by industry representatives to have development potential and steps were taken to form industry clusters (CREDC, 1998). The Cairns Regional Development Corporation (CREDC) is coordinating the process. The development and role of the CREDC is described in more detail below.

Focus on the Develop Trade/Producer Services
Given the location advantage of Cairns in relation to the Asian cities and air transport systems, the economic strategy recognized that there were opportunities to develop and export specialized trade/producer services. A study was commissioned to examine the prospects for developing tourism, environmental and cultural management, education and medical services (Daly et al., 1996). The study used Porter's (1990) Diamond Technique to analyse the competitiveness of key producer services, in terms of factor conditions, demand conditions, networks and industry structure. The analysis identified specific weaknesses in infrastructure needed to support the development of these services, and highlight opportunities for developing some producer services. Education, environmental management, business tourism, mining and tropical agriculture services are considered to have export development potential.

Import Substitution
In recognition of the growing imbalance in regional trade discussed earlier in the chapter, opportunities to reduce imports to the region are considered a high priority. The study of import substitution (Roberts & Lanarch, 1996) showed limited opportunities for total import substitution industries because of economies of scale, local market demand, transport, R&D and marketing cost issues. The research identified opportunities to combine import substitution with the development of new export industries. Several new industry activities involving marine services, agricultural engineering, construction, mining and tourism support services have significant development potential. The CREDC is facilitating the development of some of these opportunities.

CAIRNS REGIONAL ECONOMIC DEVELOPMENT CORPORATION

The Economic Development Strategy was completed in early 1997. However, the withdrawal of federal funding support to the CREDC left the Strategy without an Organization to oversee its implementation. It had always been assumed that a public sector agency like the CREDO would have custodianship of the strategy. Without ongoing funding support, the economic development strategy would go the way of many other regional strategies prepared with commonwealth funding and remain a strategy never to be actioned. Several regional leaders had been concerned for some time at the lack of business people involved with employment and economic development leadership in Far North Queensland. After many consultations the chief executive of the CREDO successfully managed to convince other industry leaders to participate in a restructured industry-led organization.

An FNQ Regional Development Network Economic Summit was held in November1997 where community leaders from the region took a major step forward by seeing the need for change in the way economic development was undertaken. The purpose of the Summit was to identify problems and set in motion actions to reverse the downturn in industry, stimulate confidence and develop industry strategies into the next century.

Representatives of the region's fifteen major industrial groups made presentations to the summit in relation to: (a) current economic status; (b) future prospects and opportunities; and (c) constraints and obstacles to future growth and assistance needed by industry. The major outcome was that while most industry leaders could outline today's problems, few could enunciate a clear plan for their industry over the next five years covering future prospects. The need for a strategy to reposition the region in Asia was a major issue. There was consensus for the need to maintain the benefits of the brand name "CAIRNS" and that it remained the focus for marketing and promotion of the region. There was also a general dissatisfaction with the current bureaucratic government processes. Time delays, poor decision making and deferment all make the business of doing business more difficult.

There was confusion over who should manage the Far North Queensland Regional Economic Development Strategy (FNQREDS). While the existing public sector orientated FNQ Regional Development Organization had the charter to facilitate the recommendations of the Strategy, industry agreed to get involved in economic development by focusing on the identification of the region's comparative competitive advantages. This led to the recent completion of a research project on benchmarking the competitiveness of the FNQ region (Roberts, 2000).

There was general agreement on the need for a replacement group/hub/organization to ensure the issues identified at the summit and of importance to the future economic development of the region were picked up and acted upon. Industry agreed there was a role for a coordinating body to call industry together as and when necessary, to deliberate and act upon issues of significant importance to regional development and to disseminate information across industry sectors. Industry agreed to regular summits to discuss issues and developments across industries.

The clear message is for the business community of Far North Queensland to make things happen. Competition outside the region has grown and it is up to regional business to compete more effectively in the future. The summit provided the opportunity to assess where the community is in terms of industry competitiveness and to consider collectively where it wants to go in the future. The prevailing themes expressed were:

- 'We should not try to be what we're not, but make a benefit of what we are';
- 'What is good for one in is generally good for all';
- 'We should support industries with potential and important ones with problems, from a whole of business and industry perspective'; and
- 'We should collaborate far more effectively for future economic development'.

Agreement for a new approach to employment and economic development in Far North Queensland was strong. Business leaders indicated their support for the establishment of a new industry led economic corporation. Follow-up briefings from over 50 influential business people together with the 1997 Northern Development Industry Association annual conference confirmed the need for the strategic partnership.

Role of the Cairns Regional Economic Development Corporation

The Cairns Regional Economic Development Corporation (CREDC) was established in 1998, and has become the forum to catalyse industry. The corporation is a limited liability company. Funding for the corporation comes from its 500 plus members, government grants and commercial activities. There are 15 voting positions on the Corporation's Board and each industrial sector holds equity in the new Economic Development Corporation. The guiding principles that govern the activities of the corporation are shown in Table 3. Government and the community are represented by non-voting members. The Board is chaired by an independent chairperson. The Corporation is supported by a chief executive, administrative staff and five part-time cluster facilitators.

The Corporation also facilitates generic marketing, cluster trade missions, cluster joint-venturing and strategic alliances. The role of industry is to adopt a global outlook and to have a strong commitment to the cluster concept. Industry must cultivate multiple alliances to develop or have access to cutting-edge technology.

Table 3. Guiding Principles of the CREDC.

Target clusters that increase economic wealth with multiple impacts on consumption.
Focus on quality employment opportunities with increasing wage rates.
Promote collaboration principles for economic development.
Facilitate international and domestic strategic alliances and joint ventures between industries and clusters.
Diversify the economy in industries that can be world competitive.
Assist firms that, whenever possible, use local firms for services and supplies.
Work with educational institutions to enhance local skills and training programs.
Create opportunities that assist all segments of the workforce.

Far North Queensland Industry Clusters

The FNQ Regional Development Network Strategy for Tradeable Services study (Daly et al., 1996) identified 15 service industries for potential clustering (See Table 4). Tourism, transport and agribusiness services demonstrated strong elements of clustering. Most other industries showed potential to support the development of small-scale industry clusters. These service industries, combined with the region's traditional industries, were intended to form the nucleus of the clusters. There was an expectation not all the clusters identified would succeed. However, as the level of enthusiasm is high, each cluster should be given the opportunity to succeed. The list is not exclusive and if other industries wish to participate, they will be welcome.

Guidelines adapted from the Greater Tucson Strategic Economic Plan (1996: 17) were used for, screening, approving and prioritizing firms to become part of an industrial cluster. These guidelines are shown in Table 4.

The tasks of the Corporation to facilitate clusters were detailed in the strategic planning process for the corporation and are shown in Table 5.

The clustering process, as expected, has meet with mixed success. Several industry clusters are well advanced in their development (see Table 6):

Table 4. Guidelines for Developing Industry Clusters in FNQ.

Firms that are stable or are from growth industries.
Industries with the capacity to become world competitive.
Industries that have a unique competitive advantage.
Firms that use local labour and suppliers.
Businesses that are export oriented.
Firms with the best potential to joint venture internationally.

Table 5. Task of the Corporation.

Provide facilitation venues, secretarial support and organize cluster meetings.
Prepare finance submissions for cluster formation activities.
Establish initiation focus groups with 15–20 people from each industrial sector.
Facilitate detailed cluster mapping for each industry.
Develop a comprehensive statistical industry profile for each cluster.
Assist each cluster to develop a strategic and business/operational plan.
Provide assistance with accessing market intelligence.
Conduct industrial cluster benchmarking for world competitiveness.
Promote skills, teambuilding and a learning environment.
Develop cluster specific training in partnership with business and education.
Enhance school and industrial cluster partnerships.
Develop cluster marketing including individual web pages.

(1) The marine industry cluster, centered around the region's A\$120 million fishing industry, has established a company, "Eco Fish", which represents the interests of the industry. It has over 150 members, and raises funds from a membership fee and a boat levee on fishing vessels depending on size. The company is involved with: (a) promoting the interests of the industry; (b) research; (c) expanding export markets; and (d) developing education courses with the local technical college and public relations firms.

(2) The education cluster has established a company "Cairns International Education Providers" to collaboratively market regional education services into Asia.

(3) "Cairns International Technology Enterprises" was established to represent and promote the interest of IT industries in the region.

(4) Other cluster companies are likely to be formed for the film and television cluster, environmental industries and agribusiness.

The operations of the industry cluster companies are funded almost entirely from cluster members. The CREDC provides training programs and other

Table 6. Selected Service Industries for Cluster Development in FNQ.

Natural Resource Management	Transportation	Cultural/Arts/Film Services
Information Technology	Education Services	Business Services
Tourism/Hospitality	Property Development	Agribusiness
Marine Services	Mining Services	

support to facilitate the development of the new cluster companies that have been formed in the region. Several of the cluster companies have been successful in securing international contracts for industries in the region.

LESSONS LEARNED FROM THE STRATEGY TO GO GLOBAL

Encouraging Industries to work together is hard work, as it requires each industry to develop long term plans and to identify its hard and soft infrastructure needs. The establishment of the CREDC as a non-profit corporate entity owned by over 500 businesses and organizations has been a major success story in collaborative economic development effort. The ownership of the corporation has had to be continually cultivated to make sure business stays committed to the process. The CREDC model is not unique, but it has worked very effectively in providing a catalyst and instilling a sense of business and community ownership over the future direction of economic activities in the region. The success of the model is that it has galvanized businesses into working collaboratively and competitively, which in turn has provided the resources and focus needed to develop new international business opportunities for industries in the region. Most other regions in Australia lack cohesive industrial and regional development organizations, and are losing business development opportunities as a consequence.

An important lesson learned from implementation of the strategy was ensuring community leadership understood the economic development roles performed by existing agencies, and that those roles be defined. Given the relatively scarce resources available for economic development in FNQ, and most other regions, it is paramount that duplication of effort is avoided. Specific roles for implementing strategies should be left to those organizations that are already fulfilling these strategies most effectively. The role of the strategic partnership for employment and economic development created by the CREDC has been to concentrate on achieving long-term goals and objectives related to its overall business mission and/or business competencies. The critical challenges in this process have been: complacency due to the previous success of the economy; procrastination over the need for change; self interest of existing organizations and personalities; understanding the regional politics; and motivation of business leadership to lead economic development.

The cluster driven approach to economic development has met with considerable success, but it has had some failures. Fostering an interest in the cluster process was difficult. The experience tells us that successful clusters only work when: industries want to do it; industries manage the process themselves; they have some initial successes to keep them interested; and they find ways of keeping all members involved. The role of the CREDC as a cluster facilitator has been one of education and support, not cluster leadership. This has been an important lesson, with the CREDC having to say to some industrial clusters that, if they were not prepared to take responsibility for leadership, it would withdraw support. In the case of the film industry cluster this threat finally brought the industry in the region together.

Redefining the role of the CREDC as a teacher or coach that supports the development of industry partnerships, rather than a leader or principal facilitator of economic development processes, has been an important change of mind-set in economic development thinking for the region. Most regional organizations in Australia still consider their primary role as leading and initiating economic activities, leaving industry to follow up on opportunities. The difference in Cairns is that industry clusters have collectively formed registered companies that actively seek new opportunities for their industry. The role of the CREDC is to mobilize resources and support from outside each industry to enable opportunities for trade and investment to be realized.

The CREDC web site (www.credc.com.au) has played a key role in global presentation of economic development opportunities for the region. Considerable research went into designing the site, especially the types of information potential visitors, customers and investors might seek. The web site is designed as a virtual information center, containing basic information on the region, data bases of business and business links, local news and information, research, strategies and on-line access to government services. The website and html pages have also been designed to maximize hit rate possibilities, which makes it one of the most heavily used sites in the region. The web has brought considerable new international business activities to the region; however, one important lesson in web site promotion is that customers expect rapid and often detailed responses to inquiries. Having one of the best economic development web sites in the country may attract considerable web user interest, but ensuring quality and prompt delivery responses from organizations and businesses linked to the web site is an issue that was not considered carefully. The CREDC is embarking on an informal program of education and quality assurance to improve the rate and quality of responsiveness to inquiries through the corporation's web site.

Regional development organizations are increasing the use of the web to promote broader national and international investment and trade opportunities. The lessons learned from the Cairns experience is that the same quality of service must be assured in delivery as is given to marketing and promotion. Competitive advantage is about quality and reliability of service. It is important that regions develop monitoring systems that ensure organizations maintain high quality service responses to inquiries or marketing over the net. The net opens up great possibilities globally for regional economic development. However, reputations for poor quality of service can be very detrimental to business and image. This is an issue the Cairns Region is very conscious of as it seeks to capitalize upon the opportunities being opened up by the virtual economy.

CONCLUSION

The Cairns region is a remarkable success story of a community that has transformed itself from an economic backwater into a global player. National economic reforms and other events forced the region to recognize that, if it was to have a future, it needed to develop links with the international economy and embrace the challenges of globalization. It has done both very successfully. The development of the International Airport by the Cairns Port Authority was the single most important event in the region's history. It launched the region into a new orbit, which is now highly integrated with the international economy and its future firmly focused on expanding its links and trade with North America, Europe, Asia and the rest of Australia.

Planning has played a key role in the economic recovery of the region following the crisis in growth management in the early 1990s. The FNQ 2010 regional planning process, developed over seven years, has provided a stable and sustainable framework for managing the future development of the region. The uniqueness of the regional plan is that its governance structure relies on collaboration and partnerships to achieve desired development outcomes, rather than a statutory framework that introduces regulation and an added level of regional bureaucracy. The collaborative planning approach embraced by the region has resulted in a more multi-sector, integrated, flexible and responsive approach to change management and development.

Community consultation has played a key role in gaining acceptance of planning as a valuable tool to manage complex development issues facing the region. The process has ensured that the community is much more informed about issues that affect them and the economy – especially global and national events. It has also ensured community values and the maintenance of regional identity are embedded into decision making processes that affect the future development of the region. The motto of the region – "a stunning location for serious business" – reflects the aspirations of a community that understands the value of its assets and how to market these to global businesses and investors.

The economic strategy laid down an approach to economic development that focuses on the development of industrial clusters, building the export capacity of selected producer services and seeking to develop opportunities for import substitution industries to address a growing regional trade imbalance. Specific attention has been given to developing regional industrial competencies that focus on innovation, entrepreneurship, learning, information and leadership. These will be critical to the future development of the economy.

The role of the CREDC has been pivotal in building regional capacity and coaching industries to continually develop the competencies and adjust strategies needed to maintain competitive advantage. The future of the region is firmly fixed on developing its human capital base, diversifying its core industries and competencies, and becoming more integrated with the global economy. The success of the Cairns region must be attributed to the vision of a few leaders in 1984 to look beyond the parochial boundaries of localism and embrace the challenges of globalization. That vision, the spirit of entrepreneurship, the "can do attitude", the maintenance and marketing of difference, and the understanding of place in the world is what makes Cairns a unique region in Australia.

REFERENCES

Abbot, J. (1995). Quality Strategic Planning for South East Queensland. *Australian Planner, 32*(3), 135–138.

Blurton Russell & Associates (1991). Report on Development Issues in the Cairns Area. Office of the Coordinator General, Cairns: Queensland Government.

Cairns Economic Research Unit (1994). Baseline Economic Profile of the Cairns Region. Townsville: James Cook University.

Cameron McNamara. (1986). *Economic Development Plan for Far North Queensland*. Brisbane: Department of Business, Industry and Regional Development.

City of Tucson (1996). *Greater Tucson Strategic Economic Development Plan*.

Cairns Regional Economic Development Corporation (CREDC) (1998). *Industry Clusters: Competing Collaboratively – A New Way Forward*. Cairns: CREDC.

Daly, M., Roberts, B., Logan, M., & Cummings, W. (1996). *The Tradeable Services Strategy*. Cairns: FNQ Regional Economic Development Network.

Daly, M., & Stimson, R. (1993). Tourism Funding and Investment, Cairns Tourism Strategy. *Cairns Regional Tourism Strategy*, Position Paper No. 10. Brisbane: Premiers Department.

Department of Tourism, Small Business and Industry (1996). *The FNQ Regional Economic Development Strategy*. Brisbane: Department of Tourism, Small Business and Industry.

Duke, A. (1993). Cultural and Social Tourism Issues. *Cairns Regional Tourism Strategy*, Issues Paper No 9. Cairns Region Tourism Study Position Papers. Brisbane: Queensland Government.

Far North Queensland Regional Economic Development Network (1997). *Far North Queensland Regional Economic Development Agencies*. Cairns: Cairns Regional Economic Development Corporation.

Far North Queensland Regional Planning Advisory Council (1998). *FNQ 2010 Regional Planning Project: Integrated Regional Strategies for Far North Queensland*. Cairns: Queensland Department of Local Government and Planning.

Ferguson, E., Harvey, J., Byrne, F., & Rogers, W. (1947). *The Tourist Resources of Queensland and the Requirements for their Development*. Report by the Queensland Tourist Development Board, submitted to the Queensland Parliament 1947. Brisbane: Queensland Government Publishing Office.

Hassell and Associates (1992). *The Competitive Economic Advantage of Regional Australia – Case Study: Cairns*. Adelaide: Hassell and Associates.

Horwarth and Horwarth (1993). Economics of Tourism. *Cairns Region Tourism Strategy*, Position Paper No. 4. Brisbane: Queensland Government.

Kelty, B. (1994). *Developing Australia: A Regional Perspective*. A report to the Federal Government by the Taskforce on Regional Development. Canberra: National Capital Printing.

McKinsey and Company (1994). *Lead Local Compete Global: Unlocking the Growth Potential of Australian Regions*. Canberra: Office of Regional Development, Department of Housing and Regional Development.

National Centre for Studies in Travel and Tourism (1993). *Visitor Forecasts*. Position Paper No. 1. Brisbane: The National Centre for Studies in Travel and Tourism.

National Institute for Economic and Industrial Research. (NIEIR) (1998). On-line Regional Economic Information; Far North Queensland Region. Melbourne: NIEIR.

Office of the Coordinator General (1994). *Cairns Regional Tourism Strategy*. Brisbane: Queensland Government.

Porter, M. E. (1990). *The Competitiveness of Nations*. New York: McMillian.

Regional Planning Advisory Committee (1996). *Far North Queensland Regional Growth Management Framework*. Brisbane: Queensland Department of Tourism, Small Business and Industry.

Regional Planning Advisory Committee (1998a). *Strategic Directions and Regional Priorities for Far North Queensland*. Brisbane: Department of Communications and Information, Local Government and Planning.

Regional Planning Advisory Committee (1998b). *Draft Integrated Regional Strategy*. Brisbane: Department of Communication, Information, Local Government and Planning.

Roberts, B. (1996). The Changing Structure of Regional Economic Development in Far North Queensland. *Urban Futures*, *21*, 1–8.

Roberts, B. (2000). *Benchmarking the Competitiveness of the FNQ Region Economy*. Brisbane: Queensland University of Technology.

Roberts, B., & Daly, M. (1995). *The Internationalisation of the Far North Queensland Regional Economy: Capabilities*. Report for Far North Queensland Region Economic Development Strategy and Department of Tourism, Small Business and Industry: Australian Housing and Urban Research Institute.

Roberts, B., & Lanarch, A. (1996). *Import Replacement Strategy*. Report for the Far North Queensland Regional Economic Development Organisation. Cairns: CREDC.

Roberts, B., & Stimson, R. (1998). Multi-sectoral Qualitative Analysis: A Tool for Assessing the Competitiveness of Regions and Developing Strategies for Economic Development. *Annals of Regional Science*, *32*(4), 1–25.

Stimson, R., Daly, M., Jenkins, O., Roberts, B., & Ross, S. (1996). *Tourism in Australia: An Overview of Trends, Issues and Prospects*. Occasional Paper, No. 23. Canberra: Bureau of Tourism Research.

Stimson, R., Jenkins, O., Roberts, B., & Daly, M. (1998). The Impact of Daikyo as a Foreign Investor on the Cairns-Far North Queensland Regional Economy. *Environment and Planning A*, *30*, 161–179.

4.   'MODEL SINGAPORE': CROSSING URBAN BOUNDARIES

Victor R. Savage and C. P. Pow

ABSTRACT

Singapore has often been noted for its efficient urban management strategies. This chapter studies the planning policies and government leadership underpinning the development of this city-state, focusing on four main areas: effective urban provision through health care, education and public housing; long-term planning of the built environment and environmental management; pursuing urban competitiveness in the global economy, and managing state-social relations and cohesion. In addition, the challenges confronting Singapore are also discussed. Fundamentally, we argue that the success of cities ultimately rests on sound management strategies as well as effective and responsive urban governance.

INTRODUCTION

In both mass media reports and academic writings, Singapore enjoys the reputation of being a highly developed, prosperous and well-ordered city-state. This exceptional standing can be attributed to a number of "world-class" achievements of the city-state, most notably its highly competitive economy (being ranked first by the World Economic Forum in 1999) and robust economic performance with an annual average growth rate of 9% since 1965. Equally impressive are: (a) the highly successful public housing program with one of the world's highest rates of home ownership at 90%; (b) a highly

International Urban Planning Settings: Lessons of Success, Volume 12, pages 87–121.
Copyright © 2001 by Elsevier Science Ltd.
ISBN: 0-7623-0695-5

efficient port (ranked as the world's busiest port since 1986, with a shipping tonnage of 877 million gross tons in 1999); (c) an international airport that enjoys international reputation as the "World's Best Airport" (voted *by Business Traveller* and *PATA Travel News*) and also the renowned national flagship carrier, Singapore Airlines (SIA); and (d) an efficient and corruption-free public administration which has been placed in top ranking for consecutive years by the Political and Economic Risk Consultancy (PERC), and which, in its latest report, rates Singapore first among other Asian countries for its 'effective economic policies and high quality political leadership' (*The Straits Times*, 26 June 2000: 1). Indeed, this small island-nation has drawn such keen interest from around the world that its Foreign Ministry had to create 80 positions just to deal with inquiries and tours from visiting foreign officials and dignitaries who come to study the "Singapore Model" (Naisbitt, 1996: 172). This chapter aims to highlight the key elements underlying Singapore's "success story" and to draw on several important lessons as well as challenges confronting Singapore in the new global era.

Several unique preconditions need to be considered when examining Singapore's urban development. One particular aspect is the size of the city-state (659 square kilometers with 3.9 million people) (see Fig. 1).

Unlike most urban centers, Singapore is a "city" and a "state". Consequently, this conflation between the 'urban' (municipal) and 'national' (state) presents conceptual problems when making comparisons with other urban domains. For example, even among Southeast Asian countries, Singapore is unique because the government does not have to contend with rural population issues and the perennial problems of uneven development or the uncontrolled rural-urban migration that plagues countries like Indonesia, the Philippines and Thailand. However, without a rural hinterland, Singapore relies heavily on external sources for all of its necessities (including water, energy and food) and consumer products. In addition, the city-state is also heavily dependent on foreign trade due to its inherently small domestic market. Under these circumstances, Singapore is vulnerable to the changing global and regional political and economic conditions.

VIEWS ON SINGAPORE'S SUCCESS

The history of Singapore and its phenomenal growth and transformation from a British colonial outpost to the present thriving global city-state has been recounted several times by numerous authors (see Turnbull, 1977, 1989; Sandhu & Wheatley, 1989; Chew & Lee, 1991; Low, 1998). Numerous reports and articles have also attempted to capture the essence of Singapore's "Success

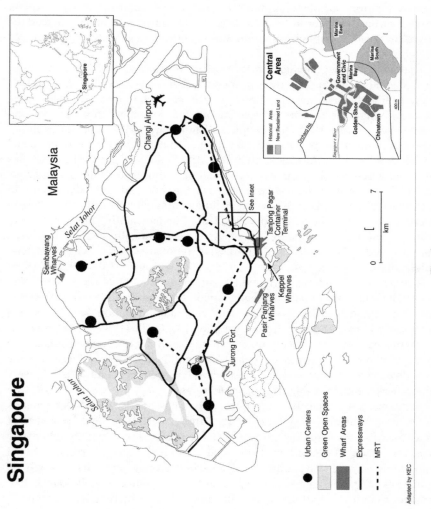

Fig. 1.

Story" on paper (see, for example, Castells, 1992; Naisbitt, 1996: 173; Mahbubani, 1998: 183–187; Tommy Koh, 1998: 204–209). *Asiaweek* recently summarized Singapore's success in catchy bite-size formulas as encompassing the five F's: forward planning, financial might, firm control, full commitment from everyone, and fear of failure. These five tenets are said to have helped the city-state weather through economic crises and political strife (*Asiaweek*, 24 March 2000).

Undoubtedly the dominant role of the government has been the most fundamental factor underlying Singapore's progress. As noted by Singapore's prominent ambassador-at-large Professor Tommy Koh (1998: 208), 'the single most important factor in the making of the Singapore miracle is good governance'. Since 1965, the People's Action Party (PAP) and its enduring power in politics and government have propelled the city-state's economic and social development. Modeled after the British labour party, the PAP has followed a democratic socialist ideological platform. One of the cornerstones of their political mandate has been their emphasis on and faith in planning. In fact, the PAP has constantly used planning as a major political tool in nearly every aspect of Singapore's development. Fundamentally, these plans are underpinned by the logic of pragmatism and rationality which has been variously described as 'one of purposive rational action [and] means-end calculation . . .' (Chan & Evers, 1973: 317; see also Hill & Lian, 1995: 188–193). The emphasis on rational and pragmatic ideology has enabled government policies to be implemented with utmost efficiency. Equally vital is the fact that the political system and civil administration have remained steadfastly honest and free from corruption. As Quah (1994: 153) observed, discipline is not a serious problem in the civil service and 'bureaucratic corruption in Singapore is incidental and not institutionalized because the incentives to be corrupt among civil servants has been reduced by the relatively high salaries and favorable working conditions'.

Fundamentally, one of the most important hallmarks of Singapore's political-administrative system is its strong belief in and practice of "meritocracy". As a guiding principle, meritocracy, complementing other state doctrines such as "multiracialism" and "multiculturalism", ensures equal opportunities for all. The ability to advance in whatever field is based solely on achievement, merit and hardwork, regardless of ethnicity, religious belief, gender or family background. More fundamentally, the meritocratic system has enabled capable local people to develop to their fullest potential and contribute to the society. For example, government scholarships are awarded yearly to deserving students based on academic results while the employment and promotion of officers in the civil service are judged on academic qualifications and work performance. Equally important has been the long and uninterrupted rule of the PAP which has enabled many of the long-term government policies to be carried out successfully. Without the presence of strong opposition parties, many of PAP's earlier key national policies (and at times controversial rulings), such as the Land Acquisition Act (1966) which empowered the government to acquire any land deemed necessary for national development, or the Industrial Relations Act (1968), which curtailed the bargaining power of workers and trade unions, were spared from being hassled in the parliament.

While critics have pointed to the somewhat 'rigid' and 'authoritarian' style of government management, paradoxically, state policies in Singapore are far from static. Often overlooked in the analysis is the ability of the government to continually adapt and respond to the changing external and internal environments. Contrary to conventional criticisms relating to the ossification of bureaucratic systems in most cities, Singapore's administration can be characterized as one which is marked by (economic) flexibility and adaptability, tempered with a strong sense of pragmatism. This is most evidently captured in the recent comments by Senior Minister Lee Kuan Yew on Singapore's challenges in the new cyber-economy: "Societies must be flexible in re-inventing and refining their economic system . . . if we do not change fast enough, we are going to miss so many chances, we'll kick ourselves for it" (in *Asiaweek*, 24 March 2000).

Having laid down some of the key elements and conditions underlying the Singapore model, this chapter now focuses on four main issues that underscore the role of effective and responsive urban governance in Singapore's growth and management. These four major areas are identified as: (1) urban provisions in terms of health care, education and public housing; (2) urban environmental planning which is aimed at providing a clean and pollution-free city; (3) creating and maintaining Singapore's economic competitiveness in the fast-paced global economy; and (4) the management of state-social relations and the fostering of a sense of community among citizens in what has been characterized as the 'turbulent global era'.

URBAN PROVISIONS: HEALTHCARE, EDUCATION AND PUBLIC HOUSING

While many different yardsticks have been used to measure urban success, cities should ultimately be judged by their ability to provide for the people their basic needs, such as food, shelter, health, education, and a healthy living environment. Under the People's Action Party's (PAP) governance since 1959, three areas have underscored their socialist democratic ideology in the national plans, namely: health, education and public housing. In all three areas, Singapore has fared well and is now widely acknowledged by policy makers worldwide to have set high standards for the delivery of urban services. Despite the government's avowed beliefs not to follow the 'welfarist models' in many countries in Europe and North America, the PAP government has, in fact, since taking power in 1959, heavily subsidized housing, health, and education programs.

Health Care

Singapore has one of the best health care systems in the world. In the World Health Organization's (WHO) Year 2000 worldwide analysis on health care provisions, the city-state was ranked sixth, ahead of many developed countries like Japan and the United States. In particular, Singapore did well due to a number of factors including greater autonomy in public hospitals, the existence of medical savings accounts and medical insurance schemes (such as the 3Ms of Medisave, Medishield and Medifund) as well as subsidies for low-income patients (*The Straits Times*, 21 June 2000: 3). The high ranking by the WHO is further supported by other statistics, for example, the long life expectancy rates (78 years old in 1999) and low infant mortality rates (3.8 per 1,000 live births) in Singapore. Government expenditure for national health care currently stands at S$4,194 million (US$2,467 million) or 2.7% of GDP which works out to S$1,240 per capita (MITA, 1999: 250). More impressively, childhood infectious illnesses and contagious diseases such as tuberculosis have been virtually eradicated through systematic mass immunization programs over the years. Recently, the Ministry of Health (MOH) has also embarked on mass health screening at subsidized rates for those aged 55 and above to check for abnormalities such as diabetes, high blood pressure and high cholesterol (*The Straits Times*, 15 March 2000: 1). To prevent overburdening the state, Singapore's health care financing philosophy is based on individual and family responsibility (partly funded through compulsory medical saving and insurance), coupled with public subsidies to keep basic health care affordable (Koh, 1998: 207).

Education

The government also attaches great importance on education and training. Education is considered by the government to be the most important means of inculcating national values and to train the workforce for maximum economic productivity. Over the years, Singapore's education system has gone through three major changes beginning with the British colonial system, followed by the Malaysian system (1963–1965) and finally the independent Singapore system. Besides these macro-political changes, the education system has also been tailored to suit the changing economic realities in Singapore. For example, in the 1960s, universal primary education was offered to train workers for jobs in the labor-intensive industries. Technical subjects were later introduced into secondary schools to develop the manpower needed in the rapidly industrializing economy. Since 1965, as Singapore's economy moved into high-tech and high value-added industries, the government has responded by increasing the enrolment for tertiary education (Koh, 1998: 205).

The continuing importance attached to education is reflected in the government expenditure on education for financial year 2000/2001, which stands at S$5.95 billion (US$ 3.5 billion) or 20.52% of total public expenditure, second in place only after defence at S$7.4 billion (US$4.3 billion) or 25.6% of total government expenditure. In fact, during its first nine years in power, the PAP government spent nearly one-third of the national budget on education and had achieved universal free primary education by the time of independence (Turnbull, 1997: 299). The general literacy rate per 100 residents aged 15 years old and above was 93.1% in 1998 (MITA, 1999: 36).

To equip students with innovative and creative thinking skills in the new knowledge-based economy, the Ministry of Education in 1997 launched the "Thinking School, Learning Nation" vision which plans to 'equip students with skills, knowledge, values and instincts to face future challenges' (MITA, 1999: 208). Beyond the school environment, the plan hopes to promote a culture of continual learning. Major initiatives include changing the assessment modes in schools and encouraging critical and creative thinking skills in the young. Based on the masterplan for information technology (IT) in education, students will be required to spend at least 30% of curriculum time accessing electronic resources and working on computers (MITA, 1999: 208–209). The government has also embarked on one of the most ambitious educational programs (S$2 billion or US$1.2 billion) in the world that will make the "virtual classroom" a closer reality for students of every age. Trials have already been conducted in selected schools on the use of mini-computer laptops (known as 'eduPADs') which are jointly developed by the Ministry of Education, Kent Ridge Digital Lab and CET Technologies Pte Ltd (*The Straits Times*, 18 September 1999: 38). Aimed at developing innovative ways of using IT in teaching and learning, these portable mini-laptop computers are installed with educational software and are also equipped for internet access. The use of computers is set to further revolutionize the educational system in Singapore.

Housing

As with many cities in the developing countries, Singapore has faced challenges in housing. In the 1950s and 1960s, nearly 45% of Singapore population lived in slums and squatters were the hotbeds of disease and crime. When the PAP government took over in 1959, housing was a major political priority of the government, and a mass public housing program was initiated in 1960 with the establishment of the Housing Development Board (HDB). The HDB was a continuation of the colonial government's housing authority, the Singapore Improvement Trust (SIT), which in its 32 years of existence had only built 23,000 units of public flats while the HDB in its 30-year period has built more than 600,000 homes. Approximately 86% of Singaporeans now live in Housing Development Board (HDB) flats, with nine in 10 residents owing their homes compared with only 9% in 1960 when HDB was established (MITA, 1999: 181).

The issue of public housing, however, goes beyond the mere provision of homes for people. To understand the rationale for public housing, one needs to look at the scenario when it was initiated. Public housing has a significant impact in three areas that are environmentally related: (a) it provided an alternative to slum and squatter dwellings that were rampant in Singapore in the 1950s and 1960s; (b) it provided an alternative means of improving public health and hygiene; and (c) it helped to create a clean and livable environment that provided the underpinnings for social and economic development. Under the HDB, public housing was constructed to provide clean, healthy and hygienic environments for citizens. This to a large extent was a reflection of the government's quasi-deterministic planning notions of controlled functions and regulations arising from designed urban form (Cherry, 1988). The official thinking at that time was to produce low cost public housing which would in turn mean a healthier population requiring lower medical expenditure (Savage, 1992: 193). The leadership also believed that the better residential environments would ensure a more productive labor force with greater prosperity and a higher standard of living for the people. Indeed, as Chua (1997: 1) noted, 'the materially tangible and highly visible presence of good social housing (in Singapore) is a powerful symbolic monument which testifies to the efficacy of the government in power and contributes significantly to its legitimacy to govern.'

Concerted effort has been made to solve housing problems and promote home ownership. For example, the 1967 Land Acquisition Act has enabled the state to acquire private land at below market rates and redevelop the land for building HDB flats. In order to encourage as many people to own flats as possible, Singapore's public housing are priced at below market rates and sold at prices within reach of the population. The regular financing terms are set at an initial 20% down payment, with 25 or 30 years to pay the remaining cost in installments (Owyang, 1998: 149). The Central Provident Fund (CPF), Singapore's social security system, is used by Singaporeans to purchase their flats. Under the CPF scheme, every employee is required to put 20% of his or her pay in the CPF account. The employers (both public and private) are then required to match the same contribution, which works out to a total of 40%, one of the highest saving rates in the world (Reutens, 1995). The CPF cannot be withdrawn until retirement but can be utilized for financing healthcare, education and shares investments and most importantly for buying HDB flats. Under the Public Housing Scheme, the cost of a new flat may be paid for with existing CPF savings or future contributions. Family co-owners may also pool their CPF savings to buy a flat (Reutens, 1995: 30–31). Through the concerted efforts of the HDB and CPF Boards, homeownership in Singapore has risen tremendously.

Social Cornerstones Underlying Economic Progress

Indisputably, the socially entrenched housing, education and health-care policies have been an important cornerstone underlying the city-state's economic progress and will continue to remain as an important factor governing the political legitimacy of the ruling PAP government. While apparently eschewing the "welfare state" model, the PAP government has nevertheless provided substantial public subsidies in these areas and in turn made Singaporeans more productive. While the government is reluctant to extend any more social securities and "safety nets" beyond the existing provisions (purportedly to discourage the "government-dependent" mentality and to foster a greater sense of risk-taking and entrepreneurial confidence), any "rolling back" of the state's subsidies in urban provisions and services is likely to be met with political consequences. For example, the government's attempts to increase the privatization of health care was met by strong disapproval of the masses which was clearly registered in the drop in support for the PAP government in the January 1997 general election (Savage, 1999: 165). Similarly, in a protracted debate in 1996, the opposition parties led by Dr Chee Soon Juan had tried to provide statistics on health care which charged that the government was providing no subsidies at all (*The Straits Times*, 8 Aug 1996). Although the opposition parties' claims and accusations were later publicly discredited by the government's Cost Review Committee, it is clear that the PAP government's legitimacy and enduring power rests on its role as the provider of affordable urban needs as well as prescient urban planning policies.

URBAN PLANNING: THE GARDEN CITY

The unchecked growth and development of cities have often posed serious environmental concerns in many countries. The rapid growth of Asian "mega-cities" (over 10 million people) has brought in its wake several problems including urban sprawl, overcrowding, poor sanitation, environmental pollution and a general decline in the urban quality of life (see Awang et al., 1995; McGee & Robinson, 1995). Fortunately, Singapore is able to avoid these problems as the government has long acknowledged the need for long term environmental planning and control. In fact, long before the Earth Summit in Rio 1992, the Singapore government had already embarked on a "clean and green" environmental campaign. This was due largely to the special circumstances of the city-state (being small and densely populated) which 'obliged Singapore to practice "sustainable development" long before it became recognized as important . . .' (Hui, 1995: 13). The success of these environmental policies is clearly evident today. For example, a recent air pollution report by the Ministry of Environment (ENV) placed Singapore among the world's top 15 "most livable" cities (*The Straits Times*, 5 March 2000: 36).

Notwithstanding the recent haze problems resulting from neighboring forest fires in Indonesia, the annual mean concentration of five traditional pollutants – sulphur dioxide, nitrogen dioxide, particulate matter, carbon monoxide and ozone are well within the standards set by the World Health Organization and the United States Environmental Protection Agency (USEPA) (MITA, 1999: 256). In addition, Singapore's level of polycyclic aromatic hydrocarbons (PAHs) – carcinogenic agents from incomplete combustion by motor vehicles were found to be lower than those in Hong Kong as well as some U.K. and Canadian cities (*The Straits Times*, 5 March 2000: 36). Singapore's clean and healthy environmental record is, however, not incidental, but requires the concerted effort and political will of the government and its public agencies.

Like many developing countries, Singapore experienced many urban environmental problems in the past. Fortunately, institutionalizing environ-mental pollution control was recognized as early as 1970 with the formation of the Anti-Pollution Unit (APU) under the Prime Minister's Office as well as the establishment of the Ministry of the Environment (ENV) in 1972, one of the earliest Environmental Ministries established in the world then (Savage, 1992). The ENV was formed to improve sanitation services, public health and to prevent water pollution. In 1986, APU was transferred to the Pollution Control Department (PCD) of ENV. The key elements of ENV's strategies are long-term planning, preventive control of environmental quality, effective legislation and enforcement, adequate provision of environmental infrastructure and the use of appropriate environmental technology (Hui, 1995: 14).

Water Pollution

Generally, the ENV has followed a three-pronged strategy to control air and water pollution, which includes the monitoring of air and water quality; environmental planning control, and enforcement control of sources of pollution (Hui, 1995: 17). The most notable success in reducing water pollution has been the massive clean up of the Singapore River which began in 1977. As a result of waste disposal by industries, farms and itinerant hawkers, the Singapore River and its Kallang basin catchment area, soon degenerated into open sewers and rubbish dumps over the years. The massive cleaning-up program, first initiated in 1980 by then Prime Minister Lee Kuan Yew, took 10 years and involved various state agencies, including the Ministry of Environment (ENV), Urban Redevelopment Authority (URA), Housing Development Board (HDB), Port of Singapore Authority (PSA) and the Parks and Recreation Department (now National Parks Board). Contrary to most public perceptions, the involvement of numerous public agencies was far from harmonious and in fact generated problems in co-ordination as well as differences in opinions between different governmental bodies. It was thus not coincidental that the massive river cleanup project had come under the central control of the Prime Minister's Office. By the time of the 10 year period, about 90% of the pollution load identified was eliminated from the catchment area (Hui, 1995: 19). Notwithstanding the initial difficulties and inter-agency conflicts, the successful cleaning-up of the Singapore River bears a strong testament to the political will and commitment of the government towards building a clean and healthy environment.

Air Pollution and Transportation

In a highly urbanized city like Singapore, motor vehicle emission is a significant source of air pollution. Over the years, vehicular numbers in Singapore have been rising steadily with currently more than 600,000 motor vehicles on the road (LTA, 2000). To tackle these problems, the government has adopted innovative traffic management measures such as the Vehicle Quota System (VQS) and the Certificate of Entitlement (COE) scheme to control the growth of vehicle population and fuel consumption. Under the VQS and COE systems, the number of new vehicles allowed for registration is pre-determined annually, taking into account the prevailing traffic conditions. To register a new vehicle, the owners are first required to bid for a Certificate of Entitlement (COE) from the Vehicle and Transit Licensing Division of the Land Transport Authority (LTA). The COE prices are subjected to market conditions with prices ranging from a few hundred dollars (for motorcycles) to over S$30,000 for the luxury car category. The high prices of the COE thus serve to deter people from owning private vehicles and opt for public transport facilities.

Overall, the urban transport policy in Singapore centers on the provision of a reliable, efficient and affordable public transportation system including the Mass Rapid Transit (MRT) rail system and public bus services. Currently public bus services are run by three bus companies operating 251 routes with a fleet of over 3,000 buses which cater to the majority of commuters (MITA, 1999). In addition, the electrically propelled MRT train system, which comprises 48 train stations, has networks extending to most parts of the Singapore island, including suburban residential estates. A second major North-East MRT line is now under construction which will add another twenty kilometers to the existing 83 kilometers of train routes. In 1998, the government also decided to construct a S$1.75 billion Marina Line consisting of a 13 kilometers underground railway line which will serve the new downtown area (*The Straits Times*, 13 June 1998).

Through comprehensive urban transport policies, the government is thus able to effectively control vehicular population and air pollution in Singapore. In addition, the government also introduced strict legislation and incentives which encourage vehicle owners to improve their vehicle engine and fuel consumption. The use of unleaded petrol was promoted in February 1990 through a differential tax system which made unleaded petrol 10 cents per liter cheaper than leaded petrol. Since 1 July 1991, all petrol-driven vehicles in Singapore had begun using unleaded petrol. In addition, all in-use vehicles are required to undergo periodic inspections to check for their road worthiness and exhaust emissions, failing which vehicle owners are not allowed to renew their road tax (Hui, 1995: 23).

Garden City Concept

Fundamentally, the Singapore government realized that effective environmental management has to begin with sound environmental plans. Without a long-term perspective with regards to environmental related issues, it is almost impossible to maintain effective environmental management and sustainable development

(Savage, 1995: 167). In 1965 the Singapore government introduced the Garden City concept to guide planning and development of a clean and green city. As noted by Savage (1998), at the root of this planning ideology is the government's quasi-environmental deterministic belief that the creation of an *ideal* urban form can generate or elicit certain desirable behavioral as well as social and political responses. The search for an ideal community is tacitly, if not explicitly, reflected in urban planning. Specifically the Garden City demonstrates in Singapore a 'neo-utopian ideal of reconstruction' (Savage, 1991: 73) and of human's power over nature and the cultural imprint of human creativity and technological prowess in the high-rise built landscape. The first political outline of this neo-utopian Garden City was sketched by the then Prime Minister Lee Kuan Yew in 1980 as a green shady city filled with fruits and flowers, a city worthy of an industrious people whose quest for progress is matched by their appreciation for the beauty of nature. The harshness and concrete hopefully will be softened by nature's trees, flowers and birds (*The Straits Times*, March 22 1987).

Having eradicated the filth and squalor of unhygienic slum and squatter settlements and successfully implementing its Garden City concept, the government's planning objectives in the 1990s shifted towards creating a higher quality life with the release of the Revised Concept Plan (1991) and the Singapore Green Plan (1992) by the Urban Redevelopment Authority (URA) and Ministry of Environment (MOE), respectively. Unlike the URA's 1971 Concept Plan which focused on 'hard' infrastructure development, such as the building of public housing estates, airport and mass-rapid transit, the 1991 Revised Concept Plan places an emphasis on developing Singapore into a "world-class city" which is 'spiced liberally with cultural and creative centers' (URA, 1991). This includes building a performing arts center called the *Esplanade-Theatres On The Bay*, new entertainment districts at Bugis-Selegie Road area, more parks and recreational areas, as well as waterfront homes. In the latter case, whereas previously the state had been reluctant to release coastal land for housing, selected sites have now been identified for waterfront housing, for example at Simpang, Tanjong Rhu, Kampong Bugis, the Singapore River, and on the island of Buran Darat, off Sentosa (Perry et al., 1997: 291). Unlike other national plans which dealt with only land areas, the 1992 Green plan included sea areas (Blue plan) to take into account the increased 300 km coastline (formerly only 140 km). While the Green Plan focuses on environmental issues relating to the setting aside of state land for nature areas and parks, as well as improvements and enhancements to environmental infrastructure and public health, the Blue Plan looks into the building of sea-fronting public housing satellite towns (e.g. Simpang), more resorts, marinas, water sport areas and snorkeling sites (coral reef conservation).

Urban Conservation

It has been well acknowledged that in recent years the conservation of historic urban landmarks and heritage has been accorded greater attention by the Singapore government. However, as many commentators noted, since independence in the 1960s and until the early 1980s, massive urban redevelopment took precedence as the means to propel the city-state towards economic growth and progress, often with little regard for the conservation of urban heritage. The economic imperatives of the day was best summed up by the comments of the Chairman of the National Heritage Board Lim Chee Onn, who analogously described that: 'there was simply no time to rearrange the furniture in the sitting room while pressing matters have to be attended in the kitchen. Indeed on quite a number of occasions there were fires in the kitchen that had to be put out promptly. In the 1960s and 70s, it was (thus) not surprising that conservation did not feature highly, if at all, in our national agenda' (quoted in Perry et al., 1997: 253).

The significant shift in urban conservation policy and stimulus for conservation efforts occurred in the mid-1980s when Singapore was searching for new economic directions, which resulted in the formation of the Tourism Task Force. Recognizing that the eradication of historic places had led to the destruction and loss of the 'Oriental mystique and charm' symbolized in old buildings and traditional trade, a US$223 million plan was promptly incorporated to 'revitalize' the ethnic enclaves in Chinatown, Little India and Kampong Glam, the Singapore River, as well as to rebuild and restore historic districts, such as Emerald Hill and Bugis Street. Arguably, while these high-profile conservation projects have undoubtedly rekindled local interests and renewed debates on urban heritage issues, the government's conservation policies have not gone unchallenged. As critics frequently lambasted: 'heritage conservation (has) become intimately connected with redevelopment strategies designed to cater to tourist demands for uniqueness and urban aesthetics' (Perry et al., 1997: 257). More specifically, the authenticity of many urban conservation projects has also been called to question. For example, the historic ethnic enclaves at Chinatown and Kampong Glam which have been conserved and revitalized under the Singapore Tourism Boards' "New Asia" theme have often been criticized for the "commodification" or "kistchification" of local ethnic cultures and urban form. Similarly, the lack of co-ordination between different government ministries and statutory boards with each pursuing different agendas may have also mitigated the successful implementation of urban conservation programs. A more major shortcoming is the absence of public consultation and the "top-down" approach in many conservation plans. Significantly however, since the late 1980s, there has been greater public participation and consultation in urban planning through the involvement of private sector architects as well grassroots participation in regular public feedback sessions organized by government planning agencies. This will be further elaborated in the following section.

Public Participation

In an unprecedented move in the late 1980s, the Urban Redevelopment Authority (URA) began soliciting for public input and feedback in its concept planning as well as in the implementation of the 55 Development Guide Plans (DGPs) which set out the detailed plans for the entire island. Interested representatives from professional bodies such as architects, surveyors, academics as well as the general public were invited for regular dialogue sessions and public exhibitions which display the planning proposals. For example, in the planning of Kampong Bugis and the Simpang new residential estate in 1989–1990, the URA and the Housing Development Board (HDB) invited the Singapore Institute of Architects (SIA) to undertake alternative planning of the two sites and then publicly exhibited the planning proposals from both public and private agencies (see Chua, 1992: 343–347). A simple survey was also conducted with members of the public who visited the exhibition to assess the general preferences for the plans. Since then, other sites such as the Chinatown conservation area, Joo Chiat, Jurong and Changi areas were also subjected to similar planning procedures. In addition, the development plans and guidelines are also published and widely disseminated to developers, professionals and the public through the media, government gazette, dialogue sessions and public exhibitions which provide greater transparency and openness of the planning system (URA, 1999: 35).

Evidently, urban planning in Singapore has undergone significant quantitative and qualitative changes over the past three decades. As discussed earlier, while planning in the past followed an 'ecological pragmatic' approach (Savage, 1992: 207) and was primarily concerned with the eradication of pollutive environment and the engineering of a neat and well-ordered Garden city-state, there has been a significant shift in recent years to incorporate greater public participation, "diversity" as well as the "repackaging" and "reimaging" of new working and living spaces. Indeed, the recent URA publication (aptly entitled 'Home.Work.Play') envisions that the new cosmo-politan Singapore will need high quality housing apartments, a series of "play spaces" including trendy night spots and other recreation and consumption spaces catering to the young professionals. In terms of the cityscape, whereas in the past the planning authorities had disapproved of neon street lighting and billboards, the URA has recently commissioned private advertising company Pearl and Dean International (S) Pte Ltd to look into revamping the image of the Bugis-Selegie entertainment district with brightly illuminated electronic screens and neon advertising signs (URA, 1997).

While it is clear that significant transformations in the urban landscape are underway, how does one make sense of these changes and what are the implications for the population at large? Undoubtedly, with increasing education and income levels, one of the primary concerns in the minds of the planning authorities is the ability to address the rising expectations and growing discontent among young Singaporeans for a higher standard of living, beyond just basic housing provisions. One major area for example is the aspiration for young professionals to own their own private properties. As reflected in a 1996 survey on 418 young Singaporeans aged between 21 to 30, homeownership, in particular owning private properties like condominiums or houses, ranked high among respondents with 25% expressing that it is very important to own private property, while 35% felt that it is quite important to do so (*The Straits Times*, 27 June 1996). In the Housing Development Board's (HDB) recent study on residential mobility and housing aspirations, it was further revealed that within the next five years, one third of HDB households are likely to move to bigger and more expensive homes (*The Straits Times*, 22 June 2000: 3).

However, the high demand and speculation from property investors have driven private property prices beyond the reach of many young Singaporeans. Notwithstanding governmental measures to curb property speculation and price inflation such as enforcing an 80% financing limit on mortgage loans as well as taxing income gained from property transactions, it is inevitable that private property will always be out of reach for the majority of the population. For the government, helping young Singaporeans fulfill the so-called 'Singapore Dream' of possessing material comforts such as private houses, and cars, as well as a higher quality of living environment has taken on greater political significance as education and income levels of the people rises. In particular, the generous land sales programme recently announced by the Ministry of National Development (MND) may be viewed in this context. Significantly, the release of land for 6,000 private homes and 3,000 Executive Condominiums (a hybrid class of public and private housing with resale and other restrictions) in year 2000 is aimed at keeping land costs in check and the eventual sale prices of private homes affordable to aspiring 'upgraders' (*The Straits Times*, 3 June 2000: 23).

While planning has paid due attention to the preferences and desires of the higher-income group of professionals and skilled workers, it is important to ensure that this is not achieved at the expense of the other less privileged people. In particular, urban planning and infrastructures should continue to look after the needs of other sectors of the population including the lower income group, the growing number of elderly people as well as the disabled. With Singapore's population targeted to reach 5.5 million by the middle of this century, judicious planning and management of urban spaces is increasingly more important and urgent. Another area of concern is the extent to which the popularity and legitimacy of the government's approach to urban planning has been accepted by the population. With a better-educated population desiring to have more say in the public decision-making process, it is clear that the technocratic planning culture and the 'top-down' approach will no longer be passively accepted by the people. To draw from a few recent examples, the Singapore Tourism Board's (STB) grand plans to redevelop Chinatown into a theme tourist district and the planned demolition of the historically significant National Library at the city-center have drawn public criticisms and debates in local newspapers. Clearly, while advocates for a 'bottom-up' approach had been ignored by planning authorities in the past decades, changes now have to be made to the political culture of planning to include greater public consultation as well as private sector involvement.

URBAN COMPETITIVENESS: SINGAPORE IN THE NEW GLOBAL ECONOMY

Recent global restructuring has heralded the rise of a new economy which places a high premium on the production of knowledge and information technology (Drucker, 1992; Knight, 1995). Arising from the imperatives of the new economy, one sees the increasing importance of the "world city" or "global city" which are conceptualised as key strategic points or 'Neo-Marshallian nodes' in the global urban hierarchy (Friedmann, 1986; Sassen, 1991; Amin & Thrift, 1992; Brenner, 1998). Within this global system, the importance of urban centres is measured in terms of their economic control functions and competitiveness, with New York, London and Tokyo standing head and shoulders above other cities as global command centres. These three cities act as key sites in the co-ordination of global capital flows, labour exchanges as well as information processing and management beyond territorial boundaries. Increasingly, urban policy-makers realise that for cities to remain competitive, they must be able to "plug" into the global economy and exploit the "global space of flows" (Castells, 1989).

In this context, Singapore's government has taken a proactive stance in the promotion of urban competitiveness by implementing national development strategies which situate the city-state in an advantageous position in the global economy. One of the early key strategies in Singapore's economic management has been diversification. The city-state's economy is based on several pillars: finance and banking, high-tech industries, tourism, trade, transportation and communications and services. After the 1985 economic recession, the government reviewed its economic policies and promptly diversified its economy in order to strengthen the resistance against economic fluctuations. "Economic flexibility" and "nimbleness" became the buzzwords among government agencies. In addition, despite its high cost in both land and labour, Singapore remains an attractive and viable economic location to do business. In 1999, Singapore was ranked first by the World Economic Forum (WEF) in global competitiveness. Similarly, the Economist Intelligence Unit (EIU) has also awarded Singapore top place for its competitive business environment among 16 contending Asian countries (MITA, 1999: 8). What the Singapore government offers to foreign companies is a total package which provides a conducive environment for business activity. This package involves political (security, peace, law and order), economic (sound infrastructure, efficient services, good communications) and environmental (clean, green landscapes) advantages (Savage, 1999). It is this combination of "goods" that make Singapore continually an attractive place for companies to do business.

Government Strategies

In recent decades, with an increasingly global economy, the government has also responded with the implementation of several strategies. As noted by Yeung and Olds (1999), Singapore's global economic strategies can be analysed in three main areas. Firstly, the city-state had sought to serve as a centre for the spatial agglomeration of high-value added and high-tech investments in leading industries. Secondly, since the mid-1980s, the government has also been actively seeking regional headquarters of leading global corporations to locate in the city-state, thus enabling Singapore to become an international business hub. Thirdly and more recently, Singapore has begun to regionalise its domestic economy, generating intra- and inter-regional interdependencies. For example, the Port Authority of Singapore (PSA), a government statutory board, has secured participation in ten port projects in the coasts of China, Italy, India, Portugal, South Korea and the Middle East since setting up its International Business Division in 1996. By Year 2007, PSA targets to handle at least 10 million TEUs outside of Singapore and earn at least a third of its revenue from overseas projects (PSA, 2000). In sum, these three key government initiated strategies have contributed significantly to the urban competitiveness of Singapore in the global economy.

As Singapore positions itself as an international business hub, it has also become more vulnerable to global market forces. The recent economic crisis in Asia (1997–1999) is a good case in point. Starting with Thailand, the currency depreciation spared no country in the region, spreading rapidly to engulf Indonesia, Malaysia and the Philippines and eventually Hong Kong, Australia and the European markets as well. Though the currency crisis did not hit Singapore very badly, the Singapore dollar fell 20% against the U.S. dollar. With Singapore's sound fiscal policies and zero national debt and budget deficits, the city-state was able to weather the economic crisis much better than the other countries in the region. Nevertheless, the economic debacle certainly served as a poignant reminder of the problems resulting from economic globalization and what it means to be living in an inter-related world. Drawing lessons from the economic crisis, Singapore has further prepared and bolstered itself for the new global economy. The government has begun to step up its efforts, which include keeping the economy broad-based and diversified, deregulating financial services, accelerating telecommunications liberalization as well as opening up other parts of the economy such as power, electricity supply and even garbage collection to private companies.

Privatization and Restructuring of Financial Institutions

The privatization and restructuring of public enterprise started in the 1990s following the report of the Public Sector Divestment Committee (PSDC) which was released in 1987. Privatisation in Singapore serves two main objectives: firstly, the listing of privatised public enterprises or government-linked companies, such as Singtel or Singapore Airlines, is able to broaden and deepen the Singapore stock market which is very small and thin, after the Kuala Lumpur Stock Exchange (KLSE) delinked Malaysian counters from the Stock Exchange of Singapore (SES) in 1991. Secondly and more importantly, the divestment of public ownership is aimed at introducing greater competition as well as to inject stronger private sector entrepreneurship which are seen as the main engines for growth in the competitive global economy (see Low, 1998:

157–158). More recently, global economic forces have further precipitated the liberalisation and deregulation of many key economic sectors.

In the financial and banking sector for example, some of the concrete policy changes include the introduction of 'Qualifying Full Bank' (QFB) privileges for foreign banks to increase competition in the local banking sector; issuing more restricted banking licences, as well as allowing greater flexibility for offshore banks to operate in Singapore (MAS, 2000). In addition, local banks such as the Development Bank of Singapore (DBS), Overseas-Chinese Banking Corporation (OCBC), United Overseas Bank (UOB) and Overseas Union Bank (OUB) have also been granted greater autonomy and operational flexibility with the removal of the 40% restriction on foreign ownership, as well as the revision of bank regulations. For instance, the recent decision by DBS to levy a $2 surcharge on POSB accounts with less than $500 was upheld despite severe criticisms from the public. What is noteworthy here is that while the government is mindful of the local population's opposition to the $2 levy, the Monetary Authority of Singapore (MAS) has stopped short of intervening in what has been rationalised as 'market forces' at work (*The Straits Times*, 10 May 2000: 40).

To make the banking sector even more globally competitive, the MAS is currently urging local banks to restructure and consolidate their operations. As revealed in a press statement, the MAS noted that due to the small domestic market, local banks which lack the economies of scale must consolidate and upgrade their operations and services in order to compete effectively and operate globally (*The Business Times*, 19 May, 1999: 2). Since 1998, two major bank mergers have occurred, most notably the Development Bank of Singapore's (DBS) acquisition of government-linked Post Office Savings Bank (POSB) (making them the largest Southeast Asian bank with total assets of S$93 billion), and the merger between Keppel and Tat Lee Bank. In 1999, the Keppel Tat Lee Bank (KPT) further signed a strategic alliance with the one of Ireland's leading financial institutions, the Allied Irish Banks p.l.c. (AIB) with the latter taking up a 24.9% equity stake. With mounting pressures in the coming years, it is inevitable that more bank mergers will occur. In line with MAS's restructuring policies, local banks are also required to dispose of their non-financial businesses (i.e. non-core assets which exceed 10% of the company's capital) by 2004 (*The Straits Times*, 22 June 2000: 1). Faced with intensifying globalisation pressures and the lessons learnt from the recent financial crisis in other countries, the move is clearly aimed at getting banks to focus on their core businesses and to reduce risks posed to the banking sector. In addition, the pace to further liberalise the financial sector is also evident in the loosening up of rules and regulations on foreign listings in the Singapore

Exchange as well as providing greater foreign access to the Singapore Exchange which is targeted to be fully liberalised by 2001 (MAS, 2000).

Liberalisation of Telecommunications and Media Industries

In other areas, liberalisation of the media industry was given a further boost with the granting of new licences to two brand new English language newspapers. *Project Eyeball*, an integrated print and cyberspace news publication which targets net-savvy young professionals and *Streats*, a morning tabloid focusing on the commuting public, is to be launched soon by Singapore Press Holdings (SPH), Singapore's leading newspaper publisher (*The Straits Times*, 7 June 2000).

In an attempt to further deregulate the media industry and to introduce greater competition, the government has also offered newspaper licences to broadcaster Media Corporation of Singapore as well as offering TV and radio licences to SPH (*The Straits Times,* 6 June 2000: 1). A S$50 million (US$30.5 million) SPH Mediaworks was also set up to run two independent TV channels which will 'cater to the lifestyles of people in the new economy' (*The Straits Times*, 9 June 2000: 1). Most significantly, the government has recently brought forward the full liberalisation of the telecommunication industry by two years to April 1, 2000. As noted by Mr Yeo Cheow Tong, the Minister for Communications and Information Technology, the introduction of full market competition is aimed at strengthening the global competitiveness of the local telecommunications industry and to help position Singapore as a leading infocomms hub (*The Straits Times*, 30 March 2000: 1). In this regard, the government has lifted both direct and indirect foreign equity limits for all public telecommunication services licences with immediate effect. Successful new entrants are thus free to decide on the types of network systems and facilities they wish to build and the types of services they wish to offer. Currently, there are three main providers (Singtel, Mobile One and Starhub) and a growing number of facility-based and service-based individual licensees, such as global carriers like AT&T Worldwide Telecommunications Service Singapore, MCI WorldCom Asia and FLAG Telecom (IDA, 2000).

Fundamentally, by further opening up the regulatory environment in almost all sectors and welcoming 'foreign talents' into the city-state, the Singapore government clearly has its sights aimed at becoming a globally competitive player. As the latest PERC report credited: 'the (Singapore) government has come to the conclusion that in order to make Singapore more competitive in the future, the time has come to relax its controls and become less protective of industries like banking and telecommunications' (*The Straits Times*, 26 June 2000: 1).

Foreign "Guest" Workers

In the management of human resources, the government's "open door" policy has also welcomed foreign guest workers or 'foreign talents' such as IT specialists, financiers, bankers and engineers to work in Singapore. Significantly, foreigners now account for one-fifth of Singapore's population, with some of them occupying top positions in local banks and companies, such as Mr John Olds, Vice-Chairman and Chief Executive Officer of the Development Bank of Singapore (DBS) and Mr. Flemming Jacobs, Group President and Chief Executive Officer of local flagship logistics and shipping company, Neptune Orient Lines (NOL).

The arrival of foreign guest workers under the government's open door policy does not only comprise highly-skilled managers and professionals. In fact, low-waged unskilled or semi-skilled immigrants, such as domestic helpers and construction workers, also form a significant proportion of the labor force that represents the "under-belly of globalization" in many cities. Currently, there are more than 200,000 foreign construction workers (mainly from Thailand, Myanmar, Bangladesh, India and China) and more than 100,000 foreign domestic workers from the Philippines, Sri Lanka and Indonesia in Singapore (*The Straits Times*, 12 February 1999). However, these groups of low-status immigrant workers in Singapore are often relegated to the most transient of categories such as work permit holders or "residual" work-force which are subjected to the 'use and discard' philosophy (Yeoh & Chang, 2000, forthcoming). In stark contrast to public discourse on "foreign talents", these immigrant workers are often portrayed as potential sources of social problems such as crimes, vagrancy or the "invasion" of public spaces, with little references to their values and contribution to the society. As Yeoh and Chang (2000) correctly observed, despite the rhetoric of globalization, there are 'definite limits to cosmopolitanism in Singapore's vision of a global city'.

New Knowledge-Based Economy

In the global economy, rapid technological advancement is closely linked to the emergence of "knowledge-intensive" industries (Castells & Hall, 1994). Consequently, the strengthening of the knowledge-base of cities has acquired tremendous importance (Drucker, 1992; Knight, 1995). In recent years, great interest and attention has been focused on Singapore's transition into a new knowledge-based economy. For example, a recent report by the United States Embassy on Singapore's investment climate noted that the city-state is now rapidly shifting to a knowledge-based economy through a mix of active manpower development, infrastructure enhancement and market liberalisation (*The Straits Times*, 11 August, 1999: 40). In the new competitive environment, the state has responded by formulating several broad-ranging plans and initiatives aimed at 'reinventing' Singapore into an 'advanced and globally competitive knowledge-based economy competing on the basis of innovation and knowledge' (MTI, 2000). Greater emphasis will be placed on human resource management and the nurturing of intellectual capital and the leveraging of science and technological innovation as key competitive edge. Known collectively as the KBE strategies, it calls 'for workers to become KBE workers, for policies to be KBE-friendly, for schools and universities to nurture KBE technologies' (*The Straits Times*, 12 Jan 2000: 58). In essence, these plans aim to strengthen and even revolutionise the country's capabilities in industry, technology, entrepreneurship as well as education and training.

Specifically, two main sectors, manufacturing and services, are seen as the twin engines of growth for the Singapore economy. Five strategic plans have also been mapped out to ensure that these two engines are well-positioned for the new knowledge-based economy:

(1) *"Industry 21"* aims to develop knowledge-driven industries which will comprise 40% of Singapore's GDP annually and create 20,000 to 25,000 jobs. The Economic Development Board (EDB) will attract investments in high-growth, high value-added industries with a focus on electronics, chemicals, life sciences and engineering clusters. To reduce the vulnerability and to broaden the economic base, EDB will also encourage a balanced mix of manufacturing activities within each cluster.

(2) *"Trade 21"* plans to make Singapore the global city of international trade and services. Trade and Development Board (TDB) aims for Singapore's trade in goods to grow by 4–6% to reach S$500 billion (US$ 289 billion) by 2005. At the same time, service exports are projected to expand by 5% yearly to S$43 billion (US$24.9 billion). Besides strengthening traditional services such as trading, financial services, logistics and tourism, new high growth services like education, health-care, info-communications and media have been identified.

(3) *"Tourism 21"*, the Singapore Tourism Board's blueprint for the development of the tourism industry, aims to make Singapore a world class tourism destination as well as a premier business centre. In 1998 total tourism revenue was $8.3 billion (MITA, 1999: 312).

(4) *"ICT 21"*, the Information and Communications Technology Plan, aims to harness ICT for national competitiveness. The National Science and Technology Board (NSTB) will develop the research and development capabilities of research institutions and support Singapore as a key value-adding node that is connected to the key business, financial and ICT hubs of the world.

(5) By building a world class financial center, Singapore aims to be a full service provider in capital and money market activities and a regional hub for retail and wholesale banking activities.

In addition, a new "Technopreneurship 21" committee headed by the Deputy Prime Minister Tony Tan, which involves high-level government officials and private sector expertise, has been formed to develop entrepreneurial high-tech businesses in Singapore. This joint initiative covers four areas including: (a) revamping the education system to encourage creative thinking and learning as well as developing the two local universities into 'world-class' research institutes; (b) infrastructural development such as building of a Science Hub with state-of-the-art technology and facilities to attract international talents working in knowledge industries; (c) reviewing rules and regulations to remove obstacles to technopreneurship; and (d) setting up of a US$1 billion Technopreneurship Investment Fund to attract venture capital activities to Singapore (NSTB, 2000).

With Singapore's physical limitations (small size and population; no natural resources), it is thus not surprising that the government places great emphasis on the development of human resources and invests heavily in knowledge-intensive research and development (R&D) programs. The National Technology Plan, for example, targets to increase R&D expenditure over the years to about 2% of the gross domestic product (the current R&D expenditure is about 1.35%). Government expenditure on R&D is spread over the private sector (about 50%), tertiary institutes and other government related bodies. Singapore's technology related growth in the future is targeted in the microelectronic sector: electronic systems, IT, materials technology, manu-facturing technology, biotechnology and energy (Corey, 1993). Between 1992 and 1999, the NSTB provided S$1.2 billion (US$700 million) for R&D. The NSTB funding has helped to initiate 55 R&D centers worth more than S$1.8 billion (US$1.04 billion) and created over 2,500 high-end jobs (*The Straits Times*, 12 June 1996: 26). Currently, Singapore's R&D expenditure stands at S$978.13 million (US$ 565.4 million) or 3.37% of the total government expenditure for financial year 2000/2001 while the number of research scientists and engineers (RSEs) has continued to grow, reaching an estimated

13,599 in 1999, an increase of 7.5% from 1998. The ratio of RSEs per 10,000 labor force has thus increased to 68.8, higher than the target set forth for year 2000 at 65 RSEs per 10,000 (NSTB, 2000). In total, the Gross Expenditure on R&D (GERD) including both public and private sector expenditures on R&D has also grown to S$2.8 billion (US$ 1.6 billion), up 12% from 1998.

In tandem with efforts to develop Singapore into a global city, the government has also launched a comprehensive cyberspace package in order to "plug" the city-state into the new cyber information era. Known as "Singapore One", developments are underway to link the whole island's resident population into one system. Singapore One arises from the national IT 2000 plan which aims to integrate 800,000 households centrally to two service providers, Singapore Telecommunications and Singapore Cable Vision. The objective of Singapore One is to create a seamless integrated system of cyberspace in which just about every activity can be performed from the workplace, school and home: online shopping, studying, watching movies and other entertainment programs, video-conferencing, paying bills and receiving all sorts of information (see Savage, 1999). Singapore One can thus be seen as the logical outcome of the government's strong support in IT development over the years. In the 1990 World Competitiveness Report, Singapore was already ranked first in IT usage and management amongst nine other developing countries in the world. A recent IT household survey by Infocomm Development Authority of Singapore (IDA) shows that almost three in five or 59% of homes in Singapore had a computer. This figure is higher than the U.S. (54%), Australia (47%) and even Japan (42%) (*The Straits Times*, 21 January 2000: 74).

Limitations On The Role Of The State

Over the last three decades, Singapore's economy has experienced tremendous growth, accompanied with constant restructuring of its economic strategies, most recently witnessed in its repositioning for the new high tech economy. While Singapore's political leaders and economic planners have generally been credited with setting the conditions in which growth has been maintained, there are clearly limitations to the role of state intervention.

As Singapore makes its transition into the fast-paced new economy, analysts are already sounding their warning that the long cherished ideas which had underpinned Singapore's economic success in the past decades (such as forward planning, firm governmental control, fear of failure) may paradoxically become a straitjacket hindering future growth (*Asiaweek*, 24 March 2000). In addition, it is feared that ideas such as risk-taking, entrepreneurial spirit and creativity which are valued in the New Economy may be missing in the character of the general workforce which have been accustomed to strict government controls over the years. As Senior Minister Lee Kuan Yew stated, to be sure to survive in the intensifying global economic race, a "major mental overhaul" is required to change the government-dependent mindset of the people. Clearly, this includes not only the restructuring and deregulation of the economic sectors but also relaxing governmental controls and curbs in the political and social sphere in order to foster a greater sense of independent inquiry, freedom and creativity. Ultimately, whether Singapore is able to prosper and succeed in the coming decades will increasingly depend on the 'people factor' which includes the management of talents as well as the human 'heartware'.

URBAN COMMUNITIES AND SOCIAL COHESION: MANAGING GLOBAL-LOCAL TENSIONS

It has been contended that globalization and the rise of the global city have been accompanied by rising local tensions and contradictions which potentially destabilize and erode the internal cohesiveness of urban communities and widens social polarization within cities (Sassen, 1991; Hamnett, 1994). For the Singapore government, maintaining a cohesive society poses a daunting challenge without having to deal with global-local cultural dialectics. Yet, it is the global-local tensions and their impact on local social relations that are likely to pose major challenges for maintaining Singapore's national cohesion in the future.

Divisive Tendencies of Globalization

Indeed, the Singapore government has expressed great concern over the divisive tendencies associated with globalization and the New Economy. The Prime Minister Goh Chok Tong in particular warned of the potential division of the population between the so-called "heartlanders" (lower income and lower skilled workers) and "cosmopolitans" (highly skilled and mobile professionals who are in demand in the global market place). Recent parliamentary debates have also been dominated by concerns over the possible emergence of an underclass of old and underskilled workers who have been left out of the fast-paced new knowledge-based economy (*The Straits Times*, 13 October 1999). In addition, the Deputy Prime Minister Lee Hsien Loong also brought attention to the widening gap between top and bottom income earners in Singapore as the economy globalizes (*The Straits Times*, 13 April 2000: 1).

In particular, he noted the disparity between the highly skilled citizens who enjoy 'First World wages' and the lowly skilled who earn 'Third World wages'. This observation was further confirmed in a recent report by the Department of Statistics (DOS), which highlighted the worrisome trend of the widening income disparity between the top and bottom segments of the population. According to the report, in 1999, households in the top 20% earned 18 times more than those in the bottom 20%, an increase from the ratio of 15 in 1998 (*The Straits Times*, 31 May 2000: 1).

Clearly social and economic polarization is not unique to Singapore, as evidenced by the burgeoning number of case studies documenting the widening local disparities in many Anglo-American and Asian cities (see for example Fainstein et al., 1992; Baum, 1999; Marcuse & Kempen, 2000). Singapore's situation is further exacerbated by its diverse multi-ethnic population comprising 77% Chinese, 14% Malays, 7.6% Indians and 1.4% classified as other races (MITA, 1999). In particular, the cultural and economic marginality of minority ethnic groups such as the Malays and Indians have raised concern among local ethnic communities as well as the government. Paradoxically, the meritocratic principle adopted by the state is sometimes perceived by critics to be endorsing the "survival of the fittest" ideology which marginalized "under-achiever" ethnic minorities and hence justifying their economic and cultural backwardness (see Li, 1989; Rahim, 1998). Since the 1980s, the government has attempted to redress the issue of ethnic differentiation by promoting several ethnic-based self-help organizations through public funding and support. This includes the MENDAKI (Council for the Development of the Malay-Muslim Community), the Singapore Indian Development Assistance Council (SINDA), the Eurasian Association (EA), and the Chinese Development Assistance Council (CDAC). Despite government initiatives and intervention at promoting minority interests, flashpoints are occasionally ignited as exemplified in the recent debates over the implementation of compulsory primary education with its effect on the potential demise of traditional Islamic schools (*madrasahs*). Unmistakably, at the root of the *madrasah* debates are wider issues concerning the dialectical roles and values of local tradition and practices in the much-vaunted "global modernity".

As policy makers are grappling with the implications of the widening income disparity and global-local dialectics, there are also worries that technology-savvy local professionals and talents who can choose to make a living elsewhere in the borderless economy may not feel obliged to stay and contribute to Singapore's progress. To stem the rising tide of young officers leaving public service, a major overhaul of the civil service reward system was recently announced with civil servants receiving an average pay rise of 13% or more (*The Straits Times*, 30 June 2000: 1). In particular, the annual pay of promising young officers ("Superscale G" category) in the elite administrative service will increase by 50% (from S$242,000 to S$363,000) while the annual salaries of ministers and senior civil servants will also increase by 12% (from S$861,000 to S$968,000) to match the top earners in the private sector (prior to the salary revision, Singapore already had among the highest ministerial pay rates in the world). While the logic of pegging ministerial salaries to competitive market rates is compelling for the purpose of attracting and retaining top talents in the civil service, it does raise serious doubts about the integrity and (misplaced) motivations of politicians who may be perceived to be driven by money and profits, rather than more noble goals of nation-building and serving the interests of the people. More pointedly, as the opposition members of parliament charged, 'running Singapore is not like running a private company' (*The Straits Times*, 1 July 2000). Yet, the recent pay revision can be seen to be sending the wrong signal to young Singaporeans who aspire to join the civil service. More critically, in face of mounting evidences of rising income disparity, the government needs to ensure that the civil service pay raise issue will not fuel political disgruntlement and politics of envy among the general population, especially lower-income people.

In the wake of the impact of globalization in all sectors and the resultant concerns on Singaporean society, the government has undertaken various measures including macroeconomics and social policies, ranging from providing skills retraining or upgrading for workers, to giving rebates in HDB rental, utilities, services and conservancy charges, as well as personal tax rebates to help reduce household income inequalities. In October 1997, Prime Minister Goh Chok Tong announced the formation of a 'Singapore 21' Committee comprising a 10-member panel to suggest new ideas to make Singapore a 'global city and the best home for Singaporeans' (*The Straits Times*, 20 October 1997: 1). Specifically the committee is looking at the intellectual, emotional, spiritual, cultural, and social needs of Singaporeans. According to the Prime Minister, the Singapore 21 vision will focus on the 'heartware of Singapore' including exploring amongst other things issues dealing with patriotism, rootedness, sense of community and nationhood (*The Straits Times*, 20 October 1997: 1). To be sure, government initiatives like "Singapore 21" represents the latest in a long list of national policies and campaigns that were launched since the early days to socially and culturally embed the citizens and to promote multiracial harmony in the society. These wide-ranging government initiatives include: (a) the highly successful public housing program which promotes inter-racial living and interaction; the bilingual education policy with English as the common lingua franca and a second 'mother-tongue' language; (b) compulsory national service for all male citizens to foster a sense of espirit de corps; and (c) a series of other national education programs aimed at inculcating national identity and cohesion. In the sphere of politics, the Group Representative Constituency (GRC) concept, which makes it compulsory for all political parties to field a multiracial slate of candidates for elections, is aimed at ensuring minority representation in the parliament (see Mutalib, 1995: 32–35).

Devolution and Civil Society

Given the contemporary thinking on globalization and notions of a borderless world as well as the hypermobile flow of talents, capital and knowledge, it would seem that the Singapore government's programs are out-of-sync with current developments. Indeed, as Trade and Industry Minister George Yeo himself noted, unlike in the old industrial world where people were at the mercy of a monopolistic government, the new global economy and techno-logical advancement are now forcing big governments to devolve power to the lowest level in order to optimize domestic consensus and international competitiveness (*The Straits Times*, 27 January 2000). In raising these issues, the PAP government is cognizant of the political implications of globalization. For example, the Ministry of Community Development and Sports (MCDS) has recently reviewed the functions of the Community Development Councils (CDCs) in charge of individual HDB precincts and granted them greater autonomy in terms of the administration of public assistance and other short-term financial-help schemes. In particular, CDCs under the leadership of a full-time mayor will now oversee the planning and location of community-based services such as childcare, student care and family service centers.

The objectives behind the recent policy to grant CDCs greater powers are twofold: (a) firstly, by delegating operational and planning functions to the CDCs, the role of the Ministry of Community Development and Sports (MCDS) will be streamlined, thus freeing government officials from the day-to-day running of local communities in order to tackle other larger national issues; and (b) secondly, and more importantly, the newly empowered CDCs will now act as local focal points for promoting local volunteerism and community development and are also more responsive to local grassroots needs. In the West Coast and Tanjong Pagar residential estates, for example, residents can speak directly to CDC officers during office hours via video-conferencing facilities installed at the void decks of their flats (*The Straits Times*, 27 May 2000). Without doubt, the CDC is part of the government's program to facilitate the development of 'heartware' to enhance social cohesion and community bonding amongst Singaporeans. In a somewhat "celebrated" decision, the government has also designated a "Speakers Corner" at a public park in Hong Lim Square (modeled after London's Hyde Park) which allows Singaporeans the freedom to air their views, albeit within certain restrictions (*The Straits Times*, 20 March 2000: 1). The idea for a Speakers Corner, first mooted by Senior Minister Lee Kuan Yew himself, demonstrates that policy makers and political leaders are mindful of the need for greater freedom in the public sphere.

While the recent moves by the government to devolve its power and allow for greater public freedom may be seen as a sign of the gradual loosening up of political control of the PAP government, critics have been quick to point out that the government is only willing to liberalize without further democratization (Chua, 1998; *Asiaweek*, 24 March 2000). In particular, political scientist and current Singapore's Ambassador to the United States Chan Heng Chee (1993) noted that 'while the PAP leaders are experimenting with liberalization, that is, with the creation of 'space' and the tolerance of dissent . . . they do not have democratization in mind in the meaning of competing bases of power' (quoted in Chua, 1998: 76). However, as Singapore makes its transition into the fast-paced new economy where diversity and creativity are two key values, the government may well have to jettison its old ways of managing the people. As Deputy Prime Minister Lee Hsien Loong noted in a recent interview with Fortune magazine, one of the main challenges facing Singapore is to be able to accommodate and even encourage diversity and different views which are required for progress and yet have a center which can hold the diversity of the system together (*Fortune Magazine*, 25 Jan 2000).

To this extent, the civil society has an increasingly important role to play in Singapore's development. While in the past, efforts at promoting civil society have been met with considerable political suspicion and even censure, the PAP government now clearly considers the presence of civil society as a key to a more vibrant society essential for Singapore's transition to the new knowledge based economy. In particular, an increasingly complex civil society can be seen emerging which includes the arts community (e.g. The Necessary Stage); voluntary welfare organizations (Action for Aids); the women's movement (AWARE); the environmental movement (Nature Society of Singapore); professional bodies (Singapore Institute of Architects; Association for Muslim Professionals); gay communities (People Like Us); independent political commentators (The Roundtable); and virtual communities on the internet like the Singapore Internet Community (or Sintercom).

As was observed by two local sociologists, people from different ethnic and social backgrounds are now increasingly engaged in a plurality of issues who talk with each other and public authorities. This sense of mutual engagement attests to the growing vibrance of a complex civil society and an evolving sense of community bonding across different social groups, independent of official encouragement (Kwok & Chua in *The Sunday Times*, 28 November 2000: 41). While various commentators may be optimistic about the vibrance of civil society, there are however clear limitations. For example, the application for permit to stage a public gay forum by a local gay community group was recently rejected by the police and the Home Affairs Ministry on the grounds of preserving conservative values in the society. Application by gay communities such as 'People like Us' to be officially registered have also been repeatedly rejected by the authorities despite several appeals to the Home Affairs Ministry and the Prime Minister. Clearly, the freedom of civil society remains circumscribed, especially by local legislation such as the Societies Act, which explicitly proscribes political roles for these organizations (Chua, 1998). Yet, it must be acknowledged that in the so-called 'borderless world' mediated by high technology, it is imperative that the government continues to engage with and support the activities of civil society in order to promote greater civic participation and to strengthen the state-society bonding. As noted by the Minister of Trade and Industry George Yeo (in Ooi & Koh, 2000: 21): 'in the past the state was hard while the society was soft. In the web world, the state and society exist in parallel'. Notwithstanding the various skeptical and critical assessments of the evolving civic and political cultures in Singapore, building trust and synergy between the state and society will be an important challenge for the government and the people in Singapore. If the recent survey by the Institute of Policy Studies (IPS) is any indication, it may augur well for the emergence of a greater sense of national rootedness and pride among Singaporeans. The survey, conducted with 1,451 people, found that two-thirds of Singaporeans are willing to die defending their country in the event of war. Further, Singaporeans were also ranked second in terms of their national pride behind countries with much longer histories like Austria (first) and the United States (a tie with Singapore) (*The Straits Times*, 19 February 2000: 1).

REFLECTIONS

The success of cities, as this chapter has argued, is underpinned by sound management strategies and effective government leadership. Clearly, the tasks of city officials are far from simple, as urban issues and problems are multifarious and are increasingly being determined by the complex interaction between global forces as well as local conditions. While the "Singapore model" has served the city-state well, it is not a universal model that can be readily applied elsewhere. Nevertheless, some general lessons may be offered in closing.

(1) Firstly, fundamental to the success of the city-state is the government's early recognition and commitment towards key urban provisions, in particular housing, education and healthcare. As demonstrated in this essay, these three areas, often neglected or overlooked by city officials, are crucial to maintaining a productive local labor force which is essential for the economy. It is amply clear that grand economic strategies would ultimately be unsustainable in the long run without adequate provision for the local population and work-force. This is particularly true in the case of Singapore where human resources are critical to the development of the city-state. In the new 'people-driven' Knowledge-Based Economy, long-term investments in housing, education and healthcare must continue to be a priority on the agenda of city governments.

(2) Secondly, long term strategic planning has been critical for Singapore's success. Rather than rely on fortuitous circumstances, planners have adopted pragmatic yet flexible and nimble approaches to planning. As highlighted in this chapter, the Singapore government has not been stubborn to resist changes even if it means jettisoning long cherished ideas or tenets. This is most evident for example in the recent liberalization and deregulation of key industries and the devolvement of government powers to "local" levels as with the case of the Community Development Councils (CDC). This flexible and pragmatic approach has also meant that planning will not be encumbered by intractable ideological differences or opinions.

(3) Lastly, and above all, underlying Singapore's management strategy is the strong adherence to the meritocratic system which enables the civil administration to tap into a wide array of talents, regardless of race, family background or any other social ascriptions. Notwithstanding certain misgivings of the system, meritocracy has undeniably enabled the constant renewal of high-quality public sector leadership by recruiting the "best" and the "brightest" into the civil service.

While Singapore has performed well in the past four decades, the challenge for the city-state currently is to 'reinvent' itself and chart its own future agendas and development trajectory in order to meet new challenges and unforeseen problems in the 21st century. Unlike in the past where it could leap-frog difficulties by taking well-trodden paths and adopting time-tested policies, the city-state must now find its own innovative solutions to many contemporary problems. This is especially crucial now that the city-state has been widely regarded as a leader in various fields. One clear endorsement of Singapore's world leadership position can be seen in the strong support given by the international communities for the city-state's election into the United Nations Security Council (UNSC), the most powerful body of the United Nations (*The Straits Times*, 3 July 2000). Once elected, Singapore together with 14 other council members will decide on major international issues from authorizing peacekeeping missions and economic sanctions to electing the next UN Secretary-General. As noted by commentators, for a small city-state like Singapore, it has certainly "punched above her weight". Unmistakably, the "Singapore model" has truly come of age.

REFERENCES

Amin, A., & Thrift, N. (1992). Neo-Marshallian Nodes in Global Networks. *International Journal of Urban and Regional Research*, *16*(4), 571–187.

Asiaweek (24 March 2000). Hong Kong: Asiaweek Ltd.

Awang, A., Salim, M., & Halldane, J. F. (Eds) (1995). *Towards a Sustainable Urban Environment in Southeast Asia*. Institute Sultan Iskandar of Urban Habitat and Highrise.

Baum, S. (1999). Social Transformation in the Global City: Singapore. *Urban Studies*, *36*(7), 1095–1117.

Brenner, N. (1998). Global Cities, Global States: Global City Formation and State Territorial Restructuring in Contemporary Europe. *Review of International Political Economy*, *5*(1), 1–37.

Castells, M. (1989). *The Informational City: Information Technology, Economic Restructuring and the Urban-Regional Process*. Oxford: Basil Blackwell.

Castells, M. (1992). Four Asians Tigers with a Dragon Head: A Comparative Analysis of the State, Economy and Society in the Asian Pacific Rim. In: R. Applebaum & J. Henderson (Eds), *State and Development in Asian Pacific Rim* (pp. 333–370). Newbury Park, Calif: Sage Publications.

Castells, M., & Hall, P. (1994). *Technopoles of the World*. London; New York: Routledge.

Chan, H. C., & Evers, H. D. (1973). Nation-Building and National Identity in Southeast Asia. In: S. N. Eisenstadt & S. Rokkan (Eds), *Building States and Nations: Analyses by Region* (Volume 2) (pp. 301–319). Beverly Hills, Sage Publications.

Cherry, G. E. (1988). *Cities and Plans*. London: Edward Arnold.

Chew, E., & Lee, E. (Eds) (1991). *A History of Singapore*. Singapore: Oxford University Press.

Chua, B. H. (1992). Planning the Built Environment. In: L. Low & M. H. Toh (Eds), *Public Policies in Singapore, Changes in the 1980s and Future Signposts* (pp. 334–351). Singapore: Times Academic Press.

Chua, B. H. (1997). *Political Legitimacy and Housing Stakeholding in Singapore*. London; New York: Routledge.

Chua, B. H. (1998). State and Society: Ambling Towards Greater Balance. In: A. Mahizhnan & T. Y. Lee (Eds), *Singapore Re-Engineering Success* (pp. 69–81). Singapore: Oxford University Press for The Institute of Policy Studies.

Corey, K. E. (1993). Using Telecommunications and Information Technology in Planning An Information-Age City. In: H. Bakis, R. Abler & M. Roche (Eds), *Corporate Networks, International Telecommunications and Interdependence: Perspectives from Geography and Information Systems*. London: Belhaven Press.

Drucker, P. (1992). *The Age of Discontinuity: Guidelines to Our Changing Society*. New Brunswick (USA): Transaction Press.

Fainstein, S., Gordon, I., & Harloe, M. (1992). *Divided Cities: New York and London in the Contemporary World*. Cambridge: Blackwell.

Fortune Magazine (25 Jan 2000). New York, NY: Time, Inc.

Friedmann, J. (1986). The World City Hypothesis. *Development and Change, 17*, 69–83.

Hill, M., & Lian, K. F. (1995). *The Politics of Nation Building and Citizenship*. London; New York: Routledge.

Hamnett, C. (1994). Social Polarisation in Global Cities: Theory and Evidence. *Urban Studies, 31*(3), 401–424.

Hui, J. (1995). Environmental Policies and Green Planning. In: G. L. Ooi (Ed.), *Environment and the City: Sharing Singapore's Experience and Future Challenges* (pp. 30–46). Singapore: Times Academic Press for The Institute of Policy Studies.

Knight, R. (1995). Knowledge-based Development: Policy and Planning Implications for Cities. *Urban Studies, 32*(2), 225–260.

Koh, T. (1998). *The Quest for World Order: Perspectives of a Pragmatic Idealist*. Singapore: Times Academic Press for The Institute of Policy Studies.

Li, T. (1989). *Malays in Singapore: Culture, Economy and Ideology*. Singapore: Oxford University Press.

Low, L. (1998). *The Political Economy of a City-State- Government-made Singapore*. Singapore: Singapore University Press.

Mahbubani, K. (1998). *Can Asians Think?* Singapore: Times Editions Pte Ltd.

Marcuse, P., & Kempen, R. V. (Eds) (2000). *Globalizing Cities A New Spatial Order?* Mass: Blackwell.

McGee, T. G., & Robinson, I. M. (Eds) (1995). *The Mega-Urban Regions of Southeast Asia*. Vancouver: University of British Columbia Press.

Ministry of Information and the Arts (1999). *Singapore 1999*. MITA.

Mutalib, H. (1995). National Identity in Singapore: Old Impediments and New Imperatives. *Asian Journal of Political Science, 3*(2), 28–45.

Naisbitt, J. (1996). *Megatrends in Asia*. London: Nicholas Brealey Publishing.

Ooi, G. L., & Koh, G. (Eds) (2000). State-Society Relations in Singapore. Singapore: Oxford University Press for The Institute of Policy Studies.

Owyang, H. (1998). *From Wall Street to Bukit Merah Strategies of a Corporate Leader, Entrepreneurs of Asia*. Singapore: Times Edition.

Perry, M., Kong, L. L., & Yeoh, S. A. (1997). *Singapore a Developmental City-state*. New York: John Wiley and Sons.

Quah, J. S. T. (1994). Improving the Efficiency and Productivity of the Singapore Civil Service. In: J. P. Burns (Ed.), *Asian Civil Service Systems: Improving Efficiency and Productivity* (pp. 152–185). Singapore: Times Academic Press.

Rahim, L. Z. (1998). *The Singapore Dilemma: the Political and Educational Marginality of the Malay Community*. Kuala Lumpur: Oxford University Press.

Reutens, L. (1995). *The CPF Story-40 Years Serving Singapore*. Central Provident Fund Board.

Sandhu, K. S., & Wheatley, P. (Eds) (1989). *Management of Success: The Moulding of Modern Singapore*. Singapore, Institute of Southeast Asian Studies.

Sassen, S. (1991). *The Global City – New York, London, Tokyo*. Princeton University Press.

Savage, V. R. (1991). Singapore's Garden City: Reality, Symbol and Ideal. *Solidarity, 131/132*, 67–75.

Savage, V. R. (1992). Human-Environment Relations: Singapore's Environmental Ideology. In: K. C. Ban, A. Pakir & C. K. Tong (Eds), *Imagining Singapore* (pp. 187–217). Singapore: Time Academic Press.

Savage, V. R. (1995). Urban Environmental Planning: the Singapore Experience. In: A. Awang, M. Salim & Halldane, J. F. *Towards a Sustainable Urban Environment in Southeast Asia*, Institute Sultan Iskandar of Urban Habitat and Highrise.

Savage, V. R. (1999). Singapore as a Global City: Change and Challenge for the 21st Century. In: L. Low (Ed.), *Singapore Towards A Developed Status* (pp. 140–169). Singapore: Oxford University Press for Centre for Advanced Studies, NUS.

Teo, S. E., & Savage, V. R. (1991). Singapore Landscape: A Historical Overview of Housing Image. (pp. 312–338). In: C. T. Chew & E. Lee (Ed.), *A History of Singapore*, Singapore: Oxford University Press.

Teh, C. W. (1975). Public Housing in Singapore: An Overview. In: S. H. K. Yeh (Ed.), *Public Housing in Singapore A Multidisciplinary Study* (pp. 1–12). Singapore: Singapore University Press.

The Business Times, various issues, Singapore: Singapore Press Holdings.

The Straits Times, various issues, Singapore: Singapore Press Holdings.

Turnbull, C. M. (1977). *A History of Singapore, 1819–1975*. Kuala Lumpur, Oxford University Press.

Turnbull, C. M. (1989). *A History of Singapore, 1819–1988*. Singapore: Oxford University Press.

Urban Redevelopment Authority (1991). *Living the Next Lap: Towards a Tropical City of Excellence*. Singapore: URA.

Urban Redevelopment Authority (1997). *Singapore's Entertainment District*, Singapore: URA.

Urban Redevelopment Authority (1999). *Home.Work.Play.* Singapore: URA.

Yeoh, S. A., & Chang, T. C. (2000). Globalising Singapore: Debating Transnational Flows in the City. *Urban Studies* (forthcoming).

Yeung, W. C. H., & Olds, K. (1999). Singapore's Global Reach: Situating the City-State in the Global Economy. *International Journal of Urban Sciences*, *21*(1), 24–47.

ELECTRONIC REFERENCES

Infocomm Development Authority (IDA) (official website) Online. Available HTTP: http//www.ida.gov.sg (15 June 2000).

Land Transport Authority (LTA) (official website) Online. Available HTTP: http://www.lta.gov.sg/about/index.html (10 June 2000).

Monetary Authority of Singapore (MAS) (official website) Online. Available HTTP: http://www.mas.gov.sg/newspeeches/170599a-c.html (15 June 2000).

Ministry of Industry and Trade (MTI) (official website) Online. Available HTTP: http://www.mti.gov.sg/public/infocentre/feature_article_index.cfm (15 June 2000).

National Science and Technology Board (NSTB) (official website) Online. Available HTTP: http://www.nstb.gov.sg. (10 Jun 2000).

Port of Singapore Authority (PSA) (official website) Online. Available HTTP: http://www.psa.com.sg/intlbiz/index.html (10 June 2000).

5. THE LONG BEACH STORY: A CALIFORNIA CITY REPOSITIONS ITSELF

Manuel Perez and Richard A. Watson

ABSTRACT

Long Beach, a coastal port on the southern flank of the Los Angeles metro area, is an extraordinary example of a secondary city that has succeeded in reinventing itself over the decades, in the face of downturns and problems that might have seemed insurmountable.

Originally a suburb for Los Angeles, Long Beach came into its own as variously a naval port, oil drilling center, aircraft manufacturing hub, and tourist town. The shadow of Los Angeles, ecological problems resulting from oil drilling, the collapse of the defense industry, earthquakes, and decline of tourism have all buffeted the city at one time or another. By the 1970s Long Beach seemed down and out. Through a combination of far sighted city officials and effective interaction with community and businesses, Long Beach developed a series of plans to make the most of its comparative advantages (location, climate, people), and minimize its disadvantages. The city thus is now on the rise, with a striking reversal of urban decline, and poised for a major role in this century.

International Urban Planning Settings: Lessons of Success, Volume 12, pages 123–155.
2001 by Elsevier Science Ltd.
ISBN: 0-7623-0695-5

INTRODUCTION[1]

Situated adjacent to the City of Los Angeles, Long Beach has had difficulty being recognized as one of the United States' major urban centers. Long Beach's role as a "second city" can sometimes prevent us from seeing the unique contributions that such a city can make to an entire region and to a national economy. The Port of Long Beach, which competes directly with the Port of Los Angeles, is well known to trading companies throughout the world. The port has been the number one container port in the United States in the past five years, moving over 60 million metric tons per year. In 1999, the port accounted for approximately $89 billion in trade. The Port moves more than the equivalent of 4.4 million 20-foot cargo containers per year.[2]

Long Beach receives worldwide attention once a year when it hosts the Long Beach Grand Prix, a motor racing event that attracts over a quarter of a million spectators and millions of viewers.[3] Utilizing city streets along the shorefront, the Grand Prix serves to introduce Long Beach to the worldwide viewing public via television and periodicals.

Long Beach has consciously repositioned itself by choice and by necessity. Demoralizing difficulties became unique opportunities to demonstrate a social resolve and creative responses that created a paradigm shift in urban development. Among these existential choices were the problems and benefits of rapid urbanization, oil extraction, and the declining segment of the economy dedicated to national defense.

COMMON BEGINNINGS

A Sunny, Coastal Southern California Setting

Long Beach is situated approximately 30 miles south-southeast of the City of Los Angeles (see Figs. 1 and 2). It is named after a long south-facing beach that makes up part of San Pedro Bay. It enjoys the mild Mediterranean-type climate that characterizes most of Southern California. The prevailing daily breeze from the southwest gives Long Beach markedly better air quality than most of the communities in the South Coast Air Basin of Southern California.

Long Beach developed first as a "bedroom" community to Los Angeles, secondly as an alternative center of commerce and industry, and, most recently, as an independent major economic and political competitor to Los Angeles. Long Beach often defines itself in relationship to Los Angeles, but, due to the close proximity of the two cities, Long Beach has had much difficulty emerging

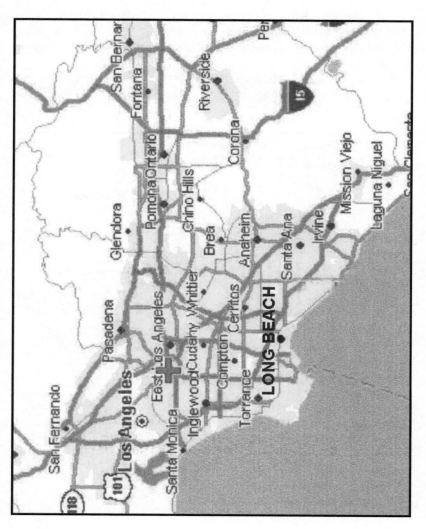

Fig. 1.

from LA's shadow. Unlike Chicago's "Second City" position to the geographically more distant New York, Los Angeles' preeminent position on the Pacific Rim, adjacent to Long Beach, has made it difficult for Long Beach to stand out as a distinct urban center. Consequently, Long Beach recognizes that its self-identity is inextricably tied to Los Angeles. That does not mean, however, that Long Beach has not been able to achieve unique and significant advances on its own.

Long Beach is a city of nearly one half million inhabitants and it occupies a unique position in the urban development of the United States. Of all of the

Fig. 2.

cities that were originally the outskirts of other major cities, Long Beach is the largest independent city that began as a suburb. Long Beach had a population of 438,771 in 1992, making it the 31st largest city in the United States, slightly larger than Kansas City, MO (pop. 431,553) and smaller than Portland, OR (pop. 445,458). The year 2000 Census is expected to place the population of Long Beach at approximately 500,000. Its growth and development has been a mixture of good luck and timing.

Although Long Beach began as a speculative venture to sub-divide Spanish land-grant ranchos into individual home lots for Midwesterners escaping harsh weather, it continued to grow and develop its own character. Today, Long Beach is on the threshold of defining how the American suburban development model can be translated into the traditional world-city model.

The original European colonization of Long Beach, like most of the Southwest, took place under the Spanish. The settlement of California occurred late in the history of Spanish colonial development; subsequently, the resources and population allotted to this effort were limited. Most of the settlements were focused around the Missions, which were entrusted with Christianizing the native population. Pueblos and Presidios were created to provide for commerce and military centers. Colonization was meant to be self-sustaining – requiring little support from the Crown and, in turn, providing contributions of raw material for the "Mother Country."

The vast region of "Alta California" was distributed among a few major landowners. The grants of land from the Spanish Crown to her soldiers and minor officials took up large areas of land. This was the way the land that later made up the City of Long Beach was apportioned.

The Ranchos

The original European landowner, Manuel Perez Nieto, a Corporal in the Spanish expeditionary forces, was granted the rancho in the lands of "Los Coyotes" in 1790. The rancho covered 300,000 acres "from the hills above San Gabriel Mission to the ocean and between the San Gabriel and Santa Ana Rivers." At that time the San Gabriel River emptied into the ocean near the current Long Beach – Wilmington border. The padres at Mission San Gabriel complained that the Nieto grant interfered with their territory, and the shifting river (the metes and bounds boundary) kept changing the Western boundary with the rancho owned by Juan Jose Dominguez. Nieto's land was reduced to 167,000 acres. Nevertheless, when he died in 1805, he was the wealthiest man in California (DeAtley, 1988: 21). In 1833, following Mexico's secession from Spain in 1821, Nieto's heirs became the first sub-dividers, partitioning the vast rancho into six ranchos: Los Coyotes, Las Bolsas, Palo Alto, Santa Gertrudes, Los Cerritos and Los Alamitos. The latter two would become the territory of the cities of Long Beach, Lakewood, Signal Hill, Paramount, Bellflower and part of Compton.

Rancho Los Cerritos became the property of Manuela Nieto de Cota. This Rancho was later sold to Jonathan (later Juan) Temple, a Reading, Massachusetts native. Temple, one of the "Yankee Dons" who converted to Catholicism and married into prominent California families, owned the Rancho from 1843 to the mid-1860s, when he sold it to the Bixby family (DeAtley, 1988: 22–30). Rancho Los Alamitos went from the Nieto heirs first to Governor Jose Figueroa, who had approved the subdivision. The ranch was then sold to Able Stearns, a Lunenberg, Massachusetts native, followed by a short holding period by W. S. Lyons, who acquired the land upon Stearns' default on a loan. The Rancho finally sold to John Bixby in 1862. The Bixby brothers then controlled both of the Ranchos that made up the territory that later became Long Beach.

Ranchers as Developers

The first house in what is now Long Beach was built in 1878 by Archibald Borden at 1st and Pine. In 1880, Jotham Bixby approved a plan devised by William E. Willmore to subdivide 10,000 acres of Los Cerritos into farming acreage with a 350-acre townsite, to be called American Colony. A Los Angeles newspaper reported receiving a map for the colony from Willmore that year. On the map, the townsite was unnamed and included a tract for a university. Willmore was believed to have been trying to lure the Methodists, who were about to choose a home for their University of Southern California. They chose Los Angeles.

Needing to find potential settlers, Willmore attempted to attract Midwestern farmers who would recognize the appeal of growing crops year-round. As Glenn S. Dumke describes in his history of the area, 'Willmore employed every possible advertising method: he listed his land with the California Immigrants Union, advertised in more than a hundred newspapers and thirty-five magazines throughout the nation, and employed a recruiting agent whose job it was to organize excursions to the 'American Colony,' as Willmore had dubbed his project' (Dumke, 1944: 70).

By May of 1884 it became evident that Willmore would not be able to make the required payments to J. Bixby and Co. He was paid $8,000 for the improvements he had made, paid the requisite one dollar consideration and concluded his obligation to Bixby. Within a month, the town abandoned

Willmore's name. Shortly afterwards, the real estate firm of Pomeroy and Mills purchased the township lands from J. Bixby and Co paying $240,000 for the site of Willmore City, the American Colony and some additional acreage not included in Willmore's option.

Looking for a new name, they first called the area Crescent City. The wife of a local shopkeeper lobbied for the name "Long Beach." Although a number of residents would have preferred Los Cerritos or Cerritos Beach as an acknowledgement of its Rancho heritage, the name Long Beach stuck and the management syndicate became the Long Beach Land and Water Company.

THE GLORY YEARS

Resort Suburb of Los Angeles

During the 1880s period of westward expansion, interior cities such as Pasadena saw a tenfold increase in population. Long Beach, though, was less accessible, and did not experience the same growth. In order to attract visitors and settlers, improvements had to be made. The first was with the horse drawn rail line that connected Long Beach to Los Angeles. Affectionately know as the "Get Out and Push" (GOP) railroad, this rail line was sold to the Southern Pacific Railroad, a company that could provide a steam train to service the line. With the building of the130 room Long Beach Hotel in 1884 and the Iowa Villa Hotel the following year, the Southern Pacific had a destination for the Midwestern immigrants.

By 1887, outside interests began taking note of Long Beach. Investors from San Francisco and Los Angeles with close ties to the Southern Pacific Railroad formed the Long Beach Development Company. They paid $250,000 for the interests of Long Beach Land and Water Company. The Company also acquired 800 acres of adjacent salt marsh.

With the interest shown by the Southern Pacific, talk of a harbor development on the west end, and a population exceeding the 500 person minimum, the community was incorporated as a city of the sixth class on January 30, 1888. By March 2, 1888 the town was formally organized. Among the first acts was to declare saloons and gambling houses 'dangerous to the public health or safety.' On November 8, 1888, a fire destroyed the Long Beach Hotel. Col. Charles Crocker, the majority stockholder in the Long Beach Development Company, died. His heirs did not share his interest in Long Beach.

In 1900, Long Beach had a population of 2,252 residents and an area of 3.1 square miles. It had a reputation as a prohibitionist, camp meeting town with modest hotels. The layout followed much of what had been set in place by Willmore. Charles Rivers Drake arrived from the Arizona Territory, where he had amassed a sizable bank account handling contract work for the Southern Pacific Railroad. Drake bought 40 acres in the unincorporated Signal Hill area and an almost solid strip of beach frontage from the east end of Long Beach all the way to what was then the mouth of the Los Angeles and San Gabriel Rivers. Drake organized the Seaside Water Company to oversee his land holdings, and the Long Beach Bath House and Amusement Company to oversee his developments. His initial development idea was a massive salt water bathhouse at the beach. First, however, he needed a way for the bathers to come to Long Beach.

Drake, utilizing his familiarity with the Southern Pacific, contacted Henry E. Huntington, proposing an electric trolley line to connect Long Beach to Los Angeles. Many residents, fearing a change in the quiet lifestyle they enjoyed, fought the idea of providing easy access to Los Angeles. They fought permitting the electric line to invade the sanctity of the peaceful and God-fearing little city. The opposition failed and Huntington's bid to provide an interurban line from Los Angeles – as well as local service – was accepted. He withdrew from the Southern Pacific and declared that the new trolley would be known as the Pacific Electric.

To many people, the real birth of Long Beach was July 4, 1902. On that date, the Pacific Electric line inaugurated service from Los Angeles. It also marked the completion date for the bathhouse. An estimated 60,000 people came to Long Beach that day. They guaranteed the success of Drake's bathhouse, "The Plunge," and precipitated an irrevocable change in the character of Long Beach.

The Pike

Needing to create an attraction that would bring visitors to Long Beach, Drake and his transportation associates found the perfect destination, "the Pike on the Silverstrand," a collection of amusements and concessions along the board-walk. The Pike became the premier amusement on the beach in Southern California. Similar to Coney Island in New York, the Pike offered carnival rides and attractions year-round and was a model for today's controlled entry amusement parks. People could dance at the Majestic Ball Room, ride the merry-go-round, take in a show at the Rialto Theater, eat at one of the many food vending facilities or swim at the Plunge

Prompted by the competition from the "Race Through The Clouds" in nearby Venice, the Pike's first roller coaster, built in 1907, was replaced in 1914 by the famous "Jackrabbit Racer." It, in turn, was replaced in 1929 by the legendary "Cyclone Racer," which operated until 1968 (Berner, 1982: 26). The last half of the twentieth century saw the end of the Pike and a major redevelopment project undertaken on the adjacent land. The seedy collection of beer bars, pool halls and tattoo parlors was demolished by the City of Long Beach in 1968. While the Pike site is being considered for new development, the neighboring area remains undeveloped.

Studios in Long Beach

Well before the development of the well-known Hollywood studios, Long Beach was home to Balboa Studios, which produced the movies of Roscoe "Fatty" Arbuckle and the Keystone Cops (DeAtley, 1988: 66). The studio required its players to live in Long Beach and the city served as a frequent backdrop in these films. However, Long Beach's conservative Midwestern sensitivities and the libertine lifestyle of the movie industry would prove incompatible.

Through the end of the First World War, the movie industry was the number one employer in Long Beach. Ultimately, Balboa Studios overproduced, creating inferior movies by the dozens in an attempt to maintain cash flow. The sensational trial of Fatty Arbuckle, accused in the death of a young starlet, marked the point where the movie industry truly became an undesirable neighbor. While some of the buildings that housed Balboa Studios stand yet today, movie production moved out. Since then, Long Beach has served as the location for a number of movie premieres and can still be seen as an urban backdrop in movies and on TV.

Discovery of Oil

Long Beach sits astride the Newport-Inglewood seismic fault line. While not as significant as the infamous San Andreas Fault, this fault line has played a significant role in defining the geologic nature and topographic appearance of Southern California. Fault zones experience periods of folding, earthquakes and subsidence. Each of these evolutionary processes has played a major part in the recent history of Long Beach.

The first impact to be noticed was the discovery of oil on Signal Hill on June 23, 1921. While not the first major find in Southern California, this oil field has been one of the most productive – and continues to this day to produce significant quantities of oil. The City of Long Beach and the State of California – through a tidelands agency – continue to receive royalties for the extraction of oil under State and City lands. With the advent of slant drilling, the oil companies were able to extract oil beneath the City of Long Beach from man-made offshore islands.

The oil islands in Long Beach harbor also serve to separate the noisy oil well operations from the desirable residential water-view sites along the beach. The islands are designed to contain spills and prevent other potential pollution from reaching the ocean water. The drilling towers, mounted on tracks that access each of the well heads, have been disguised as attractive "high-rise" structures. Some people, unaware of their true function, express an interest in renting an apartment in those off shore towers.

Aircraft Industry

Boeing Aircraft Company, currently the largest employer in Long Beach, is also the largest private employer in Los Angeles County. The modest beginnings of this major industry took off early in the 20th Century, with Glenn H. Curtiss' one-mile flight over Dominguez field (northwest of Long Beach), on January 10, 1910 – billed as the first airplane flight on the Pacific Coast. The region has been home to the aircraft industry ever since, although the recent consolidation of manufacturers has caused the departure of many industry companies from Southern California.

One of those observing Curtiss' exploits was Iowa-born and Long Beach-raised Earl Daugherty. The former bookkeeper left his profession to build the first area airport and begin the construction of airplanes in Long Beach. Daugherty Field was initially located on leased land. Recognizing the growth potential in the aircraft industry, '. . . in 1921, Earl and his father bought a patch of marshy land at Willow Street and American Avenue, built an 80-by-100 foot hangar, and moved the private airport to that location' (DeAtley, 1988: 63).

In 1924 Daugherty and his friends, Al Ebrite and J. J. Montijo, formed part of the City of Long Beach aviation commission. The city sought enlargement of Daugherty Field, but it already represented a $50,000 private investment to Daugherty. He suggested establishment of a Municipal Airport at Spring Street and Cherry Avenue on 80 acres owned by the water department. The new Municipal Airport would later be named for Earl Daugherty and serve as the necessary attraction for Douglas Aircraft. Donald Douglas moved his production facility to Long Beach in 1940. The defense efforts during World War II allowed Douglas Aircraft to grow and draw numerous workers to Long Beach. In 1967 Douglas merged with its St. Louis-based competitor, McDonnell. The McDonnell Douglas Corporation, in turn, was acquired by Boeing in 1997.

Navy Town

In 1919 the Navy was divided into Atlantic and Pacific fleets. The Pacific fleet anchored in San Pedro Bay without any designation as a base or port. Long Beach built its own Navy Landing in 1926 and was selected over Los Angeles as the home port of the Pacific Fleet in 1932. As Richard DeAtley wrote, 'The official designation brought the navy population of the city to 2,224 officers and 26,587 enlisted men. More Navy families made their home in Long Beach than any other city in the United States' (DeAtley, 1988: 80). The presence of the Navy provided economic benefits to the city during the Great Depression. In addition, the Navy provided much needed security forces immediately following the Long Beach Earthquake on March 10, 1933 (discussed further in the next section).

The Navy did not begin building facilities in Long Beach until 1940. Much of the intervening delay was due to conflict created by the competing City of Los Angeles, and California's two senators, who favored San Francisco (DeAtley, 1988: 92). The Navy also made it necessary to expand the breakwater protecting the harbors of Long Beach and San Pedro.

World War II brought Long Beach into prominence as a military facility. The navy base included the largest dry dock on the West Coast. The U.S. Naval Drydocks began operation in 1943, ultimately repairing over 800 ships and utilizing 16,400 workers (DeAtley, 1988: 92). With the Navy in charge of the port during the war, the sobriquet of "Navy town" was even more appropriate for Long Beach. The Navy's influence over Long Beach waned in the late '60s. The "peace dividend" to Long Beach at the end of the Vietnam War was a marked down-sizing of forces in the area. Long Beach is reputed to have incurred the greatest impact of any city in the United States as a result of the Federal base closures. Infighting with the Ports of Los Angeles and San Francisco, recently joined by the Port of San Diego, continues over the re-use of the naval facilities.

DECLINE AND FALL OF LONG BEACH

Oil Depletion and the Sinking City

The same forces that provided the vast pools of oil under Long Beach, and much of Southern California, also created two major detrimental impacts to the Long Beach community. The first was the earthquake of 1933; the second was the gradual subsidence of the Long Beach oil field.

The Long Beach earthquake, which measured 6.3 on the newly created Richter Scale, actually had an epicenter six miles deep, and three and one half miles southwest of Newport Beach – immediately south of Huntington Beach. Long Beach lent its name to this catastrophe due to the extensive damage suffered in this emerging metropolis. The destruction of most of the unreinforced brick structures, particularly the public schools, led to substantial changes in the building code requirements for the region. The Field Act, requiring additional assurances of earthquake safety for schools and other public buildings, was passed by the State Legislature shortly thereafter.

The second major natural disaster to visit Long Beach was much more protracted in its impact – the gradual subsidence of the area as oil was being extracted. 'Parts of Long Beach had been literally floating on oil. And since the oil was being pumped out, the city dropped under its own weight' (DeAtley, 1988: 98). Initially noticed during the early 1940s, subsidence became pronounced by the end of the decade. The epicenter of subsidence dropped over 30 feet by the end of that decade. The drop in elevation had tremendous impact on the infrastructure of the area. Sewers, both sanitary and storm drains, actually reversed in their slope. By the early 1950s proposals were made to inject ocean water to reverse the subsidence.

Arguments arose over who would pay to stabilize or reverse the subsidence. In addition, the subsidence that had occurred benefited the navy base and the port by creating a deepwater port without having to dredge. Thus, not all waterfront users wanted the land brought back to its original elevation or to pay for the anti-subsidence pumping. The land depression also caused a continuing economic depression in the City of Long Beach. 'Time magazine had called Long Beach the "Sinking City," and the media, with its penchant for pithy tags, latched on the term' (DeAtley, 1988: 101).

While the harbor was now able to accommodate supertankers and deep-draft modern aircraft carriers, the damage to Long Beach's reputation sped up the flight of many businesses to the newly developing suburbs. During the 1960s and early 1970s, Long Beach reached new depths (pun intended) in its physical condition and self-image.

Socio-Economic Decline and Gangs

From 1900 to 1950 Long Beach had more than a hundred-fold increase in population, from 2,252 to 250,767. During the second half of the 20th Century the population has again doubled to approximately 500,000. While the growth appears constant, the growth has been marked by major spurts and changes in the demographic characteristics of the residents of Long Beach. Like many of the cities experiencing growth in the second half of the 20th Century, Long Beach has become the home to ethnic minorities, refugees from economic and political upheaval in other parts of the world, particularly Latin America and Southeast Asia.

Loss of Lakewood

The Ku Klux Klan had been active in Long Beach, during the 1920s and 1930s. 'Amid all the prosperity, there was a moral poverty in Long Beach' (DeAtley, 1988: 74). Long Beach, like most of Southern California and much of the nation, institutionalized segregation through racial covenants in land deeds. These covenants prohibited the sale of property to anyone who was not a member of the Caucasian race, and often even excluded anyone who was not a member of a Protestant denomination. The racial covenants, which were finally declared unconstitutional in 1948, prevented many otherwise qualified families from purchasing a home in Long Beach. The growth of the defense industry during World War II and the rapid suburbanization of the region in the years immediately following, created a demand for housing that was not available in Long Beach.

D. J. Waldie, in his award winning book, *Holy Land*, describes how three entrepreneurial developers: Mark Taper, Lou Boyar and Ben Weingart, purchased 3,500 acres of farmland and built '. . . something that was not exactly a city' (Waldie, 1996: 4). The important qualities of this new form of suburban development were:

- affordable entry-level homes ranging in price from $7,825 to $9,700;
- a 154 acre, $100 million regional shopping center (but no industry); and
- affordable financing (including no down payment for veterans) which did not discriminate on the basis of religion (notable because Taper, Boyar and Weingart, as Jews, could not buy into Long Beach).

Lakewood later resisted inclusion into Long Beach. When it incorporated in March of 1954, it had a population estimated at 70,000, making it the sixth-largest city in California, and the largest-ever community to incorporate in the state (DeAtley, 1988: 95). Lakewood began the process of the incorporation of communities that relied on the County of Los Angeles to provide most of the municipal services. These so-called "contract cities" do not have their own police, fire, or even planning and building officers – choosing instead to have the County, through the Sheriffs and Fire Departments, as well as planning and building and safety Departments, provide those services. It also marked the beginning of a trend away from established cities toward the new suburbs.

Growth Moves to Orange County

The 1950s and 1960s were the decades that marked the significant national shift toward suburban growth. The suburban development of Southern California, aided by the federal investment in freeways, pushed growth further and further out. The major impact felt by Long Beach was the abandonment of the central city shopping area in favor of new regional shopping centers, and the gradual slowing of residential growth. No longer subject to racial covenants, Long Beach experienced growth in its minority population, and an almost equal amount of "white flight" during the decades of the 1960s and 1970s.

Orange County absorbed much of the white flight in Southern California. The nearby Orange County City of Huntington Beach saw its population increase from approximately 11,000 to over 120,000 in the decade of the 1960s. By 1980, Huntington Beach, with a population of 170,505, was the 85th most populous city in the United States. Anaheim and Santa Ana ranked 63 and 69, respectively, with populations of 219,311 and 203,713. In the 1990 Census, Santa Ana and Anaheim reversed their rankings to 52 and 59, with a population of 293,742 and 266,404, respectively. Huntington Beach, while dropping in ranking to 90th, grew to 181,519 (U.S.Bureau of Census).

From 1960 to 1980, Long Beach grew a scant 17,166 (4.7%) – increasing from 340,168 to 361,334. By 1980, Long Beach realized that its population, commerce and industry were moving to the newer suburbs – particularly Orange County. The late 1970s not only marked the nadir of Long Beach's confidence in itself, and particularly in the Navy's presence, but it led to a resolute change in the goals and activities of the city.

Abandonment of the Red Car Lines

Long Beach began as a suburb to Los Angeles. The impetus to its growth was the creation of the Pacific Electric Railway. Histories of the development of "Streetcar Suburbs" have been well documented (Warner, 1962). The Pacific Electric, which began strictly to promote the sale of home lots for its owner, Henry Huntington, became the most extensive interurban railway system in the world (Friedricks, 1992). The 1902 line from Los Angeles to Long Beach as well as subsequent extensions always followed the investments made by Huntington in lands that he would later subdivide. Thus, the economics of the rail lines were suspect at best.

The neighboring communities of Huntington Park and Huntington Beach not only owe their initial development to the arrival of the Red Cars, but reflect the name of their developer. The arteries created by the Pacific Electric also became the preferred alignment for subsequent freeways. As more and more of Southern California became dependent on the automobile, the need for, and influence of, the Pacific Electric diminished.

Finally, on April 8, 1961 the last run of the Big Red Cars from Los Angeles to Long Beach took place. This was the last interurban line in Southern California. It had been assumed that this outmoded form of transportation would no longer be necessary. Less than thirty years later, it would be necessary to spend nearly a billion dollars to re-establish the Los Angeles – Long Beach rail line – now called "The Blue Line."

Dysfunctional Municipal Government

Long Beach's Midwestern heritage was broad and deep. Often called "Iowa-by-the-Sea," California's fifth largest city maintained a distinctly Midwestern political attitude. Although not as partisan as Chicago, nor as corrupt as Missouri's Pendergrast Machine, Long Beach did tolerate a great deal of "wink and nod" agreements.

During the nadir of the 1970s, the city experienced the revelation of institutional corruption. First, the Planning Director was indicted for accepting a pay-off to approve a project in sensitive coastal waters. Shortly thereafter, most of the elected officials declined to stand for re-election. It was time for substantial changes in the way that "Iowa-by-the-Sea" did business.

A strong, no-nonsense City Manager, John Dever, took the helm and brought in Bob Paternoster as Planning Director. The city began to deal with the planning alternatives in a straightforward and forthright manner. The new city council considered and adopted far-reaching plans to redevelop the downtown and to create a new marina. The city began a process of periodic reviews of its plans and objectives. First, however, it had to stop the downward slide that had reached new depths in the previous administration.

Abandonment of Long Beach Boulevard

Long Beach Boulevard had been the premier auto row for Southeast Los Angeles County. Dealerships representing the big three auto makers, as well as European and Japanese manufacturers, called Long Beach Boulevard home. Three distinct actions caused the auto dealers to abandon Long Beach Boulevard. With their departure, sizable sales tax revenue also left the city.

First, the neighboring city of Cerritos realized that creating an "auto mall" would generate substantial sales tax revenues without requiring substantial commitment of resources by the municipality. Although Cerritos had been reprimanded by the State courts for redeveloping fallow (but not depressed) farmland into regional serving commercial property, they seized the opportunity to provide an auto mall alongside the San Gabriel (605) Freeway. The substantive impact was to attract auto dealers to Studebaker Road, and due to the auto companies' "non-competition" agreements, they prevented other dealers from claiming nearby territories. Today, Cerritos Auto Mall is reputed to be the highest dollar volume auto mall in the United States.

Second, the construction of the Blue Line, over much of the same right-of-way that had been used by the Pacific Electric Red Cars, placed it in the median of Long Beach Boulevard. Construction during the late 1980s made it awkward for interested shoppers to view and test-drive autos, and the dated and smaller sites along Long Beach Boulevard housed smaller inventories – reducing choices in selecting models, colors, options, etc.

Third, the neighboring City of Signal Hill, utilizing its redevelopment powers to acquire and clean up oil field maintenance and equipment yards, attracted many of the auto dealers from Long Beach Boulevard. As mentioned before, non-competition agreements limited the areas into which these dealers could go. The approximately one to two mile move from Long Beach Boulevard (in Long Beach) to Willow and Cherry (in Signal Hill) did not create a major conflict with the dealers in Cerritos to the East, or Torrance to the West. Signal Hill, however, had to write down the land cost to the dealers, substantially. Revenue to the City of Signal Hill from this project may be slightly more than the cost of acquiring, clearing, remediating and marketing the sites. Ironically, the majority of the dealers have kept "Long Beach" as part of their name – even though they moved into Signal Hill.

Base Closures and Collapse of Defense Contractors

The "Peace Dividend" following the Viet Nam war was an ironic label. From the depths of the Depression, through the Second Word War and the Korean conflict, Long Beach benefited greatly from the Navy presence. The reduction in armed forces in the early 1970s, and decreased spending on defense material had a detrimental effect on Long Beach. Initially, during the 1970s, industries that had actively been suppliers to the military found their main buyer gone. The major defense contractors in the region felt the impact of reduced government defense spending. Suppliers, lacking major clients, began to move or close down. The region was no longer the attractive defense industry bulwark.

During the 1980s, many major decisions identifying base closures were made. Long Beach lost the Naval Base – which included the shipyard and base housing that had long contributed to the local economy. Additionally, the Naval Hospital on the eastern side of the city was also closed down. Long Beach lost approximately 27,600 jobs that added $6.5 billion to the local economy (City of Long Beach).

Decline of Aerospace and Corporate Takeovers

Along with the decline in defense spending, aerospace manufacturers found themselves in an increasingly competitive marketplace. Many manufacturers found themselves unable to continue in the modes that they had adopted during the Cold War. Many of these major defense contractors were, in many ways, "too big to fail." The emerging political power of the Southeastern United States has been most critically felt among defense contractors. With regional support for "open shops," lack of restrictive environmental legislation, and friendly Congressmen (many of whom control the allocation of defense dollars), major defense contractors have moved their operations south and east.

The major defense contractors in Los Angeles County – Lockheed, North American, Rockwell, Northrop-Grumman, and McDonnell Douglas – fell one by one. They each became targets for acquisition by other major aerospace contractors: Martin Marietta, Boeing, etc. They were so big, however, that their acquisitions were called mergers. While these activities were national in scope, their impact on southeastern Los Angeles County, and Long Beach in particular, was cataclysmic.

CREATING AN ENVIRONMENT FOR REPOSITIONING

Transitioning Toward a New Paradigm

Long Beach accepted and internalized the concept that planning is a process and not a product. The plans begun in the late 1970s and the citizen involvement in the planning process that accompanied them has been constantly revisited, reviewed, and revised. The tasks before the city in the late 1970s constituted nothing less than a complete makeover. The city had allowed its core to decay. The Pike had been dismantled by the end of the 1960s. Although the city had begun the process of "urban clearance," downtown was still seen as a collection of sailor bars, tattoo parlors and second hand stores. Its Civic Auditorium, which was uniquely situated, surrounded by Rainbow Pier and Rainbow Lagoon (which was filled-in in 1955), was no longer able to attract the conventions that had made Long Beach a desirable destination. A new convention center was built in the early 1970s, and work began on building a new shopping mall. Office towers were built along the West Ocean bluff. In an effort to change the city's image, the city bought the famous ocean liner, Queen Mary, in 1967. The Queen Mary was received with much enthusiasm and fanfare. However, it did not actually make any money until recently.

Role of Strategic Planning

Realizing that "quick fixes" were not available, the city undertook a formal "Strategic Planning" process in the mid-1980s. The results of that plan, developed with much citizen input – which also sought the contributions of industry and commerce representatives – provided the entire community with a simple set of achievable goals (City of Long Beach Strategic Plan). The 15 goals established to guide the city to the year 2000 recognized both assets and limitations. That the goals of this plan have been, or are being, fulfilled underscores the fact that the plan was taken seriously by residents, elected officials and city staff.

The city has recently undergone a similar process to update the goals and objectives of the strategic plan of 1986. Submitted by its volunteer committee on December 14, 1999 to the City Council, the plan was adopted on June 20, 2000. Entitled Long Beach Strategic Plan 2010, the new plan changes some of the previous emphasis on downtown commercial development into community and resident-based goals and objectives. The current areas of focus include:

- Neighborhood Development
- Education and Youth
- Community Safety
- Business Growth and Workforce Development
- Environmental Improvement

In the effort to reposition itself, Long Beach has concluded that trade, tourism, and technology, along with retail development are to be its objectives. To those ends, the city has:

- Expanded its port/harbor facilities
- Developed an enlarged convention center
- Is beginning to attract the dot com companies
- Built a new "big box" center on the former Naval Hospital site.

While it is too soon to tell if the strategic plan for 2010 will be as successful as the plan for 2000 was, the critical importance of viable planning documents is well understood and accepted in Long Beach. The City Council has internalized the planning effort by reviewing its actions, on a yearly basis, and how they further or relate to the strategic plan.

Role of Redevelopment

Tax Increment Redevelopment, as practiced in California, is uniquely structured to prevent many of the excesses of redevelopment efforts around the country. Recognizing that redevelopment often brings benefits to adjacent sites, not touched by the redevelopment agency, tax increment redevelopment allows the agency to receive the increase in property tax for an entire project area.

Redevelopment has allowed local government to put in public improvements, such as new sewers, underground electric and phone lines, re-built roads, sidewalks, etc. which will then allow the agency to re-assess the project area based on the public investment. It is assumed that redevelopment agencies will create greater value by helping private investors in building new structures and facilities. Agencies prefer to assist retail commercial development, as this not only generates some improvement in the assessed valuation, but also generates sales tax dollars (of which the state shares $1\frac{1}{2}\%$ of the $7\frac{1}{2}\%$ to $8\frac{1}{2}\%$ tax rate with local government).

Role of Elected Officials

The "Hawkeye" political structure of Long Beach had undergone tremendous change in the mid and late 1970s – due to the indictment and investigation following the Marina Pacifica debacle. The newly elected officials, filling the void left by the old guard and very aware of the past questionable practices, made it a point to perform their duties in circumspect and proper manner. Also, due to the recognized difficulties in the downtown of Long Beach, elected officials agreed that downtown was the first priority. California's tradition of non-partisan local elections, part time council representatives and the recent preference for term limits is in full flower in Long Beach. The role of political parties or machines has been missing from the local landscape. The only full-time and fully paid legislative official in the City is the Mayor. Therefore, even though council members may be required to actively participate in governance activities nearly full time, they are still dependent on their immediate and city staffs for all of the information used in their decisions. The elected officials do have the ultimate responsibility for accepting and adopting the various plans for development. By and large, they have done a good job of being creative in their approaches, while at the same time exhibiting a cautious perspective.

Role of Government Staffs

As a charter city, Long Beach has numerous powers provided by its charter and allowed by state law. Long Beach operates the typical municipal services – police, fire, public works, building and safety, etc. – in addition, it owns and operates an airport, harbor, lifeguards and marinas and numerous unique services. Long Beach has its own water and gas service and is one of only three California cities with its own health department. With the exception of telephone and electricity, Long Beach is a "full service" city.

Long Beach is able to marshal experts in a variety of fields whenever considering or evaluating potential projects. From marinas and international marketing to aerospace manufacturing, there are few areas where city staff has not had to develop a specialty in order to operate its assets.

Each effort undertaken pursuant to the Strategic Plan has been led by government staff. The Harbor Department operates facilities and volumes equal to the Port of Los Angeles with a staff of approximately 200, versus Los Angeles' 500. The Convention Center has been growing in its ability to attract large (and economically desirable) conventions. The city has not been as successful as other cities on the West Side (of Los Angeles) at attracting the dot com companies. However, the new town center that redeveloped the former Navy Hospital site – at the eastern edge of the City – has been very successful since its inception.

Role of Citizen Activists

Long Beach has sought and continues to receive the input of its citizen activists. The city has numerous boards, commissions, and committees, which solicit citizen input. Most of this input has been received in a positive manner. Other input has been more notable for its unintended consequences.

Like any municipality in the United States, meetings of city boards, commissions or the City Council attract a core group of citizens who are, or ought to be, committed. Their views run generally counter to the recommendations of city staff. Some of these activists have influenced significant actions by the City Council, its board and commissions. Nowhere is this more evident than in the city's efforts to utilize the former naval base for the storage and transport of containers being offloaded from ships.

With the closing of the Long Beach Naval Base, the city was looking forward to conversion of the site into a major container loading and storage facility for COSCO, the shipping company of the People's Republic of China, which had been a tenant of the Port for over twenty years.

The Naval Base administration and support buildings, built in 1942, had been designed by one of the first recognized African-American design architects. The buildings had never been listed as a unique or innovative example of Paul Revere Williams' designs. Paul Williams had been recognized for his ability to adapt historical styles to the new needs of society and an innovator in his use of forms and materials. One of his last efforts was the design of the "theme tower" at Los Angeles International Airport (LAX). The spider-like building, with a restaurant at its apex, remains a world-recognized symbol of LAX. There is no question that Paul Williams was a gifted designer. The Long Beach Naval Base buildings, however, were not one of his landmark projects.

The citizen activists committed to preserving the buildings were joined by numerous professionals from Los Angeles (including the host of a TV travelogue of Southern California, and an attorney who represented the group before the courts). They managed to delay the process, but in the end the transfer to the city took place. However, the preservation activists received a payment of $5 million from the port to be used to preserve and rehabilitate other historic structures in Long Beach.

The delay also gave the Port of Los Angeles the opportunity to negotiate with COSCO and others, with the hope of luring them to their facilities. COSCO was prohibited from occupying the former base site due to a "rider" offered by a Congressman from San Diego. Nevertheless, COSCO has agreed to continue to occupy space at the Port of Long Beach. The Naval Base site, however, will be occupied by the Hanjin shipping line from Korea, and serve as the home port for Sea-Launch, an innovative method of launching satellites from a ship platform at the equator.

The main objective achieved by the activists was to delay the process of transferring the Naval Base to the City of Long Beach. The port, in turn, had to add $5,000,000 to the cost of obtaining this facility. Los Angeles had the opportunity to negotiate with a number of shipping companies. Eventually, in the merger of Long Beach tenants, Maersk and SeaLand, Los Angeles was able to insure that their new home would be the Port of Los Angeles.

Role of Corporate Citizens

Immediately after the civil unrest of 1992, following the acquittal of the police officers in the Rodney King beating, business and community representatives united to deal with some of the problems that had surfaced.

A new organization, the Long Beach Community Partnership, was set up in late 1992 to focus the efforts after the civil unrest It is a broad-based community coalition designed to address the issues and concerns of the broader community. Its membership included representatives of major employers, community activists, and institutional leaders, but it purposely did not include elected officials. Recognizing the need to be effective, as well as efficient, the Community Partnership identified three areas where it felt it could have the greatest positive impact:

(1) Creation of a seamless education system where students could move from elementary to secondary schools, to community college and on to the State University, and perhaps back to teaching at the elementary and secondary school level, with a commonly accepted level of competency. Articulation of training and transferability of credits has been achieved. Seamless education has been incorporated into the three institutions: Long Beach Unified School District, Long Beach Community College District, and California State University at Long Beach. This effort has received much national attention and, in effect, is no longer part of the Community Partnership's work plan.

(2) Improving the perception of public safety by supporting community based efforts to reduce crime. The Community Partnership has been sponsoring a yearly Safety Summit that attracts hundreds of participants. The Safety Summit recognizes individual efforts by identifying "community heroes" and creative solutions in reducing crime. This yearly meeting continues to promote public safety and provides a scorecard of the community's efforts in reducing crime. Like most of the country, Long Beach has been experiencing reduced levels of crime; however, recent increases in violent crime have raised concerns within the community and the Community Partnership.

(3) Supporting economic development in the city. The Community Partnership recognizes that to have a healthy community, economically and socially, it is necessary to promote economic vitality within the city and among various segments of the economy. The impacts upon the defense-related sector of the economy have been so great in Long Beach that the main effort has been toward retention of existing jobs. While job losses in Long Beach have been severe, the creation of new and different types of jobs has allowed the city to actually improve its total population that is employed.

The key efforts in being able to attract new jobs and industry to Long Beach have been led by corporate citizens and supported by City staff. Those efforts will be particularly challenged by the anticipated departure of much of Boeing's production facilities.

Role of Professionals

The ranks of professionals in Long Beach appear typical for a city of nearly one half million population. The proximity of Los Angeles would appear to attract the individuals to Los Angeles based organizations. In most cases, however, Long Beach based organizations exist to compete with their Los Angeles based counterparts. Long Beach has long had locally based professional organizations representing architects, apartment owners, restaurateurs, doctors and lawyers. Los Angeles appears close geographically but far away, socially and culturally.

During much of the repositioning efforts of Long Beach, various organizations have benefited from the participation of qualified local professionals. This has been specifically noted among not-for-profit organization boards. The creation of Leadership Long Beach, which follows the national model, has allowed the community to educate young professionals to create a population from which the future leaders rise. It has become a requirement for all Leadership Long Beach graduates to join and assist not-for-profit organizations. While several graduates of Leadership Long Beach have run for office, it was not until this year that Rob Webb (leadership class of 1996) was elected to the City Council.

TURNING PROBLEMS INTO OPPORTUNITIES

Sinking City Becomes a Deep Water Port

The physical effects of subsidence in Long Beach have been well documented (Colozas & Strehle, 1995). In addition to the "sinking feeling" created by the press, subsidence and the corrective actions taken by the city have "elevated" the economy of the region. The first, and perhaps most significant effect of subsidence, has been to create a deepwater port without the necessity of dredging. The epicenter of subsidence has been stabilized at-29 feet. This has allowed the adjacent channels to provide sufficient draft for large oil tankers. The subsidence has also affected the Port of Los Angeles, but not as extensively, nor as beneficially.

Secondly, it was determined that replacing the extracted oil with injected water would prevent further compression of the shale and sandstone layers. It was found that by injecting heated water, the oil flows more efficiently. The result has been a more thorough and efficient extraction of the available oil. Wells that would have previously been abandoned are still able to produce significant amounts of oil.

Expanding the Port

Stabilization of the subsidence in the port area has resulted in the build up of deposited silt and sand from upland areas. In order to maintain clear shipping lanes and dock areas, it then becomes necessary to dredge. The silt and sand picked up by the dredge is generally deposited away from the channels and dock areas. Both Long Beach and Los Angeles ports have been able to use this dredge material to create fill areas that expand the area available for dockside storage. This has allowed both ports to create land and expand the available surface area to load and unload ships. Although this process is employed worldwide (and is perhaps most well known in the creation of the polders in Holland) it has been particularly effective in the Long Beach and Los Angeles harbors. The approximately 3,000 acre (1,180 hectares) Port of Long Beach is predominantly man-made.

Turning an Aging Ocean Liner Into a Tourist Attraction

The major tenant on Pier J is not a shipping company or ship repair facility. It is one of the symbols of Long Beach, the Queen Mary. When it was acquired in the late 1960s, the 30- year old flagship of the Cunnard Line was no longer the transport of choice across the Atlantic. Long Beach did not have any social or political attachment to the aging dowager. Long Beach, however, had adopted the nickname of the "Queen City" early in the 20th Century (perhaps acknowledging Los Angeles as King). It, therefore, seemed appropriate to bring the Queen Mary to the "Queen City."

Cunnard, keenly aware of the cost of maintaining a floating city, required that the boilers be removed so that Long Beach would not be tempted to sell this symbol of 1930s opulence to a discount operator. While there have been numerous proposals to sell the Queen Mary, the lack of boilers has prevented it being put back on the seas, competing with its former owner. The Queen Mary serves as a unique hotel site. While it still floats alongside Pier J, many mistakenly believe that the ship is "grounded." The large holds of the ship now serve as meeting and exhibit spaces. Its opulent ballrooms and restaurants continue to attract visitors who may or may not be staying on board the ship.

The space limitations of the ship require that additional attractions be provided on the land adjacent to the ship. Initially, a faux-English village was built to herd the visitors to the ship. An English pub and a Scottish Heritage Center provided the British flavor. The small size and dubious authenticity of the structures and their content will result in the demolition of the village in the near future to make way for new shopping and eating facilities. While a plan to achieve this has been approved by the Long Beach City Council, work has not yet begun.

Adjacent to the Village and the Queen Mary is one of the world's largest clear span domes. Originally built to house the "Spruce Goose," Howard Hughes' colossal plywood plane, the dome now serves as a film studio. The dome is in almost constant use. Due to its large size and unobstructed floor area, it accommodates large stage sets and allows filming day or night and in all seasons. Current plans for the dome, however, envision a much more public use.

The Queen Mary site, like the "Queen City", has undergone numerous additions and renovations. Although a beloved symbol of the city, it has not fulfilled its intended role as the defining attraction along Long Beach's profitable and efficient port. It remains, simply – like Long Beach – a source of great potential.

Rundown City Center Street Becomes Dining and Tourist Center

During the early portion of the 20th Century, downtown Long Beach served as the urban shopping area for southeast Los Angeles County and most of Orange County. Like many other cities in the United States, Long Beach tried to emulate the emerging suburban shopping centers by converting a city street into a pedestrian mall. Locust Avenue, located between Long Beach Boulevard and Pine Avenue, the historic key downtown shopping streets, became the designated victim. The avenue was closed off to traffic and a three-block long suburban style mall was built. Locust mall (the new name of the pedestrian street) while envisioned as a public-friendly shopping area actually became a vast no-mans-land. Pine Avenue, the home of many specialty and local serving stores, became cut off from the regionally serving stores on Long Beach Boulevard (the interurban Red Cars were removed from the boulevard in 1961).

Changing attitudes by major retailers made it impossible for Long Beach to attract a major department store to its "new" downtown. While three department stores occupied the mall, retail shopping could not be attracted to other parts of Long Beach Boulevard, Pine Avenue, or the no-mans-land of Locust Mall.

The success of nearby Pasadena and Santa Monica in revitalizing their downtowns by attracting restaurants and specialty stores provided a new model for Long Beach. Pine Avenue has become an "eating destination" for the region. Attracting diners from southern Los Angeles County and western Orange County, the three block stretch from Ocean Boulevard to Third Street contains approximately one dozen premier restaurants and many other convenience food outlets. A sixteen-screen AMC theater also serves as an attraction for the region. From its opening, the theater complex has been one of the major grossing facilities for AMC and continues to compete well with other chains. The potential competition from an equal sized complex, planned for nearby Queensway Bay, has caused concern with both the theater operators and the neighboring restaurants. Retail shopping still remains an elusive component for this area. Three major chain stores, Z-Gallery, Crate & Barrel Outlet, and L'Express Clothing, have been the only major retailers to find Pine Avenue a potential market.

Pine Avenue does, however, mark a change in the attitudes toward mixed-use development and the recycling of mid-rise retail into residential use. The through-block development of the AMC theaters also includes upper level apartments. Further north on Pine Avenue, the Kress Lofts provide "New York Style" condominiums in what had previously been a multi-story retail store. Plans are underway for a number of similar developments, converting multi-story commercial buildings along Pine Avenue, and even one on the long-forgotten Locust Mall, into residential/commercial urban lofts.

Becoming a Cosmopolitan Community

Like most of Southern California, Long Beach has become home to an increasing number of Latinos and Asians. Reflecting the California State characteristics, Long Beach does not have a racial or ethnic majority. Non-Hispanic whites are less than 50% of the population; Hispanics make up between a quarter and a third of the population; the rest are almost evenly divided between African Americans and Asian/Pacific Islanders. More specific numbers will soon be available as a result of the 2000 Census.

Numbers alone do not convey the increasingly cosmopolitan character of Long Beach. Away from the tailored tenant mix of Pine Avenue and the convention center hotel nucleus, Long Beach displays tremendous diversity in its neighborhoods. While there are enclaves throughout the city, ethnic groups tend to intermingle and yet remain distinct. For example, along East Anaheim Street, Cambodian, Vietnamese and Latino shops and restaurants with their signage in their native language and distinct alphabet co-exist and thrive. Overcoming ethnic fear and gang battles has been a prime objective of the entire city.

It is possible to purchase unique goods, which are only available because of the import knowledge of the ethnic communities, in many parts of Long Beach. It is interesting to find the number of Latino shoppers at Asian Markets and visa versa. Long Beach has also been recognized as one of the homes of "Rap" music and gave rise to a number of its prime performers including Warren G, and Snoop Doggie Dogg.

Abandoned Pike Site Planned as a Tourist Commercial Site

For over 30years, the city has been attempting to attract development to the old Pike site, the largest stretch of redevelopment urban waterfront in Southern California. While the City of Long Beach has been willing to participate with potential developers, even providing cash infusions and deferred income from the project, it has not been able to obtain the necessary development. Part of the problem is the sheer size of the potential projects.

In the late 1980s, a one billion dollar project, consisting of an 11 story office building, a 31 story hotel with 300 rooms, a 40 story residential tower with 250 units plus incidental ground level retail and the necessary parking, was proposed by developer Wayne Ratkovich. Teamed with legendary developer Jim Rouse, the guiding force behind Baltimore's inner harbor, the approximately 19-acre site required substantial infrastructure development. Unable to find financing in the economic doldrums of the early 1990s, the project became mired in nuisance suits and a protracted approval process. The project and developer were forced into bankruptcy.

Since it became apparent that only a substantial developer could absorb the heavy initial costs of developing the Pike Site, and the adjoining Queensway Bay, the city sought the appropriate player for its seaside assets. It appeared that the right developer had arrived when the Disney Company acquired the lease to the Queen Mary, as an incidental side deal to their purchase of the Disneyland Hotel.

In the midst of negotiations with the City of Anaheim over expansion of the original Disneyland, the Disney Company knew that demonstrating a viable alternative would place it in a much better bargaining position with that city. Disney proposed a new theme park for Long Beach, called DisneySea, which would combine exciting and unusual rides and attractions with activities directed towards developing a better understanding of the ocean. The plan also included five new resort hotels with approximately 3,900 rooms, specialty retail and entertainment, 400 new marina slips, a cruise ship port, and access and transportation modifications. The key to this development was a proposal to close off access to Queensway Bay and turn it into an admission-only area.

The multi-billion dollar proposal hinged on being able to obtain permission from the California Coastal Commission to charge all visitors to the waterside. The City of Long Beach sensed that Disney was perhaps trying to gain control over much of the city's beachfront assets. The City demanded that Disney declare its intentions by agreeing to a long-term lease extension for the Queen Mary site. Not having approvals in hand from the Coastal Commission, and having an agreement from the City of Anaheim for their desired expansion, the Walt Disney Company walked away from the deal. For a short time, the Queen Mary was closed, and many spoke of selling it to Tokyo, Hong Kong or Manila interests.

The current proposal for Queensway Bay consists of a visitor/entertainment commercial development proposed by Oliver/McMillan. The uncertainty of the project is defined by the fact that the current developer is DDR of Cleveland that had been brought in by Oliver/McMillan to strengthen its proposal. The scale of the project is now much more modest – currently in the $100 to $200 million range. Its potential for success is not clear at this time.

Becoming a Health Care Center

The second largest private employment sector in Long Beach, after aerospace and ahead of shipping, is health care. Long Beach is one of the region's major hospital care providers. The quality of its health care facilities is among the best in the nation. Memorial Medical Center, the largest of the hospitals. is continually cited as one of the top providers in a variety of specialties on nationwide surveys. Other service providers are also recognized for the quality of service. Unfortunately, the cost of this quality has created a drain on the resources of the various providers. Memorial remains well situated in the marketplace. Veterans Affairs Medical Center has the resources of the Federal Government. St. Mary and Community Hospital (3rd and 4th, respectively) have experienced major problems, recently. Major employers were: Long Beach Memorial Medical Center (3,706), Veterans Affairs Medical Center (2,747), St. Mary Medical Center (1,515), and Long Beach Community Hospital (1,100) (City of Long Beach Community Development).

St. Mary and Community Hospital were recently merged under the control of Catholic Healthcare West (CHW). While proclaiming that they would maintain both hospitals to serve the central and eastern sections of the city, CHW stripped Community Hospital of much of its equipment, moving it to St. Mary. When CHW announced its intent to close Community Hospital by the end of 2000, the public outcry postponed the surrender of the hospital license and the closing of the facility. Long Beach's regional significance as a health care provider is beginning to wane.

LATEST ROUNDS OF REPOSITIONING

The Naval Shipyard and The Fight over COSCO

Not unlike the battles between the Italian City States of the Renaissance, Long Beach often finds itself battling with its close port competitors of Los Angeles and San Diego. Often enlisting the support of San Francisco/Oakland and Portland/Seattle, the Southern California ports continually jockey to come out on top.

Long Beach suffered greatly during the defense downsizing. Not only did Long Beach suffer tremendous job losses (reputed to have been the most severe in the nation), but this occurred in the midst of California's most recent and severe economic recession. The City of Long Beach attributes the loss of more than 64,000 jobs and an economic loss of over $26 billion to the base closures and defense/aerospace downsizing (City Of Long Beach City Manager). Although some 7,000 jobs remain with Boeing (reducing the actual job loss to approximately 57,000) these jobs are expected to leave in 2001–2002.

Long Beach had been the Navy's dominant West Coast port. The total departure of the Navy left numerous reuse opportunities. Perhaps no reuse has been more contentious than the Naval Base. While many communities were looking for potential tenants for the lands returned to them by the Department of Defense, Long Beach already had a ready tenant for a large portion of the base site. The city sought to make 300 acres available to COSCO.

The transfer of the Naval Base to the shipping company of the People's Republic of China elicited reactions from numerous quarters. The Port of Los Angeles undertook no overt action against COSCO's lease with Long Beach (they actually wanted COSCO to move to the Port of Los Angeles). But, they must have been pleased when a San Diego Congressman, Duncan Hunter, attached wording in an appropriation bill to specifically prohibit Long Beach from leasing the former Naval Station site to COSCO.

Although Long Beach managed to keep COSCO as a tenant by swapping lease sites with Hanjin Shipping Co., the game of musical chairs did allow the Port of Los Angeles to attract the newly merged Maersk Pacific Ltd. to a 485-acre site at Pier 400. Maersk, the Danish shipping line, merged with Sealand, an American/Taiwanese shipping company. Both had been tenants of the Port of Long Beach. The new site in the Port of Los Angeles will be the world's largest proprietary container complex. The shift has allowed the Port of Los Angeles to reclaim the title as the number one container port in the United States, a distinction that Long Beach had held for the past five years.

It is anticipated, however, that Long Beach will again regain the number one ranking as COSCO expands its already sizable volume of trade between the United States and the Peoples Republic of China. There is no question that Maersk's move to the Port of Los Angeles increases extant volume. It is reported, however, that the Port of Los Angeles paid dearly to attract Maersk. And, that deal will be the benchmark for future negotiation with other tenants, in the future. Other shippers may find Long Beach more desirable.

Alameda Corridor

Not all of the relations between the ports are adversarial. A number of cooperative efforts have been undertaken by both ports – which could not have been done by one without the other. The most recent example of mutual self-interest has been the development of the Alameda Transit Corridor. The Alameda Corridor is a consolidated rail line serving both the ports of Los Angeles and Long Beach. It provides a rapid rail connection from the ports to the transcontinental rail network in downtown Los Angeles, a distance of approximately 20 miles.

The consolidated track serves the major rail carriers and gives them unimpeded access to the ports. The $2.4 billion project will create grade separations for rail traffic through the densely developed area paralleling Alameda Street. The most visible improvement will be a 10-mile long, 33 foot-deep trench just inland from the ports. East-west streets will bridge across this trench.

The Long Beach Progression of Repositioning

Long Beach has had the opportunity to reinvent itself on numerous occasions. It has managed to adapt to the changing expectations of its residents, the available resources in the region, and the expectations of the world marketplace.

- Originally, one of the first "Streetcar Suburbs" on the West Coast, Long Beach managed to maintain its identity and independence from Los Angeles. Today, Long Beach is the largest city in the United States that originally began as a suburb. Its nearly half a million residents recognize that Long Beach is not a part or appendage of Los Angeles.
- The first home of the industry of dreams – the movie industry – it was abandoned, although it remains as a ready backdrop for movies, TV and commercials. While some movie production has returned to Long Beach (particularly utilizing the "Spruce Goose" dome) it does not have the cachet

to attract the pre- and post-production segments that are essential to a "home of the movies."

- The destruction of a major earthquake was met by rebuilding, without repeating the construction mistakes of the past, in the midst of this country's Great Depression. The disaster also led to major changes in the rules governing school construction throughout the state. More significant structures of Long Beach's architectural past have been lost to redevelopment than to seismic activity.
- The U.S. Navy's Pacific Port gave Long Beach the distinct identity as a Navy town. For over 50 years the Navy and Long Beach were intertwined. The Navy's presence gave Long Beach steady and predictable economic support. When the Navy left, Long Beach had to quickly adapt the resources left behind to its new focus as the main container port on the West Coast.
- The label of "The Sinking City" was a negative image that the city is still trying to live down. However, the subsidence did provide additional draft for the newer tankers and container ships. Oil extraction, which caused that sinking, was stabilized and made more efficient by the injection of heated water and additives – increasing the yield. Long Beach pioneered the consolidation of well heads and slant drilling which reduced the number of derricks and pumps. The man-made oil islands in Long Beach harbor also stand as a unique and aesthetic approach to oil recovery.
- Home to the largest aerospace employer in Los Angeles County, Long Beach not only reacted appropriately, but also actually anticipated the departure of much of Boeing's production facility. Long Beach is now looking to see five million new square feet of high-tech industrial building providing jobs for an anticipated 10,000 employees. Its educational establishment, Long Beach Unified School District, Long Beach City College, and California State University, Long Beach have banded together to train and educate students from pre-school to mid and late-career changes.

HOW WILL LONG BEACH ADDRESS THE FUTURE?

Long Beach has demonstrated that along with the good fortune of location, weather, economic growth and social harmony, it has an indefinable yet evident resilience. While many other communities have been unable to overcome predictable or unexpected difficulties, Long Beach seems to thrive on challenge. It continues to redefine itself. Nowhere is this more evident than its approach to the expected major downsizing of the Boeing facilities.

While other communities faced with similar problems have tried to forestall the eventual closing of major employers, Long Beach has agreed to work with

Boeing to clean up existing areas and attract new industry. The cooperative response by the City has made it easier for Boeing to be a good corporate citizen even though it is greatly reducing its presence in Long Beach and Southern California.

The plans call for Boeing to consolidate production of the B717 commercial airliner on the east side of Lakewood Boulevard and redevelop the west side of the property as a 'mixed use' business park focused on technology-based companies. While a small presence will be maintained by Boeing in the production of the B717 and the C-17 military transport, some 230 acres with five million square feet of buildings will demolished and re-built as high-tech industrial space.

Named PacifiCenter@Long Beach, the new development will offer the latest in technology development standards. "The technology infrastructure is projected to include fiber-optic cable, expanded utility power, telecommunications, data center and the lifestyle amenities necessary to attract technology companies" (Boeing Company, 2000). The $600 million building project is expected to generate approximately $1.65 billion annually of economic benefit with a minimum of 10,000 new jobs. The unique aspect of this effort is the teamwork approach by both the developer and the City of Long Beach.

Today Long Beach stands at the doorway of another change. The direction chosen will not be happenstance. A great believer in strategic planning, Long Beach has defined its areas to be considered for the near and mid-future: the three "T's" (trade, tourism and technology), and retail commercial development. Knowing that planning is just simply wishing if it does not have a procedure for evaluating progress and modifying goals as external conditions change, Long Beach has developed tremendous sophistication in the strategic planning and implementation process.

Finally, Long Beach is a repository of hope. People participating in its political, social and economic arenas are able to work together, even while holding divergent opinions on where Long Beach is going. The City of Long Beach has learned to be inclusionary without succumbing to tokenism. Anglo males are still dominant, but women, Latinos, gays and other groups are participating in the decisions being made. Long Beach is a long way from perfect, but it does manage to deal well with its imperfections.

NOTES

1. In October 1999, the Pacific Rim Council on Urban Development (PRCUD) held its Annual Forum and Professional Visit in the port city of Long Beach, California. The theme of the Annual Forum was 'Repositioning Pacific Rim Cities.' Most of the participants had little knowledge of Long Beach at the beginning of the Professional

Visit. They convened in Long Beach to assess development constraints and opportunities and to examine the city's aggressive program to reposition itself by focusing on the key factors of tourism, trade, technology, and transportation. After three days of site visits and intensive meetings with local leaders, PRCUD Council members left with a greater appreciation of the city, how it has been shaped by its history and geography, and how it has consciously and successfully repositioned itself.

2. The Port of Long Beach maintains an informative web site (www.polb.com) which contains additional information.

3. The Long Beach Grand Prix has a very attractive web site (www. longbeachgp.com) which further features the race course along the Long Beach shoreline.

REFERENCES

Berner, L. (1982). *The Pike on the Silverstrand*. Long Beach: Historical Society of Long Beach.

Boeing Company (2000). Boeing Realty Corporation Opens Visitor Center for 230 Acre Development Project at Long Beach Plant West Site. Press Release (Feb. 15).

City of Long Beach, City Manager's Office (2000). *Base Closures and Defense/Aerospace Downsizing Economic Impact)*. Exhibit 5–1 (revised 2/24/00).

City of Long Beach, City Manager's Office (2000). *Report to the City Council* (2/24/00).

City of Long Beach (1986). *Long Beach 2000 Strategic Plan*.

Colozas, X. C., & Strehle (1995). Subsidence in the Willmington Oil Field, Long Beach, California, USA. In: G. V. Chilingarian & E. C. Donaldson (Eds), *Subsidence due to Fluid Withdrawl* (pp. 285–335). New York: Elsevier Science B.V.

DeAtley, R. (1988). *Long Beach: The Golden Shore, A History of the City and the Port*. Houston: Pioneer Publications, Inc.

Dumke, G. S. (1944). *The Boom of the Eighties in Southern California*. San Marino: Huntington Library.

Friedricks, W. B. (1992). *Henry E. Huntington and the Creation of Southern California*. Columbus: Ohio State University Press.

U.S. Bureau of the Census (1991). *Population of the 100 Largest Urban Places*, Tables 14–22 (1910–1990).

Waldie, D. J. (1996). *Holy Land – A Suburban Memoir*. New York: W. W. Norton.

Walt Disney Company (1990). *Preliminary Master Plan Executive Report*. July.

Warner, S. B. (1962). *Streetcar Suburbs, The Process of Growth in Boston (1870–1900)*. Boston: Harvard University Press.

6. SHENZHEN: THE PIONEER CITY IN CHINA'S ECONOMIC TRANSITION

Mark Yaolin Wang, Xiaochen Meng and Guicai Li

ABSTRACT

Deng Xiaoping's open door policy for China has offered Shenzhen a golden opportunity, growing from a small town in the shadow of Hong Kong to a prosperous economic metropolis within 20 years. Being one of China's special economic zones, Shenzhen has also played a pioneer role for China's reform program. This chapter considers the following questions: how is Shenzhen different from other export processing zones?; to what degree has Shenzhen fulfilled Deng's goals?; and what major policies and factors have contributed to Shenzhen's miracle? It is found that Shenzhen is striving to become a Chinese city with "Singapore's city environment and Hong Kong's efficiency". The dynamics of Shenzhen lie in its geographical proximity to and cultural similarity with Hong Kong. More importantly, a set of special policies and great autonomy granted by the central government have created the "Shenzhen miracle".

INTRODUCTION

Have you ever heard of the miracle that within only 20 years a small town of thirty thousand people has developed into a big city with a population of four million? That miracle has happened in China, and the name of the city is Shenzhen. In 1979, Shenzhen was designated as one of the four special economic zones (SEZs), which were an important move in Deng Xiaoping's plan for building China's unique socialist market society (Lippit, 1997; Shirk,

International Urban Planning Settings: Lessons of Success, Volume 12, pages 157–182.
2001 by Elsevier Science Ltd.
ISBN: 0-7623-0695-5

1994). Since then, young people from all over the country have swarmed to the city to join a Chinese style "gold rush". After 20 years of continuous efforts, this small coastal town in the shadow of Hong Kong has become a prosperous economic metropolis, achieved at breathtaking speed. Densely packed with skyscrapers, Shenzhen's urban appearance can hardly be distinguished from the former British crown colony of Hong Kong. Economically, the two cities increasingly are becoming a unified region, particularly since the 1997 Hong Kong hand-over, even though they are still politically separated. Shenzhen's ambitious objective of attaining "Singapore's city environment and Hong Kong's city efficiency" suggests the future development direction of this new metropolis (Lu et al., 1994).

Shenzhen has assumed the intended role of a pioneer for the whole of China. The market economy flourishes under State control; and one can see a richer China, and one can tell what China's next reform might be. Shenzhen is an epitome of what the Chinese call a "window of China". Through this window, China looks at the world and the world at China. Over the years, Shenzhen has provided the whole country with the experience, both positive and negative, of reform and of being opened to the outside world. In fact, the significance of the successful development of Shenzhen lies not only in that Shenzhen has developed into a big modern city in such a short period of time, but also in that the whole country, following the example of Shenzhen, has undergone fundamental changes. The so-called "Shenzhen experience" has guided China to transit from a centrally planned to a type of market economy. This new "Great Leap" has brought China rapid and steady economic growth, even during the Asian financial crisis of the late 1990s (Pomfret, 1997; SSB, 1999). The overall living standard of the Chinese people has been greatly improved, and China's economy has gradually integrated into the world economy (Economy & Oksenberg, 1999; Pomfret, 1996), as evident in China's increasing two-way flow of capital. Also, more and more foreigners have invested in China in all fields, and China too has invested overseas and established offshore plants (Wang, 2000; Wall, 1996). All this would not be true without the "Shenzhen experience", with Shenzhen representing the direction of China's development in the post-Mao era.

The questions this chapter poses are: (a) what made Shenzhen different from other export processing zones (EPZs) in other parts of the world?; (b) to what degree has Shenzhen fulfilled Deng's goals?; and (c) what major policies and factors have contributed to Shenzhen's miracle? The chapter briefly traces Shenzhen's urban expansion and the major changes to its urban spatial structure. It then discusses the rationale for the establishment of SEZs and the degree to which Shenzhen has attained those goals. It answers the questions:

how different is Shenzhen from other SEZs?; and what are the characteristics of Shenzhen? The policies and factors that have contributed to the Shenzhen miracle are discussed. Finally, the chapter discusses the on-going industrial restructuring of Shenzhen and major obstacles and challenges it faces for the next stage of its transition.

OVERNIGHT METROPOLIS

Up to 1979, Shenzhen was a little known small town with a population of about 30,000 located in the remote rural south of China. Deng's economic reforms and modernization program offered it a great opportunity. The geographic position of Shenzhen attracted Deng's attention. Located in the southern coastal area of Guangdong Province where the Peoples Republic of China borders Hong Kong, Shenzhen was one of five SEZs opened to the outside world (the others were three SEZs established in 1980 are Zhuhai, Xiamen, Shantou and Hainan) (Fig. 1). This was an important move in Deng's plan for building China's unique socialist society. Since then, the small town of Shenzhen has become the "hottest" place in China. According to the Shenzhen

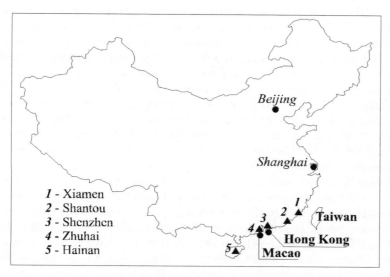

Fig. 1. Location of China's Special Economic Zones.

Notes: The SEZs of Xianmen, Shantou, Shenzhen and Zhuhai were established in 1979. Hainan SEZ was established in 1988.

Planning Bureau, its urban area has expanded almost overnight. In 1979, the urban area was only three square kilometers, and a house of five floors was the highest building. Since then, builders from all parts of the country have been attracted as development has spread rapidly across farmland and into the hills in a property boom that continues. By 1985, the urban area had grown to 47.6 square kilometers, and over 80 major urban roads were built and extended with a total length of 160 kilometers. More than 2,000 high-rise buildings were constructed. In 2000, Shenzhen had become a city of 4.05 million population covering an area of 2,020 square kilometers.

The term "Shenzhen" refers to the whole area under the jurisdiction of the Shenzhen municipal government. The Shenzhen municipality employed a three-level administrative structure: (a) municipal; (b) six urban districts – Futian, Luohu, Nanshan, Yantian, Bao'an, and Longgang; and (c) 26 street offices and 19 towns. The first four urban districts mentioned form the Shenzhen SEZ, which is a major part of Shenzhen's built-up area. The SEZ is about 327.5 square km with population of about 1.9 million in 1999 (Fig. 2). The last two mentioned districts – Bao'an and Longgang – are non-SEZ, with a population of about 2 million. In this chapter, the term of Shenzhen is used interchangeably with the Shenzhen municipality.

The CBD of Shenzhen has expanded dramatically. During the first decade (1979–1990), the Luohu District was the area where most of the construction and business activities were concentrated. During the period of 1991 to 2000, the CBD extended farther out, with the Futian District becoming a part of it. Now the Luohu District mainly functions as the financial and trading area, while the Futian District has concentrations of light industry, commerce and the information technology industry. Now skyscrapers dominate many parts of Shenzhen's urban landscape. Such rapid expansion of the urban district was possible due to the so-called "Shenzhen Speed" which refers to a fast pace of urban construction. The best example is the World Trade Plaza built at a construction pace of three floors each day (Chen et al., 1995).

Twenty years of rapid economic growth has brought Shenzhen to the forefront of major Chinese cities in terms of its overall economic strength. The Gross Regional Product (GRP) in 1999 was over 229 times of that of 1979, and the average annual growth rate has been 31.2% (Table 1). In 1999, Shenzhen's GRP was US$17.35 billion (143.65 billion RMB), ranking it sixth among the major Chinese cities. Industrial output value was US$24.47 billion fourth highest in the nation. Shenzhen is the wealthiest city in China with a per capita GDP US$4000 in 1999 (SSB, 2000). An export-oriented economy within a market framework has taken shape. Shenzhen has become one of the major host sites for transnational corporations (TNCs) and it boasts a complete range

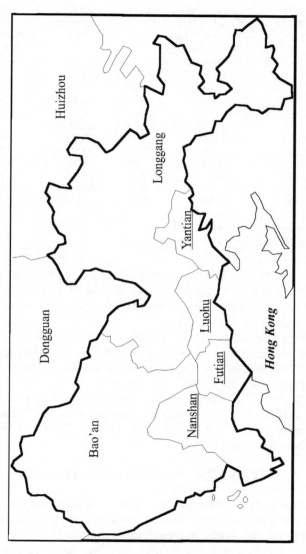

Fig. 2. Location of Shenzhen and SEZ, Guangdong, China.

Table 1. Shenzhen's GRP Output Value and GRP Growth Index.

YEAR	GDP (MILLION RMB)	GROWTH INDEX WITH COMPARABLE PRICE (GDP IN 1979 AS 100)	YEAR	GDP (MILLION RMB)	GROWTH INDEX WITH COMPARABLE PRICE (GDP IN 1979 AS 100)
1979	196.4	100	1990	17,166.6	3,439
1980	270.1	163	1991	23,666.3	4,677
1981	495.8	250	1992	31,731.9	6,230
1982	825.7	396	1993	44,928.9	8,099
1983	1,312.1	628	1994	61,519.3	10,537
1984	2,341.6	1,003	1995	79,569.5	12,960
1985	3,902.2	1,249	1996	95,004.5	15,086
1986	4,164.5	1,283	1997	113,001.3	17,499
1987	5,590.1	1,609	1998	128,901.9	20,037
1988	8,698.1	2,187	1999	143,650.7	22,882
1989	11,565.6	2,596			

Source: Shenzhen Statistical Handbook, 2000.

of industries covering over 2,000 product lines (Shenzhen Foreign Investment Bureau, 2000). Import and export of goods and services totaled US$50.42 billion in 1999, making Shenzhen the largest hard currency earner in China the seventh consecutive year (SSB, 2000).

In 1984, Deng visited Shenzhen and concluded that the developments and experiences of Shenzhen have proved that the policy to build special economic zone was correct. Shenzhen's development experience was further confirmed as a model for the rest of China. In 1992, Deng made his last visit to Shenzhen and the other SEZs, and he set a high value on the success achieved in Shenzhen. When Deng died in 1997, the Shenzhen newspaper declared that the way shown by Shenzhen in the past 18 years was the way of the new socialism in China (Shenzhen Window, 1999).

WHY SEZS? WHY SHENZHEN?

To understand the motivation for the establishment of SEZs and the reasons for emergence of Shenzhen as a metropolis within a short period of time, we need to review briefly the philosophy of Deng's reform approach.

When Deng came to power, Maoist-socialist China had experienced almost 30 years of isolation from most of the Western countries and about 10 years of cultural revolution. The main plank of Deng's reform and open door strategy was to adopt a more market-oriented economic system and to open China's door to the outside of world. But there was no model to follow as to how to test the market mechanism in a socialist country. Therefore, to reform China's socialist system and open China's door to the outside world was risky, both politically and practically (Shirk, 1994).

There were quite different approaches being practiced in different parts of the world on how to reform centrally planned economies. In the wake of their deteriorating legitimacy throughout the 1970s, the socialist countries of Eastern Europe, Latin America, the former Soviet Union, and later China, began to reassess their options for reform (Yamin & Batstone, 1995). Departing from socialism to avoid imminent macroeconomic chaos, most countries chose to reform "once and for all," abandoning previous structures of economic planning and adopting instead market mechanisms (Solimano, 1994). Nolan (1993) concludes that 'the only way to reform (the socialist system) is to go all the way to the market system, do it quickly and do not stop anywhere along the way' (Nolan, 1993: 173).

Deng opted to reform gradually or by 'crossing the river while feeling the stones' (Rozelle, 1996; Goldman, 1994). Rather than subverting any remaining institutional structures through "shock therapy", China's post-1978 government has employed strategies to both exploit existing socialist and to introduce capitalist systems. The main criticism was that 'you should jump quickly to the other side and not tread cautiously. There is no theory supporting a gradual switch of system' (Nolan, 1993: 174).

Despite ongoing criticism and debate, Deng insisted on testing his approach in Shenzhen and the other SEZs. He strongly believed that there was no universally applicable reform model, with different conditions influencing the reform process. Fortunately, China's pre-reform economic circumstances – in synthesis with predominantly unconditional civilian patronage, party support and military protection – have allowed China to forge ahead with potentially perilous revisions and to establish itself quite successfully as a "socialist market economy" with hybrid characteristics (Zhou, 1997). It has now been proved that Deng's gradualist reform and open door approach has been a most successful model, and it has been called the "Chinese model" (Economy & Oksenberg, 1999; Naught, 1996; Wang & Webber, 2000).

Objectives of SEZs

Attracting Foreign Investment, Technology and Management Skills
As a part of the reform and open door program, the establishment of SEZs had its own specific objectives and considerations. The first objective was to

promote inflows of foreign investment, technology (know-how), and management skill (Park, 1997). As mentioned above, SEZs were viewed as a window through which to introduce foreign technology, capital, and managerial techniques, as well as Western production, marketing, and information systems.

How to assess this objective is complicated. Generally speaking, foreign investment in China has been viewed very positively, both by the government and by researchers (Xiao, 1995; Park, 1997; Shuang, 1994; Song, 1994). Over twenty years of openness has made China, and particularly the SEZs and coast areas, significant destinations for foreign investment (Pearson, 1999). Indeed, by the mid-1990s China became the worlds second destination for foreign direct investment (Sun, 1998; Zhan, 1995). Foreign-funded enterprises have played a catalytic role in the process of a market-based economy, contributing about half of China's foreign trade since the mid 1990s (Economy & Oksenberg, 1999). By 1999, China held over US$15 billion in foreign exchange reserves, which was the second largest in the world.

Shenzhen attracted quite large shares of China's foreign investment. FDI has played an important role in labor-intense industry sectors. Thousands of assembly lines in Shenzhen have become a symbol of the influence of FDI. In 1999, Shenzhen had more than 13,000 enterprises with foreign investment, which have contributed a lot to the rapid development of Shenzhen industry. Calculated by comparable prices, the total industrial value reached 207.81 billion yuan in 1999, increasing 48.2% annually from 1979 (SSIB, 2000). In 1997, the gross foreign capital invested in enterprises accounted for about 73% of the investment in enterprises in Shenzhen, and the tax collected from them was about 72.5% of the independently accounted (Shenzhen Government Internet, 2000).

Special policies authorized by the central government have been used to attract foreign investment and firms. For example, SEZs offer financial, legal and infrastructural inducements to foreign investors, including tax holidays, easy remittance of profit, and prepared sites with services and buildings (see following sections). They also offer labor saving. A more important factor is their simplified bureaucratic procedures for investment, customs, and immigration.

Foreign enterprises were not only offered cheap labor but also were permitted the full control and management of their enterprises. Foreign enterprises have been allowed to adopt different employment practices and wage system. For example, foreign firms in SEZs not only can hire their own workers directly, but also they can dismiss them (Wong et al., 1995), which was never the case in the pre-1978 Maoist China.

Through joint ventures with their foreign partners, Chinese enterprises have had an opportunity to understand the world market system, to improve the quality of goods, and to develop new products. Some foreign scholars conclude that it is foreign capital that has driven China's transition to a market economy (Yabuki & Harner, 1999). While this may be a little exaggerated, it does reflect the importance of FDI in China's transition to a market economy.

However an objective of SEZs to transfer foreign technology and know-how has always been a problem (Qiao, 1996). The actual levels of technology transfer have been limited (Kumar, 1998). When foreign investment in China increased, Chinese foreign exchange reserves increased, but the direct transfer of technology has been very limited and market information has largely been controlled by foreign TNCs. Foreign firms and corporations control market information and refuse to transfer technology (Qiao, 1996).

Earning Foreign Exchange
The second objective of the SEZs was to produce goods for export to earn foreign exchange. Learning from the 'Asian Tigers' (Taiwan, Hong Kong, South Korea, Singapore) and Japan, Deng designed export-oriented industrial-ization as the SEZs' industrial strategy (Park, 1997). In Shenzhen, as well as in other SEZs, three types of processing and compensation trade were most population: (a) processing with materials; (b) processing according to samples and assembling parts supplied by investors or clients; and (c) conducting compensation trade. Overseas markets were targeted and exports became the life line of SEZs.

Shenzhen and China as a whole have fulfilled this objective. In fact, the rapid advance of foreign trade has become the most symbolic feature of China's opening under the reform and liberalization policy, and in particular its export sector (Pearson, 1999). In Shenzhen the value of exports had increased from US$9.3 million in 1979 to US$28.21 billion in 1999. Exports accounted for a large proportion of its GRP. This was also true for China as a whole, with its export dependency ratio (value of exports divided by GDP) having increased greatly since the adoption of the open door policy in 1978. Table 2 shows that exports as a proportion of GNP was less than 10% in 1978, rising to 14–15% during the first half of the 1980s, and reaching 25 to 26% during the second half of the 1980s. By the mid-1990s the export drive really reached fruition, with exports increasing to around 40% of GNP. It dropped to under 20% only after the Asia financial crises of the late 1990s.

Social and Economic Laboratory
The third objective for the establishment of SEZs was very ambitious. Deng expected Shenzhen and other SEZs to act as a social and economic laboratory

Table 2. China's Exports as a Percentage of GDP.

YEAR	%	YEAR	%	YEAR	%
1978	9.8	1986	25.5	1994	43.3
1979	11.2	1987	26.2	1995	39.6
1980	12.5	1988	26.0	1996	35.2
1981	15.0	1989	25.2	1997	35.4
1982	14.0	1990	30.3	1998	19.4
1983	14.1	1991	34.0	1999	19.7
1984	16.8	1992	35.3		
1985	23.5	1993	32.7		

Source: China Statistical Yearbook, 2000.

for China's reform and open door program. As discussed above, China's reform and opening up could not be radical as China had been a closed economy, both politically and economically, for about 30 years. To avoid unnecessary mistakes and drawbacks, Deng decided to establish SEZs to serve as centers for experimentation and observation. Therefore, it was hoped that the more market-oriented approach to business operations would be tried in these zones first, with successful experiences later being passed on to the rest of the country. This was called "crossing a river by touching the stone underneath".

Over the years the SEZs, and particularly Shenzhen, have acted as a testing ground for almost every set of reform policies. The common practice has been that if a proposed reform and new policies worked in SEZs, then such experiments would be adopted in other parts of the country. If these reform policies failed, then the problems could be identified and avoided elsewhere. Further necessary policy modification was followed-up. This has been well documented and studied (Park, 1997; Perkins, 1994; Pomfret, 1996; Wang, 1994; Wong & Chu, 1985), and it can be said that Shenzhen has provided a leading role in China's post-1978 reform program.

Confidence Building
The fourth objective of the SEZs was more political and image building related. We can call it a confidence building role. The return of Hong Kong to China had become an issue in the early 1980s, and China's leaders expected that rapid economic development, political stability and an open environment in Shenzhen would help to ease the worries of people in Hong Kong over the re-unification with China 1997. By reducing the gap between living standards of the SEZs and Hong Kong, by improving the legal framework, and by

implementing the open door policy consistently, Shenzhen helped to build confidence among people in Hong Kong and Macau (Li, 1995). This is shown in the high degree of interdependence that evolved between Hong Kong and Shenzhen before the 1997 handover (Kemenade, 1997).

It is also important that SEZs have helped the Chinese government to have a better understanding of Hong Kong, Macau, and Taiwan. Successful reunifications of Hong Kong in 1997 and of Macau in 1999, and their smooth relations with the mainland government in the post-reunification period, would be impossible without the contribution of these SEZs, which provided the Chinese policy makers in Beijing an opportunity to learn how to handle Hong Kong and Macau issues. It is said also that SEZs are an important political and economic showcase to facilitate the unification of Taiwan. In fact, the designation of Xiamen as a SEZ was an attempt to attract Taiwanese investors to build up the linkages between Taiwan and Mainland China (Park, 1997).

Accelerating Development of the Interior
Finally, the Chinese leaders also expect that SEZs can play an important role in accelerating the development of the interior regions of China. Establishment of the SEZs and giving priority to the coast areas were based on a philosophy of "let the coast get rich first", but the long-term purpose was to "let the whole of China get rich".

Shenzhen and other SEZs were viewed as engines of growth or catalysts for inland China's development (Shuang, 1994). They were expected to transfer the technology and skilled labor to the interior areas and to promote economic growth. This is a Chinese version of growth pole theory. It is arguable that Shenzhen, as well as the other SEZs, have acted as growth engines for the rest of China. While the achievements made in Shenzhen and other SEZs are undeniable, but the trickle down effect has been very limited. The Shenzhen government claims that Shenzhen provided over 2 million jobs to inland areas during the five years from 1990–1995 and that it has invested RMB 16 billion in 1,390 projects in inland areas in recent years (Shenzhen Government Internet, 2000). The migrant labor income remitted back to inland regions each year amounts to several billion RMB. But this influence has been limited, and it cannot yet be claimed that the SEZs have directly promoted inland development.

Locality and Cultural Factors
Besides these economic and political considerations, geographic locality and cultural factors are also very important elements in the establishment of Shenzhen and other SEZs. Why are all China's SEZs in southeast coastal

China? Culturally these SEZs are the home of millions of overseas Chinese. Cantonese is commonly spoken both in Hong Kong and Macau and also in Guangdong province, where the SEZs of Shenzhen, Zhuhai and Shantou are located. Xiamen and Taiwan share the same local dialect. Such a bamboo network is a very important asset for these SEZs to be integrated with Hong Kong, Macao, and Taiwan and further into the global economic system (Weidenbaum, 1996). All the SEZs were isolated geographically, remote from China's heartland of the Yangtze delta (Shanghai and the Provinces of Jiangsu and Zhejiang), and the Bohai ring (including Beijing, Tianjin, and Provinces of Liaoning, Hebei, and Shandong).

The SEZs were viewed as incubators of economic reform, permitting China to learn how to deal with market economies in a controlled environment. If the SEZs were to fail, the notion was that the government could then just close them. What this implies is that it was viewed as being risky to test capitalist management in socialist China. When Deng introduced the SEZs idea in the late 1970s, he himself had no confidence. This can be reflected by the fact that Shanghai was not listed as one of the key open areas until the early 1990s when the "Shenzhen experience" had been proven to be successful. It is well known that Shanghai is China's largest industrial city with a well-trained work force and a large pool of scientists and technicians and with extensive overseas connections. In 1992, Deng candidly expressed his regret: 'In retrospect one of my biggest mistakes was leaving out Shanghai when we launched the four SEZs in the early 1980s. If Shanghai had been included the situation with regard to reform and opening in the Yangtze Delta, the entire Yangtze River valley and, indeed, the whole country would be quite different'. Deng's regret, however, reflected the uncertainty of top China's leaders about the SEZs in the 1980s. Thus, remoteness from China's heartland was also viewed as a security factor.

Shenzhen Characteristics

The objectives of the SEZs discussed above indicate that China's SEZs are, in many aspects, similar to other Asian EPZs. These similarities include: (a) they are all export-oriented, with products being made in these zones; (b) in order to do so, special policies and regulations are adopted within SEZs, which are very different from those practiced in other parts of the country, with foreign investors also granted various preferential policies and incentives (tax reduction, exemption or holiday). However, SEZs have served as a social and economic laboratory for China's reform program. Their political/image building perspective and their role as a growth engine is not found in EPZs elsewhere in Asia. In the context of Shenzhen, the following aspects differ fundamentally from EPZs.

(1) Shenzhen is not just a processing zone but a modern metropolis with the development of comprehensive industrial sectors. Its GRP output and employment structures have been contributed to largely by the secondary manufacturing sectors, but not dominantly. Table 3 shows that, in 1998, although manufacturing (mainly assembling lines) contributed half of the total GRP and provided 56% of total jobs, the tertiary sector accounted for 48.5% of total GRP and provided 38.6% of total employment in Shenzhen.

(2) Shenzhen is not just a processing zone but is also one of the most livable cities in China, of which there are few. It is beyond this chapter's scope to explore in detail whether Shenzhen has achieved its goal of being a socialist metropolis with "Singapore's city environment plus Hong Kong's city efficiency". But most visitors are impressed by its livability. Over the

Table 3. Employment and GRP in Shenzhen, 1998.

	MILLION RMB	(%)	PERSON	(%)
Primary (mainly agriculture)	**1,645.4**	**1.3**	**45,643**	**1.6**
Secondary sectors:	**64,458.3**	**50.2**	**1,711,204**	**59.8**
Manufacturing	51,744.9	40.3	1,603,368	56.0
Construction	12,713.4	9.9	107,836 (3.8%)	3.8
Tertiary:	**62,180.1**	**45.0**	**1,106,833**	**38.6**
Banking and insurance	17,546.6	13.7	31,774	1.1
Wholesale and retail trade	10,372.2	8.1	490,581	17.1
Real estate	8,082.9	6.3	32,697	1.1
Social services	6,753.7	5.3	139,710	4.9
Post and telecommunications	5,692.5	4.4	31,944	1.1
Transportation and storage	4,289.6	3.3	34,144	1.2
Catering services	2,771.9	2.2	83,974	2.9
Health care and social welfare	1,966.2	1.5	26,598	0.9
Education and culture	1,886.0	1.5	36,210	1.3
Others	2,818.5	2.2	199,198	6.9
Total	**128,283.9**	**100**	**2,863,680**	**100**

Source: Shenzhen Statistical Yearbook 1999.

last two decades, Shenzhen's urban environment has improved and the development of its social facilities remain in step with its two-digit rate of economic growth. With a green coverage of 44%, Shenzhen has a good ecological record and has relatively clean air. It is one of few environmentally friendly cities, as well as one of the best tourist cities in China.

(3) A feature of Shenzhen's economy is its export orientation, but it is not highly dependent on foreign investment. This is not to underestimate the role of foreign investment in Shenzhen's economic miracle. By the end of 1999, the foreign business community was represented by 66 countries which had located 23,608 operations in Shenzhen with a pledged foreign investment volume of US$29.84 billion and paid-up total of US$20.04 billion. Shenzhen ranks third among cities in China in terms of paid-up foreign capital. Shenzhen has 76 of the world's top 500 TNCs and 55 foreign financial institutions (Shenzhen Foreign Investment Bureau, 2000). Foreign investment is becoming increasingly an integral part of the economic dynamo in Shenzhen, contributing a significant share of its economic growth. For example, in 1997 the increase in GRP was 16%, with 5.2% of the increase being created by foreign investment in manufacturing enterprises, which themselves accounted for 32.4% of the increase in GRP (Shenzhen Window, 1999). But this cannot lead to a conclusion that foreign capital is the dominant capital source. Over the years, Shenzhen has not been highly dependent upon foreign capital, with domestic investment being the major capital source for Shenzhen's total capital investment. In the 1980s foreign capital accounted for about one-third of Shenzhen's total capital investment, but this had dropped to 15% in the 1990s (Table 4). This contradicts the popular perceptions about the role of foreign capital in Shenzhen's development. The relatively low dependency on TNCs and on foreign capital makes it possible for the municipal government to carry out its own development plan and promote priority sectors, such as high tech activities (see the next section).

Shenzhen's Leading Position in Economic Performance

Perhaps a more explicit picture of the character of Shenzhen's development is gained from its number-one rankings on a range of indicators. It has an advanced telecommunications network and a well developed services sector to support its export-oriented economy. About 300,000 mobile phone users and more than one million pager users give Shenzhen the number one ranking in China. Shenzhen is also the city with the highest concentration of financial services and the most complete range of financial service categories, and it has

Table 4. Capital Investment in Shenzhen 1990–1995 (million yuan).

YEAR	TOTAL [1]	FOREIGN CAPITAL [2]	[2] AS % OF [1]
1990	4,998	1,641	32.8
1991	5,862	1,236	21.0
1992	7,689	872	11.4
1993	12,181	1,560	12.8
1994	13,267	1,748	13.2
1995	13,906	2,306	16.6
1996	15,249	3,244	21.3
1997	20,294	5,226	25.7
1998	21,447	1,285	6.0

Source: Shenzhen Statistical Yearbook, 1999.

the highest proportion of workers in finance services in China (outside Hong Kong).

However, a more symbolic feature of Shenzhen's economy is its electronics industry where it ranks number one in China. Shenzhen is a home of many foreign electronics processing lines. The development of the electronics industry in Shenzhen can be traced back to the very beginning of the SEZ. The first foreign joint venture introduced in Shenzhen was an electronics project. On April 20th, 1979, the Hong Kong entrepreneur Lin Zhongqiao signed an agreement with Guangdong Overseas Chinese Farm to establish Lucent Overseas Chinese Electronic Factory. This agreement gave birth to a Chinese color TV giant Konka (in Chinese this means "propitious and beautiful") which became the synonym for color TVs with its counterpart Iris ten years later (Yang, 1988). Since then, Shenzhen has become the top electronics city in China. According to the latest statistics from Guangdong Province, Shenzhen accounted for 59% of Guangdong's total, and over 15% of the national electronics production total (Guangdong Statistical Bureau, 1999). The production of computers, program-controlled switchboards, hard disc drivers, glass bulbs and magnetic heads are the main products, with electronic toys and other low tech electronic products as secondary specializations.

Shenzhen is also ranked number one in the production of clocks and watches. Shenzhen is now the world's largest regional production center for clocks and watches. The output of various clocks and watches reached 317.9 million in 1996, of which 286.7 million were watches. About 100 million watches are exported each year (SSIB, 1997). Fyata is a well known brand. As its advertising slogan says, "once possessed, nothing else needed". Locals would say "once a processing line is established in Shenzhen, nowhere else is needed".

Shenzhen's Social Fabric
Shenzhen's social fabric is unique. The question "what is the size of Shenzhen's population?", is not easy to answer. This is due to the uniqueness of the population structure. Shenzhen is the first Chinese city with a high degree of population mobility (Kong & Yao, 1995). Among the 4.05 million population, two-thirds are so-called temporary migrants according to Chinese urban population definitions (Table 5). Temporary residents are those who have registered and who have stayed in Shenzhen for more than six months. (Some

Table 5. Population Residential Status in Shenzhen.

YEAR	TOTAL POPULATION (10,000 PERSONS) [1]	TEMPORARY POPULATION (10,000 PERSONS) [2]	[2] AS % OF [1]
1979	31.41	0.15	0.5
1980	33.29	1.20	3.6
1981	36.69	3.30	9.0
1982	44.95	9.50	21.1
1983	59.52	19.00	31.9
1984	74.13	30.61	41.3
1985	88.15	40.29	45.7
1986	93.56	42.11	45.0
1987	115.44	59.84	51.8
1988	153.14	93.00	60.7
1989	191.60	126.78	66.2
1990	201.94	133.29	66.0
1991	238.53	165.31	69.3
1992	260.90	180.68	69.3
1993	294.99	207.30	70.3
1994	335.51	241.54	72.0
1995	345.12	245.96	71.3
1996	358.48	255.10	71.2
1997	379.64	270.18	71.2
1998	394.96	280.36	71.0
1999	405.13	285.29	70.4

Source: Shenzhen Statistical Handbook, 2000.

of them are offered permanent jobs in Shenzhen and are waiting for the approval of their permanent status). For those people who plan to stay in Shenzhen less than six months, they are called the "floating population". There is no accurate data about this category. It is estimated that the floating population in Shenzhen is as high as several hundred thousands. Due to the large numbers of migrants (most of them young and single), the age structure of Shenzhen's population is the youngest among China's cities. The average age is only 27 years (temporary resident population averages 20 years) and over 75% of its population were aged younger than 35 years in 1995 (Shenzhen Population Sample Census Office, 1996).

According to Meng (1998) and others, Shenzhen's population can be classified into three groups: (a) local/dividend owner (natives); (b) elite; and (c) assembly workers.

The first group are the local residents (natives). They are the only non-migrant group. They are also the richest group in Shenzhen, with very limited education background or skill. Their wealth has come from the land they used to farm. As demand for and prices of urban land has increased, over 80% of the farmland has been converted to urban uses. Some of land transfer deals were illegal, without government approval. Most land has been used for a range of non-farming activities, including standardized or specialized factory space, restaurants and hotels, other commercial activities, as well as housing. The regular income of this group is from dividends, which are generated from the land transfer. Their second main source of income is from rents. This group builds multi-story houses to meet the needs of migrant workers for cheap housing. Most of the natives are not engaged in any formal occupation. They hire migrant workers to plant the remaining farmland.

The second group of the Shenzhen population are the elite white-collar class. They are migrants, mostly from the large cities in other parts of China, with higher education background and skills. They are an elite class, mostly managers, clerks, governmental officials or technicians.

The third group are the migrant workers, who account for over 70% of total population in Shenzhen. Currently there are over 2.5 million migrant workers in Shenzhen. They are the main labor force, mainly engaged in labor-intensive sectors, such as assembly lines for the manufacture of garments, electronics and toys (Meng, Wang & Li, 1998). On average they have nine years of education, much higher than their hometown average (Wu, 1995). This group of migrant workers is characterized as young and mostly single. They are aged mainly between 17 and 23 years. They are part of China's floating population and are attracted by the expected higher incomes (Solinger, 1999; Wang, 1998; Zhao, 1996). Generally speaking, worker's incomes in Shenzhen are as much as three times their counterparts in other regions of China. Their average monthly income has increased from about 150 yuan per month in the early 1980s to about 800 ~ 1000 yuan in 1997. But compared with SOEs workers, migrant labors are not entitled to cheaper government housing, food, medical subsidies and welfare. Most of them remit home about 2000 yuan a year, which is about 2 ~ 3 months salary (Meng, Li & Wang, 1999). They are only entitled to be temporary migrants even though most of them work in Shenzhen for three to five years. After a couple of years working in Shenzhen, most of them return to their home towns and get married. This is the labor cycle in Shenzhen: new migrants arrive and old ones return home.

WHAT MAKES SHENZHEN SPECIAL

A number of factors have operated to make Shenzhen special as a SEZ in China. It is not an exaggeration to say "Shenzhen is the backyard of Hong Kong and Hong Kong is a front office of Shenzhen". Commuting between Shenzhen and Hong Kong is very convenient. There are frequent buses, trains and ships connecting the two cities. The close trading relationship between Shenzhen and Hong Kong is growing rapidly (Kemenade, 1997; Wong & Chu, 1985). In terms of foreign investment, more than 10,000 foreign companies from over 40 countries and regions had opened businesses in the city. About 70% of those were Hong Kong based (Shenzhen Government Internet, 2000). Since the establishment of the SEZ in Shenzhen, Hong Kong has been the main source of capital and its gateway to the world (Table 6). Shenzhen now ranks No. 1 in China in export revenue, most of which comes through Hong Kong.

A second important factor is a set of special policies adopted in Shenzhen. To test the market system within China, Shenzhen was granted a series of special policies and treatments. The role of both central and local governments in Shenzhen's special policy formation and miracle has been enormous, but there is a clear division of roles. The central and provincial governments have provided a macro framework and in fact, Shenzhen has enjoyed the highest autonomy among Chinese cities since the decision-making power has been decentralized from both central and provincial governments. The municipal government set up policies and regulations and has targeted sectors for priority development of industry as well as setting priorities for urban development (Zhang & Gao, 1997).

As discussed earlier, Shenzhen has been the front line for China's market economic reform. Many reform packages were tested first in Shenzhen and then implemented nationwide. According to Li (1992), the municipal government was allowed to practice differently from elsewhere in China. Both

Table 6. Utilized Foreign Capital in Shenzhen, Grouped by Country.

YEAR	TOTAL (MILLION US$)	% ACROSS					
		HONG KONG & MACAU	TAIWAN & SINGAPORE	JAPAN	USA	FRANCE	OTHERS
1986	489.3	79	0	14	5	1	1
1987	404.5	63	1	23	8	3	2
1988	444.3	63	1	33	1	1	1
1989	458.1	63	5	22	2	7	1
1990	518.6	51	4	33	8	2	4
1991	583.5	55	1	25	12	3	4
1992	715.4	64	2	22	3	5	5
1993	1,432.2	65	4	15	10	2	5
1994	1,729.6	73	7	11	2	1	6
1995	1,735.4	61	4	18	8	5	3
1996	2,422.4	62	9	12	4	1	11
1997	2,871.6	71	3	6	8	0	11
1998	2,552.2	72	1	4	2	10	12

Source: Shenzhen Statistical Yearbook, 1999.

Shenzhen's administrative system and its industrial practice are able to adopt different management systems in order to meet the needs of the market economy. The Shenzhen government is allowed to approve construction projects of up to 100 million yuan. There is also no limitation for foreign-funded construction projects, while most Chinese cities do not have such freedom. Shenzhen is also granted a range of other autonomies in the fields of banking, financial and foreign currency management (Zhang & Gao, 1997). Shenzhen is thus a "red capitalist city." Its administrative system, enterprise management system, social security system and economic control system, and the markets for consumer-goods, production materials, finance, land and real estate, and labor employment, all have been changed according to the needs of the market economy.

Apart from a set of nationally applicable preferences, foreign investors in Shenzhen enjoy a package of exclusive incentives. Enterprises within the SEZ enjoy a variety of special tax treatments. For example, they pay only 15% of enterprises income tax while their counterparts in other Chinese cities have to pay 33%. Among these special policies, freer mobility of currency, incentives for export, and a less-bureaucratic government approval procedure are important. Foreign investors in Shenzhen are free to remit abroad their profits, dividends, bonuses and post-liquidation income. The municipal government provides further incentives to encourage export. All export companies, at the expiration of a tax exemption and reduction period, enjoy a reduced rate of 10% for income tax provided they export 70% of total output. Those newly-established foreign enterprises with an export orientation need pay only one-half of the land use fee for industrial purposes (Lin, 1990).

Perhaps the most important factor to attract foreign investment in Shenzhen has been the efficiency of the government. The Shenzhen government has been restructured and is highly efficient. The government regulated its staff according to market economic demand and has modeled its operation on Hong Kong in the pursuit of its objective for Shenzhen to mirror "Singapore's city environment plus Hong Kong's efficiency". It is among the top three most efficient local governments in China, the other two being Dalian City in northeast China and Pudong in Shanghai. This "can-do" attitude of the Shenzhen government is one of the key attractions for foreign investors to locate an overseas operation in this city (Saywell, 1999).

SHENZHEN IN TRANSITION

Being dominated by assembly and other labor-intensive manufacturing industries for years, Shenzhen realized that it should not be just a processing, labor-intensive industrial zone. Its future lies much upon more in having value-added, capital/technology intensive industries. Started from the early 1990s, the municipal government redirected its development strategy towards new and high technology (NHT) industrial sectors (Song, 1995). Its "prosper by technology" strategy was carried out by adopting a series of measures to help establish built-in research institutions and to encourage its enterprises to emphasize human capital intensiveness. A set of special policies to attract and incubate growth of NHT in Shenzhen:

(1) Individuals or institutions engaged in technology transfer, development, and related technical consulting and service activities, are entitled to an exemption from business tax. Foreign investment in activities engaged in high-tech industries are free of income tax for two years and enjoy a one-half reduction for the ensuing eight years. Having successfully absorbed the related technologies and commenced production, the high-tech projects are given three years of income tax exemption on the profit hitherto made regardless of previous tax incentives received.

(2) For the land used by high-tech businesses (projects), no fee is collected from the transfer of land-use rights.

(3) The manufacturing and operation sites newly built or purchased by high-tech enterprises are free of property tax for five years. Other projects enjoy a three year exemption from property tax.

(4) Technological achievements counted as contribution by companies with limited liability can take up as large a proportion as 35% of its registered capital pending certification of high-tech status by the Municipal Bureau of Science and Technology.

(5) Overseas-based Chinese students and professionals intent on starting technology-intensive activities in Shenzhen may transcend the residence inadequacies of the shareholder. Payment of registered capital can take the form of installments in two years in cases where it fails to be a once-off placement.

(6) Encouraging domestic and overseas venture investment bodies to make their presence in Shenzhen. Given local registration and a minimum investment ratio of 70% in the hi-tech sector, such investment entities are entitled to all the tax holidays and other incentives enjoyed by the hi-tech firms. A 3% to 5% of annual profit can be withdrawn as a risk compensation fee to make up for the loss incurred during the previous year and the current year. The remaining amount of the risk compensation fee is settled on an annual basis provided the sum does not exceed 10% of the net assets of the company.

(7) Hi-tech companies run by foreign investors (including those from Hong Kong, Macau and Taiwan) can be registered as domestic-funded ones if their capital contribution is below 25% of the registered capital (Shenzhen Government Internet, 2000).

So far, reorientation of priority industry has achieved some results. A NHT zone has been established where the Shenzhen Tsinghua (Qinggua) University Research Center is located. The municipal government also has invested 10 million yuan for a research project cooperating with the Chinese Agricultural University and the Chinese Biology Engineering Development Center in Shenzhen. Currently, five branches of NHT industries are targeted. These are electronic information, biological technique, new materials, combination of mechanics and electricity, and laser technology.

After several years of effort, industry has been restructured. In 1999, Shenzhen had over 120 NHT enterprises with an average production value 350 billion yuan, ranking it first among all cities in China (Shenzhen Science and Technology Bureau, 2000). From 1992 to 1997, NHT production value increased at a rate of 59% annually. It is estimated that NHT production value in Shenzhen accounted for more than 45% of that of Guangdong province and about half that of the Pearl River Delta (Shenzhen Window, 1999). In 1999 the value derived from high-tech businesses accounted for 40.5% of the total industrial output, the highest proportion among all of China's major cities. In the same year, the high-tech sector generated US$5.133 billion worth of exports, representing a year-on-year increase of 16%. The last three years have seen the rapid development of computer, software, telecommunications, bio-engineering, microelectronics and accessories industries in Shenzhen (Shenzhen Science and Technology Bureau, 2000).

However, the most challenging task for Shenzhen in developing its NHT industry is how to attract Silicon Valley type professionals. Every large city in China is striving to develop NHT and as IT becomes the number one priority industry of the development plans of many cities (Shi, 1999). Many other large cities are now competing with Shenzhen to attract IT professionals.

CONCLUSION

When Shenzhen, Deng Xiaoping's pet city, celebrated its 20th birthday in 2000, we could not conclude that it had fully reached its goal of being a socialist city with Singapore's urban environment and Hong Kong's efficiency. Neverthelss, Shenzhen is the fastest-growing city in China (perhaps in the world). Its miracle demonstrates a development experience of a "red capitalist metropolis", which differs from other EPZs in East and South East Asia. Its dynamics lie in its geographical proximity to, and cultural similarity with Hong Kong. More importantly, a series of special policies and a high level of autonomy liberalized it from a centrally planned economic system, and offered Shenzhen the opportunity to be Deng's laboratory for his famous theory "it doesn't matter whether a cat is black or white, as long as it catches mice". Shenzhen caught many mice and showed other Chinese cats how to catch mice. Now many cities and regions in China are seeking to follow in Shenzhen's step.

Shenzhen has become integrated into the global economic system. Its exports, TNCs and foreign investment are all important contributors to a success of Shenzhen. But it has not lost its overall development direction. Its development strategy and priority has not been influenced significantly by the actions of its TNCs. Currently, Shenzhen is striving to upgrade its economy to be human capital and knowledge intensive. Although the NHT sector is in the early stages of development, it indicates Shenzhen has a capacity of being itself.

There are a couple of issues that need to be considered for policy adjustment. A crucial question related to NHT industry in Shenzhen is how China is to avoid duplication of IT and NHT? NHT competition among Chinese cities is severe. Shenzhen, the wealthiest city in China, is competing with the largest cities of China – Shanghai, Zhongguancun in Beijing (China's Silicon Valley) – as well as with many other cities. It is impossible for China to have a hundred Silicon Valleys or IT cities. To avoid duplication of IT industries among Chinese cities, the central government has to set up NHT priority items for each of the major cities and regions. Shenzhen, with strong financial capacity, should select an "only me can do" sector to be its next targeted sector. Shenzhen also must realize that it is competing with its neighbor city state, Hong Kong. Saywell (1999) warns Hong Kong to "watch your back" and points out that 'Shenzhen is emerging as a competitor for the hi-tech business on which the territory (Hong Kong) is striving for future growth' (Saywell, 1999: 52). The previous complementary relationship between Shenzhen and Hong Kong is now shadowed by increasing competition. If the backbone of Shenzhen's miracle – the Hong Kong factor – is gone, what is left for Shenzhen?

The second issue is how Shenzhen will face the challenge when China joins the World Trade Organization (WTO). In recent years, the special policies granted to Shenzhen have been extended to other cities and regions, such as Pudong in Shanghai as well as many other cities. Although Shenzhen is one step ahead in economic reform compared with the others, it is still some way from achieving "Hong Kong's efficiency". WTO membership will make all Chinese cities stand at the same starting line to face global competition. Although Shenzhen is still called a special economic zone, it is not treated specially anymore. Jiang Zheming, the successor of Deng Xiaoping and a former mayor of Shanghai, is placing more emphasis on Shanghai's Pudong (financial center) and Beijing's Gongguancun (IT center). Without special policies or privileges, how can Shenzhen sustain its development? Can Shenzhen remain in its leading position in China's IT era?

ACKNOWLEDGMENT

The authors would like to acknowledge the generous assistance of Professors Jack Williams, Robert Stimson and Eric Heikkila. Their comments and suggestions are gratefully appreciated.

REFERENCES

Chen, B., Hu, G., & Liang, Z. (1995). *The Sphinx Riddle of Shenzhen*. Shenzhen: Haitian Press (in Chinese).

Economy, E., & Oksenberg, M. (Eds) (1999). *China Joins the World: Progress and Prospects*. New York: Council on Foreign Relations Press.

Gate, S., Milgram, P., & Roberts, J. (1996). Complementaries in the Transition from Socialism. In:
    J. McMillan & B. Naughton (Eds), *Reforming Asian Socialism: The Growth of Market
    Institutions* (pp. 17–38). Michigan: The University of Michigan Press.
Goldman, M. (1994). *Lost Opportunity: Why Economic Reforms in Russia Have not Worked*. New
    York: W. W. Norton.
Guangdong Statistical Bureau (1999). *Guangdong Statistical Brief*.
Kong, A., & Yao, N. L. (1995). Analysis of Shenzhen Economic Development and Labor Mobility
    Process. In: Shenzhen Population Survey Office (Ed.), *Collection of Shenzhen 1% Sample
    Population Survey* (pp. 62–71). Beijing: State Statistic Press (in Chinese).
Kumar, N. (Ed.) (1998). *Globalization, Foreign Direct Investment, and Technology Transfer:
    Impact and Prospects for Developing Countries*. London and New York: Routledge.
Li, H. (1992). *Glorious Achievement of 14 Years' Reforms in China-Shenzhen*. Beijing: China
    Economy Press (in Chinese).
Li, M. S. (1995). Rethinking of Shenzhen's Function and the Reality. *Economy of Finance and
    Trade*, *4*, 58–64 (in Chinese).
Lin, Y. (Ed.) (1990). *Annals of China's Special Economic Zones*. Guangdong People's Press (in
    Chinese).
Lippit, V. (1997). Market Socialism in China? *Review of Radical Political Economics*, *29*(3),
    112–123.
Lu, S. H. et al. (1994). The Economic Development and Urban Planning in Shenzhen. *Urban
    Planning Review*, *1* (in Chinese).
Meng, X. C., Li, G. C., & Wang, M. Y. L. (1999). Shenzhen's Population Structure and Economic
    Development. Paper presented at Urban Development in China: Last Half Century and into
    the next Millennium Conference, Zhongshan City, Guangdong Province, China, 6–10
    December.
Meng, X. C., Wang, M. Y. L., & Li, G. C. (1998). *Garment Industry in Shenzhen City, People's
    Republic of China*. World Bank Working Paper.
Naughton, B. (1996). Distinctive Features of Economic Reform in China. In: J. McMillan & B.
    Naughton (Eds), *Reforming Asian Socialism: The Growth of Market Institution* (pp. 273–
    296). Michigan: The University of Michigan Press.
Nolan, P. (1993). *State and Market in the Chinese Economy*. London: MacMillan Press.
Park, J. D. (1997). *The SEZs of China and their Impact on its Economic Development*. Westport:
    Praeger.
Pearson, M. M. (1999). China's Integration into the International Trade and Investment Regime.
    In: E. Economy & M. Oksenberg (Eds), *China Joins the World: Progress and Prospects*.
    New York: Council on Foreign Relations Press.
Perkins, D. (1994). China's 'Gradual' Approach to Market Reform. In: A. Solimano, O. Suinkel
    & M. Blejer (Eds), *Rebuilding Capitalism: Alternative Roads After Socialism and
    Dirigisme* (pp. 171–207). Michigan: The University of Michigan Press.
Pomfret, R. (1997). Growth and Transition: Why has China's Performance Been so Different?
    Journal of Comparative Economics, *25*, 422–440.
Pomfret, R. (1996). *Asian Economies in Transition: Reforming Centrally Planned Economies*.
    Cheltenham: Edward Elgar.
Qiao, H. C. (1996). Market and Sectoral Choice for China's Enterprise Groups to Invest Overseas.
    Industrial Economy, *4*, 2–3 (in Chinese).
Rozelle, S. (1996). Gradual Reform and Institutional Development: The Keys to Success of
    China's Agricultural Reforms. In: J. McMillan & B. Naughton (Eds), *Reforming Asian*

Socialism: The Growth of Market Institutions (pp. 197–220). Michigan: The University of Michigan Press.

Saywell, T. (1999). Watch Your Back. *Far Eastern Economic Review*, (September 16), 52–54.

Shenzhen Government Internet (2000). http://www.fdi-shenzhen-cn.com

Shenzhen Foreign Investment Bureau (2000). *Shenzhen Investment Guide* (in Chinese).

Shenzhen Planning Bureau (various years). *Shenzhen Economic and Social Development Reviews and Prospects* (White Paper). Shenzhen: Haitian Press (in Chinese).

Shenzhen Population Sample Census Office (1996). *Collection of Shenzhen 1% Sample Population Survey.*

Shenzhen Science and Technology Bureau (2000). *Shenzhen Science and Technology Scan.* Guangdong Economy Press.

Shenzhen Statistics and Information Bureau (SSIB) (1997). *Shenzhen Statistical Yearbook.* China Statistical Press.

Shenzhen Statistics and Information Bureau (SSIB) (1999). *Shenzhen Statistical Yearbook.* China Statistical Press.

Shenzhen Statistics and Information Bureau (SSIB) (2000). *Shenzhen Statistical Handbook.* China Statistical Press.

Shenzhen Window (1999). *Shenzhen SEZ Internet.* http://www.shenzhenwindow.net

Shi, G. S. (1999). Speech on Techfair in Shenzhen. http://www.moftec.gov.cn/ moftec/official/ html/about_moftec/speeches/speech5.html

Shirk, S. L. (1994). *How China Opened its Door: The Political Success of the PRC's Foreign Trade and Investment Reform.* Washington D.C.: Brookings Institution.

Shuang, B. C. (1994). Shenzhen Should be China's Growth Pole. *Economy of Special Economic Zones, 12*, 14–16 (in Chinese).

Solinger, D. J. (1999). *Contesting Citizenship in Urban China: Peasant Migrants, The State, and the Logic of the Market.* Berkeley: University of California Press.

Song, D. (1994). Evolution of Shenzhen's Export-Oriented Economic Development Models. *Shenzhen SEZ News*, (April 26, 1995) (in Chinese).

Solimano, A. (1994). Introduction and synthesis. In: A. Solimano, O. Suinkel & M. Blejer (Eds), *Rebuilding Capitalism: Alternative Roads After Socialism and Dirigisme* (pp. 1–20). Michigan: The University of Michigan Press.

State Statistical Bureau (SSB) (1999). *China Statistical Yearbook.*

State Statistical Bureau (SSB) (2000). *China Statistical Yearbook.*

Sun, H. H. (1998). *Foreign Investment and Economic Development in China 1979–1996.* Aldershot: Ashgate.

van Kemenade, W. (1997). *China, Hong Kong, Taiwan, Inc.* New York: Knopf Press.

Wall, D. (1996). Outflows of Capital from China Paris. OECD Working Paper: OECD.

Wang, H. (1994). *The Gradual Revolution.* London: Transaction Publishers.

Wang, M. Y. L. (1998). *Mega Urban Regions in China.* Beijing: Ocean Press.

Wang, M. Y. L., & Webber, M. (2000). Is China Learning from its Neighbours? A Comparison of Overseas Investment Between China and other East Asian Economies. *Chinese Geographical Science* (in press).

Weidenbaum, M. L. (1996). *The Bamboo Network: How Expatriate Chinese Entrepreneurs are Creating a New Economic Superpower in Asia.* New York: Martin Kessler Books.

Wong, C. P. W., Heady, C., & Woo, W. T. (1995). *Fiscal Management and Economic Reform in the People's Republic of China.* Hong Kong: Oxford University Press.

Wong, K. Y., & Chu, D. K. Y. (1985). *Modernization in China: The Case of the Shenzhen Special Economic Zone.* New York: Oxford University Press.

Wu, W. H. (1995). Analysis of Education Levels of Shenzhen Population. In: Shenzhen Population Survey Office (Ed.), *Collection of Shenzhen 1% Sample Population Survey* (pp. 87–92). Beijing: State Statistic Press (in Chinese).

Xiao, D. (1995). Hong Kong, Shenzhen, and Shekou: New Centre of Asian Pacific Economic Rim. *International Society and Economy, 5*, 29–30 (in Chinese).

Yabuki, S. (1995). *China's New Political Economy.* Oxford: Westview Press.

Yamin, M., & Batstone, S. (1995). Institutional obstaclers to marketization in post-socialist economies. In: P. Cook & F. Nixson (Eds), *The Move to the Market? Trade and Industry Policy Reform in Transitional Economies* (pp. 57–74). London: St. Martins.

Yang, T. (1988). *The Rise of Shenzhen's Industry.* Shenzhen: Haitian Press (in Chinese).

Zhang, S. P., & Gao, X. L. (1997). *Ten Big Systems: The Basic Framework of Shenzhen Socialist Market Economic System.* Shenzhen: Haitian Press (in Chinese).

Zhao, K. X. (1996). *How the Farmers Changed China: Power of the People.* Oxford: Westview Press.

Zhou, H. (1997). Partial Reform and Full Price Liberalization in the Short and Long Run. *China Economic Review, 8*(1), 51–65.

Zhan, J. (1995). Transnationalization of Outward Investment: The Case of Chinese Firms. *Transnational Corporations, 4*(3), 61–93.

7. CRITERIA FOR URBAN DEVELOPMENT PROCESSES: MANAGING THE VIRTUAL ORGANIZATION

Elwyn D. F. Wyeth

ABSTRACT

Improving the quality of the planning and administration of regional growth management is an important issue in many parts of the world. There is the potential to transplant established management activities associated with successful quality cultures from producer entities into those serving communities at local or regional levels. Management processes employed in the SEQ2001 Regional Growth Strategy Project in the rapidly developing region of South East Queensland, Australia, are evaluated against quality management criteria selected for their demonstrated relevance. This framework is both applicable and useful in assessing the case study and is likely to be more widely applicable as a guide for the administration of regional growth management. The incorporation of business professionals in the development process created elements of an organized structure which can be managed as a virtual organization. The chapter reports also on the evolution of the particular growth management process in subsequent regional planning projects and on the adoption of enhanced management concepts identified in the case study. It recommends how the application of management concepts may be maintained or improved in international urban settings.

International Urban Planning Settings: Lessons of Success, Volume 12, pages 183–230.
ISBN: 0-7623-0695-5

INTRODUCTION

During the past decade there has been increasing awareness of the requirement for more relevant management practices in the control of urban growth, and in the preparation and execution of urban development projects in general. Research by Jones and Ward (1994), Werna (1995: 353), Kirby (1995: 9) and others, highlight these concerns. This chapter proposes alleviating those concerns through the application of basic quality management concepts to growth management.

The author's practical involvement in both urban development and quality management led him to suggest that enhancing the management of the development processes through the application of basic quality management concepts should improve the standard of outcomes while minimizing resources required and reducing process wastage. Developing a credible test for the hypothesis involved dissecting processes and procedures for urban growth management into fundamental activities, then linking these to appropriate elements of management enhancement systems such as Quality Management. Following initial work which demonstrated the applicability of quality management systems to design (information handling) processes, Wyeth (1995) exposed the nexus between design process management and urban growth/development management.

Urban development involves many actors; some are individuals and some are organizations including governments. The process involves modifying inputs to achieve desired outcomes. They result from complex interactions of a multitude of entities and their internal systems and activities. Such interactive networks can be likened to a large, complex organization. Thus management systems which improve the efficiency and effectiveness of corporations should assist entities acting together as virtual organizations.

Growth management became a political priority in the Greater Brisbane Metropolitan Region in South East Queensland (SEQ) a decade ago due to rapidly increasing population, failing air and water quality, increasing traffic congestion, and the misalignment of the aims and ambitions of planners and politicians of adjoining municipalities throughout the region. The SEQ2001 Regional Growth Strategy Project, discussed in this chapter, arose from the communal need to solve those problems (DHLG, 1990a; RPAG, 1994).

The "design" phase of the SEQ2001 Growth Strategy Project became known as the SEQ2001-RPAG project as its government nominated "manager" was the Regional Planning Advisory Group (RPAG). The management of the project team, posited as a "virtual organization", is the focus of this discussion as a case study. Survey data were obtained from members of the project group.

Each was a member of an associated participating entity, his or her "Other Organization". After analysis of the findings, the technical success of the management of the SEQ2001-RPAG Project was evaluated against pre-selected quality criteria. Whether, and by what means, the project's outcomes may have been improved are also discussed. The ultimate success of the SEQ2001 Project is discussed, together with the progress and/or outcomes of eight subsequent regional growth management projects in the State of Queensland.

AN INNOVATIVE APPROACH TO REGIONAL PLANNING STRATEGY IN SOUTH EAST QUEENSLAND

Cities attract people for various reasons, mainly 'to live the good life' (Beaumont, 1994: 1). Rapid growth brings with it problems, both social and physical (Kirby, 1995: 8; Simpson, 1995: 1), many of which are to do with the scarcity of space (Davoudi, 1995: 374; Harvey, 1993: 93) and our methods of production (Stilwell, 1992: 56–58). Conflicts arise (Tiesdell, 1995: 231; Whalley, 1983: 2), not all of which are negative in their impacts when viewed in the long term (Dekker et al., 1992: 3). Communities may benefit positively from outcomes of conflicts that are managed properly.

The Need

During more than three decades preceding 1995, the rate of population growth in the SEQ region was consistently high (Berry, 1986: 37; DHLG, 1990a; Barker, 1993: 31; DHLG&P, 1994a: 25; Stimson et al., 1996: 1). It was caused principally by migration from southern states and it resulted in rapid urbanization of near urban areas. Urban sprawl had despoiled much of the accessible countryside within 100 kilometers north, west, and south of Brisbane, the 'prosperous city' (Stilwell, 1992: 138) of the region. Research has shown that, in such situations, 'the land and resources therein are subject to competing, often conflicting demands .... It has become integrated progressively into a particular form of settlement organization characteristic of the post-industrial age – **the regional city**. The evolution ... has created conflict and stresses, and has stimulated various adaptations of human activities' (Bryant et al., 1982: 15).

In the local context, Brisbane's "salad bowl" farming areas had been buried under houses, shopping centres and hardtop. Urbanization had initiated 'diseconomies of scale, social problems, stress, and destitution. There is loneliness, homelessness, isolation, and a breakdown of traditional notions of community which are magnified in urban settings as are transport problems.

Infrastructure follows needs instead of preceding them.' (Caulfield & Wanna, 1994: xvi) Deterioration of lifestyles may well be a combination of loss of values, status, power and resources of individuals. The grounds for stress and conflict are worse in sprawling cities than in non-urban areas.

The loss of natural environment was another obvious consequence. The people of SEQ have become more conscious of the need to preserve the natural environment, and to provide for ecological sustainability. Like Greater Vancouver's residents, they wanted "cities in a 'sea of green'", whereas they were facing 'the prospect presented by current development trends and municipal policies is more likely to result in pockets of green in a sea of city' (Kellas, 1994: 87). The potential consequences for the region of continued, un-managed, high population growth were substantial. While they were a matter of conjecture in 1990, subsequent statistics developed later by the Department of Housing Local Government and Planning and the Regional Planning Advisory Group summarized physical consequences as:

> ... the cost of providing a new and upgraded road system, sewerage and water supply, communications and other infrastructure such as education, recreation and emergency services in the region will exceed $20 billion over the next two decades . . . and that figure relates only to the cost of providing the **additional** services. It does not take into account the cost of renewing or replacing the existing infrastructures.
>
> In the absence of a growth management strategy, and based on current trends, development practices and approaches to service delivery, the region would need at least another 460,000 dwellings, another 120,000 hectares of land for urban development, an extra 4,200 hospital beds – partly reflecting the impact of an ageing population – an additional 240 primary and 120 secondary schools, and water supply head works, such as new dams, costing around $260 million.
>
> The projected growth figures imply over 300,000 additional cars on present trends, an increase in car trips almost double that at present – with a consequent further decline in public transport use.
>
> (RPAG, 1994).

Genesis of SEQ2001

Co-ordinated management of development in the SEQ region was agreed to by members of the Moreton Regional Co-ordination Council back in 1976. But this voluntary agreement failed when the State Government terminated the Regional Co-ordination Councils in June 1977 following continual opposition from sections of the major party within the governing coalition largely centered in rural local governments (Minnery, 1987).

The un-managed rapid increase in the population of SEQ was finally recognized as being potentially disastrous for its inhabitants by politicians with enough vision, courage, and power to do something about it following the election of a Labor government in November, 1989. Rather than court trouble by adopting a top-down approach to establishing a growth management process, and to circumvent the substantial political might of Queensland's Local Government lobby, it invited representatives of some three hundred stakeholder organizations, initially to assist with preparation for, and then to participate in, a conference. The aims of the subsequent South East Queensland 2001 Framework for Managing Growth Conference, held in Parliament House, Brisbane, on 7 December, 1990, were to define the issues arising from un-managed population growth, the attitudes of stakeholders, and priorities for dealing with the problems identified. It showed 'that people feared that growth and development were out of control . . . the loss of valued agricultural areas, of bushland and coastal environment areas, of the relaxed Brisbane lifestyle, and (of) the region turning into a Los Angeles type urban sprawl from Noosa to Coolangatta' (Abbott, 1996). It was a success in that it established that there was sufficient community support for devising and implementing a strategy for managing the continuing rapid population growth in the region (RPAG, 1994: 8; Stimson, 1994: 47) for it to proceed with a bottom-up design process. It was to include 'a regional economic development function' (RPAG Minutes 23.07.91).

SEQ2001 and the RPAG Process

Most invitees to the December conference were representatives of the plethora of special interest groups in the community. Many had little or no understanding of what the macro issues were or what involvement in such a project would entail. The SEQ2001 Regional Growth Strategy Project (SEQ2001-RPAG) which followed was a response to the practical and political needs of finding some method of preserving the unique amenity and lifestyle of the region while moderating and harnessing the power of the local governments. Following a series of meetings with stakeholders to devise its structure and to select representatives of various groups with "affiliated"con-stituents, the Government formed the Regional Planning Advisory Group (termed the RPAG Committee in this chapter) in May 1991.

SEQ2001 Regional Growth Strategy Project (SEQ2001-RPAG): Structure and Basic Processes

The structure of an organization and its presentation of management responsibility can indicate whether it has a quality culture, either formal or informal,. The organizational structure of the SEQ2001-RPAG "project team" is shown in Fig. 1.

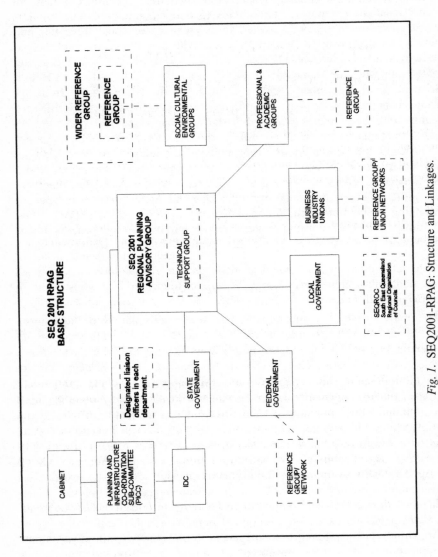

Fig. 1. SEQ2001-RPAG: Structure and Linkages.

Source: SEQ2001 Newsheet **1**, (1), November 1991, (Department of Housing Local Government & Planning).

The diagram shows the RPAG as being the focus of the process. It had direct input through its membership of fourteen persons. The number of members was limited purposefully to promote workability. The structure sought to provide cross-sectoral and multi-level governmental representation, with: nominees from the Australian Government (1 member), the Queensland Government (3 members including the Minister of Housing, Local Government and Planning as Chairman), Local Government (4 members representing Regional Organizations of Councils with the Lord Mayor of Brisbane as Deputy Chairman); and six persons from the Private and Institutional Sectors, two each from the Business/Industry/Unions Group, the Professionals/Academics Group, and the Social/Cultural/ Environmental Group. RPAG's members were supported by Reference Groups comprised of departments in the public sector, and of recognized peak bodies in the private and institutional sectors. Reference Group members sought input from organizations within their sphere and they in their turn sought ideas, opinions, and solid data from their members and the general public.

RPAG was given limited resources by State and Local Government. It relied hugely on time and resources voluntarily given by stakeholders prepared to make the effort to prepare the region for the future. Estimates of the numbers of individuals involved in the project ranged up to at least 10,000. RPAG began work in July 1991 with a budget of A\$2 million to last until the target completion date of June 1993. RPAG was depicted and promoted as managing the process. It reported upwards to the Planning and Infrastructure Co-ordination Sub-Committee of State Cabinet (PICC) which consisted of the Treasurer, the Ministers for Housing Local Government and Planning, for Transport, and for Environment and Heritage and senior departmental officials.

RPAG had a Technical Support Group (TSG) which has since been shown to have been the actual "manager". It was led by a Project Director who, together with the State Department of Housing, Local Government and Planning, was responsible for the project secretariat, for programming, co-ordinating and monitoring activities and outcomes required by RPAG, document publication, preparing draft recommendations, and financial management.

SEQ2001-RPAG's Structure as a Mechanism for Producing Decisions
Figure 1 may be re-drawn as in Fig. 2 to show supply chain relationships. It shows the various suppliers, their customers, and the interfaces between them. It shows also the policy makers, the managers, and the producers; in essence, they represent all the components of a multi-faceted corporation.

The number of entities involved was quite large and the figure does not attempt to show all of them. The complexities were huge given the technology of the day. The Technical Support Group worked closely with the five Technical Working Groups that researched and developed recommendations for policy in the specific areas of the environment, human services, transport, urban futures, and infrastructure. Working Groups were led by more or less experienced Project Managers who were responsible for data acquisition, report preparation and presentation. Working Groups needed information and data for preparation

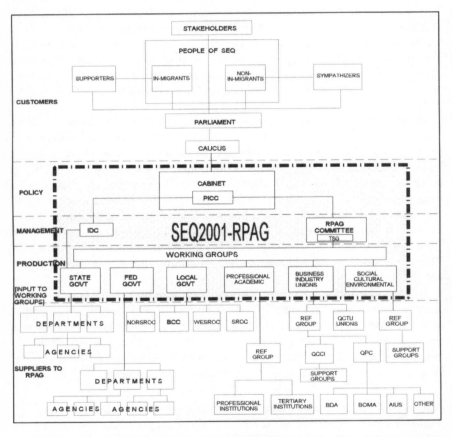

Fig. 2. The Supply Chains Through SEQ2001-RPAG and Virtual Management Structure.

Source: (Wyeth, 1998, Figure 4.8, facing page 73a).

of papers on issues, strategies, and policies. The material came from the limited standard sources available, from RPAG authorized research projects, and from Reference Groups that were convocations of sectoral peak bodies promoting the ideas of the members of their constituent organizations. RPAG and the Technical Support Group devised ideas and or requests which were then passed down the "chains" seeking data and or comments. Responses and alternative proposals had to be returned up the chains to the Technical Support Group in time to be collated, distilled and reported on before presentation at set meetings of the RPAG Committee. Usually the meetings were held only seven days after the set date for receipt of information from the supplier groups, a very limited time frame.

Shortcuts were possible when issuing material for comment through supplying materials direct to potential respondents, a resource intensive option. The same shortcuts could not work in reverse if the materials were to be kept to a manageable level. Participating entities, peak bodies, Reference Groups, Working Groups, and the Technical Support Group needed to edit and paraphrase materials submitted to them and destined for the RPAG Committee to reduce the input data to a practical assessable volume. The process was time consuming and fraught with dangers of misinterpretation, misunderstanding, manipulation, distortion, and of having material mislaid. Many participants took their ideas directly to cabinet members to circumvent this process.

Objectives of SEQ2001-RPAG

The charter of the RPAG Committee was to determine processes and outcomes; to determine the acceptability, or otherwise, of submissions from the production groups; and to report progress to the Planning and Infrastructure Co-ordination sub-Committee of State Cabinet (PICC).

The Government's brief to the RPAG Committee (RPAG, 1991a) may be summarized as follows:

(1) RPAG should take as its basic brief the submissions made to the SEQ2001 Framework for Managing Growth Conference of 7 December, 1990. These submissions had been made largely by participants in pre-conference working groups convened to discuss urbanization problems in the region and what should be done about them.
(2) The information in them should be translated into a series of Position Papers on which others might comment.
(3) When comments were received, the Position Papers were to be re-worked as Draft Policy Papers and re-issued for more comment.

(4) The process should be repeated with Draft Policy Paper's being re-worked to include relevant comments as Policy Papers.
(5) Following further public comment, the policies should be modified as appropriate by RPAG and put to the Government through the Planning and Infrastructure Co-ordination Sub-Committee of State Cabinet and Cabinet as Recommendations with Strategies for Implementation.

Distinctive Features of the Process

Queensland's local government structure differs from those in other Australian States. It has a degree of legislated independence from senior governments in return for undertaking particular responsibilities including town planning. Land management regimes in other states used State Planning Authorities or Commissions as a fourth tier of government for land-use and infrastructure planning, development and co-ordination. Up until 1995, urban and regional planning in Queensland was essentially devoid of any significant direction at state level. Although the final responsibility for approval of plans and changes to plans remains with the State, Local Government sponsored planning in Queensland is of much more political significance than in other states as planning is essentially the responsibility of individual local authorities. Queensland's Co-ordinator-General attempted to introduce Regional Planning in the mid-1970s (Minnery, 1987). Formal or institutional links between land use plans of local governments and the plans of State Government agencies for infrastructure provision did not exist until some 20 years later. Nor were there any links between the fiscal or budgetary planning of levels of government. Regional co-ordination between local authorities was at best *ad hoc*, at worst non-existent, prior to the implementation of RPAG's recommendations as part of the SEQ2001 Project (Wyeth, Minnery & Preston, 2000).

SEQ2001 was freed from the usual planning restrictions, the only ground rules proposed by the Premier in December 1990 being: (a) urban sprawl must stop; (b) open space and farmlands must be protected against further incursions of suburbia; and (c) existing urbanized areas must be used more effectively to accommodate more people, more sources of employment and education while preserving the amenity and lifestyle for which the region is renowned.

"Planners" had only a small influence on the outcome. The process was taken out of the hands of such professionals and given to the community's representatives to devise and manage. For the most part, Government deliberately sat back and watched, either through not wanting to be seen as interfering in the process, or they were not interested, or they were antagonistic to such a devolution of power. It was an experimental endeavour to gain consensus through empowerment. SEQ2001 was innovative in that the State, the funding organization, did not prescribe a methodology nor did it nominate any desired outcomes.

SEQ2001-RPAG as a Virtual Organization

Virtual Organizations
The observation by Rider (1986) that urban development project organizations are usually agglomerations of unrelated entities, typifies the early SEQ2001 team. Such agglomerations appear similar to the "multi-organizations" envisaged by Stringer (1967) and can be shown to simulate normal organizations with their policy-making, management, and production segments (Wyeth, 1998: 146; Wyeth, Minnery & Preston, 2000: 120). In today's parlance, they are "virtual organizations".

The SEQ2001-RPAG project team had three identifiable groups of components acting as policy-making units, management units, and production units. Moreover, responses to a structured survey showed that it reacted to stimuli and responded to material and human resource problems much as would any large corporation (Wyeth, 1998: 150). At the core of the policy generation group was the Regional Planning Advisory Group (RPAG). It reported upwards to the Planning and Infrastructure Co-ordination sub-Committee of State Cabinet (PICC). PICC was effectively the 'board' of the virtual organization while RPAG acted as the board of its "SEQ2001 subsidiary".

The second component of the virtual organization was its technical support structure. The directorate within the Technical Support Group was effectively "the manager" of the project organization and was responsible for implementing policies.

The third component, the producers, included the other permanent members of both the Technical Support Group and the Working Groups. These were personnel seconded from state and local governments and a few consultants and were responsible for the delivery of services and outputs/products. Working Groups were cross-sectoral and permanent staff were supplemented by part-time volunteers who represented the interests of community, environmental, business, industry, professional, academic, and union groups, and those of the various levels of government. These were supported in their turn by sectoral Reference Groups composed of representatives of peak bodies. There was an overlap of personnel of the second component of the virtual organization, the "managers" within the technical support component, with the "producers" in the third component, the representatives of the wider community.

The 'virtual organization' created to carry out the development of the SEQ2001 growth strategy project had a network of linkages connecting the Planning and Infrastructure Co-ordination sub-Committee of State Cabinet, RPAG, the Technical Support Group, the cross-sectoral Working Groups, and the sectoral Reference Groups. The limits of the connective linkages are hard to define because of the multi-layered structures underpinning the Reference Groups.

For convenience, this "virtual organization" is referred to below as SEQ2001-RPAG.

QUALITY MANAGEMENT AND ASSESSMENT OF URBAN DEVELOPMENT MANAGEMENT

Two decades ago, in an era when quality management was seen as the province of large manufacturers and engineering corporations, Crosby (1980: 13) said, 'It is difficult to have a meaningful, real-life, factual discussion on sex, quality, or any other complicated subjects until some basic erroneous assumptions are examined and altered'.

Quality Management Systems

In essence, quality management systems are risk management systems. All include control and monitoring functions and requirements for management responsibility which are enshrined in the internationally accepted ISO 9000 series of Standards for Quality Assurance (QA) systems (ISO, 1994). Some go much further into Total Quality Management (TQM) demanding both community and industry leadership and a willingness to assist others, even competitors, to better their organizations (SAA, 1992; Steeples, 1993; Kruitoff & Ryall, 1994).

Quality concepts enhance standard management systems through reducing producers' risks of providing products that customers do not want, or of finding them to be defective. They also reduce customers' risks of receiving products which are defective and/or do not meet their requirements.

Quality management criteria have been interpreted for application in complex fields, not just in assembly line manufacturing and heavy engineering whence they originated (Stebbing, 1994; Wyeth, 1994, 1995). It is now generally accepted that organizations benefit through the adoption of quality management principles (Steeples, 1993; Saunders & Preston, 1994; DBIRD

ASD, 1995; AQC, 1995; AQA, 1996, 1997, 1998). One of the most significant principles is that people must accept responsibility for their actions.

ISO 9000 Series (ISO) Based Systems

Prior to the current release of the ISO 9000: 2000 suite of standards, the international ISO 9000:1994 series of standards, and those derived directly from them, contained up to twenty "elements". Management systems of supplier organizations that incorporated the elements could be independently assessed 'against well-defined goals based on three key elements of such systems: documentation of procedures, an audit trail and demonstration of conformance' (SAA, 1992: 1). Successful assessments lead to public certification of the high standard of confidence potential customers might place in products from such organizations. The conscientious implementation of these systems results in continual improvement for the implementing entity.

Total Quality Management (TQM) Systems

In the early 1950s, J. M. Juran and W. Edwards-Deming introduced Total Quality Control which was based on leadership, customer focus, statistical quality control, and constant improvement, to the Japanese (Steeples, 1993: 5). The Japanese applied the principles, and then built on them in three very significant ways by: '(a) developing ways of involving all employees in quality control; (b) conceiving and making practical the concept of continual improvement; and (c) spreading quality control and quality improvement, to all areas of company activity' (SAA, 1992: 10).

"Total Quality Control" became "*Total Quality Management*" which provides a basis for continual self improvement of organizations (Saunders & Preston, 1994) through encouraging their members to seek continually to achieve perfection in all aspects of those entities.

Quality Criteria

Total Quality Management often requires substantial changes in workplace and management cultures. Management needed encouragement and guidance. This was given through offering prizes and or awards, the recipients being widely publicized. The criteria for assessing Japan's Deming Prize (from 1951), the Malcolm Baldrige National Quality Award (MBNQA) of the United States of America, and the Australian Quality Awards (AQA) provided guidance to management. Total Quality Management incorporates ISO based quality assurance as Operations Process Control, one of its essential elements (Kruithof & Ryall, 1994: 7).

Criteria are of consequence only if they are relevant to the matter being addressed. Therefore, it is necessary to analyze the processes usually undertaken by those involved in development management projects to determine which criteria are relevant to those processes.

Organization

Stilwell (1993: 14), suggests that for any business to succeed it must have a policy about how it will do so, it must manage and administer the implementation of that policy, and it must produce goods and or services (deliverables) for customers to generate income to provide resources to continue and to grow.

Juran (1992) provided another view: Planning is a function of senior management, that is, the CEO and the Board; control is a function of junior management; improvement is a function for all.

Community based organizations (CBOs) should embrace these basic functions to gain credibility. Saunders and Preston (1994: 9) support the proposition that CBOs should embrace quality criteria to improve utilization of their usually limited resources. They need to be able to recognize their products, their customers, and what represents 'waste' in their 'production systems'.

Appropriate Criteria: Basic Building Blocks for Decision-Makers

Management of urban development involves research, consultation, and continual decision-making by participating entities. Therefore, participating entities need management systems which incorporate appropriate quality principles to assist them to maximize the worth of their inputs.

The whole gamut of formal quality assurance criteria, total quality management criteria and auditing protocols are inappropriate for use in any practical sense with many of the volunteer based CBOs involved in urban development decision-making. Following analysis of the essential elements of recognized quality management systems, the following elements (criteria) are suggested as being appropriate for use by all entities participating in urban development data provision and decision-making processes. The criteria, and the reasons for their selection, are:

(1) Leadership: All organizations need "leadership" to provide direction and drive. Leadership is also required for engendering trust of the organization within other entities through proven "management responsibility" and

accountability. Leadership needs to incorporate planning at three levels – strategic, managerial, project/production. Each level needs to plan activities and how to integrate quality principles into them. The form of leadership may vary from the normally accepted hierarchical model in that 'in community groups, everyone is a leader, and everyone is a follower' (Wyeth, 1998: 112).

(2) Human Resources, Development and Management: The prime assets of organizations are their people. They need to be involved fully in the organization and to have their talents and knowledge developed in relevant areas in order for them to be of even greater value.

(3) Customer Focus and Satisfaction: Organizations must determine what customers need and how these needs may be met. Customer satisfaction must be assured and maintained. With community based organizations (CBOs) and non-government organizations (NGOs), this may take the form of responding reliably and credibly to requests for submissions on current events.

(4) Operations Process Control: Organizations that have extended time horizons should undertake risk management functions to minimize threats to their future well-being. They should document procedures for day-to-day activities so operational risk to the organization is minimized.

(5) Continual Improvement Through Constructive Processes: The whims of the 'market', increasing cost structures, taxes, and other social wage provisions, can prove punishing for organizations that do not improve processes, procedures, and products continually. Continual improvement relies on analysis of feedback and facts, of corrective and preventive actions, as well as on market research. The issues involved in urban development can change quickly and organizations need to have reliable systems to enable them to keep ahead of the changes.

(6) Effectiveness: The worth and the success of the integration of all the procedures should be measured and monitored. Success of organizations may be measured in various ways. For some, it is the value of their shares on the Stock Exchange. For those acting as constructive critics of urban development, success comes when governments (and others) listen to and act upon their advice.

Quality management is risk management. Organizations that are prepared to adopt its disciplines will gain from it. Organizations involved in urban development should benefit through external recognition of the high standard and credibility of their presentations and submissions.

THE OUTCOMES OF SEQ2001 AND THE RPAG PROCESS

The Vision and Objectives of SEQ2001

The Vision

RPAG prepared a vision statement but not until some eighteen months after its formation. According to many participants, the project was on the verge of collapse at that stage as it lacked direction and invigorating goals. The primary vision of all proved to be:

'South East Queensland will become internationally renowned for its livability, natural environment and economic vitality' (RFGM, 1994: 16).

The Objectives

Achieving the vision would require:

- a number of discrete, human scale regional centers – framed by a network of green open spaces;
- employment, services, commercial and recreational facilities close to where people live;
- flexible and efficient public transport and rapid transit systems;
- enhanced productivity and creativity;
- an adequate supply of affordable multi-optioned housing within an efficient, well-defined, integrated urban form;
- a rich and rewarding community life;
- preservation of the region's bio-diversity and high standard of environmental amenity;
- constant monitoring, interpretation, and management of dynamic processes of change; and
- on-going commitment by all sectors of the community working side by side with open, creative and accessible government.

The Regional Framework for Growth Management

The Regional Framework for Growth Management (RFGM) for South East Queensland is the outcome of the growth strategy project. It was published in April 1994 and has three major components: the Vision Statement (discussed above), the Regional Outline Plan, and the Institutional Arrangements. It also contains a number of Recommendations including:

- continuation and fostering of a co-operative and co-ordinated partnership approach to growth management;

- use by all spheres of government of the RFGM to manage growth in South East Queensland;
- adoption and implementation of the Vision Statement by all spheres of government;
- adoption of the Principles and Priority Actions in the Regional Outline Plan appropriate to their jurisdictions;
- adoption of the Principles and Key Implementation activities for institutional arrangements by all spheres of government; and
- the Action Plans should be assessed by all governments for implementation.

Critiques and Revisions

The SEQ2001 Regional Growth Strategy Project focused on limiting urban sprawl in the rapidly growing region of South East Queensland (SEQ), Australia. Its level of success was a matter of debate during the latter stages of preparation of the related Regional Framework for Growth Management (RPAG, 1994; RCC, 1995). The criticisms by commentators such as Booth (1993) and Stimson (1994) were of limitations and process rather than the basic concept which they supported. Waste of resources, time, and credibility during its first twelve to fifteen months of operations nearly scuttled the project late in 1992. Minnery and Low Choy (1994) showed that certain goals had been achieved despite problems and that the next phase, the implementation of the RFGM, would be critical. As will be demonstrated later, SEQ2001 now is proving successful and very worthwhile.

The project had logistical problems. The volume of material generated by participants in the project was immense. Of necessity it had to be distilled and synthesized into a set of concise recommendations responding to the Terms of Reference. The numbers of interfaces and organizations involved in the data acquisition, preparation, and presentation process mitigated against this ever being a speedy process, particularly as most of the organizations responding to demands for information were being run on entirely voluntary bases.

A supply chain linking a member of a community-based organization to RPAG contained a number of interfaces. For instance, a member of the Brisbane Development Association (BDA) would submit ideas to its relevant committee for endorsement, that would pass it to the Queensland Property Council, the relevant peak body, for consideration and forwarding to the Business and Industry Reference Group, then to the relevant Working Group, then to the Technical Support Group, and finally to the RPAG Committee, which might then endorse the suggestion and include it in its recommendations. Each interface provided an opportunity for "corrupting" the BDA member's original input (product). At each of those interfaces, each "customer" entity had the opportunity to select, amend, reject product from its "supplier" entity before acting on it and passing it further up the chain.

The process was time consuming and fraught with dangers of misinterpretation, misunderstanding, manipulation, distortion and of having material mislaid. Interviewees said that, in order to short-circuit such a process and to ensure their complete ideas reached those they saw as the ultimate decision-makers, many participants took their ideas directly to Government. Where there were disagreements within organizations, this tactic was used to undermine considered propositions put forward by their elected representatives.

Although Government proclaimed its willingness for the RPAG Committee "to manage the project", it was quite forthright in defining boundaries of goodwill. For instance, it said, 'RPAG will not perform a regional economic development function' (RPAG, 1991b) despite this activity being amongst the priorities established by the December Conference and associated submissions. This decision did more than anything else to downgrade RPAG's ultimate findings in the eyes of commentators such as Stimson (1994) and Booth (1993). Cabinet Ministers nominated either the lack of time (for research and consultation) or having too much time as the problem, not the lack of resources.

The "brief" was still incomplete at the end of the RPAG Committee's second meeting on the 16 August, 1991. Reference Groups were being established but each was setting up its own Operations Procedures and mustering its support groups. This meant that inputs necessary for finalizing the brief were often incomplete, uncoordinated, or not submitted in time to be considered. While some substantive progress was made during the first few months, it was not until 11 June, 1992, that an agreed Activity Schedule was adopted by the RPAG Committee and Cabinet.

Institutional Arrangements for Implementation

RFGM Proposals

The primary objective of the Institutional Arrangements proposed by RPAG was 'to provide an effective system for the on-going management of growth in South East Queensland which is supported by the regional community . . . .'

In order to achieve their objective, RPAG proposed some Principles for adoption by relevant parties and essential Key Implementation Activities involving the establishment of procedures and bodies. The Principles required that:

- coordinated and cooperative planning should underpin systems and processes for managing growth ensuring continued significant community involvement;
- land use planning must be linked to achievement of desired economic, social and environmental outcomes;
- management of growth should build on existing structures and processes, not add new layers;
- achieving long term goals must allow for flexibility of responses from public and private sectors to community demands and needs;
- policies, plans, and arrangements should be monitored and reviewed;
- planning and services programming should be coordinated inter-governmentally;
- growth management implementation requires overseeing at regional level;
- capacity should be maximized to increase efficiencies for all in the development system.

RPAG proposed the following Key Implementation Activities as being necessary for achieving the Objectives and to Honour the Principles :

- establish a Regional Coordination Committee, composed of representatives of the three levels of government, with clearly defined responsibilities to (a)function as the regional coordination and implementation mechanism for the RFGM, and (b) monitor and review the RFGM;
- establish a Regional Non-Government Sector Committee with representatives from human service, business, land development, trade union, and environment sectors, linked to and advising the RPAG;
- agree on an inter-governmental protocol for implementation of the RFGM;
- maintain and improve the SEQ 2001 Regional Resources Unit (RRU) as a planning resource for the Regional Coordination Committee and ensure the RRU carries out a series of (specified) tasks;
- ensure community participation embraced certain (specified) responsibilities;
- sub-regional structure plans should be developed by each Regional Organization of Councils for its area with those plans to meet certain (specified) objectives with structural mapping and sectoral strategies required together with establishing Steering Groups, convening Managers' forums, concrete support by State and Commonwealth Governments, provision for appropriate public consultation, compilation of Regional Plans through compilation of sub-regional plans at regular intervals;
- institute changes to existing procedures and policies to enable implementation of the Regional Framework for Growth Management, provide

undertakings regarding maintenance and improvement of coordinated services programs; and

- strengthen the linkages between mechanisms for financing and planning.

SEQ2001 – RPAG/RCC Transition
After some difficulties (RPAG, 1992; Wyeth, 1998: 76), RPAG produced the Regional Framework for Growth Management for South East Queensland (RPAG, 1994). It continues to be implemented in a largely unmodified form. It has survived the de-emphasizing of regional growth management by the Australian Government, two changes of State Government, and numerous changes in the politics of the eighteen local authorities which were signatories to the agreement (RCC, 1995; RRU, 1998). The strategy "design" phase concluded in July 1994 with the dissolution of the Regional Planning Advisory Group. A new entity, the Regional Coordination Committee (RCC, 1995), was appointed by the Government to act as the implementation manager of the growth management strategy. Current intentions are that implementation of the recommendations will continue to be carried out largely by local governments operating through Regional Organizations of Councils (ROCs) within guidelines developed by the responsible State Government department, now the Department of Local Government and Planning, working through its Regional Resource Unit. The Regional Framework for Growth Management was reviewed and amended in 1996, 1998 and 2000.

The project continues to provide a blueprint for devising regional growth management systems through forward planning, guidance and recommendations for co-ordination protocols for governments, communities, lobby groups, and primary, secondary and tertiary sector interests.

EVALUATING SEQ2001-RPAG AGAINST QUALITY MANAGEMENT CRITERIA

The Methodology

Various methodologies were considered for testing the argument that the application of basic quality concepts to urban growth management could enhance outcomes while reducing wastage of scarce resources. Ultimately, a "case study" protocol capable of incorporating both qualitative and quantitative data collection and analysis techniques was selected and used. The SEQ2001-RPAG Project was chosen for study for a number of reasons. These included its scale, the subject matter, the involvement of all levels of government and a very broad cross-section of other stakeholders, the accessibility of project personnel, and its being contemporaneous and "innovative". The social and physical problems caused by the continuing rapid urban growth of the SEQ region meant that findings might be pertinent elsewhere both in Australia and overseas. After determining the basic operations within the project, a survey instrument for completion by potential interviewees was prepared. This incorporated proposed assessment criteria based mainly on standard quality management assessment interrogatives.

The small cohort (36 persons) was selected to reflect the cross-section of approximately 140 senior stakeholder representatives and staff involved in the project. It included the (then) Premier of Queensland, three cabinet ministers, the Lord Mayor of Brisbane, senior members of local governments from throughout South East Queensland, and departmental officers as respondents for the government sector. Members of peak bodies representing business, industry, environment and community groups, the professions and academia responded for the non-government sector. Respondents were categorized by sectors then by sub-sectors and/or position within SEQ2001-RPAG (Wyeth, 1998: 93). All were asked to complete the questionnaire previously mentioned, and to record their opinions regarding certain matters which had come to light during earlier research and during the author's involvement with SEQ2001.

The questionnaire had three parts. The first was designed to establish the credentials and involvement in SEQ2001-RPAG of respondents as background for their subsequent responses to the second part, multiple choice Quality-based questions, and the third part requiring individual comments and or answers to management and or human resource propositions. All respondents were interviewed personally by the author. Interviews lasted for up to two hours and, with the respondent's permission, were recorded except for minor (but revealing) portions of the third part of the questionnaire.

Quantitative responses to the second part of the questionnaire were derived using a five point Likert Scale. These were converted to percentages of the possible for each criterion. The qualitative responses to part three were analyzed for key words and phrases, encoded, and quantified into a form suited to subsequent statistical analysis. Overall ratings were derived from responses given by each respondent. They were calculated as percentages of the possible aggregate of ratings against all criteria.

Performance Against Nominated Criteria

The survey data provided some results which were anticipated given the responses during interviews. Others results were quite unexpected. They are discussed in some detail later as they help to explain why the project has succeeded when so much apparently mitigated against such an outcome. The Case Study methodology proved successful in that it demonstrated that participants were reasonably consistent in their assessments of the standard of management of the project when all criteria were taken into account.

Table 1 summarizes the responses of the people in each of the categories and shows the resultant Overall Ratings of the management of SEQ2001-RPAG and of associated Other Organizations.

The results indicated some important recurring patterns. The data were sufficient to allow substantiable assessments of the management of the SEQ2001-RPAG Project, of the Other Organizations in general, and as well of the Sectors, and of the Department of Housing Local Government and Planning.

Overall Assessment Results: Differences Between Actor Groups

The results were mixed. Firstly, the overall rating of the management of the SEQ2001-RPAG Project was "fair" (61.5% of possible). Secondly, all categories of respondents and almost all interviewees assessed management of their associated "Other Organizations" as being better than that of the SEQ2001-RPAG Project.

Only six of the 70 comparisons of management capabilities in various areas (Table 1) show SEQ2001-RPAG's management as being better than that of Other Organizations. Most of the 'dissenting' assessments related to competence in Operations Process Control (OPC). Those respondents stated that SEQ2001-RPAG's documentation and implementation of procedures were better than those of their own organizations. This result was expected for "anything but organized" CBOs. When it came from some Private Sector representatives, it was quite unexpected as organizations in that sector generally were supposed to have adopted quality concepts by the mid-1990s.

Assessments by individuals varied considerably whereas those of Sectors and Groups were fairly consistent. For instance, management of the SEQ2001-RPAG Project was rated by "All Respondents" at 61.5%, within a range from about 58.7% to 66.4%, by all categories of respondents except those from the Permanent Infrastructure Co-ordination sub-Committee. "All Respondents" rated the management of the SEQ2001-RPAG Project against each criterion in the range of 57.4% to 65.1%. Taken together, these results indicate that the management of the SEQ2001-RPAG Project used the nominated quality concepts in varying degrees.

Table 1. Summary of Assessments by Sectors and Control Groups within SEQ2001-RPAG of its Management and that of Other Organizations against Nominated Quality Management Criteria.

Quality Management Criterion / Organization	People	Leadership		Human Resources		Customer Relations		Operations Process Control		Continual Improvement		Effectiveness		Overall Rating	
		RPAG	O/Org	RPAG	O/Org	RPAG	O/Org	RPAG	O/Org	RPAG	O/Org	RPAG	O/Org	RPAG	O/Org
All Respondents	36	58.83	72.60	65.14	71.67	63.97	73.20	61.44	64.42	57.39	70.89	64.92	71.83	61.53	68.83
Public Sector	18	65.11	73.56	66.39	71.11	65.72	76.39	61.67	67.83	59.89	74.11	71.72	76.28	63.93	70.30
Private Sector	10	52.80	77.60	65.00	73.50	64.50	75.00	61.20	60.60	53.50	71.20	58.00	76.00	59.40	68.81
Institution Sector	8	52.22	64.00	62.50	71.30	59.40	63.80	61.00	58.30	56.60	63.30	58.30	56.60	58.68	61.1
RPAG Committee	11	60.73	71.60	70.90	74.60	69.10	73.20	67.10	59.90	63.15	69.10	69.10	71.00	66.36	66.63
RPAG St Com'tee	6	53.60	72.00	68.00	68.00	61.00	73.00	68.20	68.20	61.40	66.80	67.80	68.00	64.07	69.30
Working Groups	20	56.00	72.60	61.75	73.00	61.40	71.00	62.20	60.10	53.05	68.95	63.30	69.60	60.22	66.33
Reference Groups	25	55.28	68.80	64.40	70.40	62.12	71.80	59.88	60.56	56.72	67.16	65.44	68.20	59.95	65.51
PICC	6	69.30	72.00	76.70	76.70	75.00	78.30	64.50	68.20	65.70	79.20	77.50	77.80	68.93	72.80
TSG	6	61.00	66.00	65.00	58.30	67.50	71.70	59.80	69.70	59.00	74.30	61.70	72.20	61.48	69.30

Source: (Wyeth, 1998, Table 1, facing page 89a).

Table 1 displays a number of general characteristics which require discussion and explanation.

First, groups within the Public Sector, or controlled by it, gave SEQ2001-RPAG's management better assessments than did other groups. Possible reasons for sectoral differences in perceptions are as follows.

(1) Most respondents were not aware of the real objectives of the project while the project's Public Sector initiators and controllers were. This inhibited the ability of many respondents to assist in the achievement of those objectives.
(2) The difficulties encountered by participants appeared directly proportional to their distance from the project's initiators and controllers which indicates poor deployment of values and objectives.

According to a Departmental respondent, 'the "control" group had to heavy some 'customers' because of their unrealistic expectations.' A Private Sector respondent put the differences in perspectives another way. 'As the project aged, it came down to a brokering exercise between State and Local Governments.' One Social/Cultural/Environment group respondent commented, 'People felt locked out. There was a barrier. Lack of time and resources limited input. You had to draw a line.' Another claimed, 'the more marginalized sections of society became quite obviously "excluded" . . . it was a land use planning exercise that did not include aboriginals.'

Information provision, vital in the consideration and preparation of authoritative, credible responses, was reported as being inequitable. Some claimed: 'The government departments were fed information that others did not get.'

Such responses suggest that a number of groups either felt left out or were left out. This led to their making negative assessments of aspects of the management of the project. Others were more pragmatic. 'The (SEQ2001-RPAG) organization had to balance outcomes with providing opportunities for discussion and debate – these two objectives were often in conflict.'

Assessment of Management of SEQ2001-RPAG Project Organization

The ratings by All Respondents, and by the Public, Private, and Institutional Sectors of the project's management against the selected criteria (leadership, human resource development, customer relations, operations process control, continual improvement, and effectiveness) are set out in descending order in Table 2.

Table 2. Performance of the SEQ2001-RPAG Project Organization's Management.

RANK ORDER	CRITERION	GROUP	ALL RESPONDENTS	PUBLIC SECTOR	PRIVATE SECTOR	INSTITUTIONAL SECTOR
1	Human Resources		65.14	66.39	65	62.5
2	Effectiveness		64.92	71.72	58	58.3
3	Customer Relations		63.97	65.72	64.5	59.4
4	Operations Process Control		61.44	61.67	61.2	61
5	Leadership		58.83	65.11	52.8	52.22
6	Continual Improvement		57.39	59.89	53.5	56.6
	Mean Overall Rating (% of Possible)		61.53	63.93	59.4	58.68

The mean overall rating (61.53%) indicates that SEQ2001-RPAG's inherent quality management system had reached the level of "Substantial Implementation;" that is, there was a recognizable quality management system in place but it was incompletely documented and only partially functioning. The data showed also that some "much needed" improvements to management were made to good effect immediately after the Mid-Term Review (MTR) in November 1992. Fig. 3 shows the results.

The assessments by all sectors of SEQ2001-RPAG's implementation of Operations Process Control procedures were similar. Ratings against all criteria by the Private Sector were similar to those given by the Institutional Sector. They were lower than those given by the Public Sector. In all cases, the Public Sector's assessments rated above the established average and exceeded those given by the other sectors.

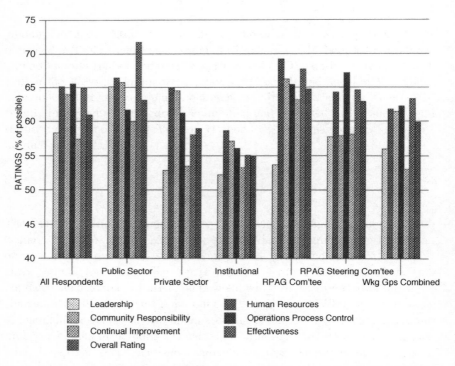

Fig. 3. Ratings of the SEQ2001-RPAG Project's Management by Sectors and by Specialist Sub-Groups.

Public Sector: General Assessments of SEQ2001-RPAG's Management
The results indicate that the Public Sector respondents, including thirteen from
the Queensland Government (eight of whom were associated with Department of
Housing Local Government and Planning), were more satisfied with SEQ2001-
RPAG's management than others were. This was either (a) because
SEQ2001-RPAG's management matched the public service model more
closely than it did models recognized by people outside the public service, or
(b) because the outcomes met their expectations more closely than they met
those of others. The Public Sector respondents included those who had initiated
the project. Most of them thought the project achieved somewhere between
60% and 70% of what they had hoped for though a few thought its outcomes
were far beyond their greatest expectations. Some suggested that more could
have been achieved with better leadership during the first half of the project,
and or better appointees to senior executive project positions.

Organizational Accountability
The Government's primary objective was relatively minor. As the Department's
Director General of the day said in an interview, 'It sought to achieve at least
a general commitment from stakeholders to work together for growth
management of the region.' It was pleasantly surprised when this and other
more problematic objectives were actually achieved. These included the
successful development of quite strong, though not binding, protocols for inter-
governmental and stakeholder co-operation and consultation concerning
planning for infrastructure and broadacre developments. SEQ2001 originated
in the Public Sector, in Queensland's Department of Housing and Local
Government. The Regional Planning Advisory Group, and its Steering
Committee formed after the Mid-Term Review in November 1992, each had
more Public Sector members than the aggregate of persons from other sectors.
The Director General of the Department of Housing Local Government and
Planning was the officer formally accountable to government for the project's
success or failure. This officer was the de facto "managing-director" of the
Regional Planning Advisory Group (RPAG) of which he was only an ex officio
member. RPAG was chaired by the Minister of Housing Local Government and
Planning. This arrangement resulted in very mixed perceptions among
respondents about who was running the project and just how much authority its
recommendations would have.

The initial perception was that the project was to have "whole-of-
government" involvement (that is, cutting across the interests of individual
ministries). This proved erroneous. The Departments of Transport (DoT), of
Environment & Heritage (DEH), and of Primary Industries (DPI) were heavily

involved, probably through self-interest. The Department of Business Industry and Regional Development (DBIRD) provided limited data and research facilities. Their involvement was not always seen by participants as being of a constructive nature, as shown by the following comments:

'Departments were very influential in Working Groups.'

'Those (Departments) that had not worked through issues (with us) sent in heavies to influence particular meetings.'

'DoT was pushing "predict and provide". It should have been looking for concepts for better transport systems.'

There is evidence also of attempts to frustrate the project for reasons related to the internal workings of the State's Public Service, as shown by the following comments:

'Treasury and Cabinet wanted to maintain control of it.'

'Some personalities and egos got in the way. (Departments) did not want to admit they were wrong.'

'Departments weren't interested.'

'The (State) Public Service thought it was a joke.'

The SEQ2001-RPAG team worked against this background, largely unknowingly, to bring an "innovative", "overdue" growth management study to a "credible", "worthwhile", and "politically acceptable" conclusion. The negative attitudes of officers in supposedly supportive Departments must have affected the spirit of individual participants as well as limiting the overall effectiveness of management of the project.

The survey data indicates that Public Sector project personnel had either less idealistic, or more realistic expectations, of the project's outcomes, or both. Others had hoped for more. It became evident that they lost faith in SEQ2001-RPAG's management when it did not deliver outcomes that would satisfy their expectations.

Serving Cabinet Ministers rated SEQ2001-RPAG's management at about 75% of the best rating possible. By their own admissions, they were not particularly close to the day-to-day running of the project and their recollections were influenced by outcomes, rather than by knowledge of the minutiae of the project. The main complaint of Cabinet Ministers was that the project's extended time frame (three years) provided opportunities for those with vested interests to undermine legitimate gains made through consultation and negotiation by the elected representatives of the community groups.

With more involvement and responsibility for the day-to -day management of the project, senior officers within the newly created Planning and Infrastructure Co-ordination Sub-Committee of State Cabinet assessed the operation more harshly, probably more realistically. They rated management of the project at slightly less than 60% of the best achievable, which is similar to the rating given by the Institutional Sector. The ratings of the management of related Public Sector "Other Organizations", such as Cabinet, the Government, and the Ministry, were similarly disparate.

Assessment of Management of Other Organizations

Ratings by "All Respondents" of management of Other Organizations (Table 3) proved quite dissimilar to that for SEQ2001-RPAG. The values for assessments of management of Other Organizations average 10% more than those for assessments of SEQ2001-RPAG's management. The least difference (2.98%) occurred in assessments of use of Operations Process Control.

Respondents' assessments of management within their own Institutional Sector organizations (Universities, Non-Government Organizations, and Community Based Organizations) are substantially lower than those by respondents in other groups. The low ratings for Effectiveness and for Operations Process Control reflect comments from interviewees that their organizations lacked resources thus limiting their ability to research, prepare, and present ideas and submissions. Lack of resources was also given as a reason for not having OPC which was considered "resource hungry" during the setting-up stage of a project, and too time-consuming thereafter. This comment was made: 'Volunteers just want to get in there and do things. They don't want to be slaves to process'.

The common assessment of the development and improvement of human resources in "Other Organizations" was about 72%. One might have expected lack of resources to preclude such activities in many of the organizations in the Institutional Sector. It appears that organizations see development and improvement of their members as being essential to the continued credibility and existence of the organizations.

The Private Sector respondents' high ratings of Leadership, Customer Relations, and Effectiveness within their organizations were expected as these are essential to their viability and competitiveness. The similar ratings for Public Sector organizations suggests that management attitudes are similar in both sectors.

Quality Review and Leadership Enhancement

Areas Nominated for Improvement of Management of Other Organizations
Participants' nominations of areas for improvement of SEQ2001-RPAG's management were dissected into elements then categorised under quality

Table 3. Order of Performance Against Particular Criteria – Other Organizations.

RANK ORDER	CRITERION	ALL RESPONDENTS	PUBLIC SECTOR	PRIVATE SECTOR	INSTITUTIONAL SECTOR
1	Customer Relations	73.20	76.39	75.00	63.8
2	Leadership	72.60	73.56	77.60	64.00
3	Effectiveness	71.83	76.28	76.00	56.60
4	Human Resources: Development and Improvement	71.67	71.11	73.50	71.30
5	Continual Improvement	70.89	74.11	71.20	63.30
6	Operations Process Control	64.42	67.83	60.60	58.30
	Mean Overall Rating	68.83	70.30	68.81	61.18

criteria. Of the 104 nominations received, "Leadership" (33 comments) was the most nominated element followed by "Customer Relations" (24), "Effectiveness" (18), "Human Resources" (16), "Operations Process Control" (11), and "Continual Improvement" (2). Two said "No improvement" was needed.

Only 67 nominations were received from respondents for improvements to management of "Other Organizations". Five said none was needed and three said "Maybe" improvement was needed. "Effectiveness" (20 nominations) was the main issue, then "Leadership" (17), followed by "Human Resources" (14), "Customer Relations" (11), "Operations Process Control" (4), and "Continual Improvement" (1).

These are shown as percentages in Fig. 4.

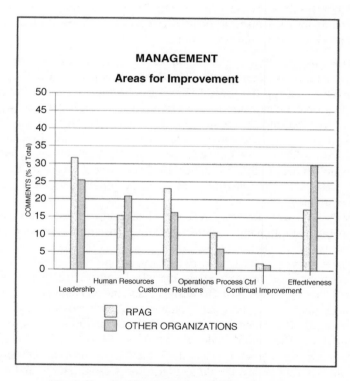

Fig. 4. Required Improvements in Management.

Unexpected Results

Some unexpected results were obtained. These include the following:

(1) Operations Process Control: an indicator of management competence.

Analysis of the data also showed that an organization's competence in Operations Process Control (as defined herein) indicates its overall management competence. In other words, organizations with well implemented, functioning ISO9000 based quality systems probably will have good management systems. The data indicated that no such correlation exists between overall management competence and management's performance against any other criterion. That is, an organization's overall management competence is indicated better by its performance in the area of Operations Process Control than its performance against any other single management criterion (as nominated) (Wyeth, 1998: 99).

(2) Success without a "Leader"?: The level of concern about leadership in SEQ2001-RPAG and in most Other Organizations led to detailed investigations because of potential effects on the overall effectiveness of the process. The results are summarized as follows.

The actors in SEQ2001-RPAG could be categorized, as proposed by Nix (1965), at least in the early months. The Deputy Premier was the "Legitimizer." The Director General, the Project Director (Co-ordination), and the chairmen of the Regional Organizations of Councils were "Effectors," as were most members the Steering Committee. Leaders of the Technical Support Group, some Working Groups and some Project Groups, are probably best categorized as "Activists." Following the retirement of the Legitimizer in early1992, "leadership" faltered. By November 1992, and the Mid Term Review, the project was deeply troubled. It was "largely process oriented rather than outcome oriented".

After the Mid Term Review (MTR), the leadership, its goals and aspirations, and implementation changed quite radically. Substantial improvements were soon noted.

The new pattern of leadership moved out of the Nix mould. There was a group consciousness among participants which recognized the opportunity it presented "to save South East Queensland" and the absolute necessity to bring the project quickly to a successful conclusion. A focused, synergic leadership team emerged. It worked quite successfully as an informal power-sharing multi-umvirate. The team included the Minister of Housing Local Government and Planning, the Director General of the Department of Housing Local Government and Planning, the Project Director (Co-ordination) and some non-government members of the RPAG Steering Committee. It had strong backing from the Regional Organizations of Councils. The data indicate a subsequent substantial improvement in other elements of the project team's management.

Who was the Leader?

The responses to the set questions regarding leadership, especially to those which asked: "Who was the Chief Executive Officer (CEO)?" and "Who was the Leader?", indicate systemic confusion (at least until the Mid Term Review) about who was driving the project or whether anyone was, who was managing it, and what it was all about anyway. For example, the question, (a) "Who was the CEO?" engendered 11 quite different answers; and (b) "Who was the Leader?" engendered 21 quite different answers. (Wyeth, 1997, 1998).

In essence, no one person or partnership was recognized by more than a few respondents as being either "the leader" or "the CEO". Contrary to standard management theory which requires clear definition of leadership in organizations for their success, the "virtual organization" that was the SEQ2001-RPAG project team, brought the very complex project to completion, more or less successfully, with ill-defined leadership.

Leadership: Comparing that in SEQ2001-RPAG with that of Other Organizations

There were significant differences between respondents' assessments of SEQ2001-RPAG's leadership and that of their Other Organizations. The leadership of the Other Organizations was generally described as being both well-defined and well regarded. For the most part, the leadership of the project team was not described so. A number of respondents commented that defective leadership had prejudiced the potential worth of SEQ2001-RPAG. The "poor decisions" included: (a) appointments of unsuitable senior staff; (b) lack of departmental participation; (c) inflexible process and vague outcomes; (d) inappropriate project strategies adopted; (e) limitation of content; and (f) failure to establish objectives and to deploy them throughout the organization.

By contrast, most respondents were reasonably satisfied with the leadership of their own organizations except for the academics who were scathing in their criticisms.

When asked about leadership style, some respondents said "strong" leadership would have precluded "ownership" of the project by the wider community and, therefore, its willingness to implement its recommendations. Others suggested that strong leadership, properly used, would have allowed ownership by others while producing better outcomes more efficiently.

Assessments of Aspects of Leadership

Five aspects of leadership were investigated. SEQ2001-RPAG did well in meeting its "Community Responsibility" but less well in providing a "Planned Approach".

However, the organization's performance in creation of clear values for the organization; deployment of those values throughout the organization; and understanding variation and management by use of appropriate facts and data were rated overall as "poor" during 1991–1992 before the Mid-Term Review.

The ratings improved to "above average" following a visioning exercise during the Mid-Term Review which resulted in creation of clear values and associated objectives and their subsequent wide deployment. According to a number of respondents, the visioning exercise should have been undertaken sooner so that participants could have agreed on goals and objectives and then worked towards them. Others suggested that the visioning exercise would not have been successful unless the "leaderless" "waffle time" had preceded it. This allowed participants to come to understand the complexities of growth management and to consider the underlying issues before trying to provide answers. The assessments of individual Leadership Aspects were quite different to those of Leadership as a whole. Public Sector and Private Sector assessments of the use of a Planned Approach by leaders favored those of their Other Organizations by 17% and 14%, respectively, while that of the Institutional Sector favored the leadership of SEQ2001-RPAG by 5%. The reason for these differences in perceptions may be related to differing approaches to this activity in the various sectors. All sectors appear to have assessed that SEQ2001-RPAG's planned approaches were barely adequate.

Groups as far apart philosophically as the Planning and Infrastructure Co-ordination Sub-Committee of State Cabinet and the Academics noticed measurable improvements in all aspects of the SEQ2001-RPAG's leadership following the Mid Term Review.

Summary: Quality and Leadership

The overall performance of SEQ2001-RPAG's management might have been enhanced if leadership problems had been identified and resolved earlier. Goals, objectives, and values needed to be established early to maximize time available for productive development, to minimize wasted effort and resources, and to create realistic expectations in the minds of participants..

Despite being a "virtual organization", the management of SEQ2001-RPAG benefitted through improvement to its leadership which included radical restructuring of its forms and functions. The basic quality management activities which appear to have brought about the changes included an in-depth review of all aspects of the organization and its procedures, and the development of a mutually agreed vision as a goal for all. They were long overdue. As with Quality in other spheres, there is a need for a group will to succeed if a project involving a number of quite disparate entities is to achieve its full potential. A good leadership culture is likely to engender such a will to succeed.

Management, Leadership, and Continual Improvement

Some respondents commented of SEQ2001-RPAG that 'it was a great first attempt and a lot of good things came out of it but it could have been done better'. Though the perceived effectiveness of management of Other Organizations generally was better than that of SEQ2001-RPAG, its management was rated more highly than that of seven Community Based Organizations and NGOs.

Leadership

Assessments of SEQ2001-RPAG's management rated its Leadership at 59% and its Continual Improvement activities at 57%. The average ratings for Other Organizations were significantly better (Leadership 73%, Continual Improvement 71%) especially in the Public and Private Sectors. This indicates that the emerging quality consciousness in both those sectors was improving management. A majority of respondents commented that SEQ2001-RPAG and or their respective Other Organizations needed improved leadership while very few called for improvement in Continual Improvement.

Human Resources

Formal questions regarding Human Resources focused on the involvement of people in their organizations and their development by those organizations. Involvement was rated quite well by most. However, a senior officer of Department of Housing Local Government and Planning said, 'It was hard to encourage involvement of people through (unstated) circumstances'. Development was rated from "poor" (36%) to "good" (69%) for SEQ2001-RPAG personnel and generally as "good" for those of most Other Organizations.

The comments about lack of resources and other difficulties in this area were more revealing: 'If we went through this process again, there would need to be resources to place sector representatives inside the Technical Support Group to provide information back (to the support groups). The government departments were fed information that others did not get.'

Customer Relations (CR)

The results indicated that entities such as those in the Business and Industry Reference Group or in Local Government, relied on good customer relations out of necessity. The ratings for "Customer Relations" abilities within such categories of "Other Organizations" were consistently high demonstrating acknowledgement of the need for best practice in this area. Their representatives were critical of SEQ2001-RPAG's performance in this area. Respondents from within the State Government generally, and also from the Professions to some extent, thought the project's customer relations were quite good. Others thought much less of the project's CR which suggests that the State's ideas of what constitute good CR practices must be quite different from those of the "real world". The attitudes towards CR of State Government and the Professions may be attributable to attitudes which developed from relationships where customers and clients are "dependants". In Business, Industry and Local Government, the reverse is true. Organizations are dependent on their customers for their long term viability.

The ratings given by the Social/Cultural/Environment and Tertiary sub-sectors may be due to the fact that the true natures of their "customer attitudes" are still being defined and their use of CR is yet to become sophisticated.

Operations Process Control (OPC)

OPC within SEQ2001-RPAG was rated better than that of Community Based Organizations, NGOs and some Professions that did not use documented procedures. Respondents from those organizations agreed that improving the OPC could enhance their efficiencies and make them more effective. However, most did not think their organizations could, or would, allocate the resources necessary for establishing, documenting, and maintaining procedures. Representatives of Business, Industry, Local Government, State Government, and some Institutions rated their use of OPC as much better than that of the project team though Sectoral averages were fairly consistent.

Continual Improvement (CI)

Respondents perceived that there was a need for SEQ2001-RPAG's management to embrace CI in order to enhance the effectiveness of both permanent and casual (volunteer) staff. There was some debate as to whether this happened as a natural function of the process. Some stated that SEQ2001-RPAG had sought CI and had devoted resources towards such activities.

Other Organizations had embraced CI to some degree. However, some of the Peak Bodies, convocations of smaller, less influential entities, did not have individuals as members and left the responsibility for CI with each of their member organizations.

Effectiveness

SEQ2001-RPAG's effectiveness was damaged through having "disjointed processes", "unfocused processes", and "being slow, too slow". It needed "quicker action", "quicker production", "the Steering Committee earlier", and "to embrace technology". "Problem" appointments, failure to establish goals and objectives at the beginning of the project, and failure to appoint a "manager" as Project Director, all reduced the effectiveness of its management.

However, SEQ2001-RPAG did have specific successes despite having its effectiveness compromised, probably for the same reasons that its leadership born of group consciousness ultimately triumphed. The successes included:

* co-operative problem resolution procedures were put in place;
* awareness of regional planning issues in particular, and of planning processes in general, was raised;
* Regional Organizations of Councils (ROCs) were established, i.e. Local Government was authorized, and expected, to work regionally or sub-regionally;
* the RFGM and its implementation including the products from the Working Groups;
* intra-governmental and inter-governmental co-operation achieved in matters of regional planning; and
* infrastructure needs were identified.

The statistical evidence (using the Chi Square test) shows some strong links between several essential quality management criteria and the resultant effectiveness of management. For instance, the link between continual improvement and effectiveness generally [$x^2 = 5.71$, DF $= 1$, p $= 0.02$], between continual improvement and effectiveness for customers [$x^2 = 6.85$, DF $= 1$, p $= 0.03$], and between continual improvement and effectiveness for stakeholders [$x^2 = 8.42$, DF $= 1$, p $= 0.02$]. Taken together, these linkages suggest strongly that organizations that practice continual improvement are more likely to be effective than those that do not. Another proven linkage was that between operations process control and effectiveness [$x^2 = 4.05$, DF $= 1$, p $= 0.05$]. Neither human resource development nor leadership (surprisingly) correlated significantly with effectiveness.

This may be interpreted as meaning that management systems that incorporate and utilize certain essential quality elements are more likely to be effective than those without such elements.

IMPLICATIONS OF THE CASE STUDY

Management and Quality Concepts in the SEQ2001-RPAG Project

A number of general conclusions may be drawn.

(1) The effectiveness of SEQ2001-RPAG's management was probably dependent upon a number of activities. These were nominated, in the terms of the previously "selected criteria" as continual improvement (particularly as assessed on behalf of customers and stakeholders), operations process control, and (possibly) customer relations.

(2) A person's assessment of SEQ2001-RPAG's management of particular activities was probably directly related to his or her depth of involvement in the project, and consequently, to his or her knowledge and understanding of the constraints in place.

(3) While not statistically proven, there is much data, including statements from some of those nominated as "leaders", which suggest that there was a direct link between SEQ2001-RPAG's performance and the standard of its leadership.

(4) If the alleged poor management of participating CBOs and NGOs from the Social, Cultural, and Environmental groups was improved, they could be more effective.

The RPAG nominated by government to manage the preparation of the Regional Framework for Growth Management, was "managed" by others at the direction of the Planning and Infrastructure Co-ordination sub-Committee of State Cabinet and or Cabinet itself. The effective manager of the SEQ2001-RPAG project was a sub-group of Project Directors and Co-ordinators within RPAG's Technical Support Group. From time to time, those Project Directors were instructed directly by their "controllers" who by-passed RPAG when it suited them. The other members of the Technical Support Group were "producers". The responses provided by the representatives of those two sub-groups within the Technical Support Group revealed consistent divergences of opinions regarding the standard of management of the project. The "directors" were much more positive than were the "producers".

The reports of difficulties experienced by the members of the RPAG in leading the project, demonstrated a lack of understanding of the functions of an "advisory" body. Its authority was limited. Real control over the project's direction lay elsewhere. The misunderstanding of its role probably arose from the fact that the SEQ2001-RPAG Committee was told to "get on with it" without any real assistance or direction initially. Both the Minister for Housing Local Government and Planning and his Director General said that the "hands off" approach was deliberate in that they did not wish to be seen as overtly influencing processes and outcomes. The evidence shows that this tactic was subsequently seen by both men, and by others, as being inappropriate and that some clearer direction and leadership should have been given.

In theory, SEQ2001-RPAG's effectiveness could have been better had its other management activities been performed better. Despite their stated reservations and despite the low ratings given to many of the other management activities, most respondents assessed the project's management as being effective.

The leadership of SEQ2001-RPAG has been shown as being difficult to define. It seems that after SEQ2001-RPAG's Mid-Term Review in December 1992, leadership manifested itself through an informal power-sharing "collective". A participant from the social care institutions said: 'There was a huge amount of goodwill around the table. You could not have stuck at it otherwise. Cross-sectoral co-operation was at a level we never dreamed we could achieve.'

SEQ2001-RPAG ultimately devised an acceptable "strategy" through the co-operative consciousness of a cross-sectoral group of those dedicated to the need to manage growth in SEQ. The project's management had achieved its goals through:

- an innovative Human Resource initiative which gave fundamental insights into urban growth management problems, and possible solutions, throughout the West Coast of the USA and Canada to thirty representatives of a broad cross section of stakeholders;
- recognizing the need to make significant enhancement of management at the Mid Term Review and then acting on that knowledge, particularly as far as its leadership was concerned; and
- bringing together (belatedly) an agreed project plan which, together with the subsequent Mid Term Review, engendered renewed commitment to achieving *the vision* for long term sustainability of the lifestyle that is the hallmark of South East Queensland.

The exercise has proved effective and has been recognized as such in that the bulk of the recommendations emanating from it are being implemented.

Lasting benefits, such as enhanced inter-governmental co-operation, were born of it. The results may have been better if:

- the leadership had not made "poor decisions regarding appointments, strategies and content";
- "supplier organizations and client entities had agreed on a scope and standard of input to be provided that would be significant yet suited to the resource capabilities of the supplier" (problems of Human Resources and Operations Process Control);
- the management had monitored the satisfaction levels of its major customers and adjusted matters to maintain them at a high level (Customer Relations);
- the process had been time effective, clear and easily understood, not "disjointed", "too complicated", "difficult to change", and not subject to corruption through short circuiting (Operations Process Control);
- the final product, the desired outcomes, the vision, had been defined early in the project (Strategic Planning within Leadership), that is, if they were not known then they should have been established quickly and deployed widely (Leadership and Operations Process Control);
- the process had embraced human resources (Improvement and Development) as a means of making all participants more effective and valuable to the organization; and
- the process had promoted Continual Improvement of attitudes, procedures, and products.

The responses to the structured questionnaire and to questons during subsequent interviews indicate that managements of most of the Other Organizations involved in the project relied on good customer relations, voluntary human resources, and continual improvement for their continued success in most cases. They were concerned with leadership and effectiveness of their organizations. They recognized that their resources were few. Leaders were loath to introduce into their "informal" organizations the additional discipline that good management requires because it could deter members from becoming involved. Well-managed Community Based Organizations and NGOs which had good funding, good research facilities, and well developed administration systems were more effective than those with limited resources and which relied heavily on volunteer staff and used deficient, sometimes ad hoc, management systems.

The question remains: "Would SEQ2001-RPAG have benefitted if support organizations had been more conscious of, and had implemented, quality management procedures?"

The probable answer is "Yes".

As mentioned previously, most respondents agreed that the SEQ2001-RPAG project had succeeded. The data indicate that it could have been even more successful had SEQ2001-RPAG formally adopted basic quality management concepts in a number of areas in its first months and encouraged associated Other Organizations to do likewise.

Recommendations for Improvements

As a virtual organization SEQ2001-RPAG relied for its success on the goodwill and integrity of all the entities within the network. Participating organizations in such networks need impeccable internal management systems if they are to service adequately the other organizations in the network (their customers). The findings of the study demonstrate that by operating as a virtual organization in a loosely coupled fashion, a group may accomplish its aims and objectives provided each entity in the network knows the overall goals, its role and responsibilities, what is expected of it, and what the roles and responsibilities of the other organizations in the network are.

For the group to be most effective, each organization must be committed to the basic quality adage of "doing it right, first time, every time". The results indicate that effective management requires satisfaction of a number of management criteria. That is:

- each entity probably needs good leadership, though the form of that leadership may vary;
- each entity should pursue continual improvement of its internal operations, its people, and its management of interfaces internally and externally;
- each entity should involve and develop its human resources;
- each entity should implement operations process controls to plan ahead, to design, to resource, to produce, to monitor, and then to review and upgrade frequently; and
- each entity should utilize customer relations to assist in assessing whether the proposed outcomes of its ventures will prove satisfactory for itself and for its "customers".

Transfer of information is the key process and needs focused management. The following comments may be of value.

(1) Firstly, a project organization, a macro-system, will operate at its full potential only if the management systems of all of the participating organizations (micro-systems) operate to their full potential. Prevention and reduction of the risk of failure requires commitment, integrity, accountability, and discipline by all those involved in the project. This

means that people need to recognize that their activities directly affect the actions of others.

(2) Secondly, early phases of projects must be completed successfully if later phases are to proceed at maximum efficiency. The prime requirement for the success of any "project" is to determine accurately at the outset the preferred outcomes; that is, to agree on the statement of requirements which becomes the brief.

(3) Thirdly, problems faced by communities relating to rapid population growth are a mixture of those that affect a few individuals and those that affect the community as a whole. CBOs that wish to be effective and to provide positive, credible inputs into solving community problems, would benefit from establishing simple, sound management systems. This should translate into credibility and respect for organizations which adopt them. A struggling but well managed organization is far more likely to enhance its credibility and to attract outside funding than those that muddle along.

(4) Fourthly, there are non-confrontationalist systems and methods available for working through urban development problems. Such methods require all parties to accept certain disciplines. The adoption of procedures based on the previously nominated criteria should bring about results acceptable to all parties with minimal waste of time, effort and resources and, hopefully, more equitable outcomes. The selected criteria may also form the basis of a purpose-made quality (risk management) system for organizations with limited resources and or short life expectancy.

(5) Finally, in order to simplify the implementation of the preceding recommendation, a simple, effective management system incorporating quality principles for use by community-based organizations and individuals needs to be developed in order to allow them to play more effective roles in debates about the futures of their communities. It may be possible to adapt one of the many proprietary software systems now on the market as an inexpensive method of making the necessary procedures and their explanations readily available. Local Governments could supply them to community groups as part of their community welfare programs.

The research findings certainly have practical applications for managing planning processes in the Australian context. However, the underlying philosophy of ensuring that care is always taken in processing information and in decision-making has universal application. It should be capable of adoption by organizations anywhere in their endeavors to ameliorate the problems generated by rapid urbanization.

POST SEQ2001-RPAG REGIONAL GROWTH MANAGEMENT PROJECTS IN QUEENSLAND

In late 1989, during a helicopter ride over the region, the obvious extent of the spreading tragedy of urban sprawl came as a shock to the new Minister for Housing and Local Government. He reacted swiftly to devise a viable system of growth management. The outcome, the Regional Framework for Growth Management for South East Queensland (RPAG, 1994), has become an essential element in development management for the region and provides a model process for use by the peoples of other regions.

Other Regional Planning Initiatives

The fundamental success of SEQ2001-RPAG has led the Queensland Government to support eight regional planning exercises in other parts of the State, most of which are on-going. While most have followed the South East Queensland model fairly closely, the Cape York Peninsula Land Use Strategy (CYPLUS) "is fundamentally different to SEQ2001".

Cape York is one of the more sparsely populated areas of Australia. Far from centres of government, its values are its natural resources and its mixture of tropical habitats. *CYPLUS* was originally set up with Australian Government funding and specific parameters, more as a resource and natural heritage management project than one with a central focus on urban development. It was managed initially by a private consultant, then the state's Department of Communications Information Local Government and Planning, before being passed to the State's Department of Natural Resources, following recognition of the true focus of the project.

The other regional planning projects are:

Wide Bay 2020	WB2020
Eastern Downs Regional Organization of Councils	EDROC
Burnett Interior Regional Organization of Councils	BIROC
Central Queensland and Northern Minefields	CQ-ANM
Whitsunday Hinterland and Mackay 2015	WHAM 2015
Townsville Thuringowa Strategy Plan	TTSP
Far North Queensland 2010	FNQ 2010
Gulf Region Development Plan	GRDP

Together with SEQ2001 and CYPLUS, they encompass 94% of Queensland's population estimated at almost 3,526 million persons (ABS, September 1999), 36% of its land area of approximately 1,727,000 square kilometers, and 60%

of its Local Governments. The remaining 64% of Queensland contains about 6% of its people and 40% of its local Governments. It is a "wide brown land".

The Results: A Few Comments
The economic aspects of regional planning and development now play a much greater part in policy formulation than was the case with SEQ2001. The FNQ 2010 scheme is supported by work of a number of experts, including Stimson, McGovern and Daly (1994) on the value to the region of tourism and associated economic development. Its Project Manager moved from the Private Sector to manage a Working Group in the SEQ2001-RPAG Project. He learned through that experience what activities and systems needed to be improved in order to reach successful outcomes more effectively. Those improvements have been incorporated into FNQ 2010's management protocols with quite significant results. According to the Regional Organization of Councils and its stake-holders, the scheme is being implemented with ever-growing confidence.

EDROC, the scheme for shires and municipalities of the Eastern Darling Downs region, was initiated by its local governments who recognized the potential long-term benefits of such an alliance. The area was growing and changing from one based on a rich wheat and wool economy into one which reflected changing markets and aspirations, and a population influx, partic-ularly around Toowoomba with its University of Southern Queensland and numerous research facilities. The eight Shire Councils involved, engaged a consulting planning firm that had participated in SEQ2001 to act as project manager and facilitator of a similar process.

The Wide Bay 2020 Regional Growth Management Framework covers an area of 22,300 square kilometers, similar to that of SEQ2001. It has a population of about 190,000 people concentrated in and around three cities, Bundaberg, Maryborough, and Hervey Bay, and is governed by ten local authorities. It includes World Heritage listed Fraser Island and the Cooloola National Park. The structure of the Wide Bay 2020 RGMF was modelled closely on that of SEQ2001. The main differences are that: (a) its implementation is being overseen by the Regional Planning Advisory Committee (RPAC) which managed its preparation, instead of being passed on to an "implementation manager" such as SEQ2001's Regional Coordination Committee (RCC); and (b) its five Working Groups include one devoted specifically to economics. . . .

. . . The Project Manager's comments are typical of those of the other projects.

> Yes, we applied lessons learned from the management of SEQ2001-RPAG and some we
> learnt along the way from our own project. The underlying (SEQ2001) format is still

appropriate. Each region will have variations based on its particular issues and circumstances. Greater coordination between projects to share experiences of what does and doesn't work could assist.

Success Beyond Growth Management

Recent interviews with participants in SEQ2001-RPAG have shown universal recognition of the achievements of the project during the implementation phase. While opinions vary, it appears that implementation is improving with time. While there have been formal reviews of processes and outcomes, the generally acknowledged success of the project and unexpected gains made in the region's long term viability may be illustrated by the following example:

> The Government shares meat-processing rights with the private sector throughout the region with State and private sector meatworks almost side by side in some shires. Some months ago, the State decided to close a number of its facilities and to allocate their quotas to a single international processor that proposed to establish one central processing facility in the region. To minimize job losses and to enhance their long term viability, established local private sector processors suggested apportionment of the State's quota among them. This was refused.
>
> The consequent threat to the local economies of two shires, where the State's processing works were scheduled for immediate closure, led the mayors to lobby the Government, but they were unsuccessful. They took the matter to their sub-Regional Organization of Councils which then took the matter the regional organization, the South East Queensland Regional Organization of Councils. Following debate, SEQROC forwarded it to the Regional Coordinating Committee with a strong recommendation for its review based on the need to preserve the viability of local industries throughout the region. The RCC supported the recommendation. Four cabinet ministers, members of the RCC, convinced Cabinet of the inappropriateness of the Government's proposed action so the original decision was overturned. Local Governments working together had saved their local economies.

Governments and the private sector throughout SEQ continue to work with each other for the good of the region using the Regional Framework for Growth Management developed through the SEQ2001 mechanism. This is clear evidence of the on-going success of the project that had almost collapsed within a year or so of its commencement but which was rescued using basic quality management mechanisms and the shared vision of the cross-sectoral shared leadership that completed the RFGM in 1994.

Though somewhat modified, it remains in place and functioning in this new millenium.

REFERENCES

Abbott J. (1996). *Preparation of the SEQ2001 Regional Framework for Growth Management*. Report to the Australian Planning Officials Group by the Regional Resource Unit, Department of Local Government and Planning, Brisbane.

AQA (1996). *Australian Quality Awards 1996 – Assessment Criteria*. Australian Quality Awards Foundation, St Leonards, NSW, Australia.

AQA (1997). *Australian Quality Awards 1997 – Assessment Criteria*. Australian Quality Awards Foundation, St Leonards, NSW, Australia.

AQA (1998). *Australian Quality Awards 1998 – Assessment Criteria*. Australian Quality Awards Foundation, St Leonards, NSW, Australia.

AQC (1995). *Australian Quality Awards 1995*. The Quality Magazine, Australian Quality Council, *4*, 6.

Beaumont, R. (1994). Metropolis of the Future – Direction, Growth and Sustainability. *Metropolis Now – Getting it Right* conference papers. Brisbane Development Association, Brisbane: 1–6.

Booth, G. (1993). Comments on Proposed Regional Framework for Growth Management. Paper presented at *SEQ2001 Workshop*, Building Owners and Managers Association, Brisbane, Australia. November 1993.

Bryant, C. R., Russwurm, L. G., & McLellan, E. G. (1982). *The City's Countryside*. Longman, London: 15.

Caulfield, J., & Wanna, J. (Eds) (1995). *Power and Politics in the City: Brisbane in Transition*. Macmillan Education Australia, South Melbourne.

Cornick, T. (1991). *Quality Management of Building Design*. Butterworth Architecture Management Guides, Butterworth-Heinemann Ltd.

Crosby, P. B. (1980). *Quality is Free – The Art of Making Quality Certain* (p. 13). Mentor Books ME2585, Penguin Books, New York, USA.

Davoudi, S. (1995). Book Review: Conflict in Urban Development. *Cities, 12*(5), 374–375.

DBIRD, & ASD (1995). *Quality Assurance Quick Guide*. Purchasing, Policy and Research Unit, Administrative Services Department and Quality Development Unit, Department of Business, Industry, and Regional Development, Brisbane.

Dekker, A., Goverde, H., Makowski, T., & Ptaszynska-woloczkowicz, M. (1992). *Conflict in Urban Development* (p. 3). Aldershot: Ashgate.

DHLG (1990a). *SEQ-2001: Framework for Managing Growth*. Conference, Parliament House Brisbane, 7 December 1990, Department of Local Government and Housing, Queensland.

DHLG (1990b). *Population Issues for South-east Queensland*. SEQ2001 Conference Papers. Policy, Planning and Research Division, Department of Housing and Local Government, Brisbane.

Doxiadis, C. A. (1971). *Ekistics, An Introduction to the Science of Human Settlements* (pp. 431–460). London: Hutchinson.

Harvey, D. (1993). *Social Justice and the City*. Oxford: Basil Blackwell. Reprint: 97.

Heath, T. (1995). Design as Reason. *Discourse 95*. Research Concentration in Design and Construction Studies, Queensland University of Technology, Brisbane, Australia: 4–8.

ISO (1994). *ISO 9001:1994* (AS/NZS ISO 9001:1994) Quality Systems – Model for quality assurance in design, development, production, installation, and servicing. Homebush, NSW: Standards Australia.

Jones, G. A., Ward, P. M. (1994). The World Bank's 'New' Urban Management Programme: Paradigm Shift or Policy Continuity? *Habitat International*, *18*(3) 33–51.

Juran, J. M. (1992). *Juran on Quality by Design, The New Steps for Planning Quality into Goods and Services*. New York: Free Press.

Kirby, A. (1995). A research agenda for the close of the century. *Cities*, *12*(1), 9.

Kruithof, J., & Ryall, J. (1994). *The Quality Standards Handbook*. Information Australia, Melbourne.

Minnery, J. R., & Barker, R. (1998). The more things change . . . Brisbane and South East Queensland. *Urban Policy and Research*, *16*(2), 147–152.

Minnery, J. R. (1987). *Co-ordination and the Queensland Co-ordinator-General*, Master of Public Administration Thesis, Department of Government, University of Queensland, Brisbane.

Minnery, J. R., & Low Choy, D. (1994). Planning the outward growth of Australian capital cities: SEQ2001 – A brave bold experiment or regional planning too late? *Urban Policy and Research*, *12*(3), 200–212.

Nix, H. L. (1974). *The Community and its Involvement in the Study Planning Action Process*. HEW Publication No CDC 78–8355, U.S. Dept. of Health, Education and Welfare, Bureau of Health Education and Bureau of State Services, Atlanta, Georgia 30333.

RCC (1995). *South East Queensland Regional Framework for Growth Management 1995*. SEQ 2001 Regional Coordination Committee, Department of Housing, Local Government and Planning, Brisbane.

RCC (1998). *Regional Framework for Growth Management, 1998*. Regional Coordination Committee, Queensland Department of Local Government and Planning, Brisbane.

Rider, R. (1986). Planning as a multicentric process. *Town Planning Review*, *52*(2), 181–201.

RPAG (1991a). *Minutes of Meeting Number 1 of the Regional Planning Advisory Group*. 23 July 1991, Regional Resource Unit, Department of Local Government and Planning, Brisbane.

RPAG (1991b). *Minutes of Meeting Number 2 of the Regional Planning Advisory Group*. 16 August 1991, Regional Resource Unit, Department of Local government and Planning, Brisbane.

RPAG (1992). *Mid Term Review Report*. SEQ2001 Project, Regional Planning Advisory Group, Department of Housing Local Government and Planning, Brisbane.

RPAG (1994). *The Regional Framework for Growth Management for South East Queensland*. Regional Planning Advisory Group, Department of Housing Local Government and Planning, Brisbane.

RRU (1998). *SEQ2001: Institutional and Implementation Arrangements Review – Discussion Paper*. SEQ2001 Regional Resource Unit, Department of Communications and Information Local Government and Planning.

SAA/SNZ HB66 (1995). *Quality Assurance Explained*. Standards Australia, Homebush, NSW.

Saunders, I. W., & Preston, A. P. (1994). *A Model and Research Agenda for Total Quality Management*. Australian Centre in Strategic Management, QUT, Brisbane.

Silverman, D. (1970). *The Theory of Organizations: A Sociological Framework*. Heineman, London.

Simpson, R. (1995). Sustainable development issues for Brisbane and the South East Queensland. Region. *Pacific Rim Council on Urban Development Conference papers*. Brisbane, Australian Housing and Urban Research Institute, Brisbane.

SAA (1992). *HB35 Stepping Stones*. Standards Association of Australia with J. Trelfall, Strathfield, NSW.

Stebbing, L. (1994). *Quality Management in the Service Industry*. Ellis-Horwood, Chichester, England.

Steeples, M.. M. (1993). *The Corporate Guide to the Malcolm Baldrige National Quality Awards* (2nd ed.). Business One, Irwin, Homewood, Illinois.

Stilwell, F. J. B. (1992). *Understanding Cities and Regions: Spatial Political Economy* (Vol. 33, pp. 56–58). Pluto Press, Leichhardt.

Stilwell, F. J. B. (1993). *Economic Inequality – Who Gets What in Australia*. Pluto Press, Sydney.

Stimson, R. J., Minnery, J., Kabamba, A., & Moon, B. (1996). *Sun Belt' Migration Decisions: A Study of the Gold Coast*. Canberra: Bureau of Immigration Multicultural and Population Research, AGPS.

Stimson, R. J. (1994). An Evaluation of the South East Queensland 2001 Study. *Queensland Economic Forecasts and Business Review, 3*(1), 47–60.

Stimson, R. J., McGovern, M., & Daly, M. T. (1994). *Cairns Region Tourism Strategy – Position Paper No. 10*: Tourism Funding and Investment, Australian Housing and Urban Research Institute, Queensland University of Technology, Brisbane.

Stringer, J. (1967). Operational Research for 'multi-organizations', *Operational Research Quarterly, 18*, 105–120.

Sudjic, D. J. (1994). The Metropolis – Present and Future. *Metropolis Now – Getting it Right Conference papers* (pp. 103–104). Brisbane Development Association.

Tiesdell, S. (1995). Tensions between re-vitalization and conservation – Nottingham's Lace Market. *Cities, 12*(4), 231–241.

Werna, E. (1995). The Management of urban development, or the development of urban management? Problems and premises of an elusive concept. *Cities, 12*(5), 353–359.

Whalley, D. L. (1983). *Approaches to Locational Conflict Analysis: An Application to Housing Rehabilitation in Minneapolis*. Ph.D. Thesis, University of Iowa, University Microfilms International, Ann Arbor, Michigan: 2.

Wyeth, E. D. F. (1994). *Quality in Urban Development. PRCUD '94 Conference papers*. Pacific Rim Council on Urban Development, Taipeh, ROC.

Wyeth, E. D. F. (1995). Quality Management in Urban Development. *Discourse '95*. Research Concentration in Design and Construction Studies, Queensland University of Technology, Brisbane.

Wyeth, E. D. F. (1997). Quality Leadership for Entities Involved in Decision-Making Processes in Urban Development. *Fourth National Research Conference on Quality Management Papers*. University of Technology Sydney/Royal Melbourne Institute of Technology.

Wyeth, E. D. F. (1998). *Quality Management for Urban Development: Potential Benefits of Introducing Quality Concepts into the Management of Activities such as the SEQ2001 Regional Growth Management Project*. Master of Applied Science (Research) thesis, Queensland University of Technology, Brisbane (unpublished).

Wyeth, E. D. F., Minnery, J., & Preston, A. (2000). Application of Quality Management Criteria to Regional Growth Management: Lessons from South East Queensland. *Cities, 17*(2), 111–121.

PART II

PARTICIPATION, PARTNERSHIPS AND RENEWAL

8.   AGAINST HARBOR RECLAMATION IN HONG KONG: LESSON OF SUCCESS

Chi Wing Ho

ABSTRACT

While the urban fabric of Hong Kong may not be the most attractive, few would disagree that Hong Kong has one of the most spectacular natural harbor and mountain settings. Since Hong Kong's founding in the 1800s, successive harbor reclamation has taken place to meet the growing needs of the city and by the 1980s almost one third of the original Victoria Harbor was already reclaimed. Yet in another move to increase land supply to meet urban needs and financial returns, the then Colonial Government had proposed to launch several major harbor reclamation projects which, if implemented, would reduce the harbor to a river. This raised serious concerns among the normally passive community. Suddenly, various voluntary concern groups began to express their dissatisfaction through various mediums and to stop what could only be termed excessive harbor reclamation. For the first time in its history, this represents a major success for advocacy planning and community action in Hong Kong, a place more renowned for its laissez faire economic policy and community apathy. This chapter analyzes the political culture of Hong Kong for planning and urban development and reviews the current planning system and the role of community planning in Hong Kong. The Hong Kong Government's plans for 'extensive' harbor reclamation and the issues for and against reclamation are discussed, and the chapter

International Urban Planning Settings: Lessons of Success, Volume 12, pages 233–258.
2001 by Elsevier Science Ltd.
ISBN: 0-7623-0695-5

presents the advocacy planning efforts and community actions against the Government's proposal, which eventually led to the reduction of the Government's reclamation plans. Gains from this lesson of success and the future planning direction for Hong Kong are discussed in light of its objective to enhance its urban competitiveness to rank among other world cities such as New York, London and Tokyo.

INTRODUCTION

The "image" of a city is comprised of its natural setting and building and infrastructures. While the built form of Hong Kong may not be the most beautiful, few would disagree that Hong Kong has one of the most spectacular natural harbor and mountain settings (Victoria Harbor and Peak) among major world cities. Since Hong Kong's founding in the 1800s, the success of Hong Kong has been closely tied to its trading and financial activities around the waterfront of Victoria Harbor. However, from the 1800s, successive harbor reclamation has taken place to meet the growing needs of the city and by the 1980s almost one third of the original Victoria Harbor was already reclaimed. Yet in another move to increase land supply to meet urban needs and financial returns, the then Colonial Government had proposed to launch several major harbor reclamation projects which, if implemented, would seriously undermine the natural setting of Hong Kong.

This raised serious concerns among the normally passive community. Suddenly, various voluntary concern groups began to express their dissatisfaction through channeled objections, alternative proposals, public signature campaigns, news and television coverage and even legislation to put a stop to what could only be termed "excessive harbor reclamation". Yet the Administration of the Hong Kong Special Administrative Region (HKSAR) would not give in, even after the change of government in 1997. Further actions were launched and the Government's "excessive" harbor reclamation plans were given hundreds of formal objections and the Legislative Council refused to approve funding for even the initial site investigations. After finding it impossible to advance their original plans, the Government suddenly yielded to public pressure and announced much-reduced reclamation plans in the middle of 1999.

For the first time in Hong Kong's history, this represents a major success for advocacy planning and community action in Hong Kong, a place more renowned for its laissez faire economic policy and community apathy. This chapter analyzes the events and reasons for the Government's position and the public reactions. It studies the theoretical workings of advocacy planning in the political and social settings of Hong Kong and the community's search for an ideal urban form, which could enhance the urban competitiveness of Hong Kong as a world city in the next century.

POLITICAL CULTURE FOR PLANNING IN HONG KONG

To appreciate the interrelationship of planning and development in Hong Kong, it is first necessary to understand the fundamentals of the political interest, economic and community values in the city state (Castells, 1988; Ho, 1992). These provide interesting comparisons to the planning and decision-making system in the United States and other city-states like Singapore (Lo, 1995, Fulton, 1991; Hall, 1989; Fong, 1988; Geiger, 1975). In Hong Kong, development policies and planning regulations are designed to give maximum freedom to private initiatives in the true tradition of laissez-faire and free enterprise. Developments are evaluated in terms of economic progress and engineering efficiency and not in human dimensions, often accepting damages to the natural environment as a necessary price to be paid. The transformation of Hong Kong from an export center to an international business and financial center has justified the means (Ho, 1991; Taylor, 1989). However, with the growing affluence and aspiration of the people, there is now a demand among certain sectors of the community for greater participation in the improvement of their environment (Yeh, 1993).

The Spirit of the Place

Ever since the famed American economist, Milton Friedman, shot his television documentary *Free to Choose*, praising Hong Kong as the world's most open economy, the bustling urban activities and the glittering commercial complexes have become synonymous with the creed of laissez-faire (Friedman, 1997). Hong Kong's "genius loci" or "spirit of the place" is based on a generally free society. Since the post-World War II recovery, this spirit has served Hong Kong well, but not without its physical and social consequences. Despite its magnificent harbor and mountain setting, the general built environment of Hong Kong is less than desirable. This has prompted the American landscape architect Lawrence Halprin to comment: 'Hong Kong should be, by any world planning criteria, a loathsome slump . . .' (Halprin, 1991). This is not without justification, as the greater part of Hong Kong's urban fabric is of rather low quality in design and maintenance not to mention any cohesive relationship of building and space (Ho, 1992).

Political Decision Making Process

To understand the existing decision-making process in planning and development in Hong Kong (which is based on the past Colonial system), it is
necessary to understand its political administration system in practice.

> Hong Kong's public decision –making is based on the classic British system . . . such as a
> cabinet in the form of the Executive Council, and a parliament in the form of the Legislative
> Council-but there is little democratic basis to these bodies. Even today, elected
> representatives do not govern. They merely act as watchdogs to the executive. As for the
> Executive Councilors, they advise the Governor and therefore are strictly answerable to
> him. He appoints and removes them at his pleasure . . . . The Governor in Council is
> supported by the civil service. Senior civil servants devise policies, but put them to the
> Executive Council for endorsement, and implement them. If legislation is required, the civil
> service drafts a Bill to put to the Legislative Council. If public expenditure is involved, a
> request for funding will be put to the legislature (Loh, 1997: 9).

In 1996, under the last years of the then Colonial Government, Hong Kong had
its first elections where all legislators were returned by either direct or indirect
elections. However, it is important to note that the representatives were not
elected to govern in Hong Kong. Loh further commented (1997: 9):

> People see themselves as bystanders rather than participants in the political processes. They
> feel powerless. It is a hallmark of the paternalistic style of government that such a small
> number of people are so confident about balancing the multitude of interests of this
> community without seeking any meaningful participation by the community.

Planning Consultation System

The Town Planning Ordinance, Chapter 131, first enacted in 1939, governs
Town planning in Hong Kong. The aim of the Ordinance is 'To promote the
health, safety, convenience and general welfare of the community by making
provision for the systematic preparation and approval of plans for the lay-out
of Hong Kong . . .' (HKSAR, 1999). From the Ordinance, it could be
interpreted that planning in Hong Kong is meant to be legalistic, physical and
efficient but not necessarily humane and community-oriented. In Hong Kong,
planning is carried out in a three-tier system comprising the territorial
development strategy, the sub-regional development strategies and the district
plans. It is under the Port and Airport Development Strategy in the territorial
development planning that the Government's proposed 'extensive' harbor
reclamation plans were first approved in 1989. Both the territorial development
and sub-regional development strategies are subject to public consultation
before their approval by the Executive Council and Committee on Planning and

Development, respectively. However, it is only the statutory district plans that are required to be exhibited for formal public comments and objections (Planning Department, 1998).

Advocacy Planning and Community Participation

In the past, strong opposition was raised to the inadequacy of the public consultation process on two grounds. First, important development options, such as the preferred harbor reclamation plans, were made by the government planners and endorsed by the Executive Council or their committees. The public was only "informed" of these final plans as a gesture of public consultation, because they were not presented with any other options nor were they invited to contribute in each stage of the planning process. Secondly, it may be difficult for the public to understand or to react to the technical reports and "economic benefits" presented, but the Government is satisfied with this form of token participation. Some academics (Wong & Pun, 1994) argued that there would only be meaningful participation in the plan-making process in Hong Kong when the public was able to take active part in the process.

However, given the successful laissez-faire economic policy of Hong Kong, which forms the "spirit of the place", there are many who hold the view that the form of community participation and struggles among the vested interest groups in Western countries would be inappropriate and inefficient for the growth of Hong Kong. What, then, is a proper balance between efficiency and meaningful public participation in the planning system in Hong Kong? (Ng, 1997).

Effective Public Participation
The role and advantages for greater public participation in the planning process in Hong Kong are argued by Mok (1988) as follows:

- Improving the quality and quantity of service provisions;
- Effecting changes in the priority of government activities and increase the amount of social investment;
- Widening the circulation of government information to reach the public and speed up the process of administrative decentralization;
- Improving the neighborliness;
- Strengthening the citizen's capacity for self-determination, self-actualization, and problem-solving;

• Producing a number of indigenous community leaders who possess the capacity to undertake the political negotiation.

Arnstein (1969) stated that meaningful citizen participation means citizen power in the form of citizen control, from delegated power to partnership. Placation, consultation and informing will only amount to tokenism. However, citizen participation is sometimes seen as another form of power bargaining as vested interest groups manipulate innocent participants for their strategic gains. Public participation on developments could also be a long drawn process, which often results in compromising rather than an optimum solution (Fulton, 1991). Interested parties must also be competent and well informed to act on issues which are important to their community. Given the general political apathy in Hong Kong, high expectation for effective participation by the general lay public may be difficult to realize.

Community Actions Against Harbor Reclamation
This brings back the search for the appropriate balance between efficiency and citizen control for public participation in planning and development in Hong Kong, given the special political economy of the place. During the Colonial era, the public seldom raised serious voices when they were "informed" of major developments such as the new towns, the relocation of the new international airport and other major harbor reclamation projects. Yet, in another move to increase land supply to meet urban needs and financial returns, the then Colonial Government proposed to launch several major harbor reclamation projects which, if implemented, would reduce the harbor nearly to the width of a river.

However, the Administration had gone too far this time, especially when the general public can witness what the other reclamation sites (such as the ongoing West Kowloon Reclamation Project) has done to Victoria Harbor. Major issues such as the minimum extent of reclamation for the essential infrastructures; the sustainability of the city with high concentration of activities around the Harbor; the development of the rural New Territories versus the Central; and the environmental impact of the proposed "excessive" reclamation were not properly addressed (Ho, 1996).

Suddenly, various voluntary concerned groups began to express their dissatisfaction through channeled objections, alternative proposals, public signature campaigns, news and television coverage and even legislation to put a stop to excessive harbor reclamation. The following section of this paper examines the history and issues on harbor reclamation and the success of community actions to prevent the Government from turning the magnificent Victoria Harbor into a river.

THE "EXCESSIVE" HARBOR RECLAMATION PROPOSAL: A CASE STUDY[1]

History of Harbor Reclamation in Hong Kong

Historically, Hong Kong carried out successive reclamation along its waterfront to meet its social and economic needs, as illustrated in Fig. 1. In the 1970s, a new town development program, which involved extensive acquisition of private agricultural land and large reclamation projects, was launched. The momentum for further economic growth in the 1970s through the 1990s, mainly arising from Hong Kong's close links with China, demanded more land for future development.

Since the 1980s, the Government has undertaken various planning studies, including the Territorial Development Strategy and Review (TDS), the Port & Airport Development Strategy (PADS) (Ng, 1993) and Metroplan. Following these and other studies, the current 'extensive' reclamation program, which

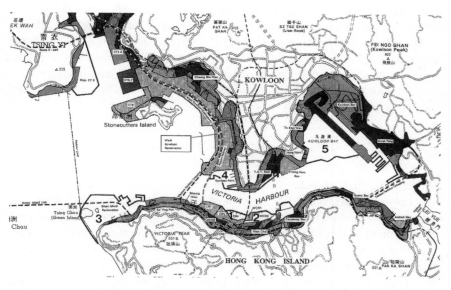

Fig. 1. Historical Reclamation in Victoria Harbor, Hong Kong.

Shaded areas: various phases of harbor reclamation from 1800s to 1993, Planning Department.

* Refer to Table 1 for numbers and names of proposed reclamation projects.

Table 1.   Harbor Reclamation Projects Commenced or Proposed (1995).

Projects	Area (ha.)	Date
Projects Under Construction as of 1998	449.3	1996–97
Proposed Medium and Longer Term Harbor Reclamation Projects:		
(1)* Central Reclamation Phase III	30	end of 2000
(2)* Wanchai Reclamation Phase II	48	1998–2002
(3)* Green Island Development	186	1996–2003
(4)* Kowloon Point Development	48	Feasibility Study 1995
(5)* South East Kowloon Development	300	Feasibility Study 1995
Sub total of proposed reclamation	612	
Total	1,061.3	

* Refer to Figures 1 and 4 for numbers and locations of proposed reclamation projects)

amounts to about 1,062 hectares in the harbor area, was proposed. This is indicated in Table 1 and Fig. 1. From the 1800s to 1994, about 5,400 hectares, around Victoria Harbor and other waterfronts of the Territories were reclaimed. Within the Victoria Harbor itself (between Green Island and Lei Yue Mun), about one third of the original harbor area was already reclaimed by the 1980s. If fully implemented, the current committed and proposed reclamation would further reduce the size of Victoria Harbor to approximately one half of its original size in the 1800s.

Making a Choice

The current harbor reclamation program, which amounts to about 1,100 hectares or approximately 25% of the area of Victoria Harbor in the 1800s, can only be considered excessive, especially when compared to other good port cities around the world like San Francisco, Sydney and Vancouver. This unprecedented action, if fully implemented, will turn Victoria Harbor into a sea channel, with the narrowest point only 860 meters wide. While it is necessary to maintain the economic and urban growth of Hong Kong, which may require limited amounts of harbor reclamation, such needs must be balanced against other important social and environmental factors. These include: aesthetic values, sense of place, natural features and landscape, physical and mental health, level of civic pride, cultural heritage and international prestige.

Government's Key Positions on Reclamation and Alternative Viewpoints

The following summarizes the Government's key positions (G) on the need for the reclamation plan. Against these issues, alternative viewpoints (A) have been expressed by various professionals, academics, environmental bodies and community groups.

To Accommodate Population Growth
G: To accommodate the projected population of 8.1 million by the year 2011.
A: Future population projections are based on assumptions accepted in the Territorial Development Strategy Review (TDSR). Government should present alternatives on growth centered on harbor reclamation versus other urban areas and the New Territories. Their implications should be studied with the view to reducing harbor reclamation.

To Promote Hub Functions
G: Hong Kong is to be the center for financial, business, tourism and professional services for the Pearl River Delta
A: Yes, but how much commercial space is needed and what is the best way to plan for it will require further studies with a view to reducing harbor reclamation . . . policies for various kinds of developments on reclaimed land and optional locations should be studied. To maintain a land bank by reclamation "for timely release" to meet future needs will not justify the "extensive" reclamation as planned.

Restructuring the Metro Area
G: To restructure the obsolete and high density neighborhoods of the Metro Area, to provide new transport links, shortfall in community and recreational facilities, and 'solution spaces' for future urban renewal projects . . .
A: Sound principle, but realization remains to be seen. If sites are sold piecemeal to the highest bidders, it may not provide the "solution spaces" for urban renewal and new projects may even aggravate the pressure; a coordinated policy is needed and the proposed Urban Renewal Authority may be in the right direction. Open spaces provided in the reclaimed areas are too distant to alleviate the congested old neighborhoods and the quality of some of the open spaces are questionable as they are cut off by major roads and flyovers.

New Transport Infrastructure

G: To provide land for the extension of strategic road and rail networks and associated facilities to meet rising demand.

A: Yes, should be limited to essential strategic facilities, and more efficient space design as a good part of the proposed reclamation are taken by proposed roads, utilities and infrastructures ... in the Central Wanchai Project, for example, 44% of the reclaimed land has been planned for roads ... more innovative urban design concepts such as limited car zones for the Central Reclamation Project could be considered.

Clearing Environmental Black Spots

G: Certain proposed reclamation has the potential to eliminate highly polluted 'black spots' in areas where the tidal flows are weak.

A: Effective only to a certain extent in a local context, reclamation to cover up polluted seabed may not be a solution to this environmental problem.

Harbor Reclamation Versus Development in the New Territories

G: Assembly and resumption of large sites in the land-based NT is very expensive and time consuming, especially in comparison to the many easy advantages of reclamation. The Government has identified some 2,000 ha in the New Territories and 1,000 ha through reclamation as potential strategic growth areas ... both suitable land-based sites and reclamation would be required over the long term.

A: The issue of decentralization is complicated. Minimum reclamation should be discussed through new alternatives that could meet strategic growth needs while preserving the quality of the harbor.

Reclamation and the Environment

G: Studies at the strategic and specific project level have been conducted to ensure that potential environmental impacts (water quality, dust, noise and ecological) of reclamation are minimized and appropriate mitigation measures taken where necessary.

A: Environmental impact should not be limited only to quantifiable factors, as there are other important but not easily quantifiable factors, such as aesthetics, traditional values and sense of place and continuity that are equally important to the well being of the community.

Scenic Value of the Harbor

G: The port functions will be shifted westward leaving Victoria Harbor to become a central amenity area with long waterfront promenades and associated squares and new forms of modern architecture on either side.

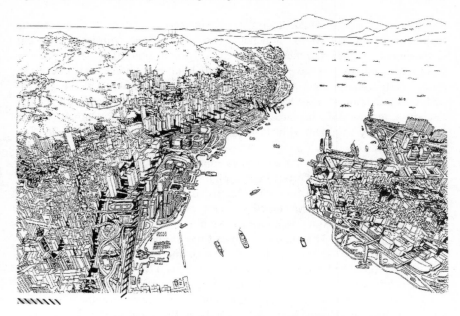

Fig. 2. "Excessive" Harbor Reclamation Proposal by the Government.

A: The key issue here is the desire to preserve the original shape and size of the harbor, our natural asset and cultural heritage which once destroyed is irreversible; harbor amenities are good but could be designed in a form that respects the old harbor. Different approaches to recognize the harbor, as the focus of life in Hong Kong, are essential. Ship captains have also expressed doubt over the suitability of the western harbor for anchoring.

It was with these arguments that the Government supported its initial "excessive" reclamation plans prepared by an engineering-led consultancy team. The plans are illustrated in Fig. 2.

COMMUNITY ACTIONS AGAINST HARBOR RECLAMATION

The Community's Initial Response

In 1995–1996, the Administration was eager to put forth their proposed Harbor reclamation strategy as part of the "Rose Garden" vision plan in the lead up to the 1997 hand over to China. A number of exhibitions and consultation sessions with various groups were launched. The public was "informed" of the Government's grandiose scheme prepared by the consultants but no alternatives were presented nor was the public consulted about their choices. This began to raise a certain alarm among selected groups in the community as the general public could now witness how Victoria Harbor was being eaten up by the already ongoing 340 hectares massive West Kowloon Reclamation (the feasibility study commenced in 1990 and reclamation completed by 1996 (See Fig. 1).

Leading the fight were certain professional and environmental groups who were more aware of the Government's plan. Under the then colonial rule, the Administration's position remained defensive and the groups were asked to present alternatives for their objections. This led to the first advocacy planning study by the Hong Kong Institute of Architects under "Alternative Harbor Reclamation Study."[2] The main objective of the Study was to review the issues on the need for the "excessive" harbor reclamation, the Institute's position on the various proposed harbor reclamation projects (Table 1, Fig. 1), and to illustrate urban design options for minimum reclamation in the Central Wan Chai Project while retaining the Government's expected development potential gains. An alternative considered in the Study is illustrated in Fig. 3. The main criteria for the design options include:

• Integrated multi-level circulation systems;
• Efficient service roads to be partly absorbed into the projects;
• Compact but qualitative and meaningful open space;
• Better urban form to identify the character of an area;
• More intensive developments in the CBD where justified;
• Government sales of sites based on design merits as well as price.

Save the Harbor Campaign and the Protection of the Harbor Bill

By this time, the Government's proposed harbor reclamation plans aroused strong awareness among the general public and special interest groups, including shippers, ferry operators, fishermen, environmentalists, planners, architects, other professional groups and political parties. Wide coverage and interest on the issue appeared in the press, radio and television. Leading the campaign was a civic group called the Society for Protection of the Harbor (SPOH) chaired by a vocal lawyer. The Society launched a public campaign with the logo "Stop Reclamation, Save Our Harbor" (Fig. 4). The public campaign collected over 100,000 signatures opposing the reclamation (Chu, 1999).

On March 13, 1996, the Legislative Council passed a unanimous motion condemning the reclamation:

> That this Council recognizes, and urges the Government to recognize, that Victoria Harbor is a unique and irreplaceable public asset, that excessive depletion of the harbor is irreversibly damaging to both the natural and human environment of Hong Kong, and that all Hong Kong people have a rightful interest in the harbor; and this Council further urges the Government to withdraw its grossly excessive plans for reclamation in the harbor and to take urgent measures instead to protect and to preserve the harbor and to ensure that further development in the harbor, if any, will be strictly limited, openly planned, and accountably carried out.

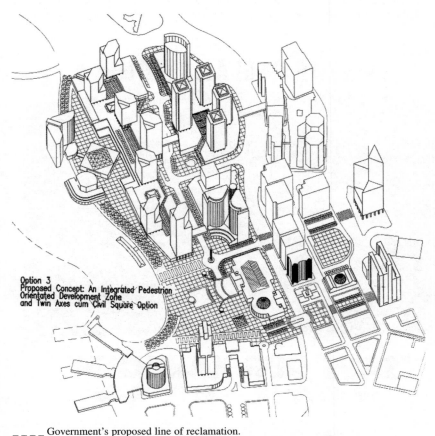

Option 3
Proposed Concept: An Integrated Pedestrian
Orientated Development Zone
and Twin Axes cum Civil Square Option

_ _ _ _ Government's proposed line of reclamation.

Fig. 3. Alternative Urban Design Proposals by the HKIA.

However, during this process, the Government did not concede in its proposal or prepare to entertain alternatives.

> It raises the question: what is the purpose of public consultation if Government neither heeds public views nor even the opinion of the Legislative Council? In the circumstances, the only lawful avenue left to Hong Kong people to stop reclamation is by new legislation (Chu, 1997: 52).

From this experience, it is clear that the Government's public consultation process is not meaningful. Chu further commented:

> It is too much for the Government to expect the ordinary public to have the time to read the bulky papers, the ability to understand the complex issues and the expertise to comment on them. Besides, the consultation process is usually carried out too late: only when

Fig. 4. Poster for Save Our Harbor Campaign.
(Refer to Table 1 for names of proposed reclamation projects).

Government has already decided on the proposals and plans are in an advanced state of preparation. Government's approach has been to convince the public of its proposal without giving genuine alternatives (Chu, 1997: 54).

In early 1996, the first Protection of the Harbor Bill was submitted as a Private Members Bill but was rejected because of technical grounds. The second Protection of the Harbor Bill was reintroduced in November 1996 and was eventually adopted as an Ordinance on June 30, 1997. Section 3 of the Bill provides that:

(1) The Harbor is to be protected and preserved as a special public asset and a natural heritage of Hong Kong people, and for that purpose there shall be a presumption against reclamation in the harbor.
(2) All public officers and public bodies shall have regard to the principle stated in subscription (1) for guidance in the exercise of any powers vested in them (HKSAR, 1997).

Government's First Response and a Hundred Flowers Bloom

After the excitement of the hand over in July 1997, the new Government of the Hong Kong Special Administrative Region quietly published a draft Central District (Extension) Outline Zoning Plan No. S/H 24/1 in May 1998, with no material change in the extent of the reclamation in the Central Wan Chai Area as originally proposed (Fig. 2). By showing the reclamation plan in sections, the information supplied by the Government was misleading as it gave the impression that there was an apparent decrease in the overall reclaimed area. During the two months exhibition period of the draft plan for public inspection, a number of professional bodies including the Hong Kong Institute of Planners, the Hong Kong Institute of Architects, the Hong Kong Institute of Engineers, the Hong Kong Institute of Landscape Architects, the Hong Kong Institute of Surveyors as well as the various green groups, political parties, developers and the business community and concerned individuals, submitted objections to the newly released Central District (Extension) Outline Zoning Plan as part of the consultation process.

To carry the notion one step further, several interested groups went to the extent of preparing alternative professional schemes at great expense for the consideration by the Government in their objections. These included the Alternative Central District (Extension) Reclamation Proposal, Study 2 by the Hong Kong Institute of Architects (HKIA, 1998), Central Wan Chai Reclamation Alternative Scheme by the CWR Study Group (CWRSG, 1998), and a Hong Kong Central Waterfront Development Concept Plan prepared by the American architects Skidmore Owings & Merrill International under the sponsorship of a major local developer (SOM, 1998). An exhibition of all these proposals drew large crowds and the public was exposed to more imaginative concepts based on different priorities other than economic and engineering efficiency.

A Statement to the Executive Council

In December 1998, the author, along with other pressure groups, was invited to a meeting with members of the Executive Council and the following statement was presented by the author:

> In his Address to the Legislative Council on 7 October, 1998, the Chief Executive of the Hong Kong Special Administrative Region (HKSAR) Tung Chee Hwa has said: 'The Government will step up its efforts to protect the environment to enable our people to enjoy a better and healthier quality of life. It will also help enhance our reputation as a pleasant destination for tourists and for international business travelers, and will make Hong Kong a more attractive place for highly-skilled professionals to live in . . . .' In the same Address on Tourism, he also said: '. . . Tourists come here for the same reason they go to Paris, to Istanbul or to Rio de Janeiro – there is nowhere else like it . . . .' While on 9 December, 1998, in a speech to the Hong Kong Association of Banks, the Chief Executive Tung Chee Wah talked about a 'mismatch between the understanding of our professional planners . . . and the views that many in the community have about what sort of development is acceptable.

The Chief Executive's objectives of a better physical environment and quality of life can be fulfilled by the proper planning and development of the strategic Central Wan Chai Reclamation Project (as well as the Kowloon Point and Kowloon Bay); that is, to make Hong Kong a beautiful world city to rank among New York, London, Paris and Rio de Janeiro and to compete with other city states like Singapore, which has consistently ranked top as an "attractive place for foreign investment and highly skilled professionals to live in." To achieve this competitive edge, one of the top priorities for Hong Kong is to preserve our natural heritage-Victoria Harbor, to foster a sense of Place for the Central Area and to design our unique harbor front as cultural and recreational amenity areas.

The planning of the Central Wan Chai Reclamation Project CWRP (between Central Reclamation Phase I and the Convention Center Extension plus Causeway Bay) must meet the following criteria:

(1) *To protect Victoria Harbor as a place of public interest for the people of Hong Kong:* the world famous Victoria Harbor, with Victoria Peak as the backdrop, forms an everlasting image of Hong Kong for tourists, business visitors and locals alike. It is both functionally and environmentally essential for the welfare of the community. The Government's proposed

excessive reclamation schemes will be detrimental to the quality of life in Hong Kong

(2) *To provide for human needs*: the development of the Central Wan Chai Reclamation Project goes beyond the basic engineering and economic needs because it is the last strategic location that could provide a central place for the arts, recreation, culture and entertainment so that Hong Kong can compare with the theatre districts of London, the Central Park of New York. We need to provide a better environment for the enjoyment of the people.

(3) *To generate an urban design vision of Hong Kong for the 21st century*: rather then to follow the past conventional two dimensional land use and engineering planning approach, the irreplaceable CWRP will provide tremendous opportunities to redesign Hong Kong as a City of the 21st Century with exciting urban forms and spaces, such as waterfront civic squares, tree lined promenades, cultural and civic complexes, boulevards, architectural interests and activity nodes. The Plan for the CWRP must relate to the natural and important features of Hong Kong. We need an urban design vision and policy support for its implementation so as to strengthen our position as Asia's leading international center for tourism and financial services.

Due to a lack of proper public consultation in the past, it appears that much valuable time; resources and efforts have been spent on the Central Wan Chai Reclamation Project without any clear-cut consensus.

There are two ways to go forward:

(1) *To start afresh*: that is, to redesign the entire project with greater openness, perhaps through an open or invited competition, given the necessary criteria, resources and constraints; or

(2) *To drastically modify the existing Government plan*: that is, to drastically reduce the excessive reclamation and to take into account some acceptable criteria under the guidance of a neutral steering group. The Government must provide genuine alternatives for the community to evaluate.

Government's Retreat

Under the existing Town Planning Ordinance, the appointed Town Planning Board has to give preliminary consideration of objections by any persons affected by the draft plan so exhibited within the said period of two months. The Town Planning Board received a total of 76 objections to the Draft Central District (Extension) OZP. The majority of the objectors considered the extent of the proposed reclamation too excessive. Many considered the land use proposal violated the principle of "presumption against reclamation" in the Protection of the Harbor Ordinance and that it should be reduced to accommodate the strategic transport links.

After preliminary consideration, the Board was prepared to re-consider the extent and the land uses of the reclamation. It was accepted that the Government would undertake further studies to determine the minimum practical reclamation option while the Board would proceed to hear the objections. (TPB, 1999). Fourteen objectors made further written submissions for the Board's consideration including four objectors who have presented new or revised schemes in their further submissions. The main points raised in the further written submissions included: (a) misinterpretation of the Protection of the Harbor Ordinance; (b) provision of commercial land based on Office Land Development Strategy is not justified; and (c) narrowing of the harbor is not acceptable. In early 1999, several sessions for collective hearing for the professional bodies, political parties, environmental groups, and individuals and organizations were held by the Town Planning Board.

A Major Change in Policy and a Victory for the Community

Having considered the objectors' further submissions and the comments of the relevant departments, the Government has finally accepted the view that the draft plan should be amended to partially meet the objections based on the reduced reclamation extent. The new reclamation limit will be significantly reduced from 38 ha to about 23 ha to meet the essential transport infrastructure, re-provide the affected waterfront facilities and accommodate the waterfront promenade and suitable sites for the necessary civic and leisure amenities, which would enhance the central harbor as a special public asset and natural heritage.

In June 1999, in an almost unexpected 180-degree turn in position, the Government issued a statement on the Vision & Goals for Victoria Harbor 'to make Victoria Harbor attractive, vibrant, accessible and symbolic of Hong Kong – a harbor for the people and a harbor of life.' (TPB, 1999: 1). The position was made official, when in July 1999 the Government released the amended Draft Central District (Extension) Outline Zoning Plan S/H24/1 showing a reduction of 14.67 ha in the critical waterfront reclamation and a major waterfront promenade in lieu of the original commercial developments. While significant work on the implementation of the Plan remains to be followed, it represents a great lesson of success for the Hong Kong community, which has fought hard for this issue for the last five years. For the first time in its history, this revised plan represents a major success for advocacy planning and community actions in Hong Kong, a place more renowned in the past for its laissez faire economic policy and community apathy.

PARTNERSHIP IN MAKING HONG KONG A WORLD CITY

The "Against the Harbor Reclamation" campaign over the past five years resulted in a major reversal of planning policy by the Government. It is a significant milestone in the planning process and political history for the Special Administrative Region after the hand over in 1997. Several planning issues and policy changes that the community as a whole has gained can be observed.

Planning for Growth and Efficiency vs. Quality and Humanity

In the past, urban development and reclamation were evaluated in terms of economic growth, revenues generated and engineering efficiency and not in human dimensions, often accepting damages to the natural environment as a necessary price to be paid. It was not long ago that Government officials' main concern over harbor reclamation was the cost efficient of the sea walls and the building up of a land bank for timely disposal for maximum returns. The various harbor reclamation feasibility studies/master plans were led by engineering consultancy firms and up to 44% of the proposed land uses were taken up by roads, which often resulted in non-integrated parcels for development.

However, the growing affluence and the presence of a large educated middle class in Hong Kong have caused fundamental changes in community values towards growth and efficiency. Equally important are concerns over environmental protection, cultural and leisure amenities, conservation and quality of the built environment and participation in the planning process. Although mainly led by professionals and the green groups, these attitudes were fully manifested throughout the "Against Harbor Reclamation" campaign. For instance, the Protection of the Harbor Bill was drafted to prevent indiscriminate reclamation and to require the Planning Department to resort to reclamation only when it is necessary, that is, for building essential infrastructural facilities, and not commercial uses for profits (Chu, 1997). In one of the proposed alternatives, the "Hong Kong Central Waterfront Development Concept Plan" (SOM, 1998), the entire harbor front was recommended for recreational uses and cultural amenities.

This led to the Government's statement on the Vision & Goals for Victoria Harbor 'to make Victoria Harbor attractive, vibrant, accessible and symbolic of Hong Kong – a harbor for the people and a harbor of life' (TPB, 1999: 1). The battle for a more humane environment for the people and not traffic and engineering dominated proposals, however, remains to be resolved in the detailed planning and implementation stage.

Certainty vs. Public Participation

In Hong Kong, development policies and planning regulations are designed to give maximum freedom to private initiative in the true tradition of laissez-faire and free enterprise. For example, Hong Kong operates under a flexible system of statutory plans and planning application where most developments in the urban areas are seen as of rights. In the case of a planning application for a change of use or an increase in plot ratio, a premium to reflect the increase in land values is payable upon any successful application.

When the rules are straightforward and well understood, it eliminates all uncertainty and reduces the time required for planning approval. This will enhance land values, and, in turn, lower development costs. These "certainties" enable developers to pay very high prices for their land; coupled with a strong market, property developments in Hong Kong are one of the most efficient, profitable, and spectacular among world cities (that is, until the 1997/99 Asian financial crisis), but not without consequence on public interest and environmental quality. Nevertheless, the majority of the development and design community supports the current system. Wan further stated that

> Certainty relies on the simplicity of the planning system, it will be understandable by most people, and there will be few areas of ambiguity. Equally important is that the system will not be radically changed. If the system has to be changed, the changes will have to be evolutionary rather than revolutionary. The changes must be in the direction of removing uncertainty. The changes must have to occur at the right time (JHKIP, 1997: 12).

This leads to the question of the degree to which public participation at the territorial, sub-regional and district planning levels should be conducted. Participation in Hong Kong should be efficient and not become a political issue between vested interest groups, as often is the case in cities in North America.

The degree of public participation in the planning process could vary from complete citizen control to the act of 'informing' (Arnstein, 1969). Others (Skeffington, 1969) view meaningful public participation in the land use planning process as the act of sharing in the formulation of the policies and proposal through the giving of information by the planning authority and of an opportunity for the public to comment on that information. It is argued here that the degree of public participation in Hong Kong should be a balance between the "spirit of the place" and an efficient and effective system which allows the public to take an active part in the plan-making and approval process without jeopardizing the "certainty" and "flexibility" of the current planning system. Throughout the "Against Harbor Reclamation" campaign, the professionals, green groups, political parties with the endorsement of the middle class and the general public mainly led the process. Future participation should aim at widening its base but avoid becoming a political game of manipulation.

Planning for the People in Hong Kong?

Mainly as a result of the "Against Harbor Reclamation" campaign and the leadership of an enlightened new Secretary of Planning, Lands and Environment, the Planning Department has introduced major changes in the public consultation process. For example, in 1999, the Department conducted fourteen public forums (mostly attended by professionals) and eight exhibitions (for the general public) on various planning studies. Fifteen outreach programs at the high school level were also conducted. The feedbacks were analyzed to gauge public opinion from a wider base in the formulation of development plans and proposals.

In addition, the Planning Department and the Town Planning Board has formulated a vision statement for the Harbor and waterfront areas to be "a Harbor for the people and a harbor of life". A "Harbor and Waterfront Plan" was commissioned to translate the visions and goals into feasible plans. The Office of the Secretary of Planning, Lands and Environment is also planning to launch an international urban design and development competition for development proposals for a world class arts, cultural and entertainment center in West Kowloon Reclamation (Fig. 1).

'We believe that planning is for the people and therefore we need to listen to the views and ideas of the public', declared Bosco Fung, Director of Planning, who highlighted four major changes in the planning consultation process including: First, the need to start consultation as early as possible. Second, a wider use of open forums to consult the public. 'Thirdly, community consensus can only be built up when we share a common understanding of the issue. We have not only made consultation materials easily comprehensible but also distribute them through a variety of media such as the internet and videos' Fung said, and 'Finally, we have taken a more proactive approach to meet the general public, representative bodies, interest groups, stakeholders and professionals to solicit their views on various planning studies and development proposals' (PD, 1999: 1).

Such major change in policy and approach in the planning consultation process is hardly conceivable under the executive-led Government and the community is now led to believe that a partnership has been fostered in making Hong Kong a world city of the new century.

Partnership in Making Hong Kong a World City

A World Class City for Hong Kong?

While the laissez-faire policy might have served the economy of Hong Kong well, the minimum intervention approach in planning needs to be reexamined if Hong Kong is to improve its competitiveness in the quality of life, housing, environmental quality and tourist attractions so as to stay competitive with other world cities. In his 1999 Policy Address, the Chief Executive of the Hong Kong Special Administrative Region said:

> I firmly believe that Hong Kong should become the most cosmopolitan city in Asia, enjoying a status comparable to that of New York in North America and London in Europe. Both New York and London are cosmopolitan cities with great depth of talent in culture, technology and education. They are vibrant economies and possess the financial strength to serve the region and the world at large in areas such as finance, trade, tourism, information industry and transport, while being home to numerous multi-national enterprises. Hong Kong already possesses many of the key features common to New York and London . . . . On the other hand, we must admit that Hong Kong lags behind other international world class cities in many respects, in particular human capital and living environment[3] (HSARG, 1999: 15–16).

The International and Urban Competitiveness of Hong Kong

This begs the question as to how competitive is Hong Kong when compared to other world-class cities. Currently, Hong Kong is lagging behind in overall urban quality when compared with other world cities such as Paris, New York, London. In 1999, the Geneva-based World Economic Forum had just dropped Hong Kong from second place in 1998 to third place in its annual ranking of the most competitive economies. The report rated Hong Kong only 21st in micro-economic competitiveness and the index of innovation placed Hong Kong in 24th place behind Taiwan (17th) and Singapore (14th), and much lower on the quality of life and housing, despite Hong Kong commanding the most expensive property prices in the world.

Models of urban competitiveness have included ten factors to rate the competitiveness of metropolitan areas: (a) cost of living, (b) local labor, (c) housing, (d) crime, (e) health care, (f) transportation, (g) education, (h) the arts, (i) recreation, and (j) climate. Of all these factors, housing, transportation, recreation, infrastructure, built environment, real estate prices and more important, their inter-relationship, certainly have something to do with the quality of life in cities.

In a recent attempt by Rondinelli and Vastag (1998) to measure the international competitiveness of metropolitan areas using the indicators of the Metropolitan International Competitiveness Assessment Model (MICAM), 11 cities from three continents were selected, including New York, San Francisco, Seoul, Beijing, Shanghai, Bangkok, Tokyo, Hong Kong, Singapore, London, and Frankfurt.

In 1994, Hong Kong was ranked 1st in *Fortune Magazine*'s ratings (Saporito & Martin, 1994), and in 1995 it was ranked 6th. In this report, Hong Kong was placed 5th among the 11 major metropolitan areas. Although Hong Kong is seen as being strong on national competitiveness and openness of its trade regime, its urban conditions are not as competitive as those of many North American and European cities, with Hong Kong being seen as moderately weak in terms of skilled labor and research cooperation between companies and universities. The city state still ranked relatively low on trade related infrastructure and transportation and is one of the most expansive cities in the world in which to do business because of its high rental costs and high cost of living. Environmental conditions are also poor compared to other world cities in Europe and North America.

Partnership in Making Hong Kong a World Class City
In a society which takes pride in its successful laissez-faire economic policy under an executive-led Government, major changes in the direction of partnership and proactive involvement in urban design require a different policy and structural approach. The economic, social as well as physical meaning of urban design in Hong Kong in relationship to its standing as a world city will have to be re-examined. This will lead to a broader meaning of urban design in Hong Kong such that it could gain wider support from a greater part of the community. The following components will be necessary in the new partnership if Hong Kong were to improve its urban competitiveness and built environment so as to be comparable to other world cities:

• Policy support from the Chief Executive Officer and Executive Council;
• The roles of the political parties, Legislative Council, Urban Council and District Boards;
• Greater concern among related professionals and institutes;
• Wider community participation;
• A more positive interest from the development community;
• Redefining the economic, social and physical meaning and implication of urban design for greater community acceptance.

The issue of minimum harbor reclamation in Victoria Harbor is a major one that concerns every citizen of the city-state. The success of the "Against Harbor Reclamation" led to the Administration's subsequent reversal in position and has opened up a new chapter in the history of public consultation. It has started the beginning of a new partnership to enhance the quality of life in Hong Kong. As Hong Kong and other major Asian capital cities are attempting to recover from their current recession and looking towards the status of a world city among New York, London and Tokyo, their urban planning model and achievements will be among the decisive factors.

NOTES

1. The case study is adapted from the "Study of Alternative Minimum Harbor Reclamation Strategies" proposed by the Hong Kong Institute of Architects, 1996 in which the author was the Planning Consultant.
2. The author was commissioned as the Planning Consultant for the Study in 1996–1997.
3. The 1999 Policy Address on 6 October by the Chief Executive of the Hong Kong Special Administrative Region, the Honorable Mr. Tung Chee Hwa.

REFERENCES

Arnstein, S. R. (1969). A Ladder of Citizenship Participation. *Journal of American Institute of Planners, 8*(3).
Castells, M. et al. (1988). *Economic Development and Housing Policy in the Asian Pacific Rim: A Comparative Study of Hong Kong, Singapore, and Shenzhen Special Economic Zone*, Monograph 37, Institute of Urban and Regional Development, University of California, Berkeley.
Central Wanchai Reclamation Study Group (1998). *Central-wanchai Reclamation Alternative Scheme*. Central Wanchai Reclamation Study Group, Hong Kong.
Chu, W. K. S. (1997). Strategic Planning and Harbor Reclamation. *Journal of the Hong Kong Institute of Architects, 9*(2nd Quarter), 52–55.
Chu, W. K. S. (1999). Is Harbor Reclamation Really Necessary. *Journal of the Hong Kong Institute of Architects, 20*(2nd Quarter), 50–55.
Chui, E. W. T., & Ng, M. K. (1999). From Colony to SAR: Advocacy Planning in the Executive-led Policy of Hong Kong. *The Asian Journal of Public Administration, 20* (December), 173–202.
Fong, P. E. (1988). The Distinctive Features of Two City-state's Development: Hong Kong and Singapore. In: P. Berger & H. Hsia (Eds), *In Search of an East Asian Studies Development Model* (pp. 220–238). New Brunswick: Transaction.
Friedman, J. (1997). *World City Futures: The Role of Urban and Regional Policies in the Asia-Pacific Region*. Occasional Paper No. 56, Hong Kong Institute of Asian-Pacific Studies, Hong Kong.
Fulton, W. (1991). *Guide to California Planning*. Solano Press, Point Arena, Ca.

Geiger, T., & Geiger, F. (1975). *The Development Progress of Hong Kong and Singapore.* Macmillan, Hong Kong.

Hall, P. (1989). The Turbulent Eighth Decade: Challenges in American City Planning. *Journal of American Planning Association, 55*(3), 275–282.

Halprin, L. (1991). The Collective Perception of Cities. In: L. Taylor (Ed.), *Urban Open Spaces.* London: Cooper Hewitt Museum.

Ho, C. W. (1992). *Planning Policies & Real Estate Developments: Hong Kong, Singapore and U.S. West Coast Cities.* Working Paper 576, Institute of Urban and Regional Development, University of California, Berkeley.

Ho, C. W. (1992). Comparing the Qualities of the Urban Environment in Hong Kong and Selected Cities. *Planning and Development* (JHKIP), *8*(2), 31–39.

Ho, C. W. (1996). *A Response to Territorial Development Strategy Review 96: the Option for a Minimum Harbor Reclamation and a Balanced NT Development Pattern.* Society for Protection of Harbor, Hong Kong.

Ho, Y. P., & Lin, T. B. (1991). Hong Kong Structural Adjustment in a Free-trade, Free Market Economy. In: H. Patrick & L. Meissner (Eds), *Pacific Basin Industries in Distress: Structural Adjustment and Trade Policy in the Nine Industrialized Economies* (pp. 257–310). New York: Columbia University Press.

Hong Kong Government (1997). *Protection of the Harbor Bill.* Government Printer, Hong Kong.

Hong Kong Institute of Architects (1998). *Alternative Central District (Extension) Reclamation Proposal Study 2.* Hong Kong Institute of Architects, Hong Kong.

Hong Kong SAR (1999). *Town Planning Ordinance.* Government Printer, Hong Kong.

Lo, F., & Yeung, Y. M. (1995). *Emerging World Cities in Pacific Asia.* United Nations University Press, Tokyo.

Loh, C. K. W. (1997). Efficiency vs. Public Participation in our Planning System. *Planning and Development* (JHKIP), *13*(1), 9–11.

Mok, H. T. K. (1988). Citizen Participation in Hong Kong Planning. *Planning and Development* (JHKIP), *4*(1), 27–33.

Ng, M. K. (1997). Beyond the Efficiency vs. Public Participation Debate: Implications for Land Use Planning System in Hong Kong. *Planning and Development* (JHKIP), *13*(1), 5–8.

Ng, M. K. (1993). A Case Study of the Port and Airport Development Strategy (PADS) in Hong Kong. *American Institute of Certified Planners' Casebook 7.* American Planning Association.

Planning Department (1998). *Annual Report.* Planning Department, Hong Kong.

Planning Department (1998–99). Various *Newsletters.* Planning Department, Hong Kong.

Planning Department (1998). *Urban Design Guidelines for Hong Kong* (unpublished). Planning Department, Hong Kong.

Rondinelli, D. A., & Vastag, G. (1998). Urban Economic Growth in the 21st Century: Assessing the International Competitiveness of Metropolitian Areas. In: R. E. Billsborrow (Ed.), *Migration, Urbanization and Development: New Directions and Issues* (pp. 469–514). Norwell, MA: Kluwer.

Saporito, B., & Martin, J. (1994). The world's best cities for business. *Fortune, 130*(10), 112–124.

Skeffington, A. M. (1969). *People and Planning: Report of the Committee on Public Participation in Planning.* HMSO London, and p. 1.

Skidmore Owings & Merrill International (1998). *Hong Kong Central Waterfront Development Concept Plan.* Hong Kong: Swire Properties Ltd.

Taylor, B., & Kwok, R. Y. W. (1989). From Export Center to World City: Planning for the Transformation of Hong Kong. *Journal of the American Planning Association*, *55*(3), 309–322.

Town Planning Board and Design Division (1999). Various Town Planning Board papers (unpublished). Hong Kong: Planning Department.

Wan, M. Y. (1997). Planning System in Hong Kong: Efficiency vs. Public Participation. *Planning and Development* (JHKIP), *13*(1), 12–14.

Wong, J., & Pun, H. C. (1994). *A Study of the Planning Law of Hong Kong and Role of Public Participation in Land Use Planning*. Working Paper Series no. WP94012. Business Research Center, School of Business, Baptist College.

Yeh, A. G. O. (1993). Urban Development of Hong Kong in the 21st Century: Opportunities and Challenges. In: Y. M. Yeung (Ed.), *Pacific Asia in the 21st Century: Geography and Developmental Perspectives* (pp. 69–103). Hong Kong: Chinese University Press.

9.   A PARTNERSHIP APPROACH TO URBAN RENEWAL IN BRISBANE

Trevor Reddacliff and Robert J. Stimson

ABSTRACT

Urban renewal is a challenge that will be faced on a greater scale by cities across the world. Usually initiated through the role of the state, it is one of a large number of processes through which transformation is occurring in the inner city areas of big cities. This chapter discusses change in the inner city of Brisbane, Australia's third largest metropolitan city region, where there has been a population turnaround as the processes of economic and social change and new public policy initiatives facilitating urban consolidation are generating a rekindling of interest in the old inner city suburbs attracting new residents and new investments. The chapter focuses on the successful initiative by the Brisbane City Council in 1991 to commence a 20 year program of urban renewal in Brisbane's inner north-eastern suburbs through a public-private-community partnership approach that has facilitated very significant levels of private sector investment in redevelopment projects in a planned way so as to avoid market flooding and without massive public sector spending on icon projects. The urban renewal planning process has focused on lifestyle outcomes, with project design and delivery occurring through a brokerage role by an Urban Renewal Task Force.

INTRODUCTION

Transformation of inner city areas is an increasingly important theme in the literature on urban change. The focus is on inner city change not only on the

International Urban Planning Settings: Lessons of Success, Volume 12, pages 259–293.
2001 by Elsevier Science Ltd.
ISBN: 0-7623-0695-5

problems of the inner city as has been the case in much of the analysis of inner urban decline in many of the large cities in the United States, but also on the revitalization occurring in the inner city areas of many large metropolitan areas. This paper looks at inner city change that is being facilitated in Brisbane, the capital city of the State of Queensland and Australia's third largest metropolitan region, through a public policy intervention known as the Urban Renewal Task Force (URTF) which was initiated in 1991. The chapter discusses the broader planning context that has generated a considerable focus on inner city redevelopment through urban consolidation aimed at stemming the tide of metropolitan regional growth occurring predominantly through urban sprawl. It examines the planning objectives and achievements over the first nine years of what is envisaged as a two decade program of urban renewal focused on Brisbane's inner north-eastern suburbs which adjoin the Central Business District (CBD). In particular, the chapter highlights the way the URTF has used a precincts planning approach through a public-private-community partnership whereby a low-cost public sector facilitated planning and development process has generated significant levels of private sector investment in a staged manner to create urban renewal with a focus on livability.

The geographic location of Brisbane in Australia and of the inner city URTF renewal area is shown in Fig. 1.

FRAMEWORKS FOR STUDYING INNER CITY CHANGE

Brisbane is typical of many rapidly growing metropolitan city regions in Australia, the U.S. and Canada in that its growth has been dominated by the process of suburbanization. However, unlike the common situation in many cities in the United States, the big cities in Australia have not experienced the same magnitude or scale of inner city decline; in fact, the Central Business Districts (CBDs) have remained strong and for some time many inner city areas have been regenerated as desirable places to live.

Theoretical Explanations

Inner city change, including urban renewal, is a complex and multi-faceted phenomenon. Researchers have put forward three explanatory frameworks for studying it:

(1) Production-based theories are built around on the one hand arguments to do with opportunities to invest in housing redevelopment, and on the other hand arguments to do with the restructuring of economies as a result of

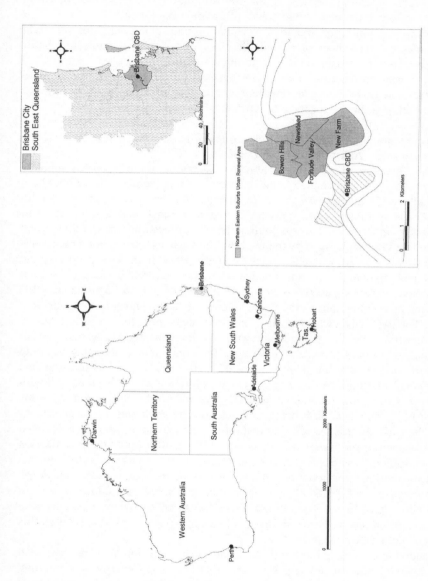

Fig. 1. Geographic Location of Brisbane in Australia and the Inner City URTF Renewal Area within Brisbane City and South East Queensland.

forces of globalization and the transformation from the old industrial economy to the new services and information economy.

(2) Consumption-based theories revolve around changing lifestyles and amenity preferences of the middle class, and involve certain households choosing the "cosmopolitan" offerings of the inner city.

(3) Theories on the role of the state focus on public policy interventions to facilitate inner city redevelopment, and include urban boosterism aimed at creating an image for the city through 'showpiece' projects.

A recent study analyzes inner city transformation occurring in Brisbane (Stimson et al., 2000) within these frameworks.

The phenomenon of "gentrification" has been long studied by urban scholars as a process of social change in the inner city, and has been studied within both the (1) and (2) frameworks above. In Brisbane this process became evident in the 1970s as middle class households began to move into a selected small number of inner city suburbs adjoining the CBD renovating the old timber and tin cottages once inhabited by the working class. This gentrification process has been widely studied, with early work by Smith (1979) in the U.S. proposing the 'rent gap' hypothesis as an explanation. Later research by Ley (1986) on Vancouver in Canada and by Badcock (1989) on Adelaide in Australia provided international comparative empirical evidence of this explanation of gentrification. The hypothesis was that inner city localities where there was a disparity between the potential ground rent with development and the actual present ground rent would provide a motivation for reinvestment once that rent gap exceeds a critical value. However by the early 1980s, new scholarship had developed a far broader meaning of gentrification (Sassen, 1991) linking it with processes of spatial, economic and social restructuring. Smith and Williams (1986) also noted the link between residential rehabilitation in the inner city and the shift towards the services and information economy and the associated transformations of class structure, as well as the shift towards the privatization of consumption and of services provision in the inner city. In addition globalization has spurred city governments to facilitate and often sponsor the redevelopment of parts of the inner city landscape, including redundant waterfront land, in a wave of urban boosterism to produce new spaces catering for recreation and tourism, shopping, offices and residential living. Often this was on public-owned land.

Later, the increasing interest in sustainable urban development has sharpened the focus on the relationship between urban form and energy consumption, with some espousing the benefits of urban consolidation and redevelopment of inner city areas through urban village renewal and redevelopment projects

(Newman, Kenworthy & Vintila, 1993) to attract people back to the inner city and turn around population decline so as to achieve more efficient use of inner city infrastructure.

This overall reorientation towards issues to do with the revitalization of the inner city has taken on a wider concern with "reurbanization", including the repopulation of the inner city as well as its revitalization. Borgegard and Murdie's (1993) study of Stockholm in Sweden provides an interesting example of these issues.

Public Policy Promoting Urban Consolidation

By the late 1980s in Australia a considerable public policy debate had emerged on the processes and forms of metropolitan growth and development, with governments at all levels – Federal, State and local – coming together to promote urban consolidation policies and practices in metropolitan regional planning. In 1991 the Better Cities Program was initiated as a partnership program between all three levels of government to promote a more integrated approach to the planning of Australia's cities, providing funding for demonstration projects involving planned and cooperative approaches to urban development. It was a five year A$816 million program that involved projects across the nation. A number of the specific projects sponsored through the Better Cities Program involved urban renewal, including the URTF project in Brisbane's inner north-eastern suburbs.

The Better Cities Program represented one of the rare occasions on which the Federal Government in Australia has made a policy incursion into urban planning and development. Not surprisingly it was an initiative taken under a Labor government (which is Australia's equivalent to a social democratic government), and it is also significant that the program was closed down in 1996 by the new Federal Liberal-National government (which means conservative government).

However, in the early 1990s the Federal Labor Government also had taken other policy initiatives concerned with urban and regional development, including encouraging State Governments to take metropolitan regional planning initiatives aimed at developing frameworks to achieve more sustainable forms of urban development. That public policy push involved promoting urban consolidation, which it was claimed would enhance the efficiency of providing urban infrastructure through reducing the rate of outer suburban growth by diverting population and jobs back to inner city localities through renewal, redevelopment and densification within the existing urban areas. It has attracted its share of critics, notably Troy (1996).

But the impacts of the broad set of processes of urban change, especially those affecting the inner city – globalization, demographic shifts, and new lifestyle preferences, the growth of services in the post-industrial society, and the impacts of public policy initiatives for inner city redevelopment – have become increasingly apparent in Australia's major cities during the last decade as reurbanization has begun to turn around decades of population decline in the inner city areas of Sydney (Daly et al., 1997), Melbourne (O'Connor et al., 1997) and Brisbane (Stimson & Taylor, 1998). Some commentators have painted graphic pictures and made rapturous claims about these trends, such as Reynolds and Porter (1998) in their piece on Melbourne's inner-city revival. But O'Connor (1998) provides a more sobering and statistically based analysis taking a metropolitan regional perspective of the impact of reurbanization in Melbourne, as do Stimson et al. (2000) in their work on Brisbane. Nonetheless, there is now ample evidence to show that an inner city population turnaround is occurring in all the big metropolitan cities in Australia, and that it is occurring as a result of a mixture of the processes of change encompassed within the three theoretical frameworks discussed earlier to explain the processes of inner city transformation.

INNER CITY CHANGE IN BRISBANE: THE DEMOGRAPHIC AND PUBLIC POLICY CONTEXT

Metropolitan Growth and an Inner City Turnaround

The greater metropolitan city region known as South East Queensland (SEQ) that has evolved rapidly over the last three to four decades has been referred to as Australia's "sun-belt metropolis" (Stimson, 1992). On world standards, the rate of growth of the SEQ region has been high at an average of 3.7% per annum over the 20 years to 1996. The overwhelming majority of the growth in this metropolitan regional population, which is projected to increase further from 2.1 million in 1996 to reach over 3 million by 2016, has been achieved through outer suburban expansion and growth outward from Brisbane in three corridors towards the tourism centers of the Gold Coast to the south and the Sunshine Coast to the north, and to the west to encompass the old industrial and mining city of Ipswich and its hinterland.

Over the two five year census periods between 1986 and 1996, the Brisbane Inner sub-region at the centre of Brisbane City Council (which once encompassed all of the metropolitan area) accommodated only 4.6% of the increase of 573,000 that occurred in the population of the SEQ region. However, after a period of population decline from the late 1960s to the mid

1980s, population of Brisbane Inner has increased significantly from a low of 337,500 in 1986 to reach 374,500 in 1999, an increase on average of 2.5% per annum in just 13 years, with 10,000 of that increase in population occurring in just three years between 1996 and 1999 (Fig. 2). This represents quite a significant population turnaround, but it is being experienced unevenly across the 65 suburbs which comprise Brisbane Inner. However, despite this population turnaround, the Brisbane Inner share of the SEQ region's population continues to decline, accounting for only 17% in 1996 compared to 28% a decade earlier in 1986, and the Brisbane Inner area accommodated only 4.6% of the total population increase of 573,000 that occurred over that decade.

Planning Initiatives

It was within the context of the rapid growth occurring in the SEQ region and population loss that had been occurring throughout the 1970s and 1980s in the inner city areas of Brisbane that a number of planning studies were undertaken from the late 1980s.

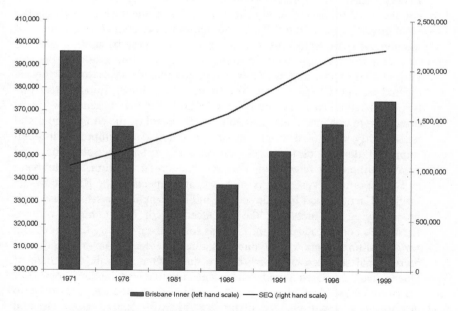

Fig. 2. Trends in the Population of Brisbane Inner and the SEQ Region, 1971 to 1999. *Source*: Stimson et al., 2000.

(1) First, under a Liberal Administration, Brisbane City Council initiated a study called "Inner City Action" in 1989. Focusing on a group of 20 inner city suburbs surrounding the CBD, this project had the goals of improving the living environment for residents, promoting community participation in local area planning and neighborhood improvement schemes, and addressing issues to do with work in, and travel to and through the inner city suburbs. In 1990 Brisbane City Council also initiated the "Brisbane Plan" project, which had the broader focus of developing proposals for the economic, environmental, demographic, social and technological futures for the development of Brisbane City within the broader SEQ regional context. Inevitably this project provided a considerable focus on strategic planning and development issues in the CBD and the inner city areas where about two-fifths of the jobs in the SEQ region were then located.

(2) Second, in 1990 a newly elected State Labor Government initiated an innovative approach to developing a new regional development, planning and management strategy for the SEQ region. Known as "SEQ2001", over the next few years a Regional Framework for Growth Management (RFGM) and a Regional Outline Plan were developed through a collaborative process involving the State Government along with all the local governments in the SEQ region, and with the formal involvement of the Federal Government, plus representation from the business sector and the community sector. This planning strategy and the planning process known as SEQ2001 and the RPAG (Regional Planning Advisory Group) is the subject of Chapter 7 by Wyeth in this volume. Importantly, this SEQ2001/RPAG process proposed a RFGM that was based on a set of principles to enhance the sustainable development of the SEQ region, and it explicitly promoted future urban growth and development through improved density performance, encouraging urban consolidation, and creating improved integration between residential location, employment and transportation systems. As such, specific aspects of the RFGM and its proposed actions had both direct and indirect implications for Brisbane's inner city areas, including the enhancement of the dominant role of Brisbane's core area around the CBD as for state capital city functions, and for providing high order business, health, education, cultural and recreational services and facilities for the SEQ region and the State of Queensland. A related State Government initiative was the development of a new Integrated Planning Act (1997) which requires local authorities to develop new town or city plans that identify desired environmental outcomes that are consistent with the RFGM and for which performance indicators are identified.

(3) Third, in 1991 the newly elected Labor Administration in the Brisbane City Council, which subsequently has progressed to win a fourth term of government at the 2000 local government elections, initiated over the next few years a series of planning studies which have had a theme of achieving "livability". In 1995 the Council published its "Brisbane 2011: The Livable City for the Future" plan. This plan envisaged a future population for Brisbane City of 900,000, a substantial increase from its population of 764,930 in 1991, which the Council's planners estimated would require an additional 96,000 dwellings (over and above replacements of demolitions and renewal) by the year 2001, of which 25% would be contributed by in-fill development, 15% through urban renewal at major sites, and 60% through greenfield residential development. Thus the "Livable City" plan had a significant focus on urban consolidation to accommodate growth within Brisbane City, which was an objective consistent with those of the State Government's SEQ2001/RPAG RFGM plan. But to achieve this inevitably explicit public policy interventions would be required, which were to include:

- formally designated areas for comprehensive planning for urban renewal (which was in the form of the URTF);
- amending the provisions of the Brisbane City *Town Plan* to facilitate in-fill development and diversification in existing inner city residential areas;
- encouraging high-rise residential development and medium-density redevelopment housing in designated localities;
- a concerted effort to develop Local Plans for comprehensive planning including redevelopment of designated localities, including the creation of urban villages.

THE URBAN RENEWAL TASK FORCE (URTF) INITIATIVE AND APPROACH

Genesis and Objectives

One of the early initiatives of the incoming Labor Administration in the Brisbane City Council in 1991, was to establish in July of that year an Urban Renewal Task Force (URTF) to investigate opportunities to revitalize the inner north-eastern suburbs of Brisbane. In October of that year, the URTF released the Urban Renewal Report – Inner North-Eastern Suburbs Brisbane, which set

out a new vision for the suburbs of New Farm, Newstead, Teneriffe, Bowen
Hills and Fortitude Valley. This urban renewal area is large covering 730
hectares. This initiative was an important one, representing the beginning of a
long-term commitment by Brisbane City Council to a program of urban
renewal. As well, the Council has committed to a much wider range of planning
initiatives promoting a facilitating urban consolidation.

Table 1 sets out the URTF's objectives for this project, the processes for
urban renewal, current problems in the target area, and the vision for the
redevelopment area.

The broad objectives of the urban renewal program were to:

- Revitalize the inner north-eastern suburbs of Brisbane;
- Implement urban consolidation and reduce urban sprawl;
- Improve employment opportunities, access to services and facilities, and
  appropriate housing choice in the area;
- Improve coordination between levels of government and the private sector;
- Improve private sector participation in development.

The URTF's report prepared in just a few months responded to a range of
problems common to inner city locations in many cities. It recommended
development strategies and implementation procedures to accommodate a
population of 30,000 in these inner north-eastern suburbs over the next 20
years. A "Master Plan" was proposed to be funded through private and public
sector initiatives. The URTF was then to proceed to document public feedback
and commission a number of planning and feasibility studies, after which, the
report said, there would be a strong basis for decision making and strategy
implementation. The key to successful urban renewal was seen to be a 'strong
relationship between employment, housing, public transport and social
infrastructure' (Urban Renewal Task Force, 1991: 9).

Characteristics of the Urban Renewal Area

These inner north-eastern suburbs had a population in 1986 of just 12,000,
which had declined by 13% over the decade 1976 to 1986. Household sizes had
been reducing, and the proportion of one- and two-person households had risen
to 78%. But despite these changes, the area had remained more densely settled
than elsewhere in Brisbane, with densities reaching 34 persons per hectare
compared to an average of around 10 for the metropolitan area, with 53% of the
population in the area living in medium-density dwellings compared to an
average of 7% in the metropolitan area. Of course in world terms, and even in
terms of inner city areas in some of the other large cities in Australia, these
densities are low.

A little over one-third of the population of these inner north-eastern suburbs had been born overseas, with Italians being the dominant immigrant group, followed closely by immigrants from England and New Zealand. Italian and Chinese were the most common foreign languages spoken in the area.

There had been a substantial increase in the incidence of white-collar workers since the mid-1970s, to account for well over one half of the resident

Table 1. The Urban Renewal Task Force.

OBJECTIVES OF TASK FORCE

The objectives of the Task Force are to:

- Focus on the inner north-eastern suburbs including Fortitude Valley, New Farm, Newstead, Teneriffe and Bowen Hills as a pilot for revitalization of inner-city areas.

- Deliver a master plan, development strategies and procedures for implementation, based on practical solutions and viable investments to achieve a population of 30,000 people over the next 20 years.

PRESSURES FOR URBAN RENEWAL

The recommendations of the Urban Renewal Task Force respond to:

- High population growth in South-East Queensland.
- Population decline or stagnation in inner city areas.
- Changing social patterns.
- Obsolete land usage.

- Recognition of the costs of urban sprawl.
- Underutilized physical and social infrastructure.
- Ill defined development directions.
- Non viable commercial investments.

CURRENT PROBLEMS

The project area is variously characterized by:

- Chaotic heavy traffic.
- Visual pollution.
- Extensive industrial obsolescence.

- Poor social image.
- Inadequate public transport.
- Limited sewerage infrastructure.
- Inaccessible river frontages.

VISION FOR REDEVELOPMENT

- Increase residential population with a range of housing and employment opportunities, improved traffic arrangements, efficient public transport and adequate social infrastructure.

- Create attractive living environments and enhance the quality of life.

Source: Urban Renewal Task Force, 1991.

workforce, with around one-in-five working in the CBD and a further one-in-ten in the adjacent Fortitude Valley, an old retail-commercial arm adjoining the CBD which had been experiencing considerable urban decay for some decades. However, there remained a high proportion of low-income households and subsidized housing in the area, so that affordable housing would be an issue for the URTF.

The area was relatively well served by public transport, particularly Fortitude Valley and New Farm, but the Newstead and Teneriffe precincts had relatively poor access to buses and none to trains. These were likely to be the areas where highest residential intensity redevelopment could occur. Traffic congestion was a major problem, with the main roads to the northern suburbs of Brisbane converging on the Fortitude Valley and from the Story Bridge, which brought traffic from the eastern suburbs to the CBD. And heavy vehicle movements were a problem, exacerbated by the existence of a number of major industries in the area in addition to substantial cross-city-center freight traffic through Fortitude Valley.

The area contained a large number of buildings and sites of heritage significance, indicative of the area's diverse and colorful history. The Fortitude Valley precinct contained pockets of "sleaze" activities typically associated with urban decay. The riverside precincts of Newstead and Teneriffe contained redundant uses such as woolstores with preservation and redevelopment potential. New Farm had been undergoing extensive change over the last thirty years as medium- and high-density construction (including some high-rise residential towers) had occurred, and this development was of a largely functional architectural style that was not compatible with or complementary to the existing colonial timber-and-tin "Queenslander-style" housing character-istic of the suburb. The Bowen Hills and Teneriffe precincts had visually prominent hills that are significant landmarks.

Overall the provision of infrastructure in the area was reasonable, although urban renewal would impact on utility capacity, and upgrading of the trunk water supply and sewer system would require in excess of A$100 million.

Around one-fifth of the land in the urban renewal area was zoned for industrial purposes, with many obsolete industrial land use functions present, and in addition there were a number of large manufacturing industries located on sites unsuitable for expansion and which were creating transport access difficulties. The now disused Mayne railway yards provided an opportunity for redevelopment or industrial relocation.

Existing retailing served the local populations, although the Fortitude Valley retail center had once served wider areas with high order functions. It had been experiencing over a long time a diminution from what was once its major regional shopping strip status which included department stores. However, it had developed as a small Chinatown, and the Brisbane City Council had redeveloped part of the Valley as a Mall. Entertainment and leisure activities had also developed in Fortitude Valley, including "vicarious" recreation functions associated with the sex industry.

Some office redevelopment had occurred as spillover from the CBD, and a wide range of established, but relatively small scale, arts and cultural facilities were located in the area. The area was attracting the in-movement of arts and cultural communities and New Farm was attracting the gay community. There was evidence of gentrification with rising housing and land costs, particularly in New Farm, once a working class inner city suburb. The area had a few significant areas of open space, including New Farm Park, but generally local open space was lacking. Riverfront access was generally poor. Thus, at the beginning of the 1990s when the URTF was established, these inner north-eastern suburbs of Brisbane represented an inner city area in transition that was ripe for a major urban renewal initiative.

Figure 3 provides an aerial panorama of the area.

The Task Force Management and Funding

The URTF formally began as a Brisbane City Council initiative on 19 July, 1991. It received the support of the Deputy Premier and Minister for Housing and Local Government in the Queensland State Government. The Task Force was structured to incorporate both public and private sector interests in urban renewal. The Council provided A$9.85 million funding over the first three years, 1991/92 to 1993/94. A considerable impetus to the project occurred when the Federal Government allocated A$31 million in 1992/93 to support the urban renewal program under the Better Cities Program (which was a A$816 million national program). The Federal Government was given representation on the Task Force.

Figure 4 illustrates this partnership approach, indicating how the Task Force provided links between all levels of government, the development industry, professional reference groups, and – very importantly – the local community.

The Task Force has had the same Chairman since its inception. It has a small professional staff of about 9 to 12 forming the Project Team, which includes planning, marketing and administrative staff. Importantly, the Task Force office was located in Fortitude Valley in the commercial heart of the urban renewal area. The Task Force meets every fortnight to review planning, projects and programs.

Aerial photograph showing major sites in the Urban Renewal area.

Note: RNA Showgrounds and Mayne Railway Yards are located within Bowen Hills, which is not fully shown in this photograph.
The whole suburb of Bowen Hills is however included in the Urban Renewal area.

Fig. 3. Panoramic View of the Inner North-Eastern Suburbs Urban Renewal Area Looking South Towards Brisbane's CBD.

A feature of the URTF has been its relatively low level of public sector funding, which amounted to A$47.28 million over the period 1991/92 to 1999/2000, of which only A$11.51 million (20%) went to administrative and operational expenses, including planning studies. Other areas of expenditure have been: (a) A$7.88 million on local area and community improvements (14%); (b) A$4.25 million on land acquisition (7%); (c) A$25.5 million on sewerage and related infrastructure (44%); and (d) A$8.11 million on low-cost housing (14%). Brisbane City Council's expenditure on the project has been A$26.27 million, which represents 46% of total expenditure over the first nine years of the project. The investment potential for the 20 year timeframe for the URTF project was estimated at approximately $4 billion.

The Better Cities Program funding of A$31 million over five years was provided subject to criteria and arrangements relating directly to that program's objectives, which sought to tie all aspects of the urban development process together. This Federal initiated program had set out to encourage and

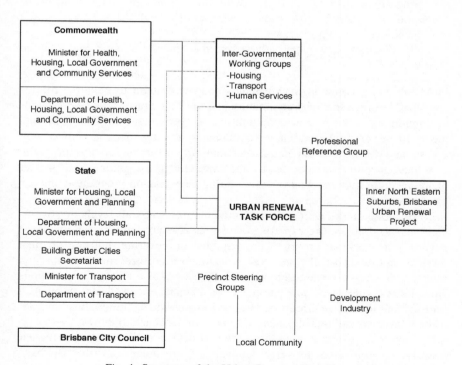

Fig. 4. Structure of the Urban Renewal Task Force.

demonstrate 'best practice' for urban planning and management at all levels of government, supported the provision and upgrading of essential infrastructure, recognized the links between urban environments and their impact on the health and well-being of people living in cities, and pursued social justice objectives including housing choice and affordability. For this particular urban renewal project in Brisbane, A$22 million was provided for sewerage infrastructure improvements, A$8.1 million for low-cost housing provision, and A$900,000 for environmental improvements.

Consultation and Inter-Governmental Liaison

Following the October 1991 release of that initial *Urban Renewal Report*, the URTF embarked on an intensive public consultation process. This involved:

- the distribution of 2,000 reports and 5,000 information pamphlets;
- holding more than 20 meetings with the public, government agencies, community groups, professional associations and landowners, which involved over 3,000 people; and
- public displays, newspaper advertisements and an attitude and opinion survey.

In March 1992, community consultants, who were seen to have the role of "brokers" between the local community and the Task Force, with backgrounds in community activism and community arts, were engaged. This team had the tasks of providing the local community and the general public with access to information and details relating to the urban renewal program, coordinating public responses to the detailed investigations and master planning studies, and setting up an on-going participation program to suit the local precinct.

To facilitate inter-governmental coordination between all levels of government and to draw on the expertise of various relevant public agencies, three government working groups were established covering housing, human services and transport. Private sector consultation occurred not only through private sector representation on the Task Force, but also through negotiations with local landowners and property developers, as well as through a Professional Reference Group representing professional, community, environmental, business and industry bodies, to provide feedback to the Task Force on urban renewal planning initiatives. The Task Force also initiated regular consultation with the Property Council of Australia and the Brisbane Development Association.

The Original Master Plan

The early Master Plan developed by the URTF adopted a precincts planning approach [Fortitude Valley, Newstead, Teneriffe, New Farm, Bowen Hills, the Mayne Railway Yards, and the Royal National Association (RNA) Showgrounds]. Planning for the redevelopment of the renewal area was based on a fundamental principle for successful urban renewal, which was to achieve a strong relationship between employment, housing, public transport and social infrastructure.

A wide range of employment opportunities were seen to include the ready access to Brisbane's CBD, plus the continuing development of Fortitude Valley as a secondary commercial center, the further development of the teaching hospitals complex at Herston, and a possible new industry park at the old Mayne railway yards. In the context of the metropolitan area, these represent a significant range of strategic employment locations, crucial for the residential redevelopment of the area.

Residential development was seen as needing to provide a variety of environments from controlled high-density towers in the precincts of New Farm, Newstead, Teneriffe and Bowen Hills, to low- and medium-rise environments near river frontages and public open space. To cater for the needs of low-income households, provision of affordable housing, and subsidized public housing was proposed, including demonstration projects.

Recognizing the high volume of through traffic and the traffic congestion problems that characterized the area, the Master Plan recommended the development of a western bypass as a short-term resolution for heavy vehicle traffic through Fortitude Valley, with a potential to improve access from the Story Bridge. It proposed high quality public transport connections between the renewal area and the CBD, including a light rail transit system. Traffic calming to enhance pedestrian amenity was proposed for Fortitude Valley.

The Master Plan proposed the introduction of new pockets for open space and public recreation in strategic locations associated with public transport corridors and stops, the connection of New Farm Park and Newstead Park with continuous public access to the river frontage, the greening of streets, and the creation of pedestrian and bikeways to enhance existing and future employment centers, including a riverfront link extending to the CBD.

The renewal area contained a large number of buildings and sites of heritage and townscape significance, and the Master Plan proposed that future Development Control Plans incorporate appropriate conservation techniques to preserve and enhance worthwhile historic environments without detracting from the viability of investment opportunities. The core of Fortitude Valley, the

Teneriffe woolstores area, the colonial residential character of New Farm, and the visually prominent hills in Teneriffe and Bowen Hills, were all identified as having particular importance.

The Fortitude Valley business center was identified as having the potential for development as the headquarters for Asian business and commerce, linked to the existing small Chinatown area. The Master Plan proposed the relocation of Brisbane City Council and State Government departments to help revitalize the commercial core of Fortitude Valley. A new tertiary arts oriented campus was suggested for the Teneriffe precincts. An industrial park was suggested for Mayne. A multi-faceted sports complex was proposed for the redevelopment of the RNA showgrounds, which was seen as providing a major civic catalyst for the renewal of the area.

The Master Plan proposed, as a general principle, that general industry and warehousing should be converted to mixed use development to provide areas of transition between residential areas and commercial or industrial areas.

It was recognized in the Master Plan that an increased demand would be placed on the physical and social infrastructure of the renewal area with the proposed population increase from 12,000 to a target of 30,000 and to serve the commercial redevelopments proposed. Anticipated physical infrastructure deficiencies included trunk sewer reticulation, water reticulation and drainage. Gas, electricity, telecommunications and trunk water supply services could be expanded to meet the anticipated new demands. Anticipated social infra-structure deficiencies include childcare and secondary education facilities, while primary education facilities were considered adequate.

From the outset, the URTF recognized that property development is market driven and sensitive to timing. For those reasons for the first phases of the urban renewal program five major precincts were identified, each with a separate market focus and separate development strategies. However, it was recognized that each precinct could not be developed in isolation, there being a need for complementarity. For example, the revitalization of Fortitude Valley would be dependent on the success of the Newstead-Teneriffe precincts and efficient public transport to the CBD, connecting to the Valley.

Planning for all the precincts also had in common a process for consultation with landowners from the outset, with further involvement in consultative processes of residents and business associations.

As the redevelopment of the inner north-eastern suburbs was anticipated to extend over a 20 year period, thus involving several cycles in property market conditions, implementation was to provide for feasible opportunities to proceed in the short-term, while detailed planning was to proceed for other opportunities over the longer-term. The Task Force saw the adoption of mixed zonings as being fundamental to the urban renewal process, the maintenance of property values, and to enhance amenity in the project area.

Supposed Financial Benefits of Urban Renewal

Funding for urban renewal generally has involved an initial grant for resumption and improvements with revenue by sales or joint venture of property holdings. This project for Brisbane's inner north-eastern suburbs would involve widespread refurbishment of an established urban environment and conversion of obsolete industrial activities to mixed use development, with the objective of maintaining land values.

The URTF developed an indicative formula, in constant dollar values (that is, base year 1991), to reconcile the impact of basic costs, revenue and shortfall, as well as to illustrate the ultimate financial benefit to government of the urban renewal program versus metropolitan fringe urban development to house the projected increase in population of about 18,000 people envisaged to be housed in the urban renewal project area. The target for overall investment in the redevelopment in the urban renewal area was estimated at A$4 billion. Table 2 sets out those calculations, which show that the reduction of fringe urban development costs by saving 6,000 households at A$25,000 per allotment would be A$150 million, with recurrent savings also occurring in relation to transport from an additional 18,000 people in the project area rather than at the urban fringe. The URTF claimed "the net gain and ultimate benefit is significant and represents a worthwhile investment by all tiers of government" (Urban Renewal Task Force, 1991: 16).

Collectively, the value of properties held by governments and the Brisbane City Council should exceed A$75 million before costs of replacement, reflecting a capacity for participation in the renewal process. The redevelopment of the Mayne railway yards also provided the potential to yield A$20 million, and by a joint venture with Queensland Rail, could contribute towards low-cost housing projects. The URTF also projected that the rezoning of industrial land for residential development with proximity to water frontages and incorporating new mixed use should maintain land values.

Financial Incentives

The URTF considered Betterment Levies, but concluded that they would be a deterrent to redevelopment in the short-term, but that as land values increased in the longer term, then the application of betterment levies should be reviewed. Also, it was considered that density bonuses on individual allotments would be counter productive in terms of overall land value without considering the impact on adjacent allotments.

In 1991, a time of economic recession, building development was seen as being difficult to finance in Australia as a result of the high interest rates of that time in comparison to other countries. Residential developments tend to be a volatile investment without the security of pre-commitment and on-going tenure, and in relation to commercial opportunities it represents poor rental yields and a reliance on capital gains, with financial institutions consequently preferring retail and commercial investments. Thus, viable residential development opportunities would be created through the introduction of attractive incentives and joint participation between the private and public sectors, with institutions being encouraged to undertake catalyst developments, particularly Queensland (local) based initiatives.

Table 2. Estimated Costs and Benefit to Government of the Brisbane Inner North-Eastern Suburbs Urban Renewal Project versus Urban Fringe Development.

COSTS
• services including sewerage, water and drainage – $40M
• Major roadworks and land acquisition – $90M
• Low income housing and social infrastructure – $60M
• Light rail and electric bus system – $60M   ... ($250M)

REVENUE

• contributions by private sector for residential, retail, industrial and commercial development
                                                                              ... $125M

SHORTFALL

• Requirement of funding by Commonwealth Government, State Government and Brisbane City Council   ... ($125M)

SAVINGS

• Reduction of fringe costs by saving 6,000 households at $25,000 per allotment
                                                                              ... $150M

NET GAIN

• Ultimate benefit to Government of urban renewal after offsetting savings on fringe against shortfall of inner city   ... $25M

Source: Urban Renewal Task Force, 1991.

As a result, the Task Force proposed incentives to reduce holding charges, building costs and delivery time. These were:

- integrated zonings for flexibility to admit commercial and retail use and improve the overall viability of development;
- bonuses of increased density to encourage amalgamation of properties and, in turn, reduce overall building and infrastructure costs;
- bonuses for retention of historic buildings;
- bonuses or subsidies for private low-cost housing and pensioner units;
- bonuses for provision of open space;
- equitable distribution of infrastructure costs among benefited parties, to reduce impact of costs on a particular development;
- deferred payment on contributions to infrastructure;
- deferred payment for purchase of government property;
- taxation benefits for contributions to social infrastructure;
- streamlining the approval process to shorten processing times for applications complying with planning objectives;
- bonuses for innovative/high quality design;
- reduction in statutory charges, including stamp duty and legal charges.

As a principle, the URTF saw that, in order to stimulate development, incentives and bonuses should be structured so as to maximize benefits for developments that proceed in the short-term.

Legislation

The URTF recognized that developers and investors need to have confidence of an established framework to facilitate immediate approval, commitment and implementation. But to ensure such confidence, there was a need for Brisbane City Council to take action to allow desired development to proceed, as well as for longer-term negotiations with the Queensland State Government and the Federal Government to improve processes. As well, there was a need for public consultation to bring the community along with the objectives of urban renewal for the project area.

The Task Force proposed a three phase procedure to facilitate implementation by the Council:

(1) Phase 1, non statutory: Council adopt the recommendations of the URTF as guidelines for interim approval, and commensurately obtain authority under existing legislation to proceed with Development Control Plans for each precinct, and commence negotiations on terms for a special Urban Renewal Act and necessary amendments to other legislation.

(2) Phase II, statutory: A Special Urban Renewal Act to provide an overall framework for planning, financial and administrative mechanisms, as well as the legal basis for approvals, and incorporate new legislation for mixed use development and joint venture arrangements.
(3) Phase III, statutory: Preferred Development Control Plans for each precinct and process in the normal manner. Landowners, developers and the community to be involved in the preparation of Development Control Plans through a process of public consultation.

It was also proposed that provisions in relation to compensation for changes to development rights as a result of amendments to the Brisbane City Town Plan be reviewed for the project area to facilitate conversion from industrial to residential without undue costs to the Council, and, in line with legislation existing in other states in Australia, to limit the potential impact of injurious affection claims.

Joint Venturing

The URTF recognized that the experience in successful urban renewal in other countries was often the result of partnership between the private and public sectors, with government involvement resulting in increased revenue for governments through taxes and shares of profits, as well as maintaining equity holdings. Generally, urban renewal through joint venturing consolidates interests, producing improved quality of environment, a wider range of housing and facilities, reduced infrastructure costs and improved values. The Task Force noted how government participation could be pursued through these avenues:

- joint venture by contribution of land holdings and infrastructure with deferred payment and share of revenue or sales when the projected and real income stream has been established;
- coordination of joint ventures by initiation of the design process and predetermined design controls;
- pre-commitments by the Council and State Government for tenancies or end purchase arrangements;
- off-budget funding schemes for physical and social infrastructure;
- pilot projects with design innovation, particularly in low-income housing;
- privatization of infrastructure projects.

Administrative Process

The URTF recognized that the main administrative requirements for urban renewal relate to the approval process and having a vehicle for on-going implementation. The approval process needed to be streamlined by improved coordination at the State level, project focus at the Council level, improved communication between State and Council departments, and new initiatives involving the Council and landowners in a joint planning process for specific urban renewal projects.

It has been common in many cities for independent corporations or authorities to be legislated and formed as the vehicle for urban renewal to provide active initiatives, project focus, direct responsibility for delivery and performance, as well as to administer projects involving government participation. Such authorities have the ability to coordinate government, supervise design and construction, recruit developers, and provide the necessary catalysts to stimulate development. The Task Force noted how in Britain a number of development corporations are responsible to government, and how in the U.S. there are examples of joint venture development partnerships responsible to the local authority. These act as brokers between government, businesses and the community. However, the Task Force also noted how the Brisbane inner north-eastern suburbs urban renewal project was different from many of these overseas examples in that a very high proportion of the land in this area was in private ownership, and an established pattern of land use, including a substantial area of housing, had been in place for a long time.

Thus, in proposing a structure for the administrative vehicle for the project, the URTF considered there were three essential criteria to take into account:

- a requirement for on-going negotiations and immediate implementation preceding any necessary formalities;
- an emphasis on refurbishment of an urban environment, closely involving the Council and State Government departments; and
- pockets of development which will require focus and coordination with the overall Master Plan.

A number of options for administering the project were considered, including an independent corporation with wide powers of planning and development or a semi-autonomous authority with powers to implement joint ventures and development. But the Task Force stated categorically that there was a 'basic requirement for the administrative vehicle to have responsibility for the initiation, delivery and performance of the overall development and specific projects' (Urban Renewal Task Force, 1991: 18) including being responsible for implementing recommendations and entering into negotiations with development prospects.

Brokering the Development Process

The URTF has acted as a broker between the private sector and government in matters of investment and development in the urban renewal area. It provides management services to applicants seeking to undertake development projects and liaisons with current and potential landowners and investors to identify development opportunities. Proposals are reviewed by the Task Force at an early stage to determine compliance with the urban renewal objectives and policies. The Task Force then provides developers and investors with relevant Brisbane City Council contacts and a program of activities. It may advise on preparation of applications, convene initial meetings of relevant public agencies, and monitor the progress of applications through the Council's and State Government's approval process.

ACHIEVEMENTS OVER THE FIRST NINE YEARS

At the time of writing, the URTF has been operating for nine years, and the urban renewal process for Brisbane's inner north-eastern suburbs is now well under way, with many clearly visible projects having been completed or in progress. It is thus timely to review the achievements at what is approaching midway through the 20 year program of urban renewal.

The Milestones

By the end of 1999, the following milestones had been achieved by the URTF for the inner north-eastern suburbs urban renewal area:

- 100% of the area's planning was completed, with operational Local Plans for Fortitude Valley, New Farm and Teneriffe Hill, Bowen Hills, and the Newstead and Teneriffe Waterfront being included in the Brisbane City Council's draft new City Plan;
- over just nine years there has been an increase in the residential population of 18%, from 11,734 to 13,833;
- over 350 residential, commercial and mixed use developments worth A$1.4 billion has been committed, with further project investment of A$1 billion under negotiation;
- developments committed represent approximately 35% of the program's A$4 billion investment potential over the first nine years of the 20 year time span for the project;

- A\$54 million had been spent on sewerage, traffic management, neighborhood shopping centers, the Fortitude Valley malls, parks, bikeways, street lighting, street trees, land acquisition, planning and administration;
- 1.6 hectares of parkland had been created;
- local area improvements involved expenditures of A\$6 million, spent on landscape and amenity improvements to Brunswick Street Mall, Chinatown Mall, Fortitude Valley footpaths, Merthyr Village, Carramar Centre, and residential landscapes;
- 1.25 kilometers of riverfront along the Teneriffe-Newstead waterfront had been opened to the public as part of an extensive promenade being built between New Farm Park and Newstead Park, which will link with the River Walk to the CBD;
- 8.85 kilometers of bikeways has been completed;
- a high speed CityCat ferry service links the urban renewal area with river transport to the CBD, and a hail-and-ride bus service operates in New Farm-Teneriffe;
- 4,160 dwelling units have been approved for development and 3,340 are constructed or are under construction, with 26 mixed use development projects approved and 21 constructed;
- there has been an 86% increase in public housing units, from 182 to 339, an increase from 43 to 160 public housing apartments, and a 30% increase in public housing seniors units from 123 to 160;
- community housing that is government funded but provided by not-for-profit community organizations, has increased from 10 to 30 units, with public owned boarding house units increasing from 0 to 120;
- 46,400 square meters of retail floor space has been constructed, 106,200 square meters of commercial floor space has been constructed, and there has been a 15% increase in the number of commercial premises, a 27% growth in net lettable commercial area in Fortitude Valley, and a 52% decrease in total commercial vacancies in Fortitude Valley.

Seven major innovative design projects have been achieved: (a) the A\$56 million Centro on James in Fortitude Valley, a mixed retail, employment and entertainment hub; (b) the A\$145 million Central Brunswick in Fortitude Valley, redevelopment of the former Carlton and United Breweries site transforming 2.6 hectares into a self-contained community for living, working and shopping; (c) the A\$35 million The Cannery, Teneriffe, project converting a 1920s cannery into a 204 unit residential complex and restaurant area; (d) the A\$16 million Greenwich Residences, New Farm, a low-rise residential development near recreational areas; (e) the A\$120 million Cathedral Place,

Fortitude Valley project, which is a gateway development, providing an imposing entrance to Centenary Park and the CBD, acting as a catalyst to invigorate and further Fortitude Valley as a place to live and work; (f) the A$10 million Sun Apartments, Fortitude Valley, a project converting the former headquarters of the now defunct Sun Newspapers into a living and shopping environment to help boost the population of Fortitude Valley; and (g) the A$90 million Mariners Reach, Newstead project of 172 housing apartments transforming a 3 hectare derelict wharf site into a new living environment on a 400 meter river frontage and promenade.

New Master Plan and Local Plans for Future Strategic Development

A new Master Plan has been prepared to cater for the changing dynamics of the inner north-eastern suburbs, building on the 1991 Master Plan. This revised Master Plan continues to provide the conceptual guide for addressing macro planning issues to achieve a strong relationship between employment, housing, public transport and social infrastructure, a formula which the 1999 report of the URTF re-emphasizes as being fundamental to every urban renewal project undertaken by the Task Force in partnership with the public and private sectors. This revised Master Plan is shown in Fig. 5.

While building on the original Master Plan, the 1999 version goes further to address numerous major urban renewal issues, namely:

- it responds to the recent planning for Bowen Hills and reinforces the strategic location of the Royal National Association Showgrounds for a major events stadium (which has been subsequently over-ridden by the decision of the State Government to redevelop the Lang Park football stadium on a cramped site to the west of the CBD, which informed planning opinion has strongly criticized favoring the URTF proposal);
- it highlights the importance of the Inner City By-Pass road project, now under construction by the Brisbane City Council, a Brisbane Light Rail project, approved by State Governments, but recently abandoned by the current State Government;
- it identifies Newstead's Riverpark, New Farm's Colonial Sugar Refinery site and Brisbane Powerhouse as major development projects.

In October 1998, the Task Force established a Community Liaison Committee to ensure the local community continued to have direct input into the urban renewal program, following completion of the Local Plans.

Local Plans

The Fortitude Valley Local Plan envisages development of a major cosmopolitan and commercial center, including initiatives to strengthen Fortitude Valley's traditional role as a commercial, cultural and employment node, and it

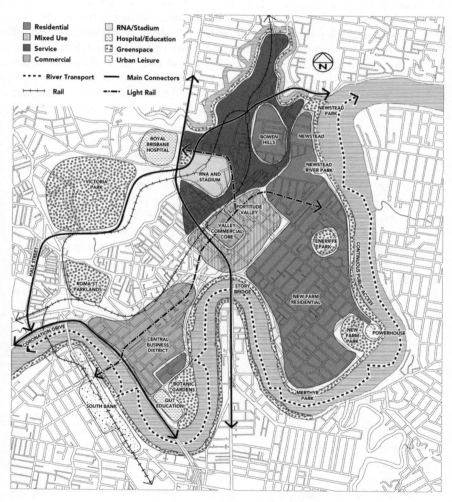

Fig. 5. 1999 Urban Renewal Master Plan.

includes provision of mixed use developments, including "shop-top" housing, the restriction of taller buildings in and around The Valley heart, and measures to ensure the scale and character of buildings complement The Valley's heritage character and its social and cultural diversity.

The New Farm and Teneriffe Hill Local Plan seeks to preserve the built character and local fabric, identifying opportunities for home-based businesses, affordable housing, art and craft galleries and shops, adult learning and cultural centers. There is provisions for mixed use activities, housing diversity, and low cost housing including the A$45 million River Gallery Apartments project on the site of the former Australian Maritime Safety Authority Service Depot.

The Newstead and Teneriffe Waterfront Local Plan seeks to preserve the historic woolstores and create an inner city suburb focused on the river. It contains initiatives capitalizing on the precinct's accessibility to the CBD and to Fortitude Valley, its river frontage, historic buildings and established services. Planning strategies comprise developing a Newstead Riverpark, A$500 million urban village comprising residences, shops and businesses, medium-scale buildings connected by streetscapes, landscaped gardens and public spaces, on a site jointly owned by the Boral company, the City Council, and the State Government, a parkland residential community development; and the A$17 million redevelopment of the Brisbane Powerhouse as a cultural and arts center. Moving industry out of the Colonial Sugar Refinery seven hectare site and moving people in through a A$200 million low to medium rise redevelopment project will be a major new project. In addition, the Local Plan for New Farm and Teneriffe Hill incorporates the A$41 million Freshwater residential development on the riverfront next to historic Amity House; the A$30 million Capricorn Wharf low-rise residential development with a 1,500 square meter park in the center to provide public access to the river; and the Amity House promenade to open up more Brisbane River waterfront.

The Bowen Hills Local Plan capitalizes on existing services to create a vibrant inner-city community on the fringe of Fortitude Valley with established transport infrastructure commuting to the CBD, and a service industry as well as residential development on the hill. The planning strategy is to create a transit-oriented development precinct by facilitating commercial and resi- dential uses hubbing around the Bowen Hills Rail Station, and supporting small scale business and industry to have a nexus with the nearby Royal Brisbane Hospital and/or to provide support services to functions in the CBD. This Local Plan recognizes the potential use of the Mayne railway yards for a mix of employment uses when available for redevelopment, it seeks to develop the Royal National Association Showground as a major events center, and it retains the role of the Breakfast Creek Wharf as a restaurant, retail and business center.

Low cost housing provision is a feature of the strategy for the Bowen Hills precinct.

Some examples of the built environments delivered by the URTF process are shown in the photographs in Fig. 6.

INGREDIENTS OF THE SUCCESS OF THE BRISBANE APPROACH TO URBAN RENEWAL

The challenge faced by the URTF has been summarized by the Task Force Chairman in these words: 'Planning is creating environments for people from all walks of life. Urban renewal is the marriage of living, work and leisure. Our challenge for the future is addressing unparalleled social change' (The Urban Renewal Task Force, 1999: 3).

The URTF approach to urban renewal has been characterized by the drive to develop a genuine partnership between government, business, the professions and the community, with the Task Force operating as an independent interface between the public and private sectors and the community. The experience to date demonstrates a perhaps surprising lack of political interference in the execution of the urban renewal process and the operation of the Task Force – at least by Brisbane City Council. There has, however, been intervention by the State Government in terms of unilateral decisions resulting in the abandonment of the proposed light rail project (which in its original concept was to service in part the urban renewal area) and a decision not to back the Royal National Association showground site for the proposed new super stadium.

The Philosophy

The planning philosophy underlying the URTF approach reflects a number of key values.

(1) First, the notion of creating sustainable human community development in the context of urban renewal has been a macro concern, with the overall planning being cognizant of macro trends in society, such as the changing nature of the household, economic transition reflecting the growth of the services economy and the clearly evident preference among a range of social groups for inner city living.

(2) Second, the planning approach has addressed community values that place a preference on relatively low-density, low-rise development, incorporating creativity in design and protecting heritage.

(3) Third, emphasis has been on people in developing the broader planning concepts as well as in the operational detail at a project level, reflected

Church Street Public Housing – Well designed housing for low-income households in Church Street, Fortitude Valley

Centro on James – Spanish Mission style commercial and retail development on James Street, Fortitude Valley

McTaggarts – A former wool storage building was redeveloped into residential apartments on the river at Tenerife

Merthyr Village – An innovative design for a bus shelter forming part of the streetscape improvements at Merthyr Road, New Farm

New Farm Village – a mix of retail and residential on bustling Brunswick Street, New Farm

Brisbane Powerhouse – Centre for the Live Arts at Lamington Street, New Farm

Fig. 6. Examples of the Built Environments Delivered by the URTF Process.

through the extensive consultation program and participation of local residents and businesses in developing the details of Local Plans for the precincts and for specific development projects. This has resulted, for example, in the managed movement out of industry before the movement of people in.

(4) Fourth, and very importantly, the execution of redevelopment projects has been carefully managed by the Task Force so as not to flood the market, moving within the capacity of the market to absorb projects.

(5) Finally, both at the macro level of planning and at the micro level of individual projects, the emphasis has been placed on lifestyle outcomes.

The process of urban renewal administered through the URTF has been enhanced through the unwavering on-going political support of the Brisbane City Council which has been led by the same Lord Mayor since 1991. This has provided continuity and a sustained commitment, a factor that has been important for the success of the project and its achievements to date.

The Brisbane Experience Compared to Others

The fourth point (4) above is important as it distinguishes between the URTF approach to urban renewal in Brisbane compared to different philosophies that have underlain some other approaches to urban renewal in other cities in Australia, notably the Docklands renewal area in Melbourne, the capital city of Victoria. The Docklands Authority has been criticized in the media as being secretive and expensive, having consumed A$50 million in operating expenses since 1995, whereas the URTF in Brisbane has had administration costs averaging A$1.6 million per annum over its first nine years. The URTF operation has been characterized by collaboration with developers on relatively small scale projects to ensure market viability in contrast to the Docklands approach which sought simultaneous competitive bidding by large consortia for the development of large precincts involving mega projects, which, not surprisingly, has led to the falling over of many proposals because of the lack of market viability to support so much at such a large scale being developed so quickly.

While the URTF has used in a sparing way a small number of catalyst projects – such as the TC Beirne building redeveloped for Brisbane City Council offices, the redevelopment of the McTaggarts by Baulderstone Hornibook, and the Mariners Reach project in Newstead by Mirvac – large scale icon projects have not really featured as part of the game plan for urban renewal. Joint public-private venturing has been used for a relatively small number of projects that are of small scale and unlike the Melbourne Docklands there is no project such as the proposed Grollo Tower (the proposed world's largest building), and unlike the Pyrmont-City West urban renewal project in Sydney there is no Star Casino. True there are publicly-funded projects, but these are of relatively small scale, such as the Powerhouse performing arts project. Rather, public funding in the Brisbane inner north-eastern suburbs urban renewal project has concentrated on infrastructure upgrading, streetscapeworks, the upgrading of existing and the provision of new open space, and in particular the riverfront public access projects.

But perhaps the most significant achievement of the URTF has been its brokerage role to facilitate the urban renewal process, to coordinate, to provide certainty for developers, and to deliver smoothly the requisite Council and State Government agency approvals. This has been an essential ingredient in the execution of the urban renewal process because, for the Brisbane inner north-eastern urban renewal area, unlike the situation in many other large urban renewal areas in other cities, approximately 90% of the total land was and remains in private ownership. This lack of large scale public land holdings, along with the market facilitating approach in underlying the node of operation of the Task Force, is reflected in the ratio of public to private expenditure of 1:26 achieved over the first nine years.

CONCLUSION

The URTF approach to urban renewal in Brisbane's inner north-eastern suburbs has been widely recognized as being successful, managing the urban renewal process within a transparent process, with a dynamic macro planning framework, and through collaborative and facilitative partnership with the business sector and the community. So far the process, the program and its projects have been remarkably devoid of media and interest group criticism; it is not perceived as a blatant political exercise; it has not produced white-elephant icon projects, and nor has it flooded the market with oversupply; it has involved relatively small investment of public resources; and it is well on track to achieve its 20 year development and investment targets.

There are, of course, questions that remain unanswered about the potential negative impacts of the urban renewal process in Brisbane's inner north-eastern suburbs. For example, it is likely – perhaps inevitable – that the transformations that are occurring in the inner city areas (not just as a result of urban renewal programs) will result in a displacement of low-income and socio-economically disadvantaged households as housing prices rise and become less affordable. Further, some claims about the impact of urban renewal on sustainability – particularly in stemming continued sprawling suburban metropolitan growth – may be overstated or over-ambitious, especially in terms of the magnitude of the share of future growth in population and households in metropolitan areas that will be accommodated through urban consolidation including urban renewal. Such issues are important and have been discussed in the work of Stimson et al. (2000) in the context of Brisbane. Nonetheless, urban renewal as one of a range of urban consolidation instruments is having success in turning around the population decline that was widespread across much of the inner suburbs of Brisbane City.

Out of the Brisbane experience to urban renewal through the URTF, it is possible to suggest a number of challenges to urban renewal in the future.

(1) First there is what we might call the "commerce factor". This involves the growth in international business and the growth of syndication to secure prime property and direct investment in large projects. The increasing requirement is for flexibility and mixed use zoning to provide the built environment spaces to accommodate the work, leisure and living requirements of the knowledge-based society, and a challenge in how to link urban renewal project phasing to a changing property market cycle.

(2) Second there is what we might call the "aesthetic factor", whereby in an increasingly global society and one where new lifestyle values are evolving rapidly, there will be a need to incorporate aesthetics in innovation in planning and building to design and deliver quality lifestyle communities which marry the old and the new.

(3) Third, there is what we might call the "people factor", for which we need to link the planning and construction of built environments to the increasingly diverse needs of a more mobile society characterized by a wide variety of household types, in which the nature of work and the role of woman are changing, in which very diverse lifestyles are evolving, and in which the community expects and has the right to be involved in the planning and design processes.

(4) Finally there is what we might call the "political factor" which relates to the changing role and limited resources of government that will require joint venturing and public-private community partnerships to provide project funding and to generate more sustainable forms of urban development and living. This will not be achieved through heavy handed unilateral approaches by government that typically generate bad planning

decisions that are difficult to reverse, and which will not be achieved by governments deviating from strategic planning frameworks that have evolved through collaborative and consultative processes because of short-term political agendas and by bowing to sectional interests.

Urban renewal will become a more important part of the dynamic processes through which our large cities evolve. The challenges remain considerable, but experimentation through mechanisms such as the URTF can help us develop innovative best practice approaches in addressing the task of planning for and executing urban renewal programs.

REFERENCES

Badcock, B. (1989). Rent Gap Hypothesis. *Annuls of the Association of American Geographers*, *79*, 125–145.

Borgegard, L. E., & Murdie, R. (1993). Socio-demographic Impacts of Economic Restructuring on Stockholm's Inner City. *Tijdschrift voor Econ. en Soc. Geografie*, *84*(4), 269–280.

Daly, M., Taylor, S., & Clark, L. (1997). *Monitoring Sydney*. Brisbane: Publications and Printing Department, Queensland University of Technology.

Ley, D. (1986). Inner City Revitalisation in Canada: A Vancouver Case Study. *Canadian Geographer*, *25*(2), 124–148.

Newman, P., Kenworthy, J., & Vintila, P. (1993). Can We Build Better Cities. *Urban Futures*, *3*(2), 17–24.

O'Connor, K. B. (1998). Understanding Metropolitan Melbourne . . . Without Being Confused by Coffee and Doughnuts. *Urban Policy and Research*, *16*(2), 139–147.

O'Connor, K., Rapson, V., & Clark, L. (1997). *Monitoring Melbourne 1997*. Brisbane: Publications and Printing Department, Queensland University of Technology.

Reynolds, J., & Porter, L. (1998). Melbourne's Inner City Revival. *Urban Policy and Research*, *16*, 63–68.

Sassen, S. (1991). *The Global City, New York, London, Tokyo*. New Jersey: Princeton University Press.

Smith, N. (1979). Toward a Theory of Gentrification: A Back to the City Movement by Capital, not People. *Journal of the American Planners Association*, *45*, 538–548.

Smith, N., & Williams, P. (1986). *Gentrification of the City*. Boston: Allen and Unwin.

Stimson, R. J. (1992). The Brisbane Strategy Plan and Growth Management in the South East Corner of Queensland. In: C. Fletcher & C. Walsh (Eds), *The Impact of Federalism on Metropolitan Strategies in Australia* (pp. 118–165). Canberra: Federalism Research Centre, Australian National University.

Stimson, R. J., & Taylor, S. P. (1998). Dynamics of Brisbane's Inner City Suburbs. *Australian Planner*, *35*(4), 205–214.

Stimson, R., Mullins, P., Baum, S., Davis, R., Gleeson, S., & Shaw, K. (2000). *Inner-City Renaissance: The Changing Face, Functions and Structure of Brisbane's Inner-City*: CD Rom publication, University of Queensland (available University of Queensland Bookshop).

Troy, P. (1996). *The Perils of Urban Consolidation*. Sydney: The Federation Press.

Urban Renewal Task Force (1991). *Urban Renewal Report: Inner North Eastern Suburbs Brisbane*. Brisbane: Brisbane City Council.

Urban Renewal Task Force (1999). *Brisbane Urban Renewal: Addressing Tomorrow 1999 Report*. Brisbane: Brisbane City Council.

10. RAILWAYS AND REURBANIZATION IN PERTH: CASE STUDIES OF SUCCESS IN URBAN PUBLIC POLICY

Peter Newman

ABSTRACT

Changes in urban public policy away from car dependence are traced in Perth through the renaissance of railways and the process of reurbanization. The case studies are developed through personal histories to illustrate the kind of political and cultural changes that are needed in such policy transitions. The context of oil scarcity is used to highlight the underlying sense of vulnerability driving public attitudes in this process.

INTRODUCTION

In 1976 I was elected as a local councillor in the City of Fremantle, part of the metropolitan area of Perth, Australia's fourth largest city. My passion was the two "r's" – "railways" and "reurbanization". But the major reaction from most of those who I had to work with in urban public policy was another "r" – be "realistic". There were apparently two fixed certainties in urban public policy in Australia – "You will never get Australians out of their cars" and "Australians love their large blocks in the suburbs". This is a story of how cities are always a good deal more complex than such simple assertions. It is also a story of hope that cities can change in ways that respond to deeper issues of urban public policy.

International Urban Planning Settings: Lessons of Success, Volume 12, pages 295–310.
2001 by Elsevier Science Ltd.
ISBN: 0-7623-0695-5

PUBLIC POLICY CONTEXT

Both urban policy and urban transport policy in Australia have tended to follow North American traditions in the past 50 years (Neutze, 1977). Land was constantly opened up on the urban fringe at new standards of reduced density and with automobile accessibility assumed. The shift outwards and hence decline of the older areas was seen to be inevitable and certainly driven by market preferences. Likewise urban transport policy was essentially a process of facilitating an ever growing stream of traffic with bigger and better roads. As buses fitted into that too, there was little else needed. Railways were a relic of another age and with about as much market pressure for them as for reurbanization.

However some dark clouds began to form in this rather sunny and simple world, starting in the 1970s. First in 1973 and then in 1979, cities around the world were faced with oil scarcity. Oil prices globally quadrupled, plateaued and then doubled again. Although life returned to normal fairly quickly, the average motorist was left with an uneasy sense of vulnerability. In discussions about the future, people in cities built around the car would now feel that some other options might be needed. Issues about location and mode were no longer quite so simple and as the century ended the oil problem has become a dark shadow over our urban future.

A range of other factors also began to impinge from the 1970s: (a) environmental issues (sprawl and air quality); (b) social issues (women working and an aging population); and (c) economic issues (the transition from an industrial economy to a knowledge-based economy). However in this paper the underlying issue of oil scarcity will be used to highlight a transition in urban public policy towards a greater role for railways and reurbanization.

Oil is the key resource which has driven the economy in the 4th Kondratiev Cycle (Freeman & Soete, 1997). As we enter the 5th cycle and create an economy around other technologies like information technology and green technologies, there will be many tensions with those who are part of the present order. Perhaps even the urban management professionals who have been trained in the technologies and techniques of the previous economy may not be as amenable to change as the general public. This is an underlying theme of the stories outlined below which show the importance of public involvement in urban public policy.

In my academic career I had studied at Stanford during the 1973 oil crisis and had been fortunate to work for a short time with an aging oil expert called M. King Hubbert. He had predicted the oil crisis back in 1956 when he first did some depletion curves on the U.S. oil reserves (Hubbert, 1965). He recognized that the key to understanding a resource like oil was the peak point in production. This he calculated for the U.S. would be in 1970 – after that they would need to turn to large scale imports.

The peak point occurred as predicted in 1970 and large scale imports to the U.S. began. By 1973 OPEC had recognized the vulnerability of the U.S. and its own opportunity to ensure a better price for the remaining decades of their own oil. M. King Hubbert was pleased to see that his methodology was correct but not happy about how he had been treated for 20 years – no serious consideration to changing cities or transport had been made in the United States, after all, cars and urban sprawl were part of the American way of life.

Hubbert also made some calculations on world oil production. He considered that a similar global oil scarcity would be felt most dramatically around the year 2000. This would be when the world's oil reserves were likely to be half used and hence production would begin to decline. A few brief decades were left for the world to prepare for a process of using less and less oil not more and more. To me the implication for cities were obvious – car dependence needed to be reduced through railways and reurbanization.

I began to write about this from my academic base which moved from Stanford to my home town and the new Murdoch University (Newman, 1975). But it was not long before I found that the pull of urban policy began to draw me into political processes. The issues of my local town were becoming a test case for my ideas but I also felt a strong need to learn about urban public policy from the inside. Key questions I sought to answer were: (a) how does change occur in political institutions on issues that are of long term consequence? (b) does one always have to be "realistic" and accept the political status quo on urban public policy? and (c) is there hope that cities can change particularly in their oil vulnerability and car dependence?

The processes of change will be discussed first in terms of railways and then reurbanization.

CASE STUDY 1: RAILWAY RENAISSANCE

In November 2000 an historic announcement was made by the Premier of Western Australia, Richard Court, of a A$1 billion rail system for the southern suburbs of Perth. The announcement was at the height of global concern over oil as prices rose and looked to be staying up. The moment was particularly historic because it ended a chapter of urban public policy in Perth which was started in 1979 by Sir Charles Court, who as the then Premier had announced the closure of the Fremantle-Perth railway. This case study is about the urban public policy transition which changed a modern car dependent city and enabled it to build a new rail system.

The Fremantle Line Struggle

As a young city councillor in the City of Fremantle, the announcement of the closure of our rail system in 1979 had come as a bitter blow. It was a powerful expression of the dominance of an urban public policy very different to the one I was hoping to enact. But, in retrospect, it also provided the basis for me to become involved in a process of urban change that few people (academics at least) are given the opportunity to do. The closure gave me the chance to be part of a movement that could reach the hearts and minds of the public and bring changes in urban public policy from the grass roots.

The closure of the Fremantle-Perth railway (a line almost 100 years old) was rationalised in the State Government's policy documents on the basis that:

(a) the replacement bus service would be better than that provided by the aging diesel trains,
(b) Perth was a car-based city and flexible buses were the best option and least costly to provide with the minimal levels of service for those who can't drive, and
(c) trains were a part of the past but were unlikely to be part of the future, witness most newly developing cities in the United States.

After some digging it also became clear that the road builders were keen to have a major highway using the railway reservation.

A few months after the announcement the 1979 oil crisis broke in the wake of the Iran-Iraq war. The drama of a global oil crisis and at the same time local facilitation of more car driving, were the perfect motivation for a public campaign focusing on the symbol of the railway closure.

After some pushing from a local politician I formed a group called "The Friends of the Railways". Volunteers to help were called for and a roller coaster ride of political activism absorbed me for the next four years. Public meetings turned into mass rallies. Huge media attention gave us all the coverage we needed (see Fig. 1). A record was cut and played regularly on local radio. A petition was gathered that produced 100,000 signatures (more than 10% of the population). Detailed studies were drawn up by our team including retired railway engineers, on how Perth could be rebuilt around a new and extended rail system. My writing stressed the looming oil crisis and the complete lack of attention to this issue by the government. I also began a research program with Federal Government support to do comparisons of the transport and land use patterns of Australian cities in relation to world cities. The work has continued as our major global contribution (Newman & Kenworthy, 1989, 1999) but its roots were in this campaign.

When the last train was run we had a mass rally and hoped one day we could return to reopen it – but we feared the end had come. The new bus service on the Fremantle rail line immediately lost 30% of its patronage despite having a more frequent service (it was slower and less direct). All advice to us was to give up – you can't win this one, be realistic. Direct action continued to highlight the issue but we also shifted tack and ensured that the Labor Party Opposition had a clear policy that they would re-open the railway and examine ways to upgrade it. The movement then became decidedly more party political in the lead up to the State election in 1983.

A turning point in the campaign came when the State Government's Director General of Transport organised bus loads of Liberal party supporters to blanket a rally organised by the Friends of the Railways, shutting out any of our rail supporters. They passed motions of support for the government. It was a moment of despair but in retrospect was probably the moral turning point in the campaign. Public anger was now palpable.

Fig. 1. Newspaper cartoon supporting campaign that buses are not the same as trains.

In 1983 the Labor Party was elected after decades of opposition and immediately re-opened the railway. The public servants who had been responsible for the policy of closure were there to help cut the ribbon.

Electrification

The old diesel trains immediately drew back the lost 30% patronage but the prospect for much further upgrading of the system looked bleak. The public servants had made estimates of the cost of electrification which put it way out of consideration. However, an independent "Electrification Inquiry" was established on which one of the retired railway engineers from Friends of the Railways was placed. The public process was being opened up a chink.

The Inquiry was able to conclude that electrifying the rail system could be done relatively cheaply (far less than the cost estimates provided by the Department of Transport) and indeed cheaper than trying to maintain the aging diesel fleet. A future for rail was at last assured.

In the year that this Inquiry was held I had been asked to take a secondment to work with the Minister for Transport. I was given the joyful task of briefing the Minister on the Inquiry's findings and preparing a Press Conference to announce the electrification possibility. The Minister shrewdly suggested that the major issue was going to be: 'what about the northern suburbs, why can't they have an electric rail too'?. The northern suburbs were the fast growing post 1960s suburbs based around the car. They had already exceeded their new freeway's capacity and local people were beginning to lobby for the Friends of the Railways' vision document which suggested a rail line should go there someday. I suggested to the Minister that if asked this question he should announce another Inquiry.

The Press Conference was a great success with huge interest from all media outlets. The first question after the details of the electrification Inquiry were spelt out was: what about the northern suburbs? 'Oh yes, we are going to have a new Inquiry on that' the Minister said. The Director General of Transport nearly fell off his seat and the next day the headline in the newspaper said "Northern Suburbs to get Rail".

Northern Suburbs Railway

The Department's policy officers couldn't quite get their minds around the possibility of a *new* rail line. Upgrading some old lines may have a little rationale but to consider a new line through suburbs designed for the car didn't make sense. In the 1960s the two rail reserves had been removed as these suburbs would never need anything other than road access for cars supplemented by buses.

All attention focused on the electrification projects which had been the subject of much discussion in the subsequent State election with considerable popular support. The re-elected Labor government then put the plan and finances together and started to think about the next stage. Such political sensitivity existed in the northern suburbs that a full public consultation process was undertaken.

However the public servants involved were convinced that an area like this could never work with a railway; the best that could be hoped for would be a busway. Thus the public surveys raised questions like – "if you had a choice between a railway with a thirty minute service and a busway with a ten minute service (and equal levels of comfort and speed) what would you prefer?" Unfortunately the public kept wanting a railway. They refused to be "realistic".

Next, a detailed study was done by consultants comparing the options with a clear preference for the Busway being outlined. A key argument was that bus-rail transfers would work against a railway and possibly even see a reduction in patronage on what the present bus service carried. In cost terms the busway was considered to be much cheaper. The politics now became very difficult – the public wanted a railway and the public servants wanted a busway. The Minister called in another Inquiry and invited an "Expert Panel" to assess the Busway option. The Expert Panel found that: (a) there was considerable undercosting of the Busway (particularly the engineering of how to accommodate large numbers of buses arriving close together in the city at peak time); and (b) there was also considerable overcosting of the Railway (particularly the transfer penalty would not be so high and better patronage could be anticipated).

The State Government welcomed the new Inquiry and announced the new railway which was built on time and on budget, opening just before they were voted out of office in 1993. The patronage in the 1990s on the electrified lines and the new line to the northern suburbs are shown in Fig. 2. They are compared to Adelaide, a similar Australian city, which has not upgraded their rail system but has remained 'realistic'.

The patronage on the Perth rail system went from seven million passengers a year to almost 30 million passengers a year in seven years. In international comparisons the total level of patronage is not huge, but the turnaround is quite dramatic. The Northern Suburbs line carries the equivalent of 6 lanes of traffic in peak hours and was built for the cost of two lanes of highway. Furthermore its stations (each architect designed) have become icons representing the

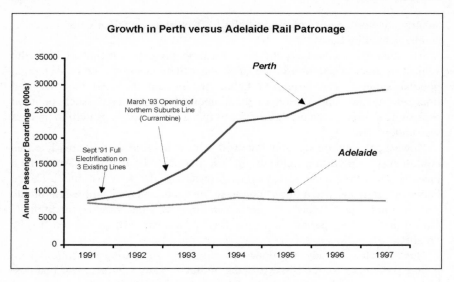

Fig. 2. Perth and Adelaide Rail Patronage, 1991–1997.

different areas along the line and are important features in a rather featureless landscape (see Fig. 3).

Southern Suburbs Railway

The remaining major missing piece of railway in the Perth region is the southern suburbs. Before being voted out in 1993 the Labor Party had begun a process to plan this railway. The new Liberal Coalition government of Richard Court was now acutely aware of the popularity of rail and when elected made it clear that a railway to the south would occur sometime. They changed the route to enable some of their seats to be advantaged and then set about planning the service and seeking how to finance it. After seven and a half years and a looming election the funding for a A$1 billion budget was put together and announced in November 2000.

The public pressure for such a policy option had become unbearable. Surveys by the government and other groups had shown that over 90% of the population wanted to see the railway extended, a mere 9% wanted to see more roads and 87% supported transferring the funds out of "road funds".

At the height of the fourth oil crisis and against all advice from their Department of Transport policy advisers, the government committed to the rail

Fig. 3. Passengers at Central Perth station entering one of the new electric trains.

option. Rail was now a bipartisan urban public policy in Perth. Not long after, at a seminar on transport futures, one of the policy advisers from the Department angrily spoke about the waste of money in the Perth rail system; it was time that politicians and the public became more "realistic", he suggested.

CASE STUDY 2: REURBANIZATION – REVITALISING OLDER URBAN AREAS

The 1976 census in Australia showed that the inner city across all major cities had entered a major decline phase. In my City of Fremantle there had been a 12% loss of population in the period 1971 to 1976. The spectre of urban decline similar to the U.S. was seen to have set in. The "doughnut effect" was freely associated with the inner area along with a sense of inevitable and irreversible decline (Kendig, 1979).

If an urban area planned to promote a public policy process designed to reverse its decline, the response was always given that Australians love their large blocks. They do not want to live in city areas in high rise blocks of flats.

The market would mean that older urban areas in Australia were not a realistic option for development.

The Fremantle Renewal

The first academic paper I wrote on this issue was written as a Fremantle councillor trying to outline a policy of reurbanization that could be implemented (Newman, 1977).

The paper suggested that the process should emphasise the benefits of living in an urban community where access to quality urban services and friends, would outweigh the private benefits of large blocks and large houses in suburban areas. Other work we undertook also showed that there would be significant savings in transport energy and infrastructure costs if reurbanization occurred (Newman, Kenworthy & Lyons, 1985). The policy framework all made sense.

Nothing happened. The planning department of the Fremantle Council themselves could not see any way to facilitate reurbanization. The housing and regulatory system were not conducive to redevelopments in an area filled with non-standard buildings, heritage qualities and awkward spaces. After a frustrating year on the Planning Committee where it seemed all we ever heard was why development did not fit, we decided to close down our planning department and advertise for a "development officer". The person appointed was a visionary planner who showed us how to plan in a way that could facilitate reurbanization (McGill & Dawkins, 1988).

The first step was to develop a clear set of goals for each area in the city – goals that reflected the character of the area and enabled it to be built on for the future. Then with a one page Plan development was invited to help fulfil those goals. Zoning was virtually abolished apart from an "urban zone" that encouraged mixed use. Finally and most importantly, the development process was dominated not by rules of density and plot ratios but of design; the development must fit the heritage qualities of the area and must look good. Design was everything.

Development was further assisted by the council actually setting out and building some housing developments to show what we were looking for. The trickle turned into a flood of projects, small and large, that began to see how a market did in fact exist. But the social processes of community building were also critical to developing that market. Artists were attracted to put their creativity into the built form and into the development of festivals and life on the streets. A desire to be part of Fremantle, to be able to walk to the "cappucino strip", to attend the Fly by Night Club, to walk down interesting (and safe) streets, to have good schools which your kids liked attending, to have places to visit – all these were part of the Fremantle revival.

The process was well underway when the America's Cup was won by Australia and frantic preparations were begun to hold the Cup in Fremantle in early 1987. Such were the strong planning principles and processes in place in Fremantle that when the development boom hit it did not ruin Fremantle – it helped to heal the wounds of decline and set in place a long term future (Newman, 1988). In 2 years, around A\$400 million of public infrastructure and social housing was built and A\$400 million of private development occurred. A new kind of architectural confidence began to be asserted which reflected the historic urban heritage of Fremantle but which was new. The "Fremantle Style" became recognized as a type of development that began to spread to other parts of the old suburbs of Perth.

East Perth and Subiaco as "Better Cities"

At the beginning of the 1980s the Deputy Prime Minister of Australia, Brian Howe, a committed urbanist and former Methodist Minister, started a new program called "Better Cities" (which is also discussed in Chapter 9 of this volume). This program was designed to demonstrate how integrated urban development in the old industrial parts of Australian cities could occur in ways that set a pattern of urban renewal. Other innovations in terms of mixed use, water sensitive design, reduced car dependence and toxic waste site remediation were all part of the A\$850 million program.

The model reurbanization projects funded under Better Cities in Perth were East Perth and Subiaco. Both were adjacent to the rail system, Subiaco in fact was built around and over the Fremantle line and became Perth's first example of transit-oriented development. Both were developed with considerable government assistance in their planning due to the complications in the land titles, the need to create infrastructure and a new plan before the private sector could envision any involvement. Both were expressions of the new urban revival in Perth using the "Fremantle Style" (see Figs 4 and 5).

Studies done before the developments were able to show in both cases that there were considerable savings in infrastructure and transport costs by making them reurbanization projects rather than doing similar development on the urban fringe (Newman & Kenworthy, 1991). In particular it was anticipated that people living in these locations would use one third of the transport fuel of those living on the urban fringe (see Table 1).

The real value of the two projects is in their urban symbolism, as I suggested in one of the preliminary papers:

Fig. 4. Reurbanization around Subiaco rail station.

Fig. 5. Reurbanization at East Perth.

Table 1. Estimated Total Transport and Infrastructure Costs of the East Perth Redevelopment Compared to Urban Fringe Development in Perth.

COST ITEM	EAST PERTH (A$ millions)	FRINGE (A$ millions)
Infrastructure and servicing		
Direct	25.665	48.025
Indirect	10.915	–
Total infrastructure/servicing	36.580	48.025
	Difference $11.445	
Capitalised annual transport costs		
Residential development	89.387	176.439
Employment development	112.471	135.678
Total transport costs	201.858	312.117
	Difference $110.259	
Total infrastructure and transport costs	**238.438**	**360.142**
	Difference between total $121.704	

Note: Annual transport costs are capitalized at the median social discount rate of 10% over a fifteen period.

> Ad hoc efforts at consolidation of existing built up areas will not be enough to curb demand for new land at the fringe or change perceptions positively about new styles of higher density, mixed land use developments. These must be supplemented by larger scale urban village projects such as East Perth which begin to demonstrate a 'phase change' in urban options and allow developers and the community to see that high quality alternatives to sprawl are available (Newman & Kenworthy, 1991: 220).

By 2000 East Perth had over 500 new housing units and Subiaco a similar number. All were selling at much higher values than expected and indeed were attracting prices as high as any other location in Perth. The issue shifted dramatically from whether such high density development would work and attract people from the suburbs back to the city, to one of how a proportion of social housing could be included. This issue remains as the city has moved rapidly to adopt reurbanization as the norm.

Other Parts of the City

Reurbanization received a spurt in each of the years when petrol prices rose due to oil scarcity and then tended to drift back out to fringe development as prices fell. Then in the 1990s across Perth new projects in reurbanization began to appear everywhere in the new urban "Fremantle Style". Not only did they appear in older suburbs but in middle, outer and even fringe locations. The higher density, mixed use developments with emphasis on pedestrian qualities and narrow streets with no garages fronting onto them, began to take over. The market was clearly there though often local authorities took exception to the "overdevelopment" or lobby groups were established to save the suburb from "infill". Nevertheless in most areas where public surveys were made there was a majority who favoured reurbanization (as long as design rules were closely followed).

One of the driving forces behind this process is the sense of vulnerability people have in new fringe suburbs. Not only is this vulnerability due to the potential to be literally stranded in an oil crisis but the sense that the value of their property may not hold up in such a future. This has become very obvious in the 1990s where property prices in inner city locations have continued their strong growth (86% in Sydney in the 1990s) but outer suburb values have plateaued and in some cases declined (see *Australian Financial Review*, 2000; Badcock & Beer, 2000).

Similar trends have been found across all Australian cities with reurbanization becoming a dominant urban process in the 1990s. Densities in all Australian cities grew in the 1990s after falling for most of the previous 90 years. In parallel with this process there has also been a falling off in the growth of car travel per capita (VKT) and a rise in the growth of rail travel. The two transport trends and the move to reurbanization seem to be closely linked. Some academics have provided leadership for the anti-reurbanization reaction (Troy, 1996; Lewis, 2000). However the market is firmly set and processes at local government level that enable subdivisions and creative infill have become more and more evident.

In Perth a new planning code was created to facilitate a more urban kind of development which was less car dependent. Called "Liveable Neighbour-hoods", it was rationalised as a better way to create community, to reduce car use and to respond to the new economy (Ministry for Planning, 1998). Demonstrations of this are now being put in place in middle and outer suburbs.

Planning agencies have not always been able to anticipate or facilitate the process however. In 1992 the Perth Metro Plan was completed after two years of preparation. It suggested that every effort would be made to ensure that 20% of all development was reurbanization of inner and middle areas but that being "realistic" it was unlikely to occur. By the time the report came out the figure was already over 30%. A similar preliminary plan in 2000 for a planning process called Future Perth suggested that they would hope to achieve 37% reurbanization; the most recent figure shows that it was already 46% in 2000.

CONCLUSIONS

Urban public policy in Perth is now considerably less car dependent in its orientation and spending priorities than it was 30 years ago. The commitment to a rail system has become bipartisan after it had once been a major political battle. At the same time the trend back to the city has been occurring to the extent that reurbanization is now almost half of all development and even some of the urban fringe housing is inner city in style.

This change has not occurred without its political pain, its creative demonstrations and its tapping of public sentiment. The reaction against car dependence has moved from being a fringe issue to a central issue. The cause of this can be argued and obviously includes elements of economic, social and environmental drivers as outlined earlier. But the rising sense that oil is becoming scarce has coincided with some of the key turning points and appears to be one of the public underpinnings to this urban public policy transition.

REFERENCES

Australian Financial Review (2000). Your Property Nest Egg Has Just Cracked, 4 November.

Badcock, B., & Beer, A. (2000). *Home Truths: Property Ownership and Housing Wealth in Australia*. Australia: Melbourne University Press.

Freeman, C., & Soete, L. (1997). *The Economics of Industrial Innovation* (3rd ed.). London: Printer.

Hubbert, M. (1965). Energy Resources. In: *Resources and Man* (pp. 157–242). San Francisco: National Academy of Sciences, Freeman.

Lewis, M. (1999). *Suburban Backlash!: The battle for the worlds most livable city*. Melbourne: Blooming Books.

McGill, G., & Dawkins, J. (1998). Fremantle Urban Conservation Success Story. In: P. Newman, S. Neville & L. Duxbury (Eds), *Case Studies in Environmental Hope* (pp. 111–120).. Perth: Environmental Protection Authority.

Ministry for Planning (1998). *Livable Neighbourhoods: Community Design Code*. Perth: Ministry for Planning.

Neutze, G. (1977). *Urban Development in Australia*. Sydney: George Allen and Unwin.

Newman, P. (1975). An Ecological Model for City Structure and Development. *Ekistics, 40*(239), 258–265.

Newman, P. (1988). Fremantle and the America's Cup. *Architecture Australia, 77*(2): 72–76.

Newman, P., & Kenworthy, J. (1999). *Sustainability and Cities: Overcoming Automobile Dependence*. Washington, DC: Island Press.

Newman, P., & Kenworthy, J. (1989). *Cities and Automobile Dependence: An International Sourcebook*. Gower: Aldershot.

Newman, P., & Kenworthy, J. (1991). *East Perth: A Model for Reduced Automobile Dependence*. Paper presented at the Ecological City Workshop, OECD Conference, Brisbane, November.

Newman, P., Kenworthy, J., & Lyons, T. (1985). Transport energy in the Perth metropolitan region: some urban policy implications. *Urban Policy and Research*, *3*(2), 4–15.

Troy, P. (1996). *The Perils of Urban Consolidation*. Sydney: The Federation Press, Leichardt.

11.   KANAZAWA: CREATING A LIVABLE CITY THROUGH HISTORIC PRESERVATION

Akihiko Tani, Mitsuhiko Kawakami and Tatsuo Masuta

ABSTRACT

Kanazawa, on the Sea of Japan in the historic Hokuriku region, is one of Japan's most successful cities in historical preservation. Originally one of the larger castle towns in the feudal era, Kanazawa was out of the mainstream of Japan's modernization after 1868. Moreover, it escaped both the destruction of World War II as well as fires and earthquakes. Hence, after World War II, Kanazawa was a prime candidate for historical preservation. The city, through government initiative and active citizen participation, started various programs from the 1960s onward to preserve historically valuable buildings as well as entire districts. In the process, the city has become a model for the nation as a whole and one of its best preserved old castle towns. Nonetheless, Kanazawa faces pressures common to all modern cities in Japan as to how to preserve inner city vitality and population, provide effective public transportation, and control suburban growth.

International Urban Planning Settings: Lessons of Success, Volume 12, pages 311–335.
2001 by Elsevier Science Ltd.
ISBN: 0-7623-0695-5

INTRODUCTION

Uniqueness of Kanazawa

Kanazawa for many Japanese is the city to visit, together with Kyoto and Nara (see Fig. 1). This is because these cities successfully maintain the rich historical environment and traditional culture. Unlike Kyoto and Nara, which are the old national capitals, however, Kanazawa evolved from one of many castle towns of the Edo Era, the period between 1603 and 1867, when the Tokugawa Shogunate controlled the nation. The nation was divided into territories under direct control of the Shogunate and some 300 autonomous provinces ruled by provincial lords. The castle town was then the capital of each local province.

While preservation of two old capitals owes considerably to the national programs of historic preservation, many other cities had difficulties in maintaining their historical character. Kanazawa is considered to be one of the few successful cases in which a castle town was developed into a large local city and yet has maintained its original historical character.

What sets Kanazawa apart from all the other castle towns is its unique process of historical development. While all the other castle towns were either burnt by major fires since the Meiji Era or destroyed by WWII air-raids, and therefore were thoroughly remodeled to suit the modern and thus Western city planning requirements, Kanazawa survived any major disasters and therefore the current central urban areas were built on the infrastructure of the old castle town. Sato (1995) studied various cities with their origin from castle towns and classified their development pattern. However, he excluded Kanazawa from his study because of its unique development process.

This situation was once considered as a disadvantage for the city. While other local cities took advantage of the changes, Kanazawa found it difficult to accommodate various development projects promoted by the national government, such as street widening and land readjustment, within the existing built-up areas and hence did not follow the same course of modernization and industrialization as many other local cities took. As a result more historic buildings and townscapes have survived in Kanazawa than in any other local cities. When the city realized the significance of its historical heritages that survived WWII, it started its own effort of historic preservation in the postwar 1960s.

Historic Background of Kanazawa

Kanazawa City is located on the Japan Sea side of Honshu, the main island, and to the north of Nagoya. Its population is ranked around 30th in the nation at

Fig. 1. Location of Kanazawa.

460,000 in the year 2000. However, the city had the fourth largest population when the Meiji Restoration occurred and did not grow as much as other local cities, especially ones on the Pacific Ocean side. The city is now ranked at the top of the list of not "most populous cities" but "most attractive and livable cities." Kanazawa's attractiveness can be attributable to its well-preserved historical heritage and local traditional culture as well as its sufficient size as a modern city and rich natural environment surrounding the city.

Kanazawa was founded in the mid 16th century, when Japan was in the civil war period. In 1583, the region fell under the control of a powerful provincial lord, Lord Maeda, and Kanazawa was built into a large castle town. After that, the city continued to be one of the largest castle towns during the Edo Era, until the Meiji Restoration in 1868. As the center of its territory with the largest rice production in the nation, the city enjoyed its economic prosperity and developed a variety of cultural activities. This was due to the policy of Lord Maeda to invest economic wealth on cultural activities rather than to build up its military might that could have invited unnecessary conflict with the Tokugawa government.

Kanazawa thus evolved on the urban structure of the largest castle town of the Edo Era.[1] The city had a population of 120,000 in the early Meiji Period, larger than the 100,000 presently living in the old castle town area. Kanazawa's population had declined gradually during the period of modernization and industrialization, as the city could not, and in a sense would not, follow the national policy. Kanazawa's unwillingness to follow the national policy was partly because of its difficulties to change the existing urban areas and partly because of its conservatism that avoided the government-driven modernization. In other words Kanazawa was not necessarily dissatisfied with the status quo.

Also, Kanazawa was excluded from the WWII bombing list of the Allied Forces, together with Kyoto, Nara and Kurashiki, on the ground that these cities had much cultural significance and limited industrial accumulation. Also, the city did not suffer from any other major disasters like extensive fires and major earthquakes. It is now a well-known historical city often compared with Kyoto. However, Kyoto is an old national capital whereas Kanazawa has grown out of a castle town like many other local cities have. Therefore, Kanazawa is a precious model for historic preservation and receives attention from other local cities as a successful model.

Historic Preservation in Japan

Historic preservation in Japan has long been promoted by the national government as one of its cultural programs. After World War II the government started to preserve historically significant buildings, such as temples, shrines and palaces, as National Treasures or Significant Cultural Assets under the Cultural Asset Protection Law of 1950. Also it started the Special Law for Old Capital Environment Protection in 1966. Then, in 1975 the government launched a new program called the "Preservation District for Groups of Historic Buildings" to expand historic preservation into townscape preservation. This is an important step towards preservation of historical environment for many non-capital cities. However, in order to be designated as a Preservation District under this program, the area has to show a certain level of concentration of historical buildings and to satisfy a set of strict conditions and rules of the program (Ohkawa, 1997; Nishimyama & Mimura, 1995). The program had designated 44 districts all around the nation by the year 2000. One of Kanazawa's historic districts, Higashi Chaya-gai, is under investigation for the next designated district.

However, the majority of other historical buildings and townscapes in Kanazawa and elsewhere, which were not so significant nor so concentrated as those in the Preservation Districts, were out of protection of these national programs and therefore bound to disappear as cities developed. Because historical buildings did not accommodate the modern life such as Western style living and car parking, many Japanese chose to replace them by new but characterless houses. As a result of these individual replacements the city's townscapes had gradually changed along with the original character of the city.[2]

Kanazawa challenged this problem by devising its own programs of historic preservation (Kawakami, 1999; Tani et al., 1999). The city enacted the Traditional Environment Preservation Ordinance in 1968 to start focusing its urban policy on historic preservation, especially townscape preservation. This is the first attempt by a local government to have an ordinance of this kind and since then Kanazawa has been recognized as the frontrunner in this field, as Tani and Masuta pointed out (Tani & Masuta, 2000).

This Chapter attempts to illustrate how Kanazawa could successfully preserve its historical environment, what has been done to make it possible, and how the city should make use of its success to deal with inner city problems and to prepare for the future. There are a limited number of publications written on historic preservation as part of urban strategies, and it is only recently that the importance of historic preservation has been highlighted (Nishimura, 1997; Ohkawa, 1997).[3]

JAPAN'S URBAN POLICIES AND LOCAL CITIES

Modernization of Local Cities

The Meiji Government was actively involved with urban policies for the purpose of increasing the national wealth and building up its military power. Japan then was far behind the Western nations as a result of its past national isolation policy, by which Japan closed its international trade and communication, except for a few limited trade partners, such as Portugal and Holland, for most of the Edo Era.

During the Edo Era a castle town was the capital of each autonomous province, which had all the necessary urban functions to act as the center of administrative and military power as well as economic activities. After the fall of the Tokugawa Shogunate, the Meiji Government centralized power and adopted an urban policy of developing local castle towns into industrial cities or transportation nodes and concentrating administrative and other central functions into Tokyo and several other regional centers, such as Sapporo, Sendai, Nagoya, Osaka and Fukuoka. For example, regional offices of the central government, military camps, and national universities were allocated among these regional centers.

Within the castle town the centrally-located castle was replaced by government buildings and public facilities, such as the prefectural office, the city hall and the central park. Also, *Buke-yashiki* (residences for the upper Samurai class) were converted to large commercial and office buildings and *Ashigaru-yashiki* (residences for the lower Samurai class) for residential uses. The structure of the castle town was totally changed as its narrow, winding streets were improved through road widening projects and its traditional wooden houses replaced by modern buildings. Urban planning in the prewar period was characterized by the two types of projects which never paid attention to historic preservation. (Fig. 2 shows Kanazawa's central areas in the Edo Era).

Postwar Development of Local Cities

These cities were further changed by World War II, during which major cities of Japan suffered from extensive damages of air raids by the Allied Forces. In addition, many Japanese cities were repeatedly destroyed by extensive fires or major earthquakes. As most buildings were wooden structures and old street configurations did not suit reconstruction, cities tended to be restructured completely. Kanazawa, however, was one of a few exceptions in this regard and thus took an entirely different course of development, especially in the postwar period.

After the War the Japanese Government changed its policy of concentration to decentralization by developing the national land almost coast to coast for economic purposes. Based on the "National Comprehensive Development Plan", a strategic plan for long-term, nation-wide development, and by utilizing various subsidies and incentives, the national government constructed the bullet train system and freeway network, and relocated the manufacturing industry from major metropolitan regions to new industrial cities, Technopolises (high-tech industrial cities) and other rural areas. Redevelopment of station-front areas and renewal of central business functions were also pursued in major local cities. As a result, local cities were divided between regional centers with increasing population and their subordinate cities with decreasing population. Furthermore, uniform development standards have altered local cities into little Tokyo's, often jeered at as the *Kintaro-Ame* phenomenon[4].

Fig. 2. Map of Kanazawa's Central Areas in the Edo Era.

Kanazawa suffered a population loss after the Meiji Restoration partly because the city was not eager to attract modern industry and partly because the National Government tended to prioritize investment on the Pacific Ocean side of Honshu. The city had decreased its population down to 80,000 in the late Meiji Period from 120,000 of the early Meiji peak. It was not until the Taisho Period (1912–1926) with the construction of Hokuriku Railroad Line and the opening of national institutions such as the Fourth High School when Kanazawa's population restored its early Meiji peak level.

The development history of Kanazawa was its modernization process (like many other castle towns). With construction of interregional links, such as Hokuriku Railroad Line and National Highway Route 8, development of urban transportation such as streetcar lines, and the expansion of Kanazawa Port which made the city ready for industrial take-off. However, the old urban areas with large historical buildings and street networks of the Edo Era always were in the way. The railroad station was placed two kilometers away from the city center and main streets were built with insufficient right-of-way, resulting in slow changes of the land use pattern. Ironically, these central areas have later become very important to the city as resources for tourism.

Urban Development Strategy of Kanazawa

Kanazawa announced various master plans one after another including the "Plan to Become a City of 600 Thousands" in the 1970s and the "Plan to Be a World City" and the "Plan to Build a New Urban Corridor" in the 1990s. These expressed the continued desire to be the regional center of Hokuriku into the future.[5] Among the strategies included in the plans were: to strengthen the city's linear corridor connecting the central commercial and business centers (Kanazawa Station, Musashigatsuji, Kohrinbo and Katamachi) by concentrating urban redevelopment projects along this axis; to extend the corridor to the west of the station up to Kanazawa Port by developing a new business subcenter with the relocation of the prefectural office and some other public facilities; and to extensively use large-scale land readjustment projects so as to accommodate increasing housing and to build circumferential roads.

There were many historical buildings that survived not only the war destruction but also the postwar development pressure in central Kanazawa. These became precious assets of the city, as many other local cities had lost their idiosyncratic character. These historical landmarks have recently been recognized not only as touristic attractions but also as urban amenities to the city residents.

Kanazawa has recognized the importance of historic preservation from the very early stage of the postwar development and adopted a policy to preserve them. The city enacted the "Traditional Environment Preservation Ordinance" in 1968, the first historic preservation legislation in Japan. It aimed to preserve the significance of the historical environment and influenced the nation's move towards historic preservation. Another big step taken by the city was its adoption of the "*Komachinami* Preservation Ordinance." This epoch-making ordinance aimed to enhance the historical image of Kanazawa throughout the city by preserving small-scale historical townscapes scattered all over the city. Also, the city is converting the old castle site into a historic park with some stone walls and turrets rebuilt to their original forms.

The "Plan to Become a City of 600 Thousands" is no longer achievable by Kanazawa alone, as its urban area has expanded far beyond the city's boundaries and its population has reached 600,000 with the surrounding municipalities of Mattou, Nonoichi, Tsubata and Uchinada included. In the foreseeable future, with the West of Station Areas fully developed and the circumferential road network completed, urban problems, such as the over-expanded urban areas and automobile reliant structure, will soon be addressed within the framework of overall city planning and new challenges will emerge to make Kanazawa's urban areas more compact and efficient. Figure 3 shows the master plan for Kanazawa in 1998.

CITY ORDINANCES TO PRESERVE HISTORIC DISTRICTS

Early Preservation Effort

Historic preservation of Kanazawa started in the 1960s when Japan's rapid economic development began. The city lost many historical buildings, which had survived through the prewar and early postwar periods, through modernization with widening of streets and renewal of buildings in the central areas. Many residents felt that Kanazawa's historical values were endangered and therefore the city tried to establish a policy to preserve them. The first attempt was to implement its own program, the "Program to Preserve Mud Walls and Gates of Samurai Residences", in 1964. This program aimed to preserve the gates and walls that surrounded Samurai residences and symbolized the status of Samurai. The specific area targeted by the program was Nagamachi, which kept the atmosphere of middle-class Samurai quarters of the Edo Era.

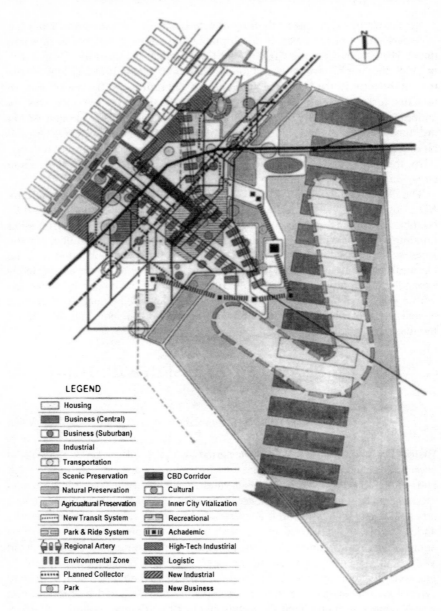

LEGEND

- 🔲 Housing
- ⬛ Business (Central)
- ◧ Business (Suburban)
- ▨ Industrial
- ▣ Transportation
- ▨ Scenic Preservation
- ▨ Natural Preservation
- ▨ Agricualtural Preservation
- New Transit System
- Park & Ride System
- 🚗 Regional Artery
- ▮▮▮ Environmental Zone
- PLanned Collector
- ▣ Park

- ▨ CBD Corridor
- ◧ Cultural
- ▨ Inner City Vitalization
- Recreational
- ▮▮▮ Achademic
- ▨ High-Tech Industirial
- ▨ Logistic
- ▨▨ New Industrial
- ▨ New Business

Fig. 3. Master Plan of Kanazawa, 1998.

Then, in 1968, the "Traditional Environment Preservation Ordinance" was passed as the first local legislation of historic preservation. Prior to that the "Special Law for Old Capital Environment Protection", a national program, had been enacted in 1966 to preserve historical environment of old capital cities, and three old capital cities, Kyoto, Nara and Kamakura, were designated. Kanazawa also wished to be included but, with its origin as a castle town rather than an old capital, it was difficult to consider Kanazawa for designation. This forced Kanazawa to devise its own ordinance for historic preservation as a means of urban planning. This was a quite rare case in which a local government invented its own tool of preservation without the backing of the national legislation, since Japan's planning administration after the Meiji Period has always been initiated and supervised by the national government. It is only a recent trend that local governments have passed various ordinances of urban planning for historic preservation, townscape conservation or community improvement through citizen participation. Therefore, Kanazawa's attempt was widely regarded as an epoch-making event.

Evolution of Preservation Ordinances

The Traditional Environment Preservation Ordinance aimed to expand the planning provision to preserve good living environments. For that purpose the ordinance took the approach of designating preservation areas, the same approach taken by the Special Law for Old Capital Environment Protection, and 13 areas, including Kenrokuen Garden, Utatsuyama Hills and areas along the Sai and Asano Rivers, with a total of 423 ha, were designated. The Ordinance called for the establishment of a special committee composed of local specialists to review large-scale building projects within the designated areas, based on the guidelines for exterior design, specifically colors, and to give the builders advice if necessary. It was intended that the ordinance perform as a design review process by the local authority. However, the Japanese administrative system does not allow local governments to be discretionary on building codes, and the uniform national policy assumes a considerable freedom for building rights as long as the building conforms to the codes. Hence, the ordinance has proven to be only advisory and thus often unsatisfactory, as in the case of non-local builders who do not conform to the local rules.

Between 1968 and 1988, 1,377 building projects were carried out in the designated areas of the Ordinance, which was 1.4% of the total number of projects completed in the whole city. Among them, a total of 143 projects were reviewed by the committee for their exterior relevance. In 1987 the "Landmark

Program", designed to preserve the exterior of historical buildings, was added and enabled the city to preserve historical buildings outside the designated areas. As a result, 45 buildings had been specified as landmarks by 1999. Therefore, the Ordinance, together with the Landmark Program, have proven to be quite effective in preserving historical environments and original townscapes.

Recent Development of Preservation Ordinances

In the 1980s and 1990s Japan experienced a nation-wide boom of city beautification movements. Local governments, with support of the national government, were eager to promote city beautification projects, including modern public buildings, attractive parks, streetscape improvements and refined public open spaces. Responding to the need for these projects, the Kanazawa's "Preservation Ordinance" was amended in 1989 to take modern urban landscape into consideration. This new Ordinance for the Preservation of Traditional Environment and Formation of Modern Urban Landscape had a two-fold strategy. It attempted to maintain the function of historic preservation and, at the same time, to balance preservation with development by the designation of areas with modern urban landscapes, such as the central business and commercial zones. Through the Ordinance, Kanazawa also intended to complement the centralized planning administrative system of Japan and to promote its own planning practices. Based on this amendment, its designated areas have increased to 32 areas with 1,599 ha, including 13 areas with 154 ha for the formation of modern urban landscapes.

By this amendment the Ordinance has also become effective in controlling the height of buildings in the city. After the national building codes introduced a volume control and abolished height restrictions by zone in the 1963 revision, medium- and high-rise buildings have invaded local cities. This phenomenon became more prominent during the so-called "bubble economy" in the 1980s and cities, with historical townscape having to cope with the situation. Kanazawa reacted promptly by reintroducing height restrictions into its own ordinance to preserve the historical townscape and to control the modern urban landscape. The maximum heights applied to buildings in the Traditional Environment Areas were 8, 10, 12, 15, 18, 20, and 31 meters, depending on the zone in the existing national system of zoning regulations, whereas buildings in the Modern Urban Landscape Areas were limited to heights of 20, 31, 45, 50, and 60 meters.

Between 1990 and 1993, 871 projects (or 5.6% of the total) were completed within the designated areas under this Ordinance. Among them, 63 projects with significant sizes were reviewed for their exteriors by the committee and the majority of them accommodated the advised changes. This evidence shows that Kanazawa's Traditional Environment Preservation Ordinance has been utilized effectively to maintain the visual quality of the city and developed as a tool to preserve the historical townscape as well as to create a balance with the modern urban landscape.

"KOMACHINAMI PROGRAM" TO PRESERVE SMALL HISTORIC LANDMARKS

How Komachinami *Preservation Ordinance Was Born*

The *Komachinami* Preservation Ordinance (*Komachinami* literally means "a small-scale historical townscape") enacted in 1994 was another unique attempt by Kanazawa within the local administrative system. Traditionally, Japan's historic preservation has two systems. One pays attention to individual buildings of historical significance and the other to groups of historical buildings forming a continuous townscape. The former is represented by the program for National Treasures and Cultural Assets whereas the latter by the program of the Preservation District for Groups of Historic Buildings. The *Komachinami* Preservation Ordinance acts as a supplemental program to fill the gap between these two systems by saving small-scale historical elements scattered in the city.

The *Komachinami* Preservation Ordinance has grown from an inventory survey of historical heritages in the old castle town areas conducted in 1984. A group of researchers identified historical buildings including 16 upper Samurai residences (*Buke-yashiki*) and 13 lower Samurai residences (*Ashigaru-yashiki*) built in the Edo Era and 33 *Buke-yashiki* and 24 *Ashigaru-yashiki* rebuilt in the Meiji Period.[6] This survey identified the architectural characteristics of these buildings and the structure of these neighborhoods.

The mayor and the city's Office for Cultural Promotion acknowledged the achievement of the survey and decided to form an official study team composed of researchers from Kanazawa University and Kanazawa Institute of Technology. The city covered the cost for the three-year study of historical buildings and structures both in Samurai and *Machiya* (townhouses for merchants and other city residents) districts. This study was not only a significant academic research but also a powerful tool to promote historic preservation. However, it was not expected that this study would be so powerful to initiate a new preservation program one year after the report was filed.

Effectiveness of Komachinami *Preservation Ordinance*

Komachinami Ordinance has a unique feature of preserving small-scale, insignificant historical elements. Kanazawa, after going through the prewar modernization process and the postwar rapid growth, retained only a handful of historic districts with significant buildings or continuous townscapes. The remaining historical elements were all small-scale and scattered in various parts of the city. The program enabled the city government to identify these historical elements to be preserved and to designate the areas as the *Komachinami* Preservation Districts. It was intended that a collection of some *Komachinami* Preservation Districts would make up a significant historic district (see Fig. 4 for examples).

In 1995, Satomi-cho of the old Samurai district and Shin-cho of the *Machiya* district were designated as the first *Komachinami* Preservation Districts. In the early stage, the city officials in charge of the Program were reluctant to meet local residents of these districts because until the 1970s old townscapes implied backwardness and old houses connoted disgrace for residents. However, it was later found out that the residents welcomed the designation and formed a local taskforce to promote the program. This fact suggests that the program was introduced at the right time to hit the turning point at which the national values began to shift from modernization and development to historic preservation.

The 39 candidate areas listed in the report of 1992, 13 for Samurai Districts and 26 for *Machiya* Districts, were examined for designation. Since the first designation of Satomi-cho and Shin-cho in 1995, six other distiricts, Mizutame-machi, Kannon-machi, Kyu-okachi-machi, Kyu-tenjin-cho, Kyu-hamagurizaka/Kyu-izumidera-machi and Hikoso/Kyu-horo-machi, have been added to increase the number of districts to eight. In these designated districts subsidies were given to improvement projects of building appearance and attached exterior structures. Eight projects were subsidized in 1995, increasing to 11 in 1996, 23 in 1997, and 38 in 1998. Among these 80 projects subsidized in these 4 years, 25 cases (31.3%) were for new construction and building exterior improvements, 12 for restorations, 11 for hedges and walls, and 8 for gates.

Until today, as a result of these individual improvements the look of the districts has been dramatically changed. For example, an old Samurai residence in Satomi-cho, which was initially planned to be demolished, was restored completely. And concrete walls were replaced with traditional mud walls. Also, an old Western-style building was saved from demolition. The program saved not only buildings and townscapes but also the community as it encouraged the residents to live on in the area.

Higashi Chaya-gai District

Tera-machi Temple District

Nagamachi Buke-yashiki District

Kazue-machi Chaya District

Fig. 4. Photos of Kanazawa's Historic Districts.

The quality of these restorations has increased gradually. There are even some cases where newly improved buildings look as if they were quite historic (see Fig. 5). This shows the effectiveness of the *Komachinami* Program as a tool for historic preservation. The program is also effective in improving the living environment and maintaining inner city population, suggesting that historic preservation is an effective tool for inner city revitalization.

CASE STUDIES OF HISTORIC PRESERVATION DISTRICTS

Higashi Chaya-Gai District

Early Attempt for Designation
Higashi Chaya-gai is one of Kanazawa's historic foci along with the old castle site and Kenrokuen Garden. It was a traditional entertainment district for the largest castle town. Its beauty and historic significance has both local and national recognition.

Higashi Chaya-gai was a highly regarded entertainment district where the rich but intelligent *Danna* (clientele) had exclusive access. *Geiko* (performing ladies) working there were also required to be refined and talented. Daughters of even Samurai families often spent some years before their marriage. *Chaya* buildings were built by first-class carpentry and therefore considered as a showcase for the cultural excellence of the times (see Fig. 6).

In 1971, Higashi Chaya-gai was considered as the first candidate district for the national program of historic preservation, the Preservation District for Groups of Historic Buildings, and a two-year survey was conducted by Kiyoshi Hirai, a professor at Tokyo Institute of Technology. However, as the residents did not consider historic preservation vital to their community and there were some delicate issues associated with the entertainment district, the residents rejected the designation. Since then historic preservation in this district has been discussed only behind the scene as if it were a taboo. It was not until 1999 when the city and the community started a basic study once again to become a designated district for the same national program.

Recent Survey
In the survey of 25 years ago, 87 of 128 units surveyed, or 68% of the total, were entertainment facilities (*Chaya*). Now after 25 years the number has decreased to 62 with a survival rate of 71.3%. Of these 62 units, 26 units were restored with facade improvements. Despite the decrease in the total number of *Chaya* buildings, the majority of the restored units are clustered along the three

Satomi-cho (Samurai District)

Kannon-machi (Machiya District)

Fig. 5. Images of Improved Townscape by Komachinami Program.

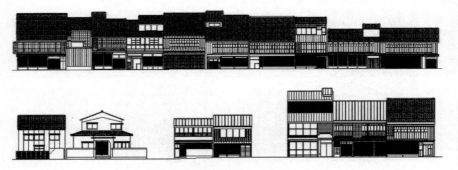

Fig. 6. Elevation of Historic Buildings in Higashi Chaya-gai.

main streets giving the impression that the district has been considerably improved. Its improved presence also can be seen from the increasing number of tourists and the popularity in tourist polls.

The new study is being conducted by a group of researchers from Kanazawa University, Kanazawa College of Arts and Crafts and Kanazawa Institute of Technology. The study covers a diversity of aspects, such as residents' expectations, facade and townscape conditions, street composition, landscape formation, building conditions, living conditions, building improvements, family composition, business situations, emergency measures, traffic conditions, and influence of tourism.

The study has revealed various problems the district faces, such as an economic slump for the *Chaya* business, the increasing number of wage earners as residents, a shrinking family size, increasing vacant units, decreasing home owners, building deterioration, diminishing historical buildings, a danger of spreading fires, touristic annoyance, shortage of parking, and emergence of new but undesirable businesses. These problems indicate that physical preservation of *Chaya* buildings alone can not sustain the district. It is important as well to address community development issues including how to convert the *Chaya* buildings to more adaptive uses, how to improve the living environment of historic districts, and how to secure sufficient parking spaces for both residents and tourists.

Now that the city government tries to assist community activities and the community leaders begin to understand the importance of these activities for the future of the district, it is expected that community improvement activities in Higashi Chaya-gai will become more active and many of the problems mentioned above will be addressed properly in the future. There is also a plan to form a taskforce for Higashi Chaya-gai, composed of researchers, community leaders and others concerned, not only for its successful designation as the Preservation District for Groups of Historic Buildings in 2001 but also for its continued success as a model case for Kanazawa's historic preservation.

Restoration of the Old Castle Town

The old castle site was seized by the military in the prewar period, and was under Kanazawa University's control from 1949 until recent years. In 1996 Ishikawa Prefecture decided to acquire the land of 28.5 ha vacated by the relocated university and to build a public park to be open in 2001. In the park, part of the castle buildings such as Hishi-yagura and Gojukken-nagaya, burnt by the fire in the early Meiji Period, are being rebuilt as they looked in late Edo Era, using traditional techniques. Imori Mote, which was buried for use as a road, is being dug for restoration. There are additional studies to rebuild Ninomaru Palace, the residence of the provincial lord, and other parts of the castle. Although some buildings and structures will be restored, the site is developed as a park to ensure public access. Because of its central location, there are proposals to build a convention center or other facilities on the site.

Adjacent to the old castle site is the location of the prefecture office scheduled to be relocated to the West of Station Area by 2003. Also, the 27 ha site to the east, which was used for the attached schools of Kanazawa University, was acquired by the city in 1998. These two sites constitute an important quarter of the city's central areas. Therefore, various studies and discussions involving citizens have proceeded as to how best these sites can be utilized for revitalization of inner city areas.

As for the previous attached schools site, the city decided to build the Museum of Contemporary Arts and related facilities for citizens' art activities. This new art center, called Hirosaka Art Village, to be completed in 2001, is intended to develop the city's modern art activities, creating a good balance between the existing rich traditional culture and the emerging contemporary culture as a modern city. The present prefectural office site is currently under study for development as a library and related facilities. This plan aims to complement the art activities of the adjacent site by adding educational and information functions and to exert a positive influence to the surrounding areas of the city center. The image of the restored buildings at the castle site is shown in Fig. 7.

INNER CITY REVITALIZATION

In many local cities where inner city revitalization is the main issue, there has been an attempt to convert historical buildings for more adaptive uses. Kanazawa created its own new program, the "Traditional Building Restoration and Remodeling Program", in 1998. This Program gives assistance to the owner of a prewar building who plans to convert it to a residential unit or a store. Six applications were made for assistance during the first seven months. The city also created another program in 1998 to assist citizens to build or purchase residential units in inner city areas under the condition in which the building conforms to the design criteria of the traditional building style. Already 35 applications were submitted for assistance in the first seven months.

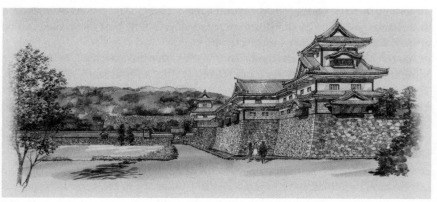

Fig. 7. Image of Restored Buildings at the Old Castle Site.

These examples show Kanazawa's commitment to shift its policy emphasis from mere preservation to inner city revitalization through a combination of historic preservation and other planning tools.

Transportation problems are also what historical cities have to cope with. Kanazawa leads the nation by adopting TDM (Traffic Demand Management) measures. One measure is a park-and-ride system to reduce inner city traffic and increase the use of public transportation. Another is the introduction of a low-deck minibus system named the Flat Bus to serve historical and back street areas and to improve accessibility of the elderly and minors to inner-city commercial areas. The buses are specially made in Germany and the first low-deck model in Japan. The system with its flat fare of 100 yen is popular among senior citizens. The first route was open for service in 1998 followed by the second route in 1999 and two other routes will be added in the future. In Japan public transportation is under a strict control by the central government and thus leaves very little room for local authorities to maneuver. Kanazawa's effort to overcome various national regulations and police controls under such centralized power structure can be highly appreciated.

Kanazawa used to have an extensive network of streetcar lines. With the advent of motorization, however, the city abolished all of them by the 1960s as many other cities did. Now many European and American cities have reintroduced surface transit such as the LRT (Light-rail Transit) system, and Kanazawa is studying the possibility to build an LRT line along the central corridor. If this becomes real, the central areas will be more accessible by pedestrians using public transportation and more favorable conditions for historic preservation will be produced.

SUCCESS FOR THE FUTURE

Reasons For Kanazawa's Success

Kanazawa is considered to be one of the most successful cases of historic preservation in Japan. Kanazawa's success in historic preservation can be attributed to the following six points:

(1) Kanazawa was developed during the Edo Era not only as the largest castle town but also as a significant cultural center by Lord Maeda.
(2) Kanazawa was fortunate to have survived World War II destruction and to avoid major fires and earthquakes.
(3) Kanazawa's location on the Japan Sea side of Honshu has made its development process slower and much more manageable than in many other cities on the Pacific side.

(4) Kanazawa was reluctant to follow the urban policy of the central government because of its conservative sentiment.
(5) The city and local communities have noticed the importance of historical buildings and townscapes at a very early stage and devised their own policy tools for historic preservation.
(6) The city is committed to retain and enhance its historic character and utilize it for its inner city revitalization and economic sustainability.

As a result the city has become not just a tourist destination but in addition a role model for the cities with historic preservation as a strategy for their urban policy. Kanazawa is now equipped with various planning tools that have been accumulated in the course of the postwar urban development. The city's commitment to historic preservation is widely acknowledged by citizens and efforts by local communities have been well coordinated.

Potential Problems

As Kanazawa continues its effort to maintain its historic character and to enhance its modern urban functions, there are, nonetheless, some foreseeable problems in the near future. First, the population of inner city areas is slowly but steadily declining and aging. There are an increasing number of vacant houses in these areas and they gradually become vacant lots, often used for parking. In some cases these vacant lots are assembled and large-scale condominium projects built, only to destroy the neighborhood character and further aggravate the situation.

Second, the inner city commercial and business functions are also declining with an increasing number of businesses having decided to relocate in suburban areas. Relocation of the prefectural office will be an additional blow to this situation. There have been a number of attempts to revitalize the inner city areas, but some of the city's projects to widen streets or to redevelop declining areas often backfire and hasten the declining process.

Third, the suburban development has become less and less dense and thus less efficient. Land readjustment projects that have been extensively used in the region tend to supply more developable land with adequate infrastructure than is demanded by the market. As a result suburban development will proceed with vacant lots built into the process. In the near future suburbs will face the same kind of population decrease and business decline that the inner city areas presently experience. In all, the city's future is not so rosy despite the city's success in historic preservation.

Ensuring Continued Success

There are some suggestions to be made based on our observation and the analysis presented in this article. The basic strategy that Kanazawa has to take is to make the city more compact and sustainable. For that purpose it is important to maintain the inner city population and to control development in the suburban areas. Without people living in the central areas, it is difficult to retain its historic character. Although historic preservation is an effective measure to deal with the problems stated above, it cannot deal with the multiplicity of the problems. It is therefore desirable to have a more comprehensive approach. We suggest that Kanazawa pursue the following three policy directions:

(1) First, it is time for Kanazawa to shift its urban development strategy from suburban development of this century to inner city redevelopment of the 21st century. Since redevelopment projects of the existing type tend to aggravate the problems, the city needs to develop a way to supply new residential units in a smaller scale and in a more flexible form within inner city areas. It is also important to improve the living environment of these areas as well as to supply basic urban functions for inner city residents.

(2) Second, it is essential to control suburban developments as they tend to cost more to the city and to leave more unused land. Although Kanazawa Region is expected to increase its population significantly until the year 2010, further development of its suburbs will make the region inefficient and thus less sustainable.

(3) Third, the city has to develop a plan to improve public transportation. A plan to build an LRT line is examined but the development along the New Corridor proceeds without any consideration of public transportation. It is important to have a clear picture of how the public transportation network will be improved when developing and redeveloping parts of the city.

Now that Kanazawa has achieved a certain degree of success in historical preservation, it is expected to shift its strategy to meet the more comprehensive goals. If Kanazawa can successfully shift its urban policy from mere preservation to more comprehensive strategies, it will certainly become the role model and therefore worth studying from the viewpoint of strategic urban development for many other cities. It is certain that the next decade will be a challenging period for Kanazawa.

NOTES

1. During the Edo Era the city of Edo, which was Tokyo's old name, was always the largest city, but, because of its status as the national capital, it was normally excluded from castle towns. The castle town was then the capital of its respective local province.

2. There are several smaller cities that have kept their historical environment as a result of the postwar decline of their economy. Examples include Kakunodate in Akita, Ohuchi in Fukushima, Tsumago in Nagano, Hagi in Yamaguchi, and Usuki in Ohita.

3. We did not compare Kanazawa to cities in other nations because of the limitation of information. There is a limited volume of literature available for international comparisons of historic cities in Japan (see Nishimura, 1997).

4. *Kintaro-ame* is a stick candy with a boy's face appearing at both ends. The face appears wherever the candy is cut. Thus, it is often use as a metaphor for the same look everywhere.

5. The Japanese City Planning Law did not require cities to have a comprehensive type of master plans until the major revision of 1992. Therefore, these plans tended to be growth-oriented with various city and prefectural projects allocated in the suburban areas, leaving the central areas untouched.

6. This survey was initiated by the researchers at Kanazawa Institute of Technology and Kanazawa University, including the authors of this article, and later supported by the city government.

REFERENCES

Board of Education (1992). *Kanazawa no Rekishiteki Kenchiku to Machinami* (Historic Buildings and Townscapes of Kanazawa). City of Kanazawa.

City Planning Committee. (1983). *Machinami & Juukankyou no Tosikeikaku* (Urban Planning for Townscape and Living Environment). Japan Institute of Architecture.

Kawakami, M. (1999). Characteristics and Planning Themes for the Preservation of Kanazawa's Historical Area. Paper presented at MIT Summer Workshop in Kanazawa.

Kobayashi, F., & Kawakami, M. (2000). Townscape Simulation and Planning Evaluation for Historical Urban Districts – A Case Study in a Japanese Castle Town, Kanazawa. Presented at 5th International Conference on Design and Decision Support Systems in Architecture and Urban Planning in Nijkerk, the Netherlands.

Masuta, T. (1998). *Bukeyashiki* (Housing of the Samurai Class). In: *History of Kanazawa*. City of Kanazawa.

Nishimura, Y. (1997). *Machinami Machizukuri Monogatari* (Stories of Townscape Preservation and Community Planning. Kokon-shoin.

Nishiyama, N., & Mimura, H. (1995). Dentoteki Kenzobutsugun Hozon Chiku ni Okeru Kekan Knri Kekaku ni Kansuru Kenkyu; Shirakawa-mura Ogimachi Gssyo-syuraku o Jirei to Shite (A Study on Landscape Management Planning in Preservation District for Groups of Historic Buildings: A Case Study on Ogimachi-area of Shirakawa-village in Gifu-prefecture. *Journal of Architecture, Planning and Environmental Engineering (Transactions of AIJ)*.

Ohkawa, N. (1997). *Rekishiteki Isan no Hozon-Katsuyou to Machizukuri* (Preservation and Utilization of Historical Heritage for Community Development. Gakugei Shppann-sha.

Sato, S. (1995). *Jokamachi no Kindai Toshi-dukuri* (Modern City Planning of Castle Towns). Kajima Shppann-sha.

Tani, A., & Masuta, T. (2000). Revitalization of Kanazawa through Historic Preservation. Proceedings for the International Symposium on City Planning 2000, City Planning Institute of Japan.

Tani, A., Masuta, T., & Shimokawa, Y. (2001). Reproduction of the Kanazawa Castle Town by 3D CG. Proceedings of International Symposium on City Planning 2001, City Planning Institute of Japan.

Tani, A., Mizuno, I., & Tsuchiya, A. (1999). Revitalization of Local Cities: Kanazawa as a Case Study. CPIJ Newsletter No. 17, City Planning Institute of Japan.

12. CONTINUITY AND CHANGE IN MACAU'S HISTORIC LANDSCAPE DURING A PERIOD OF TRANSITION

Bruce Taylor

ABSTRACT

The territory of Macau passed from Portuguese to Chinese administration on December 20, 1999. The Portuguese administration in its last years devoted considerable public resources to the restoration of landmark buildings and districts in Macau. As a result, the new government has inherited an architectural landscape punctuated with historic structures that evoke the colonial past. This chapter reviews and enumerates these activities and assesses their degree of success from the vantage points of several interest groups. It suggests that the leadership of the Macau Special Administration Region has an excellent opportunity to build on past achievements through policies that combine a pragmatic stance towards the retention and maintenance of the inherited landscape ("continuity") with a humanizing aim of spreading the benefits of preservation more widely across the community ("change").

International Urban Planning Settings: Lessons of Success, Volume 12, pages 337–369.
Copyright © 2001 by Elsevier Science Ltd.
All rights of reproduction in any form reserved.
ISBN: 0-7623-0695-5

INTRODUCTION

In January 1992 a delegation from the Hong Kong Institute of Planners made a field visit to nearby Macau, then in its 435th year under Portuguese administration. The writer – then resident in Macau – organized a roundtable discussion for the visitors with several members of the Macau Association of Architects. The exchange of views on that occasion was both provocative and instructive, and a consideration of those views forms a useful starting point for this chapter's review of how Macau has acted to preserve its historic architectural landscape during the recently-concluded period of political transition.

The first of the Macau speakers at the roundtable, the architect Campina Ferreira, gave a scathing critique of what he saw as Macau's unregulated and poorly coordinated urban development. He painted a bleak picture of a city that continually missed opportunities to manage its growth so as to enhance the quality of life enjoyed by its residents. He saw new building activity as motivated almost wholly by the pursuit of profit in the short- to medium-term. (In this he was undoubtedly correct: in the early 1990s Macau was experiencing major inflows of speculative capital, mostly from China and mostly invested in real estate.) The character of the living environment created in new and older parts of the city alike bordered perilously, he thought, on anarchy. His view was that only a firm hand at the center, guided by an all-embracing plan for the further development of the city, could steer Macau towards a future where its citizens enjoyed benefits in quality-of-life terms commensurate with what (then) was the territory's continued economic advancement.

At the same gathering another Macau architect, Bruno Soares, spoke in quite different terms. He admitted that Macau was not all it could be, but felt that all things considered, a basically non-interventionist attitude was not a bad thing for the city. Eventually the right decisions were made, he suggested; the infrastructure and facilities needed to support high-density urban living were provided one way or another by public or private action. More of a problem for Macau, thought Soares, was the prospect of grandiose redevelopment schemes that outran the administration's ability to manage and fund them. Simply put, Macau was too small a place, and its resources too limited, to run the risk of saddling itself with potential white elephants even if they were put forward by planners with the best of motivations.

"Urban success", the subject of the chapters in this volume, is a subjective construct. A city reputed to be successful in one area (say, providing chances for its residents to earn a living) might be thought deficient in another (supplying cultural amenities to support a divergence of life styles). A city embracing a thriving post-industrial economy may be home to the depressed remnants of an industrial past and a workforce unprepared to make the transition from one mode of employment to another. As is well known, even very prosperous cities typically house deprived groups – racial minorities, say – whose economic condition makes a mockery of the city's overall prosperity. "Success", in other words, is filtered through each individual's perceptual lens. Urban policies that from one vantage point are highly successful are, to another observer, indicative of fundamental failures in policy-making.

This is the case also with the subject of this chapter, the preservation of historic buildings and townscapes in the territory of Macau. From the viewpoint of a typical Hong Kong visitor, especially a Westerner, Macau is a success story. What he or she experiences as the so-called "colonial character" contributes mightily to the perception of Macau as someplace different; as a relaxed getaway from the pressure-cooker environment of Hong Kong. Yet a discerning tourist who has experienced, say, European settlements with medieval centers preserved in situ will be quite disappointed in what Macau has to offer. And to many Macau residents, historic preservation has had only a marginal effect at best on their daily life, as later sections will discuss. Little affected by the presence of a landmark church or a repaved town plaza, they go about their activities in jam-packed, grey, indistinguishable neighborhoods offering degraded living conditions and only the barest of amenities.

The divergent opinions of Ferreira and Soares echo similarly divergent views within the planning profession as to the context in which planners function most effectively. Ferreira's distaste for piecemeal development contrasts with Soares' distrust of centrally-directed plan-making. In the literature of planning theory, the rational-comprehensivist or synoptic strand (Hudson, 1979), traceable at least as far back as Daniel Burnham's well-known admonition to "make no little plans", contrasts with the incrementalist strand exemplified by Lindblom's (1959) "muddling through". Macau's initiatives in historic preservation fit within a political context where the dominant mode of decision-making favors incremental change (Lo, 1990). The Macau Portuguese administration, especially in its final years, was hesitant to initiate major reforms in political, economic, or social spheres, preferring instead to move gradually towards what the governing elite groups, at least, in both Portuguese and Chinese communities viewed as a societal consensus on appropriate directions of development. Evidence to date suggests that the political transition to Chinese administration has not led to a fundamental change in the nature of Macau's governance.

The perceived success of Macau in preserving elements of its colonial (or, more precisely, its pre-industrial, hybrid Luso-Asian)[1] architectural heritage can be viewed as a triumph of incrementalism – a true "muddle", perhaps – rather than as a victory for a comprehensively-designed preservation policy. Though to some observers this may be disappointing, it should in fact be viewed as a hopeful conclusion. It is not necessary, or even realistic, to expect a city to follow a rigidly-specified, step-by-step, formulaic process in order to attain a measure of success in pursuing an objective. This chapter enumerates some of the policy initiatives that successive Macau administrations have taken to support preservation. Some have overlapped with others; some have had a greater impact on Macau's observed and experienced urban form than others. All have been piecemeal interventions into an ongoing process of growth, development, and change. None have been put into place as part of the sort of comprehensive controlling framework over the territory's growth and development that Ferreira, rather forlornly, was asking for in 1992. But nonetheless, as the fourth section of this chapter documents, from a number of points of view these interventions can be viewed as, collectively, contributors to a real success.

What can certainly be improved, however, is the contribution that historic preservation makes to the day-to-day quality of life experienced by the residents of Macau. The challenge facing the Special Administrative Region (SAR) government is to institute policies that combine a pragmatic stance towards the retention and maintenance of the inherited landscape (the "continuity" of this chapter's title) with a humanizing aim of spreading the benefits of preservation across the community as a whole (the "change"). The Epilogue to this chapter discusses this challenge, and how the SAR authorities might act to meet it.

CONTEXT: THREE TRANSFORMATIONS

The territory of Macau until the early 1970s was, in terms of its urban form, very much in the mold of a pre-industrial city (Duncan, 1986a). The commercial center of the historic Portuguese city was on the western side of the Macau peninsula, facing the sheltered Inner Harbor and China.[2] The administrative center was the square facing the elegant building of the *Leal Senado* (municipal council). Within short walking distance of these two focal points were markets, temples, and a jumble of residences, shops, and small handicraft workshops nestled on the flatter parts of the peninsula. On the hilltops and along the waterfront Praia Grande were the landmarks of the city: the churches, fortresses, lighthouses, and public buildings erected by the

Portuguese. Planned extensions of the old city to the north adopted a more rectilinear street pattern but maintained a very similar architectural character. It is the surviving remnants of this pre-industrial settlement, characterized by a distinctive hybrid Luso-Asian architecture, that constitute the "heritage" which Macau Portuguese authorities have been so keen to retain, as a tangible and enduring aspect of the city's distinctive merging of disparate Eastern and Western cultures (Marreiros, 1991).

Government policies and programs in support of the preservation of this heritage have evolved in the broader context of Macau's metamorphosis from a sleepy (albeit historic) coastal port to a modern (albeit still very small) metropolis. Three transformations underlie this metamorphosis: one economic, one political, and a third focused on the development of infrastructure.

The Economic Transformation

Macau's economic transformation covered roughly the decades of the 1960s and 1970s. This transformation had two major sources. Like Hong Kong and many other Asian urban centers, Macau experienced an evolution from handicraft-based industry to factory industry. With Hong Kong's logical hinterland, China, closed to foreign investment, Macau was the only suitable nearby location to house industrial overspill from the British territory. Garment and textile manufacture, financed initially by Hong Kong capital, quickly established itself as the dominant local industry, accounting by 1980 for more than 80% of local export earnings (Maruya, 1999). Spatially the growth of manufacturing fueled the creation of purpose-built high-rise "flatted factories", concentrated mainly in the waterfront Manduco and Patane districts (already the home of maritime-centered business) and the newer, sparsely-populated Areia Preta district formed partly from reclaimed land (Duncan, 1986b). But Macau's pre-industrial urban fabric was also pressed into service to accommodate small-scale enterprises, many of them subcontractors to larger firms that set up their workshops in residential buildings (Sit et al., 1990).

The second source of economic transformation was the award in 1962 of the monopoly franchise for casino gambling to a new syndicate, the *Sociedade de Turismo e Diversões de Macau* (STDM), that undertook to modernize the industry. STDM introduced Western games such as roulette and baccarat to Macau's casinos, constructed new hotel-casino buildings (notably the distinctive Hotel Lisboa), and placed fast ferries and hydrofoils into service on the Hong Kong-Macau route to cut the travel time for visitors (Pinho, 1991). The results was a sharp increase in the number of visitors to Macau, mainly from Hong Kong, and a growth in tourism-related businesses generally and ancillary businesses to the gambling industry more specifically. The latter include less savory activities such as loan sharking and prostitution, along with the more visible hotels, restaurants, and pawn shops.

This economic transformation of Macau was largely complete by the early 1980s, but it has progressed little since. Garment and textile export and gambling-related tourism continue to be the local economic mainstays (Maruya, 1999). Both, however, have an uncertain future. Garment manufacturers will lose by 2005 their quotas guaranteeing access to overseas markets such as the United States, following the conclusion of the Uruguay Round of world trade agreements. Macau's casinos face competition from Australia and other regional centers, and increasingly from the unregulated world of cyberspace. Uncertainty is magnified by the forthcoming expiration of STDM's monopoly rights in 2001, and by the lack of an obvious successor to STDM's founder and patriarch Stanley Ho, the subject of much local myth and legend, now in his late 70s. From time to time proposals are put forward for restructuring of the local economy to focus on, say, back-office services, or high-tech manufacturing, or service as a conduit between China and the European Union (European Union Eminent Persons Group, 1999). None of these proposals have yet proven to be very fruitful.

One such idea, however – to encourage heritage tourism as a counterfoil to casino-related tourism – has direct implications for policies regarding preservation of the pre-industrial landscape. Government authorities have taken pains to encourage visitors to Macau to venture beyond the casinos and to experience those aspects of Macau's identity (food, entertainment, cultural festivals, as well as architecture) that distinguish it from other destinations, including Hong Kong. The success of such endeavors rests highly on the maintenance of a defining local character, of which buildings and other physical landmarks are the most enduring expression.

The Political Transformation

It is widely, and erroneously, believed that Macau's political transition from Portuguese colony to Chinese Special Administrative Region began in 1987 with the signing of the Sino-Portuguese Joint Declaration that set the 1999 handover date. In fact, the transformation began much earlier. Cultural Revolution-inspired riots in December 1966 badly shook the Portuguese colonial authorities. The Portuguese government gave in to Chinese demands that, among other things, removed all influence of the Kuomintang in Macau.[3]

More significantly for the long term, to maintain stability the Portuguese began a systematic arrangement of behind-the-scenes consultation with local Chinese intermediaries on important government decisions. In effect, Macau was governed as a Luso-Chinese condominium, albeit with a facade of Portuguese authority, with the intermediaries representing the interests of the People's Republic of China (PRC).

Portugal's revolution in 1974 led to further changes. As part of its worldwide decolonization process subsequent to the revolution, Portugal offered to hand Macau back to China. China declined, mindful of the effect that a takeover would have on sentiments in the much more politically and economically significant territory of Hong Kong. Portugal then unilaterally redefined Macau as "Chinese territory under Portuguese administration", withdrew its military forces, and introduced a new constitution, the Organic Statute of 1976, which allowed Macau a significant level of legislative autonomy. A directly elected element was introduced into Macau's Legislative Assembly at the same time – years before the 1991 introduction of directly-elected legislators into Hong Kong's Legislative Council – while the introduction of universal suffrage in 1984 induced greater political participation by the Chinese middle class.

Both Portuguese and Chinese sources have been keen to point to the spirit of harmony, or *amizade*, in which Macau's political transformation was accomplished (Cheng, 1999). From Portugal's standpoint, it could honorably withdraw from the last of its possessions and point with pride to its efforts to maintain the rights and privileges of Macau's citizens – notably the estimated 125,000 who held full Portuguese nationality. The PRC's attitude was more complex. Edmonds and Yee (1999) suggest that Chinese policy towards Macau at the time of the Joint Declaration did not differ significantly from its policy towards Hong Kong; both were to be examples of the successful application of the "one country, two systems" formula that would serve as inducements to Taiwan to accept reunification on the same grounds. After Tiananmen in 1989, Chinese attitudes began to change, and the "friendly" Portuguese authorities were increasingly contrasted with the "unhelpful" British. The appointment of Chris Patten as Hong Kong's last British Governor intensified this distinction drawn between the two colonial powers. Hence Macau's Portuguese Governor, General Vasco Rocha Vieira, was greeted warmly in Beijing while Governor Patten was vilified as a "sinner for a thousand years". Likewise, the negotiations over the building of Macau's international airport, though lengthy, were not marked by the acrimony that entered the Sino-British negotiations over the building of Hong Kong's airport at Chek Lap Kok.

From a practical standpoint, the desire of both sides to retain at least the appearance of friendly relations meant that PRC government authorities,

Macau's influential Chinese intermediaries, and the Chinese-language media rarely issued fundamental criticisms of the Portuguese administration's policies. Thus a programme to preserve historic landmarks erected by the Portuguese, even if blatantly inspired by the desire to maintain a colonial legacy, would not have been opposed by the Chinese elite. The lack of overt opposition was certainly a contributing factor to the smooth implementation of programs in support of historic preservation during the 1980s and 1990s. It also implies that a post-handover government is unlikely to make use of some of the blunter instruments available to it – for instance, the obliteration of identified colonial landmarks – in dealing with the architectural landscape it has inherited.

The Infrastructure Transformation

Early improvements to Macau's woefully inadequate pre-industrial infra-structure were mainly at the instigation of the casino syndicate STDM, which dredged the harbor and contributed to the building of a new ferry pier in the Outer Harbor, close to its flagship Casino Lisboa. Macau's antiquated electrical grid and telecommunications network were upgraded by monopoly franchise holders in the early 1980s. However, it was left for successive Portuguese Macau administrations to initiate in the mid-1980s an extensive program of public works to endow Macau with the 'infrastructural basis to sustain the autonomy of the future Special Administrative Region', to quote LUSA news agency (1999). The assumption by the colonial authorities was that with the elements of a modern infrastructure in place, serving the surrounding Pearl River Delta as well as Macau itself, the city's post-handover survival as a distinct entity – and with its distinct heritage – is all but assured.[4]

Symbolic of this transformation is the Macau International Airport, costing US$1.1 billion and opened for commercial flights in November 1995. The completion of the airport heralded an end to Macau's dependence on Hong Kong for international transportation links. Other transport-related develop-ments have included a new maritime terminal, opened in 1993, a small-scale container port at Ka Ho, and a second bridge linking peninsular Macau to the territory's two outer islands. Extensive land reclamation has produced a brand new office and residential district in the Outer Harbor and an even larger-scale scheme to enclose the Praia Grande Bay, creating two artificial lakes and several new sites for commercial and public buildings. Cultural, recreational, and sporting facilities have not been overlooked. A new Cultural Center opened in 1999, a sports stadium in 1997, and several new museums have appeared in the past few years.

Taken together, this flurry of building projects has resulted in change to the spatial character of Macau that has few parallels among cities of Macau's size (an estimated 450,000 population in 2000). However, the economic activities that play themselves out within this modernized spatial structure have, as noted earlier, changed little in recent years. The result is that elements of the new infrastructure, introduced with the intention of equipping Macau with the requisite facilities to succeed as a forward-looking, dynamic, autonomous economy, are seriously underutilized. New office buildings on the reclamations stand nearly empty. The container terminal at Ka Ho handles fewer containers than the old landing wharves in the Inner Harbor. The new bridge, though significantly easing the flow of traffic to and from the islands, handles fewer vehicles per day than does the old one. Even the international airport, which handled more than 2.2 million passengers in 1998, has been successful only as a center for serving destinations in the Asian region.

One unintended consequence of the major public investments in infrastructure – and of a property glut created by overinvestment in speculative real estate during the first half of the 1990s – has been that development pressure on the older built-up areas of Macau has slackened considerably since the 1980s. Bastos (1986) reported that Macau was losing as many as 300 old houses per year by the early 1980s. This is no longer the case. The implementation of government programs to support historic preservation has been eased immeasurably by the lessened competition from private development interests for the reuse of built-up land.

GOVERNMENT INITIATIVES IN SUPPORT OF PRESERVATION

Macau has never had an overall development plan to guide its physical growth (Prescott, 1993; Edmonds & Kyle, 1998). Various pieces of Macau's territory, mainly new reclamations, have been comprehensively planned, but mostly in isolation from each other (Taylor, 1994). "Urban Intervention Plans" were prepared for three historically-sensitive zones in the 1980s, including the "main street" of Avenida Almeida Ribeiro, but these never received the formal recognition of publication in the Macau government's *Boletim Oficial* (Official Gazette) and thus never took legal effect (Prescott, 1993). Large parts of Macau are legally subject only to generalized rules regarding such matters as building heights and plot ratios, although unofficial guideline plans may be available for some areas.

According to Marreiros (1991) formal government activity in support of preserving Macau's architectural heritage began in 1976, with the creation of the Committee for the Preservation of Macau's Heritage. In the early years of activity, most successful historic preservation initiatives involved the purchase of buildings by the government for its own use. A row of homes along Avenida do Conselheiro Ferreira de Almeida, one of the city's main north-south traffic arteries, was preserved in this way, as was the nearby walled Lou Lim Ioc Chinese garden. By contrast, there was very little success during this period in encouraging private sector involvement in preservation, and much of the destruction of Macau's pre-industrial townscape dates from the intensified period of urban expansion in the 1970s and early 1980s.

Perhaps mindful of the inherent limits of a program focused on the outright purchase of property for government use, the Macau Government has in the past fifteen years initiated a wide range of policies and programs with the common aim of encouraging the retention and, where appropriate, the active use of historic buildings, and enhancing the visual appeal of those districts that retain much of their historic character. Some of these involve the public sector directly, as a purchaser or a provider of financial incentives; others involve a greater role for private interests, with the Government perhaps in the role of behind-the-scenes persuader. The list here is not exhaustive, but is representative of the scope and breadth of public involvement in preservation.

Continuity

This refers to an effort to ensure the maintenance of a historic structure in its original use. In some cases continuity requires very little effort to achieve. Figure 1, for instance, shows Government House (*Palácio do Governo*) on the waterfront Rua da Praia Grande, which has served as the offices of the Portuguese Governor, and now the Macau SAR Chief Executive, since the 19th century. Although the overt signs of Portuguese colonial authority – the coats of arms and flags – have been removed, the building still stands and continues to be the seat of the executive-led government.

In other cases continuity has been assured through extensive (and costly) restorations. St. Dominic's Church anchors the northern end of the symbolically-important Largo do Senado, noted earlier as the center of Portuguese administrative power. The late 16th-century church received a thorough

Fig. 1. Continuity: Government House (*Palácio do Governo*) on Rua da Praia Grande, Macau. In this February 2000 photograph the Chinese national emblem has replaced the Portuguese emblem on the central pediment, while the flagpoles display the Chinese national flag and the Macau SAR flag. (All photographs by the author).

restoration and reopened in 1997, not only for worship but also as a small museum of (Catholic, and mainly Portuguese) religious art.

Facade Renovations

Private owners of historic buildings have received government support to renovate building facades. This has been especially prevalent along Avenida Almeida Ribeiro, where traditional three-story shophouses are still very much in evidence. The commercial/residential building shown in Fig. 2 is on this street. Typically although the facade is repaired and repainted the interiors are not altered. Questions can be raised as to the longer-term effectiveness of facade renovations – which fundamentally are a cosmetic exercise – in ensuring the viability in continued commercial or residential use of the buildings that receive this treatment.

Fig. 2. A commercial/residential building on Avenida Almeida Ribeiro, with renovated facade.

Adaptive Reuse

The Macau government continues to support adaptive reuse of historic buildings for new purposes. Several government departments including the Tourism Office, the Monetary Authority (equivalent to a central bank), and the Social Welfare Department occupy buildings that have been completely renovated – in one case a former hotel and in the other two a private residence. The new Museum of the City of Macau opened in 1998 in a refurbished 19th-century building within the precincts of the even older (16th-century) Monte Fortress. Private sector adaptive reuse activities include most notably the Pousada do São Tiago, a boutique hotel converted from the disused fortress of St. James.

More controversial has been the acquisition of the well-known Bela Vista Hotel (Fig. 3) as the residence of the post-handover Consul General of Portugal, and hence its closure to the public. At the same time, the former São Rafael Hospital, which the Monetary Authority had converted in 1988 for its home, became the Portuguese Consulate. Some in the community, including

Fig. 3. Adaptive reuse: the former Bela Vista Hotel, now the residence of the Consul-General of Portugal. The closure of this uniquely atmospheric hotel to the public in 1999, less than seven years after its reopening following a total renovation, is regretted by many in the community.

many Portuguese, have questioned why two of the most significant restored public buildings in Macau should be, in effect, privatized, with the explicit agreement of the outgoing colonial administration and at least the tacet approval of the incoming one.

Fragmentary Preservation

This involves the retention of elements of a historic structure, typically the facade, as part of the redevelopment of a site. Figure 4 is the most spectacular instance of this; the shell of the Banco Nacional Ultramarino headquarters building has been retained while a new, ultra-modern office tower had been built within (and above) it. Two nearby sites on Rua da Praia Grande have been redeveloped in the same way. On a smaller scale, three-story shophouse facades on Avenida Almeida Ribeiro have been retained while five-story structures – the upper two stories set back from the facade – are built behind them.

Fig. 4. Fragmentary preservation: The new Macau headquarters of Banco Nacional
Ultramarino (Portuguese National Overseas Bank).

Not all redevelopment projects using this technique are as architecturally
successful as the building in Figure 4. Any such project runs a risk that vestiges
of the historic building will appear wholly out of place in the new structure –
becoming a visually discordant rather than an architecturally congruent
element in the landscape.

Infill of New Structures

Quite frequently in the older areas of Macau a site that is potentially sensitive
in terms of maintaining the character of the historic townscape sits vacant.

Typically this is due to the destruction – in some cases the literal collapse – of the original building. In such cases developers are encouraged to construct new buildings that are visually in harmony with the surrounding historic structures. In some cases "harmony" simply means a modern building that in terms of volume, setback, color, and other such aspects is in keeping with its neighbors. In other cases, however, more explicit regulations are in force. New buildings are expected to adopt the architectural vernacular of the old, with pseudo-Iberian arched windows, covered verandas, external window shutters, and so forth.

Examples of this latter approach have occurred most notably on Avenida Almeida Ribeiro, in the Largo do Senado, and in the area surrounding the ruined facade of St. Paul's Church, a mecca for visitors. The commercial building shown in Fig. 5, while new (1999), uses stylistic motifs common in Portuguese colonial architecture (cf. Figs 3 and 4). In this case the building closely replicates the structure formerly on the site, abandoned and partly ruinous since the 1980s.

Fig. 5. A commercial building at the heart of the tourist district below the Ruins of St. Paul's. Visible at the lower right is one of the controversial monuments to Luso-Chinese friendship erected during Rocha Vieira's governorship.

Preserving Symbols

The ruins of St. Paul's Church (Fig. 6) are a widely-known symbol of Macau and indelibly associated with the city, much as the Eiffel Tower, say, is associated with Paris. To ensure that this symbol retains its prominent place in the city's public image, the Macau Government has financed the repair and cleaning of the facade, the partial excavation of the foundations of the rest of the church building, and the building of a small museum on the grounds to the rear of the facade.

Fig. 6. Preserving symbols: the ruined facade of St. Paul's Church, erected in 1602 and destroyed by fire in 1835.

"Mothballing"

This is a quite new practice, and refers to weatherproofing and structurally reinforcing the shell of a historic structure to prevent its further deterioration while decisions are taken as to its ultimate use. Two landmark structures on Avenida Almeida Ribeiro are among the first to receive this treatment: the Lok

Kok Building, once home to the atmospheric Lok Kok teahouse (Berlie, 1999), and the Hotel Cantão (Fig. 7), one of the last of the former seafarer's hotels in

Fig. 7. "Mothballing": the weatherproofed shell of the early 20th-century Hotel Cantão, in the historic Inner Harbor district.

the Inner Harbor district. Both are seen as key pieces in the commercial revival of the Inner Harbor end of Avenida Almeida Ribeiro, a prospect admittedly not yet in sight (Prescott, 1993).

Faux Historicism

The enthusiasm with which the Macau authorities have embraced heritage conservation has from time to time led to the introduction of "historic" elements that in fact have no antecedents. Such faux historicism is most often seen in an attempt to give a more "antique" feel to a district that is already rich in preserved structures. When the central Largo do Senado was pedestrianized in the mid-1990s, a Portuguese-style black-and-white pavement was introduced. There was no precedent for the use of this type of paving material in Macau; its use was simply to give the square a more "European" feel, reminiscent perhaps of a small Portuguese town. Two other squares that are highly visible to visitors, including the Largo do Templo da Barra adjoining Macau's oldest and most-touristed Chinese temple, have received the same black-and-white paving.

A more amusing example of faux historicism, in this case from the private sector, is seen in Figs 8a and 8b. The owners of the Restaurante Litoral, a restaurant serving Portuguese and Macanese food, have opted for a facade that mimics the well-known building of the Leal Senado (Figure 8a). However, as Figure 8b shows, the restaurant is only one shop front in an otherwise modern (1990s) building. The effect is comical: historical pastiche bordering perhaps on mockery, at least as jarring to the observer as would be the opposite action of placing a out-of-scale modernist building in the midst of a row of colonial homes.

GAUGING THE SUCCESS OF PRESERVATION POLICIES

The Introduction noted that the definition of "urban success" varies depending on the vantage point, and the vested interests, of the person or group making the assessment of the level of success. In Macau the driving body behind practically all of the initiatives outlined in the previous section has been the public service, working either directly through government departments (most notably the Cultural Institute) or indirectly through publicly-supported charitable bodies (mainly the Orient Foundation [*Fundação Oriente*], financially supported until the handover by a dedicated fraction of the territory's

Fig. 8a. Faux historicism: Facade of the Restaurante Litoral, a Portuguese/Macanese restaurant near the Inner Harbor waterfront. The facade mimics the 19th-century Leal Senado building, a landmark in Macau's central city

Fig. 8b. A wider-angle photograph showing the modern building in which Restaurante Litoral is located.

gambling receipts). These functionaries have no doubt viewed their intervention into the ongoing processes of growth and change as a success. The
Cultural Institute has gone so far as to organize an international symposium
"Macau Metropole" in 1998 with the behind-the-scenes aim, at least, of
celebrating its accomplishments in maintaining the city's cultural identity.

For a broader assessment of Macau's preservation policies it is necessary to
move beyond the limited sphere of the individuals and groups who design and
implement them. In this section the viewpoints of five relevant interest groups
are examined, and an attempt made to offer a balanced assessment of Macau's
actions in support of preservation.

Architects and Historians

Observers whose main concern is with the built environment as an artifact in
its own right will judge the success of a preservation strategy by its
accomplishments in retaining historic structures and districts, along with the
attributes of the built environment (visual appeal, human scale, and so forth)
that are valued by the city's residents (Taylor, 1992). Macau has been
successful, from this perspective, in retaining the monuments and landmarks –
fortresses, churches, temples, public buildings – that figure importantly in the
history of Macau seen from both European and native viewpoints. There has
been less success in maintaining the sought-after traits of the historic
townscape; the traditional built environment in many districts has been
destroyed, or persists only in fragments. But in the handful of districts where
a sense of the pre-industrial character has been retained, initiatives such as
infilling of new architecturally-harmonious buildings, facade renovations, and
adaptive reuse of buildings have succeeded in enhancing the visual appeal of
the townscape considered as a whole. The Largo do Senado – pedestrianized,
repaved, painted, and provided with comfort-enhancing amenities – is the best
example. More than ever before in Macau's modern era the spruced-up square
is a focal point of the city and a gathering place for the community.

Visitors

Visitors to Macau will assess the achievements of preservation policy in terms
of whether preservation contributes towards the pleasure of their visit. There is
no doubt that for many visitors from the regional catchment area embracing
Hong Kong, mainland China, and Taiwan, Macau's attraction is casino
gambling. Historic preservation policy is of little concern to this group. But
those with wider interests of experiencing, even superficially, a distinctive

cultural milieu (and this includes Hong Kong residents seeking a getaway from what typically is a supercharged routine of work and socializing) the "colonial" ambience created by the preserved landmarks and districts is one of the features that most defines the attractiveness of the territory. More abstract dimensions of visitors' experience, such as a claimed "slower pace of life", are not necessarily enduring – indeed, Macau residents can legitimately question whether the vaunted "slower pace" actually exists. Restored buildings, by contrast, are a constant and inescapable reminder that "this place [Macau] is not like home". Tourism policies of the Macau Government have in turn successfully built on the attractiveness of the city's architectural heritage. "We have been waiting 400 years for you" is one tourist slogan used some years ago. It rings much more true with visitors when there are indeed 400-year-old landmarks, like the Monte Fortress and St. Dominic's Church, on display for their edification.

Portuguese and Macanese Residents

A uniquely defining feature of Macau is that, while Eastern and Western cultural traditions have met and to some extent clashed there, neither tradition has in the end dominated the other (Zepp, 1991; Cheng, 1999). Macau's remaining Portuguese community, and particularly the ethnically mixed Macanese for whom the territory is home, place a very high importance in retaining their cultural identity and distinctiveness in spite of the territory's transition from Portuguese to Chinese administration. Despite their best efforts, there is no guarantee that the Portuguese language will survive in widespread use, even in government, nor that Portuguese-style education will be available to more than a limited number of local children. The significance of Portuguese visual and performing artists in the enclave's cultural scene also inevitably will fade. Buildings, however, have a permanence that languages or education systems do not, and a conscious, tangible, willful decision must be taken to destroy them. From this group's vantage point, then, the accomplishments of successive Macau authorities in supporting preservation rate as very much a success. It also is not lost on Macanese observers that in other outposts of the Portuguese maritime empire, such as Malacca and Muscat, the only reminder of Portugal's one-time presence is in the city's buildings.

Interestingly, it is in architecture that the cultural traditions of Portugal and China have fused most closely (Marreiros, 1991), creating a hybrid architecture that does not have its counterpart in, say, language (a creole tongue) or in the visual arts (Zepp, 1991). The strong criticism directed from some quarters at the Rocha Vieira administration's program of erecting monuments (Fig. 9) to commemorate the spirit of *amizade*, or Luso-Chinese friendship, can better be

Fig. 9. The controversial *Portas do Entendimento* (*Gate of Understanding*), by Portuguese sculptor Charters de Almeida, built in 1993 at the southern tip of the Macau peninsula.

understood with this in mind. The buildings of Avenida Almeida Ribeiro, although "colonial" in appearance, are not seen as icons of colonialism at all. In a very real sense they are part of the local heritage shared by every resident. The megalith appearing in Fig. 9, the work of a Portuguese sculptor, betrays no evidence of Chinese cultural influence.[5] The theme of Luso-Chinese friendship is all but invisible to the viewer who has not been previously enlightened to the symbolism. The fact that the monument celebrates "understanding" (*entendimento*), rather than imperial dominance, does not negate the local view that it is a foreign imposition: in Cheng's words 'superficial, a waste of money, a clash of culture, and above all, a superfluous repetition of the theme of *amizade*' (1999: 13).

Chinese Officials

For the People's Republic of China, Macau (like Hong Kong) is a poster child for the "one country, two systems" concept associated with the late Deng

Xiaoping, a focal point for national rejoicing over the reunification of the Motherland's sacred territory, and a model for Taiwan to emulate in due course. None of these aims is furthered by an attempt to obliterate the presence of Portuguese culture. The analogous situation occurs in Hong Kong, which similarly has moved with great caution towards erasing reminders of the British presence – not even bothering to rename Queen's Road, Victoria Park, or other features with toponyms recalling past administrations. An understated monument on the Wanchai waterfront is the only reminder of the handover to China's sovereignty. Rather, Hong Kong is building new monuments (waterfront office towers, a new government office center, Hong Kong Disneyland, and many others) to supplant, and perhaps eventually replace in the public's consciousness, those inherited from the British colonial era – a strategy to obscure rather than obliterate the legacy of the past. This strategy, it appears, has the full support of China.

The limited evidence to date suggests that Macau is following the same path, with some Portuguese monuments coopted for the SAR administration's use (the "continuity" discussed above) while new points of interest are created alongside them. By far the most visible of these is the nearly 340-meter tall Macau Tower (*Torre de Macau*), under construction by the casino syndicate STDM. Reportedly the tenth highest building in the world, the tower will dominate the skyline and create a new focal point for Macau tourism. (It will also, in what certainly is an unintended irony, dramatically overshadow the Rocha Vieira administration's *Portas do Entendimento* monument discussed above). The continued support of preservation activities does nothing to undermine the SAR administration's authority, demonstrates in concrete terms the desire of the new government to retain a multicultural identity for the territory, and (at least hypothetically) offers the prospect of both economic benefit and quality-of-life improvement. From this standpoint the accomplishments to date, then, are part of an ongoing success.

Chinese Residents

The interests of local residents have not been at the forefront of Macau's efforts in support of historic preservation. In part this is due to the focus on landmark structures that in themselves have attained historic importance, at the expense of less notable buildings that are background elements in the overall townscape observed by residents (Taylor, 1992). These landmarks have little bearing on local residents' daily lives. Fortresses, for instance, are viewed mainly be visitors. Churches are of immediate interest only to the small part of the population that is Christian. Government buildings, as on the Praia Grande, are normally passed by rather than entered; some (like the Chief Executive's residence, formerly the colonial governor's residence) are closed to the public and under guard. Chinese temples are of course more frequented than Macau's other landmarks, but even here their use is sporadic with large crowds during festival times and important religious holidays and smaller numbers of visitors at other times.

The rhythm of Macau residents' daily lives is not centered on the districts with large groups of historic buildings, with the possible exception of the Largo do Senado. Avenida Almeida Ribeiro is a major traffic artery but no longer the dominant center of commerce. The bulk of Macau's people live in modern rather than historic buildings, in districts that are either completely new (Hipodromo, near the northern border with China; Nova Taipa on Taipa island) or totally changed in character from their origins (Manduco, near the Inner Harbor; San Kio and Ho Lan Un in the north-central part of the Macau peninsula). Historic buildings intrude upon their vision from time to time, but do not dominate any part of their day-to-day experience.

What these new neighborhoods do not enjoy is the human scale of their historic counterparts. The newly-developed ones tend to be "monumental", with tall high-rise towers; the redeveloped ones are merely claustrophobic. The government's involvement in historic preservation have not enabled it to incorporate the sought-after attributes of the historic built environment into its planning of newer districts. From the residents' standpoint, then, the Macau authorities' success with historic preservation has been limited.

A Balanced Assessment

For an outside observer to balance these perspectives is not an easy task. The interests of the different groups identified above are by no means as separated as the preceding paragraphs might suggest. For instance, residents may not benefit in day-to-day terms from the presence of historic landmarks and districts. But visitors to Macau attracted by its cultural ambience support jobs in tourist-related businesses, which helps to alleviate unemployment (at the time of writing Macau's most serious social problem, supplanting public safety which was a key concern before the 1999 handover). Portuguese and Macanese residents, their fears over the future allayed in part by the authorities' demonstrated concern to support a multicultural identity, invest their own capital into businesses (restaurants, say) that employ still more local staff. Government officials charged with guiding Macau's future development can (potentially, at least) look to the lessons that historic districts provide in planning for the residential areas of the future, in the process enhancing the quality of urban life for all Macau residents.

Architectural purists, and some long-term Macau residents whose memories stretch back to when the city retained its pre-industrial form, are quick to decry the amount of the city's architectural heritage that is already obliterated and imply that preservation activities have failed. This is, on balance, too harsh a judgment. The main preserver of Macau's historic buildings before the modern era was not government policy but the happenstance of poverty. When rapid economic development began to occur as a result of the economic transformation, per capita income and spending power increased throughout Macau society. The rising expectations that Macau residents consequently held for their living conditions could not be met by the obsolescent and decaying buildings of fifty or one hundred years ago. It is not accidental that the fifteen years from 1965 to 1980 saw the greatest destruction of the pre-existing built form; the period coincides neatly with the peak of the economic transformation, which lay the foundations for Macau's modern economy.

The pre-existing machinery of the Macau colonial administration, geared as it was to incremental policy-setting and slow-paced adaptation to equally slow-paced change, and to the concerns of the elite groups within the Portuguese and Chinese communities, also cannot be seriously faulted for not putting comprehensive procedures in place to cope with the redevelopment pressures that built up over the expansionary 1960s and 1970s. The changes needed in the established decision-making processes to, say, implement a comprehensive development plan devised with input from all sectors of the community, following Anglo-American models, were too great to contemplate – the very point made by Bruno Soares to the visiting Hong Kong planners. The elite groups themselves often had interests in real estate development, or if not they at least saw the "modernization" of the community as encompassing a physical modernization as well – a process that they perhaps short-sightedly felt would be impeded, rather than promoted, by the need to take into account the preservation of the pre-industrial built environment.

Where the Macau Government can rightly receive blame is for being too slow to act when it became apparent that: (a) among the consequences of rapid economic growth, left unchecked, was the wholesale destruction of the city's pre-existing built form, and (b) that preservation was in the public interest, or at least in the interest of the several sectors of the community noted above. The legislation needed to provide a basis for preservation activities was not enacted until 1984 – far too late to turn back the destructive legacy of the previous decade's expansion. The initiatives discussed in the previous section have often been cases of "too little, too late"; potentially much more effective if only implemented earlier. "Mothballing", for instance, could have saved several structures on sensitive sites – Avenida Almeida Ribeiro, for one – that collapsed from prolonged neglect.

The other main criticism of the Macau Government's efforts at preservation is that its benefits have trickled down only slowly to the community as a whole. This is not the result of malice or purposeful decisions on the authorities' part, but perhaps because their view of the significance of preservation has been too limited. As noted before, many residents have little day-to-day contact with historic landmarks or districts. Macau's historic buildings and districts also have many lessons to offer Macau's modern-day architects and planners; for instance, the need to keep building heights in proportion to the width of streets, or the pleasing visual environment that ensues when buildings in a fundamental architectural harmony nevertheless are ornamented with exuberant details that delight the eye. There is little evidence – surely not in the massive and monumental developments that sprout on Macau's new reclamations – that these lessons have been learned (Kvan & Karakiewicz, 1998).

Yet in the end, given the piecemeal nature of Macau's planning activity, even piecemeal successes as gauged by narrowly-focused interest groups should be valued for what they are. While incremental policy-making and small-scale initiatives do not produce dramatic outcomes, they do not tend to produce dramatic failures either. Macau is a territory within a region where the pace of change is possibly unequaled in any other part of the world. To have merely retained any part of the pre-existing built environment in the face of such pressure for change should be counted as a success for Macau's Portuguese administrators. To build equally successfully on that legacy is a challenge that the Macau SAR's leaders face for the years ahead.

EPILOGUE: PRESERVATION IN THE NEW CENTURY

The year 2000 in Macau marked not only the first year of a new century but also the first year of a new government, one that no longer is beholden above all else to a foreign power. At the time of the 1999 handover there was an upbeat mood among the local Chinese community; an optimism that economic and security crises that had dominated the second half of the 1990s could be decisively addressed by the new government, together with a less well-specified but still visible confidence that a local administration ("Macau people ruling Macau") would be guided in its decisions by a concern for citizens' welfare and the community benefit considered broadly, in ways that its predecessor administration was not perceived to be.[6]

Of course most new administrations in any country – no matter whether they arise from revolution or from the workings of the electoral process in a parliamentary democracy – take office with confidence that their victory represents a mandate for change to both the accumulated body of public policy and to the accepted ways of "getting things done". Macau's SAR government is no exception. But Macau's fledgling government is constrained in ways that many others are not. Under Article 5 of the Macau Basic Law it is bound to sustain Macau's capitalist economic system and pre-existing way of life for the next fifty years (Conselho Consultivo da Lei Básica, 1993). It is likewise bound to: protect individual rights; maintain a balanced budget, a convertible currency, and a free trade policy; protect judicial independence; and maintain social welfare provision "on the basis of the previous [pre-handover] system". Most significantly for the discussions of this chapter, it is bound by Article 125 to take steps to protect Macau's cultural heritage, along with vaguely-defined points of touristic or historical interest. And beyond the legal requirements for continuity in policy, the SAR government is constrained by the inherited spirit of *amizade* that has defined relations between the Chinese and Portuguese states and between the respective communities. It is unlikely that SAR government officials would act in ways calculated to upset or seriously compromise the primacy of *amizade*.

Some would argue that these constraints on the SAR government's freedom of action represent useful shields against the public disillusionment that typically sets in after a new administration's honeymoon period, as citizens come to realize that neither policies nor procedures are receptive to change. But from the point of view of Macau officials and their powerful local and mainland backers – the former drawn mainly from the traditionally pro-Beijing business and professional elite – the Basic Law and the restraints it imposes reinforce an existing predilection towards continuity as the basis of policy-making, and bit-by-bit, incremental progression as the preferred mode of change. The concept of "one country, two systems" itself embodies a conservative, rather than a radical or revolutionary, approach to integrating capitalist foreign-ruled territories as parts of a socialist nation. The administrations of Macau and Hong Kong are led by powerful Chief Executives supported by an administrative hierarchy and a civil service that have changed little in substance from pre-handover times. The legislatures in both territories, but especially in Macau, have solid pro-government majorities. What pent-up demand for change there is within the Macau community manifests itself in protests and petitions relating to a few "hot-button" issues, notably unemployment, and not in a more broadly hostile stance towards the administration or its policies seen as a whole.

Specifically in relation to the Macau SAR government's activities in support of historic preservation, the new century and new administration will not see a radical redirection of effort away from the various initiatives noted earlier in this chapter. All indications are that the public sector's involvement in preservation will be grounded in a pragmatic stance; an accommodation to the presence of an architectural legacy, a commitment to the maintenance of that legacy as one way (and a relatively low-cost one in political terms) of demonstrating the importance to Macau of a multicultural society, and a recognition that the distinctiveness of the SAR as a built environment brings its own advantages in, say, the promotion of tourism. The architectural legacy of Macau also is the most obvious and visible feature that distinguishes the SAR from the neighboring Special Economic Zone of Zhuhai, which owing to its sheer scale is seen by some as a threat to the SAR's independent future.

We might accept, then, that the elements of a fundamentally successful program for the preservation of historic buildings and townscapes pursued by successive Portuguese Macau governments of the 1980s and 1990s will remain in place under the SAR administrations of the early 21st century. As the Introduction to this chapter suggests, this is a hopeful conclusion. It is an indication that successfully accomplishing an objective, such as preserving the key elements of a city's architectural heritage, is not predicated on continuity among policy-makers, or on maintaining a sustained level of public expenditure. It does not require the creation of a comprehensive framework for growth, such as Ferreira was calling for in 1992, although some trial-and-error experimentation probably could be avoided if such a framework was in place. It does not require communities that, for whatever reason, are wedded to political contexts in which change proceeds in incremental fashion to embrace some other mode of operation that is foreign to them, or that depends on an infeasible restructuring of the established social order.

Yet as the previous section has shown, preservation policies in Macau cannot be seen as an unmitigated success. Many citizens of Macau benefit very little from the authorities' commitment to preservation. Perhaps they live in the "wrong" areas, such as the working-class, northern industrial districts near the land border with China. Perhaps by chance their home neighborhood retains little of its pre-industrial character, or their pattern of daily activities takes them through but not into areas that have been more of a focal point for restoration. This detachment of the local population from preservation activities, although widespread, is not inevitable. There is ample scope for directing the energies of agencies and officials concerned with historic preservation towards activities that can benefit the individual resident along with the visitor or the public official. Suggested here are four approaches, which, individually or collectively, can contribute to this desired outcome.

(1) First, the SAR authorities can subtly shift the emphasis of preservation activities from a concern with individual landmark structures and largely-intact districts, which have a special attraction to visitors, to an equal concern for those less obvious elements of the historic urban fabric that remain in place. These might be in less-touristed parts of Macau, or in less visible locations (narrower streets or alleys that parallel broader ones, say). Except for the newly-developed reclamation areas, neglected historic structures exist in most neighborhoods of Macau (Fig. 10). A demonstration project on the rehabilitation of historic structures for housing, coupled with a commitment to give financial support to private owners who undertake rehabilitation themselves, could potentially induce a significant volume of restoration activity extending into many districts of the city. This is especially true in the current economic climate where the housing market is seriously overbuilt (Edmonds & Kyle, 1998), and the sites of historic buildings have much less value for redevelopment.

Fig. 10. A decrepit residential building in the midst of the half-restored São Lazáro district, the first planned suburban development outside Macau's city walls.

(2) Second, the SAR government could integrate its efforts at historic preservation more closely with neighborhood-based planning activity that focuses on the enhancement of a community's quality of life. This does not necessarily mandate the development of formal district plans, but it does call for adopting a more holistic notion of how communities are experienced by their residents. For instance, the retention of two-story historic buildings, even if few in number, can relieve the otherwise oppressive density of an area built up to six or eight storeys as a result of redevelopment. Historic preservation activity can integrate well with a program of neighborhood planning that also includes regulation of building density, management of traffic, and the creation and maintenance of public amenities. Some such activities are going on in Macau; for instance, the municipal council's work in landscaping small open spaces in built-up areas to provide neighborhood parks (Prescott, 1993).

(3) Third, an effort is needed to ensure that Macau's greater and lesser historic landmarks are observable in their best possible setting. Both visitors and residents are inconvenienced if to best view a preserved historic structure they must dodge a steady stream of cars, motorcycles, and tourist coaches. Nor does anyone except the fortunate property owner benefit when a vista crowned by the Guia lighthouse, say, is blocked by another modern high-rise. There are major benefits to stepping back from an exclusive focus on the individual structure or localized townscape and giving more attention to the broader context within which the structure is experienced. The pedestrianization of the Largo do Senado has set an excellent example that can be emulated in other, less-touristed parts of the city.

(4) Fourth, the SAR government can do more to promote the economic significance of preservation among the community at large, especially among local property owners and business leaders. Specifically this would involve working together with private sector interests to integrate restored historic structures into the mainstream of economic life in Macau – particularly the sort of less distinctive structures that would form background elements, rather than highlights, in the historic landscape. Only with increased private sector involvement will preservation of Macau's architectural legacy ultimately attain community-wide acceptance as a public interest and not a minority interest.

Implementing these suggestions would not, in itself, guarantee that the benefits from historic preservation activities in the Macau SAR would be spread broadly throughout the community. But in seeking to involve the widest spectrum of Macau residents as participants in one way or another – even if their involvement is limited to being passive observers of restored buildings in their own community – the new SAR government will do a great deal to bring preservation into the mainstream of community life. This, in the end, is the best insurance that the Macau SAR will continue to build in the 21st century on its past successes in accommodating both continuity and change in the territory's built environment.

NOTES

1. "Luso-" here is a shortened form of "Lusitania", the Latin name for today's Portugal. Hence the common forms "Luso-Chinese", "Luso-Asian", and so forth to refer to a combination of Portuguese and other influences.

2. The territory of the Macau SAR consists of a peninsula (the Macau peninsula, or more simply Macau), which is part of the Chinese mainland, and two offshore islands known as Taipa and Coloane. The Portuguese settled on the Macau peninsula, and with very minor exceptions the historical monuments and landmarks from what Marreiros (1991) calls the "Christian City" are located there. Until a bridge was built in 1974 connecting Macau with Taipa, the nearer island, the two islands were basically rural. At present there are two bridges linking Macau to Taipa, as well as a causeway connecting Taipa and Coloane. The two islands will also by 2005 be linked by reclaimed land in the so-called "Cotai" reclamation project (Edmonds & Kyle, 1998).

3. In the years after 1949 the Chinese Communist Party and the Kuomintang, or Nationalist Party, by then based in Taiwan, both vied for influence in Macau through such means as support for local primary and secondary schools (Tang, 1997).

4. For an illustrated listing of major infrastructure projects undertaken during the last years of the Portuguese administration (see Lopes, 1998).

5. Several months after the monument's completion, repairs were needed to its black marble facing. As usual in Macau, bamboo scaffolding was used to facilitate the repair work. The perceptive (and outspoken) newspaper owner and columnist José Rocha Dinis editorialized that the bamboo scaffolding should remain on the monument after the work was completed, to give the megalith more of a localized character in keeping with the spirit of *entendimento* that it commemorated (Dinis, 1994).

6. This was evident in a number of reports filed by Hong Kong and overseas correspondents in the weeks before the December 20 handover, although the optimistic tone often was tempered by a litany of the problems that the new administration would face in its first months (see, for instance, Ching, 1999).

REFERENCES

Bastos, J. L. M. (1986). Heritage Preservation Work in Macau Today. *Arts of Asia*, *17*(1), 98–104.

Berlie, J. A. (1999). Society and Economy. In: J. A. Berlie (Ed.), *Macau 2000* (pp. 20–52). Hong Kong: Oxford University Press.

Cheng, C. M. B. (1999). A Historical and Cultural Prelude. In: J. A. Berlie (Ed.), *Macau 2000* (pp. 3–19). Hong Kong: Oxford University Press.

Ching, F. (1999). The Future of Macau as Part of China. Online. Available http://www.csis.org/asia/hkupdate/hk9909ching.html (2 February 2000).

Conselho Consultivo da Lei Básica da Região Administrativa Especial de Macau (1993). *Lei Básica da Região Administrativa Especial de Macau da República Popular da China* [Basic Law of the Macau Special Administrative Region of the People's Republic of China]. Macau: Tipografia San Ngai.

Dinis, J. R. (1994). Portas da Localização [Gates of Localization]. *Tribuna de Macau*, 3 September.

Duncan, C. (1986a). City Profile: Macau. *Cities*, 4(1), 2–11.

Duncan, C. (1986b). Industrial Plant Location in the Territory of Macau. *Asian Geographer*, 5(1), 61–77.

Edmonds, R. L., & Kyle, W. J. (1998). Land Use in Macau: Changes Between 1972 and 1994. *Land Use Policy*, 15(4), 271–292.

Edmonds, R. L., & Yee, H. S. (1999). Macau: From Portuguese Territory to Chinese Special Administrative Region. *The China Quarterly*, 160, 801–817.

European Union Eminent Persons Group (1999). *Macau in the Context of EU-China Relations.* Unpublished report, 3 March 1999.

Hudson, B. (1979). Comparison of Contemporary Planning Theories: Counterparts and Contradictions. *Journal of the American Planning Association*, 45(4), 387–398.

Kvan, T., & Karakiewicz, J. (1998). Regaining the Sense of the City: Reclamation in Macau. *Urban Design Quarterly*, 65. Online. Available http://rudi.herts.ac.uk/ej/udq/65/internat.html (12 December 1998).

Lindblom, C. (1959). The Science of 'Muddling Through'. *Public Administration Review*, 19(2), 79–88.

Lo, S. H. (1990). Decision-Making in Macau: The Amnesty of Illegal Immigrants. In: D. Y. Yuan, H. K. Wong & L. Martins (Eds), *Population and City Growth in Macau* (pp. 159–165). Macau: Centre of Macau Studies, University of East Asia.

Lopes, G. (1998). Projects for the 21st Century. *Revista Macau*, Special 1998, 6–33.

LUSA [News Agency] (1999). Backgrounder – Infrastructures: Guaranteeing Autonomy in an Area of Sustained Economic Development. Online. Available http://www.lusamacau99.com.mo (26 February 1999).

Marreiros, C. (1991). Traces of Chinese and Portuguese Architecture. In: R. D. Cremer (Ed.), *Macau: City of Commerce and Culture* (2nd ed.) (pp. 101–116). Hong Kong: API Press.

Maruya, T. (1999). Macroeconomy: Past, Present, and Prospects. In: J. A. Berlie (Ed.), *Macau 2000* (pp. 123–144). Hong Kong: Oxford University Press.

Pinho, A. (1991). Gambling in Macau. In: R. D. Cremer (Ed.), *Macau: City of Commerce and Culture*, (2nd ed.) (pp. 247–257). Hong Kong: API Press.

Prescott, J. (1993). *Macaensis Momentum*. Macau: Hewell Publications.

Sit, V. F. S. et al. (1990). *Entrepreneurs and Enterprises in Macau: A Study of Industrial Development*. Hong Kong: API Press and Hong Kong University Press.

Tang, K. C. (1997). The Development of Education in Macau. In: R. Ramos et al. (Eds), *Macau and its Neighbors Towards the 21st Century* (pp. 221–238). Macau: University of Macau and Fundação Macau.

Taylor, B. (1992). Assessing the Contribution of Historic Preservation in Macau to the Quality of Urban Life. In: B. Taylor et al. (Eds), *Socioeconomic Development and Quality of Life in Macau* (pp. 241–255). Macau: Centre of Macau Studies, University of Macau and Instituto Cultural de Macau.

Taylor, B. (1994). Planning for High Concentration Development: Reclamation Areas in Macau. In: R. Ramos et al. (Eds), *Population and Development in Macau* (pp. 59–76). Macau: University of Macau and Fundação Macau.

Zepp, R. A. (1991). Interface of Chinese and Portuguese Cultures. In: R. D. Cremer (Ed.), *Macau: City of Commerce and Culture* (2nd ed.) (pp. 153–164). Hong Kong: API Press.

PART III

SPECIAL EVENTS AND NEW TECHNOLOGIES

13. WORLD'S FAIRS AND URBAN DEVELOPMENT: LISBON AND EXPO98

Mark I. Wilson and Laura Huntoon

ABSTRACT

World's fairs are complex economic, political, and planning events that combine decisions about a short-term festival with long-term land use management. While the public focuses on the glamour of a celebration, the event itself can obscure the many significant local and regional planning initiatives that can be accomplished using the world's fair as a vehicle. Many of the public spaces that grace cities today are remnants of past world's fairs. While world's fairs historically were celebrations of science and technology, more recently they have also been driven by local desires to make major investments in infrastructure and to revitalize urban neighborhoods. This chapter focuses on the urban and planning context for the EXPO98 in Lisbon, Portugal, and evaluates the post-EXPO plans and early outcomes for the site. This examination is prompted by the declining relevance of these events, and an interest in the planning and equity implications of world's fairs as ways to harness community resources for urban redevelopment. It discusses the background of world's

International Urban Planning Settings: Lessons of Success, Volume 12, pages 373–394.
Copyright © 2001 by Elsevier Science Ltd.
All rights of reproduction in any form reserved.
ISBN: 0-7623-0695-5

fairs, examines the motives and plans for EXPO98, and evaluates post-EXPO98 land use planning.

INTRODUCTION

World's fairs are complex economic, political, and planning events that combine decisions about a short-term festival with long-term land use management. While the public focuses on the glamour of a celebration, the event itself can obscure the many significant local and regional planning initiatives that can be accomplished using the world's fair as a vehicle. Many of the public spaces that grace cities today are remnants of past world's fairs. For example, the Champ de Mars and Eiffel Tower in Paris, Chicago's lakefront parks and museums, Southbank in Brisbane, Seattle's Space Needle, Golden Gate Park in San Francisco, and Flushing Meadows in New York. While world's fairs historically were celebrations of science and technology, more recently they have also been driven by local desires to make major investments in infrastructure and to revitalize urban neighborhoods.

World's fairs can be considered part of a class of ephemeral urban-based events that use a popular public event as a motivating force for a range of urban developments and activities. Other events similar to World's Fairs include the Olympic Games, sporting championships, gardening shows, and world-wide trade shows. These events share a short life-span and are characterized by a three-stage life cycle: (a) stage one is a bidding and building process; (b) stage two is the life of the event; and (c) stage three, which generally is the most variable, is the afterlife of the physical changes and economic changes which occur as a result of the event. These events are short-lived, highly popular, and can elevate the host location to international prominence. World's fairs are justified as generating export or tourism spending for the private sector, while offered by the public sector as break-even or minimal cost events that serve as development initiatives or marketing vehicles for the locality.

At the same time, expositions can also be costly and controversial events that divide host cities and nations. The residents of host cities and countries are concerned about the use of their tax revenue for events that may only benefit a segment of the community, or resistant to the delays and inconvenience of a major event in their city. Continuing problems with post expo redevelopment in New Orleans (EXPO84), Knoxville (EXPO82), and Seville (EXPO92) show that the formula does not always work. These cities saw a world's fair as a vehicle for development yet found that the long term benefits were limited and that the sites remain underdeveloped and problematic. World's fairs are still able to instill excitement and interest, and to serve as vehicles for development and identity for their host cities and regions, although the recent track record for fairs has not been as positive and successful as in the past.

Today, the proliferation of competing venues for consumer interactions with science and technology, such as museums and theme parks, and the greater accessibility of domestic and international travel, have somewhat devalued world's fairs and made them less exotic and appealing than in the past. The new and exciting attractions experienced by many at past world's fairs may well seem tame to a public with access to theme parks, and the visual stimulation of television and the Internet. World's fairs were considered popular attractions until recently, with a steady stream of expositions marking the last decade of the twentieth century; Seville (1992), Taejon (1993), Budapest (1996, canceled), Lisbon (1998), and Hannover (2000). The world's fairs of the 1990s tended to attract fewer visitors than forecast, with the very disappointing attendance at EXPO2000 in Hannover, less than half the numbers projected, suggesting that the world's fair may no longer be an attractive option for cities. The first world's fair of the next century will be EXPO2005 in Nagoya, Japan, and it could well be the last event of its type.

Despite their glamour and impact, little has been written about world's fairs as an economic or urban development phenomenon. Most common is research on the historical dimensions of world's fairs, with, for example Rydell (1984, 1993), Rydell, Findling, and Pelle (2000), and Greenhalgh (1988) addressing the social and scientific contexts of world's fairs in the nineteenth and early twentieth centuries. The historical dimension is also rich in its discussion of popular culture, and the symbolism of national and corporate pavilions. A second stream of literature addresses the architecture of fairs, with many firms and countries using dramatic design to attract attention in a visually stimulating and crowded space. Related literatures that also inform analysis of world's fairs reflect research on the Olympics, such as Hill (1992), McGeoch and Korporaal (1995), and Lucas (1992), or the growing debates about public support for sports teams and funding of stadia, exemplified by Cagan and deMause's (1998) book.

This chapter focuses on the urban and planning context for a world's fair, EXPO98 in Lisbon, Portugal, and evaluates the post EXPO plans and early outcomes for the site. Our examination of a recent world's fair is prompted by the declining relevance of these events, and an interest in the planning and equity implications of world's fairs as ways to harness community resources for urban redevelopment. This chapter proceeds first by discussing the background of world's fairs, followed by examination of the motives and plans for EXPO98, and an evaluation of post EXPO98 land use planning.

HISTORICAL CONTEXT FOR WORLD'S FAIRS

Fairs and civic events have long been held in all societies, but the world's fair as a modern institution started in 1851, with the Crystal Palace exposition in London. Crystal Palace was characterized by a large and impressive glass pavilion used to house exhibits, and established the dramatic event space as a hallmark of world's fairs. The Crystal Palace drew international and popular acclaim as a phenomenon of its time. The impressive physical and social outcome of Crystal Palace inspired a steady stream of fairs in Europe and North America in the latter half of the nineteenth century, and throughout the twentieth century. These fairs frequently created significant new urban areas, and cities such as Paris, through a series of world's fairs, created vast areas of public space over several decades. Paris can claim the Eiffel Tower, Champ de Mars, Trocadero and the Grand Palais as part of its world's fair heritage. It is significant that the concept of urban planning was closely tied to the organization and architecture of the 1893 world's fair in Chicago. Gilbert (1991) reports that the 1893 Columbian Exhibition supported the concept and construction of the ideal city, and was an example of how planning created order out of chaos.

World's fairs usually coincide with significant dates and anniversaries, such as the 1876 fair in Philadelphia to commemorate the centennial of American independence, or the 1893 exposition in Chicago, which was one year late to recognize Columbus' arrival in the new world 400 years earlier. More recently, Expo67 in Montreal celebrated 100 years of Canadian independence; Expo88 in Brisbane commemorated the 200th anniversary of European settlement in Australia; Expo92 in Seville recognized the 500th anniversary of Columbus' voyage; while Calgary's failed bid for Expo2005 was driven by the province's centenary.

The popularity of world's fairs led to the establishment of a governing body in 1928, the Bureau International des Expositions (BIE) based in Paris. The BIE awards cities the right to hold world's fairs and serves as a mechanism to prevent too many events being held. While the BIE does not have legal authority to control world's fairs, it does have sufficient stature to be a powerful governing body. Without the imprimatur of the BIE, many countries and firms would not participate in a world's fair. Currently, the BIE has 82 member nations, each of which has one vote when deciding where the next world's fair will be held. The BIE is not a democratic organization and claims no mission of representation, either geographically or in terms of population. In the run up to the intensely contested bid for EXPO2005, the number of voting member countries of the BIE doubled, with claims by both Canada and Japan that the other country was encouraging membership to improve the odds of a successful bid. In order to preserve the character of the event the BIE has decided to reduce the number of world's fairs to once every five years. The many fairs of the 1990s led to concern that the event was being overused, which minimized the value of each world's fair.

Much scholarly research on world's fairs has contrasted the surface, a celebration of science, technology, and culture, with the underlying message being that world's fairs represent the embedded beliefs, preferences, and stereotypes of their hosts and sponsors. Fairs of the interwar period, for example, celebrated consumerism, were apologists for social Darwinism and, by extension, imperialism, under the rubric of the West bringing civilization to the less developed regions of the world. The themes of fairs from the interwar period included a defense of colonialism in a modern context, the value of scientific progress and technology in advancing American culture, principally through consumerism, corporate capitalism as a force to rescue American society from the Great Depression, the use of erotic male fantasies as a symbol of modernity, and the manipulation of African-Americans with a promise of equality in exchange for African-American support of the coming World War (Rydell, 1993).

The interwar fairs themselves had an important economic development subtext because of timing. Evidence presented by Rydell suggests that the Chicago World's Fair of 1933 was an important source of both employment and pleasure for local residents. Thus the message of rejecting the old principles of 'scarcity, limitation, and sacrifice' for the new principles of 'abundance, self-fulfillment, and unlimited possibilities' (Rydell, 1993: 35) seems more persuasive when packaged as part of an event that brought both economic and moral sustenance to Americans overwhelmed by the Great Depression. Directly, and indirectly, world's fairs broadcast messages about social and political values to residents and visitors. At the same time, these events are also boosting the local economy through short-term earnings and infrastructure enhancement. These two purposes, value statements and economic development, are closely intertwined in a world's fair, making attribution of intent and purpose difficult.

World's fairs can be interpreted on many levels. On the surface they celebrate the stated theme(s) of the event, and are designed to provide an entertaining, educational, and enjoyable experience for visitors. World's fairs tend to portray the positive and popular elements of their day, and to avoid controversy and topics likely to make visitors uncomfortable. It is rare for a display or pavilion to challenge visitor standards or beliefs, and when it does, such as the European Union's landmine exhibit at EXPO98, it is a dramatic reminder of the real world outside the fair grounds. Beneath the surface of a world's fair are many organizations and interests, each with an agenda served by association with a glamorous international event.

World's fairs, along with similar high profile events such as the Olympics, offer an attractive target for governments, firms, and national organizations to achieve a variety of goals. Rationales for world's fairs are interrelated and many, including:

(1) Signaling economic achievement, or reaching the status of a developed nation: World's fairs, with their emphasis on science and technology, offer a powerful vehicle to display the achievements of countries and regions and to advertise advanced technical expertise. These fairs can also be used by organizations to shape public opinion about the role of science and technology and the advantages of progress. Recent examples of such fairs include EXPO70 in Osaka or EXPO93 in Taejon, Korea.

(2) Raising the international profile of secondary cities, using a fair to bring attention to emerging major centers that are often overshadowed by larger cities: World's fairs and the Olympics offer a dramatic route to international recognition by focusing media attention on one place for several months, and by attracting visitors from around the world. For example, EXPO88 in Brisbane, EXPO92 in Seville, EXPO2000 in Hannover, and EXPO2005 in Nagoya, Japan.

(3) Leveraging national funds for local purposes: In the national competition for public funds, many cities and regions face barriers to access, or rationing of investment by central authorities. The promise of a major international event can leverage funds for local purposes that may not otherwise occur. Public funds flowing to Atlanta for the centennial Olympics in 1996, or to Seville for EXPO92, exceeded the usual level of national expenditures for these locations.

(4) To influence public opinion, with world's fairs a powerful mechanism to direct public attention to national and local achievements and goals: EXPO93 in Korea was used to inform the public about the economic gains made by that country and the promise of future benefits through economic growth.

World's Fairs and Growth Machines

The appeal of world's fairs is that even as an ephemeral event they are seen to boost the status and position of the host location and country, and provide a temporary increase in the level of economic activity. Local attributes, most importantly the presence of an entrepreneurial culture (Andersson, 1985; Scott & Storper, 1987), are essential to locally-generated development. The context of entrepreneurship for world's fair development is the growth machine, a co-ordinated rent seeking apparatus staffed by a range of influential individuals, firms, and institutions. Molotch (1993: 50) sees the growth machine as

> ... the idea that nested interested groups with common stakes in development use the institutional fabric, including the political and cultural apparatus, to intensify land use and make money. Coalitions with interests in growth of a particular place (large property holders, some financial institutions, the local newspaper) turn government into a vehicle to pursue their material goals.

Growth machine theory rests on three premises. First, at least some aspects of urban and regional governance structures can be controlled by elites instead of by the median voter, or the political and commercial elites are able to convince the public of the desirability of the world's fair. Second, individual landowners, corporations such as newspaper publishers, utilities, hospitals, major local employers, as well as universities and perhaps other nonprofit organizations derive direct pecuniary benefit from increases in population and population density and expansion in economic activity generally and therefore favor a local growth economy. Third, the directors and heads of these institutions can cooperate to influence the actions of public officials, public agencies, and governments, ranging from local planning boards to national legislative bodies.

Growth machines can take many forms; the mechanisms by which elites control governance indirectly are not specified. The essence of the concept is the coincidence of an event possibility with a group of influential actors who each see opportunity for themselves through a shared or collaborative venture. Research on anti-growth entrepreneurs suggest that opportunities due to local political structure are more influential than economic or demographic elements in explaining the presence of an antigrowth movement in local governments (Schneider & Teske, 1993). This suggests that the institutional context (that is, governance structures) may be an important ingredient in how well a growth machine operates. The concept of growth machine is valuable as it shows how coalitions of interested elites within a city or region come together around an impressive event for community and self-gain. The expediency associated with an international event also offers ways to avoid due process. As Cabral, Rato and Reis (2000: 31) note about political issues for EXPO98, 'Any undemocratic processes that resulted from such a system of control was excused officially by the necessity to comply with the 1998 deadline.'

Regardless of the motivation for a world's fair, in general they do provide a significant source of earnings and intensified levels of economic activity. It is unlikely that a world's fair will not invigorate a local economy at least for the short-term period of the event. The question to explore is not so much if economic activity will be enhanced, but who will pay for, and who will benefit from, the event. World's fairs incorporate expenditures from many sources, ranging from direct spending by fair organizers, to government-funded infrastructure, and general housecleaning for the tide of new visitors. What is clear from our research is that recent world's fairs are not self-sufficient, but dependent upon considerable subsidy in addition to admission and merchandising revenue. The general net loss, contrasting the books balanced in the public eye, raises the issue of spending of public monies for private development. Testimony to the sensitivity of financial data on world's fairs is the significant lack of detailed accounting information on the costs and revenues associated with each fair. The differential between bearers of costs and recipients of benefits explains why it takes political motivations to raise a world's fair.

LISBON AND EXPO98

Portugal has experienced three decades of major political and social change as it has transitioned from a socialist state to a market economy and membership in the European Union (EU). During this time, the country has also confronted major economic restructuring and a shift away from manufacturing to a services economy. Portugal has also faced the challenge of its role in an integrated European market, and the ways it can best develop its peripheral location. Syrett (1995) notes that entering the European Union forced Portugal to reconsider many of its public policies, while at the same time providing funding for new economic and social initiatives. While EU membership created tensions about economic and social change, it also provided access to a unified European market and finance for development.

Today Lisbon is a major metropolitan area housing over 2.5 million inhabitants, or almost one quarter of Portugal's population. Until recently, the primacy of Lisbon was not considered as a policy issue, with little attempt made to decentralize population growth. The focus on Lisbon is captured in a local saying, quoted by Corkill (1999: 46), that 'Portugal is Lisbon, the rest is just scenery.' In fact, Lisbon's role as engine for the Portuguese depended on its ability to serve as a major concentration of economic activity. Corkill (1999) suggests that Lisbon's role of economic engine is also being challenged by Porto, Portugal's second largest city, which tends to contain private investment and initiatives, in contrast to Lisbon's foundation on public funds and industries. Nunes (1996) finds that Lisbon is too large in terms of population, yet too small in terms of its economic power for the country. One of the challenges for Lisbon is to define itself beyond national borders, and to find an economic and political position for itself in relation to the many European Union cities seeking their own place in an integrated European market.

Lisbon's internal structure and growth are the products of a long urban history. At the start of the 16th century, Lisbon was a major trade and economic force, and through the 18th century remained one of the leading centers of Europe. Baptista and Rodrigues (1996) identify modern Lisbon's growth in three zones. First, the current urban core fronting onto the Tagus River – comprising the Baixa, Alfama, and Bairro Alto – which dominated the city through the late 19th century. The second area of growth came with outward expansion from the core, characterizing the early 20th century direction of the city. The third area of development, most significantly since 1991, is the rise of the urban periphery as the location of the majority of Lisbon's residents. It is this zone of the city that is characterized by suburbanization, most highway and arterial roads, major shopping centers, and also the location of the EXPO98 site.

The pattern of urban development is evident in Fig. 1, which comprises two adjacent aerial photographs of Lisbon taken in 1998. The historic core of the city is characterized by high-density construction and narrow streets at the lower right center of the photograph, on the northern bank of the Tagus River. The April 25 Bridge spans the Tagus river, and until EXPO98 prompted a second river crossing, was the only bridge connecting Lisbon to southern Portugal. The periphery of Lisbon, now home to more than half of the city's population, forms an outer ring comprising the northern zone of the photographs. The EXPO98 site is evident as a construction zone on the banks of the Tagus River to the east (right) of the airport.

Motives for EXPO98

The initial idea for a world's fair in Lisbon is officially attributed to participants in a Portuguese government appointed commission responsible for commemorating the 500th anniversary of Vasco de Gama's voyage to India. With any significant event, however, there are many factors that shape development. The growth machine concept applies well in this case, with Lisbon's elite joining government leaders to support EXPO98. Far more important than the commemorative significance of past maritime achievements was the use of the EXPO form as a way for Portugal's leaders to achieve political goals of raising its international profile and self confidence (Corkill, 1999). With the EXPO as a vehicle for political, economic, and social change, Portugal was also aware of the risks associated with failing to conduct an effective event. The benefits of

Fig. 1. Lisbon 1998.

Source: Instituto Geografico do Exercito, Portgual.

a world's fair and the use of the event for many purposes were clearly recognized from the start. In the words of Antonio Mega Ferreira, one of the initiators of EXPO98

> ... it soon became clear that an effort had to be made to avoid the wasted results of so many previous international expositions during this century. The idea was to render useful a festive occasion – useful for the city, for the country and for the international community (EXPO98, 1998: 24).

The timing and scale of EXPO98 provided a rationale for many other projects and public activities that government and business sought. World's fairs usually provide cover or an urgent rationale for a wide variety of public and private initiatives, and a way to expedite developments that may otherwise be caught in time consuming bureaucracy or public scrutiny. The role of EXPO in Portugal's development was clearly identified by Portugal's Minister of Parliamentary Affairs, Antonio Costa, who stated the mission of EXPO as '. . . a catalyst for the co-ordination and articulation of various sector policies involving the oceans, and . . . launch a significant urban development programme' (EXPO98, 1998: 11). To provide context for EXPO98 we have identified four factors that shaped the initiation and development of the event: environment and heritage; national identity; urban redevelopment; and event capacity.

Environment and Heritage

The dominant theme of EXPO98 is the world's oceans and broader environmental issues, with the subtitle of the event "The Oceans: A Heritage for the Future". The theme revisits many elements of Portugal's powerful past, and the goal of re-establishing Lisbon as Europe's Atlantic Capital. Portugal also initiated through UNESCO, and strongly supported in the United Nations, the declaration of 1998 as the United Nations' Year of the Ocean. In 1994 the United Nations approved the designation for 1998 to be the Year of the Oceans. EXPO98 was seen as a forum for discussion and the focus of world attention on the state of the world's oceans. Beyond providing substance to national goals and identity, the mission also carried with it tangible benefits. For example, Lisbon has been chosen as the home for the European Agency for the Oceans, and it seeks to be the location for other international secretariats for oceanic and environmental research and management.

National Identity

With Portugal's entry into the European Union the country sought to establish its identity in a rapidly changing economic and political environment. Portugal's peripheral location applied not only to economic matters but also to political and diplomatic issues as well. The loss of its colonial role with the independence of Angola and Mozambique in the 1970s and need to reestablish itself within Europe weighed heavily on Portugal's leaders. The importance of national identity was evident in remarks by former president Mario Soares at the opening of EXPO98,

> Portugal is now a front-rank member of Europe and the European Union, its economy, in a growth cycle, is stronger than many of its EU trading partners and its new generations have a completely different outlook on life . . . Expo'98 is a starting block for the proud new Portugal. . . . Expo'98 is an achievement which will have a profound impact on the self

esteem and pride of the Portuguese and help to end a once too prevalent feeling among domestic intellectuals that nothing Portugal does is any good (*The News*, 1998: 1).

The importance of a world's fair as a vehicle to emphasize national identity cannot be underestimated. The rhetoric of EXPO98 very clearly addresses a concern by national leaders for the country to recognize its abilities, and to instill pride and a sense of Portugal's national esteem. Mega Ferreira captures this sentiment in his reflection on the contribution of EXPO98 to Portugal, "A people that was able to create an exposition like this one can do anything. I hope that we'll never hear 'we're not capable of doing that' anymore in Portugal" (EXPO98 Press Release 9/29/98). Simonetta Luz Afonso, Commissioner of the Portuguese Pavilion, saw EXPO98 as a way of '. . . regaining the confidence within us and the trust that other people had in our capacities' (EXPO98 Press Release 9/27/98). Very clearly, the Portuguese government, and EXPO98 officials, saw the fair as a way to establish Portugal's place in Europe, and to send a strong national message not only to EXPO98 visitors, but to the Portuguese public as well.

Urban Redevelopment

The redevelopment possibilities of a world's fair were also significant forces in the design and location of EXPO98. The revitalization of Lisbon and its region was a central factor in the development of EXPO98. Mega Ferreira describes the site as

> Antiquated industrial facilities, a tank farm, old military warehouses, an obsolete abattoir and even a huge rubbish tip were to give way to a new concept of the use of urban land that would, in the future, give back to the city a large strip of land, about 5 kilometres in length, located along the Tagus, the river that bathes Portugal's capital (EXPO98, 1998: 24).

Midway through EXPO98 Mega Ferreira evaluated the contribution of the fair to Lisbon, noting that '. . . one of the great merits of EXPO98 was to recover a part of Lisbon that was dead' (EXPO98 Press Release 8/4/98). EXPO98 provided the rationale for a major urban redevelopment that went beyond the Expo grounds themselves, and also to access national and European Union funds for Lisbon's development.

Event Capacity

A lesser consideration, but one that becomes important with the end of EXPO98, is the use of a world's fair to proclaim the ability of Lisbon and Portugal to host and manage a major international event. A world's fair provides experience for many workers and managers in ways to handle the many and diverse needs of an international population of visitors and organizations. By staging EXPO98, Portugal gains visibility for organizing other major events and the ability to show evidence of its skills. In preparing for EXPO98 Lisbon redeveloped its airport and public transport system, while private firms dealing with tourism and business services took on new challenges to serve an international clientele. The EXPO98 site has many buildings available to house future sporting, trade, and political events. Lisbon's success in bidding for Euro 2004, the European football championship, was based, in part, on its demonstrated world's fair success.

Planning EXPO98

The plan for an international exposition was submitted to, and approved by, the Portuguese government in Fall 1989. All political parties in Portugal supported the EXPO98 initiative. At the same time a formal request was made to the Bureau International des Expositions (BIE) to reserve 1998 for a world's fair in Lisbon. Lisbon was not assured of its right to hold the world's fair, and in 1991 Toronto sought to obtain the right for an exposition in 1998. The right to organize the 1998 world's fair was decided by a vote of the BIE membership, which selected Lisbon over Toronto in a vote of 23 to 18 on June 23, 1992.

Once sanctioned by the BIE, Lisbon proceeded to establish the institutional structure for developing and running EXPO98. In March 1993 the Exposition Commissariat was established '. . . to represent the Portuguese Government in all matters connected with the organization of the exposition' (Parque Expo, 1996: 34). At the same time a corporate entity, Parque Expo 98, was established as the agency responsible for carrying out the world's fair. All members of the board of Parque Expo98 were nominated by the Exposition Commissariat, making the operating entity an extension of the national government. Parque Expo is responsible for the management of the assets under its control, although its decisions are guaranteed by the Portuguese state. Cabral, Rato and Reis (2000) report that Parque Expo received considerable powers from the government, including compulsory land acquisition, special tax exemption (until 1999), and exemption from environmental impact assessment, although an impact study was conducted for the site.

EXPO98 became the core feature, and primary motivation, for the development of a brownfield site east of the center of Lisbon on the Tagus River, around the Olivais Dock. The larger project, called the Intervention Zone, was on a site that had many past uses, including a seaplane facility until the late 1940s, and multiple industrial uses, such as petroleum refinery, storage facilities and tank farms, and trash reprocessing. The site was a deteriorating industrial area with few applications and limited potential for further industrial development. The adaptation of the site for EXPO98 represents a major reuse of the land and a dramatic shift away from industry to commercial and recreational land uses. To manage the large-scale redevelopment of the site, a master plan covering 330 hectares was approved in 1994, of which a 50 hectare site along the Tagus River was the EXPO98 site. The Intervention Zone occupied land in both the municipalities of Lisbon and Loures, and while each municipality welcomed the event for its infusion of investment, both lost control of land use to the EXPO98 management entity, Parque Expo, and felt that their policies and interests were ignored (Cabral, Rato & Reis, 2000).

In 1994, demolition began on the old industrial structures on the site, and new construction was also started. Construction continued in 1995 and 1996, with the site expanded to 60 hectares during this time to accommodate a growing number of participating countries. From an initial expectation of 60 participating countries, the fair opened with over 150 countries represented. The elements of the master plan can be divided into site developments and regional developments to serve the site. Site developments included: clearing and cleaning of a brownfield site; centralized hot and cold water distribution center; pneumatic garbage transport system; and fiber optic telecommunications network for the site.

Regional developments included the construction of the Vasco de Gama Bridge, an 11 mile (18 km) bridge over the Tagus River, forming Lisbon's second link across the river. Associated road construction included improvements to Lisbon's inner and outer ring roads and the integration of the EXPO98 site and the Vasco de Gama bridge into the Lisbon region's highway system. The expectation of visitors to EXPO98 led to a major redevelopment of Lisbon's Metro system, including the construction of a new line linking the EXPO98 site to central Lisbon. The Metro station for EXPO98, Oriente Station, was built as an intermodal transportation hub serving as a common point for rail, subway, taxi and bus service as well as the provision of parking for private vehicles. Oriente Station was planned not only to handle transport for EXPO98 but also to be a hub for the commercial district and residential area to grow after the fair ended.

The completed EXPO98 site is shown in Fig. 2, which clearly illustrates the spatial organization of the site around the Olivais dock and along the Tagus River. The site featured several elements: (a) two major buildings serving as international pavilions, comprising 190 modules totaling 80,000 square meters; (b) seven major thematic pavilions; (c) restaurant and retail areas; (d) corporate displays and pavilions; (e) entertainment venues; and (f) landscaping for ten parks and gardens. One of the features of the site, the Oceanarium, was located inside the dock and linked to the shore by two bridges. Also evident in Fig. 2

Fig. 2. EXPO98.

Source: Instituto Geografico do Exercito, Portgual.

is the Oriente station, a transit hub forming a cross in the center of the photograph.

EXPO98 opened on May 22 and closed September 30, 1998. During the fair, almost 11 million people visited the grounds, with Sarmento (1999) noting a generally favorable response from over 500 visitors surveyed about their experience at the fair. The event also had a major economic impact on Lisbon, employing 7,000 people during the construction phase and 11,000 workers during the fair. The event led to investment exceeding U.S.$1 billion and enhanced GDP by 1% in 1998 and by 0.1–0.2% projected for the period 1999–2010 (Corkill, 1999). Cabral, Rato and Reis (2000) note however, that the heavy real estate focus of the Expo financial model means that most of the investment was required in 1998 or earlier, yet more than half of the expected revenues will accrue from real estate development in the period 1999–2010.

POST EXPO98 LAND USE

Unlike many world's fairs, which did not have clear plans for post event land use, EXPO98 was planned with a clear direction for later development. In fact it can be argued that more than most recent world's fairs, EXPO98 was based upon a well developed plan for site utilization. Most of the structures on the site were developed with later uses in mind, and the EXPO site and surrounding area of the Intervention Zone were designed to become a new element in urban Lisbon. The Intervention Zone now comprises the EXPO98 site, called the Park of Nations (Parque das Nações), and the residential development known as Expo Urbe. Among the goals for post EXPO land use are to revitalize a brownfield site; to reconnect part of the city to the River Tagus; and to develop a new commercial node for the metropolitan area. The development zone comprises the EXPO98 site, as well as residential and commercial areas.

EXPO98 Site/ Parque das Nações

The EXPO98 site has been redeveloped as a park and recreation area called the Parque das Nações, retaining most of the EXPO98 buildings, some in new uses planned before the fair. Public event spaces include the performance arena, SONY Plaza, and the Camões Theater, which now houses the Lisbon Symphony Orchestra. Recreation activities include the gardens and promenade along the Tagus River, as well as bicycle and boat rental for use on the site and river. The grounds have 40 restaurants, some once associated with countries participating in the world's fair, and 35 shops for souvenirs, clothing, entertainment etc. The continued use of some attractions, and the reuse of major pavilions, means that the EXPO98 site continues to function as public space after the event, contrasting past Expos where little thought was put to later use. The major buildings of the EXPO98 site and their current uses are:

(1) International pavilions took the form of modularized units that are being sold and removed from the site. In the meantime, they offer space for trade fairs and exhibitions.
(2) Oceanarium is an aquarium that formed the centerpiece for the world's fair, and continues as a major tourist attraction. It is the largest aquarium in Europe and second largest in the world.
(3) The Knowledge of the Seas Pavilion for EXPO98 focused on maritime discoveries and marine resources, and it is now the Knowledge Pavilion – Center of Live Science, a science museum run by Portugal's Ministry of Science and Technology.
(4) Pavilion of the Future exhibited scenarios for different uses of the oceans and an environmental consciousness message for visitors, and continues as an exhibit on marine conservation.
(5) Utopia Pavilion presented a fantasy multimedia show drawing on myths and stories about the oceans and sea creatures. It is now the multipurpose

pavilion of the city of Lisbon and serves as an arena for major entertainment events.

(6) Portuguese National Pavilion focused on Portugal's maritime history and discoveries, and was also the location for ceremonial events for visiting government leaders. The pavilion is now the office of the Presidency of the Cabinet.

(7) Virtual Reality was a pavilion sponsored by Portugal Telecom that presented a virtual voyage to the ocean floor, and it remains as an attraction associated with the Oceanarium.

(8) Cable Car and Vasco de Gama Tower retain their functions by offering viewpoints for both the EXPO98 grounds and the Vasco de Gama Bridge.

Expo Urbe

Plans for residential development were incorporated into the planning of EXPO98, and when the site was constructed facilities were put in place to serve future residents. Expo Urbe includes an underground technical gallery carrying telecommunications, power, water, and a solid waste removal system. Benefiting from the ability to start afresh, Expo Urbe also became the first part of Lisbon to use natural gas, facilitated by the flexibility and access afforded by the technical infrastructure put in place. The residential zones are located at the marina on the southern end of the site and at Tagus Park at the northern end of the site. The residential areas target middle and upper income residents for new apartments and housing developed as Expo Urbe. Housing ranges from moderate to high density construction, from buildings of 2–3 floors to high rise apartment buildings. Figure 3 shows the new housing and riverfront development at the southern zone of the site. Expo Urbe plans over 1 million square meters of new housing development for the site, along with the development of parks and facilities to serve the new housing. Once completed in 2010, the site will house 25,000 people in 10,000 housing units.

The commercial/office zone is located along major roads in the area and is connected to the Oriente transport hub, which now includes a major shopping center. Tenants of the commercial zone include major banks, construction firms, Portugal Telecom, BMW Portugal, Mitsubishi, and Sony. The Vasco de Gama Shopping Center contains over 160 shops, and occupies the space originally used to connect the Oriente Station to the EXPO98 entrance plaza. The residential and commercial functions of the area are well served by the Oriente transport hub, and by the road system and Tagus crossing linked to the development zone.

Fig. 3. New housing and Tagus promenade in Expo Urbe.

Source: Mark Wilson.

EVALUATION

There are a number of ways of evaluating world's fairs, depending upon the goals of the event, and on the context for its operation. Starting with the event itself, in terms of recent world's fairs EXPO98 was successful at attracting tourists, raising the profile of Lisbon, and redeveloping a brownfield site. The event made good use of its location and was able to attract a reasonable number of visitors even though it was competing with the soccer world cup in France and a public losing interest in world's fairs. EXPO98 can also claim success for longer-term benefits for the region, such as the enhanced transportation infrastructure of road and rail for metropolitan Lisbon. Portugal can also point to EXPO98 for experience and as a successful example of a major event as it successfully bid for the European football final for 2004. The massive investment and construction associated with the event did boost GDP and employment for a city challenged by its peripheral position in Europe.

Analyzing EXPO98 identifies a number of factors important to the planning of future world's fairs:

(1) The site for EXPO98 was well chosen. It held the potential to be an attractive district of Lisbon, and the fair provided the resources and motivation for the cleaning of a major industrial area that showed little viability maintaining its traditional function.

(2) The EXPO98 site was developed with considerable attention paid to post-Expo function. Most major buildings either maintained their function or were transformed for new uses. For many Expos, buildings are either demolished and not replaced, leaving vacant land, or deteriorate through lack of use and create negative amenity values for surrounding areas.

(3) Integrating new residential and commercial uses around the EXPO98 site provided population presence and growth to support the post Expo functions. As many Expo sites are large tracts of land in locations distant from their city cores, the ability to provide residential life is essential if a site is to be economically and socially viable.

EXPO98 was not a financial success. As commonly occurs for such events, the organization responsible for management has little incentive or, often, no legal requirement to make public its accounting. While EXPO98 closed in October 1998, it was not until July 2000 that any financial data were released, and the results led to a major political scandal with claims of fraud and misuse of funds. Associated Press (2000) reports an audit of EXPO98 found that the event cost U.S.\$1.1 billion, with a loss of U.S.\$531 million. Organizers were criticized for cost overruns on infrastructure projects and poor management of contracts. In his discussion of the rationale for world's fairs, Alfred Heller (1999: 5) notes that '. . . every world's fair is a financial failure, though some are more creative in their accounting than others'.

EXPO98 can also be assessed in broader terms, such as the opportunity cost of the resources used. The heavy public investment represents a transfer from taxpayers to the organizations and workers benefiting from EXPO98, and serves to bolster the Lisbon economy, which already had the highest income levels in the country. It also caused some controversy by redirecting resources to one major location and by focusing on middle and upper income groups in Lisbon. EXPO98 was the rationale for funding to flow into the northern sector of Lisbon, with resources drawn from Portugal and European sources. The funding issue is not straightforward, however, as Portugal was able to utilize European Union funding for much of the infrastructure development. This means that the event provided Portugal with a reason to seek additional EU funding, representing a transfer from wealthier parts of Europe to Portugal. As Lisbon will soon lose its eligibility for EU structural funding as its income level approaches 70% of the EU average, EXPO98 can also be seen as a political move to capture EU funds when future eligibility is in doubt.

The urban impact can also be seen several ways. The Expo Urbe development will offer an attractive new residential and commercial center for Lisbon, but by locating major new housing, transport, and commercial facilities away from central Lisbon, the EXPO site has the power to redirect the future development of the city. The ring road system and new bridge across the Tagus, combined with the suburbanization of population, may well re-orient Lisbon away from its core to its periphery, with new development enhancing middle and upper income residents at the cost of lower income groups living closer to the city center. The compelling need for new housing for low-income groups and for residents of deteriorated housing in the inner city contrasts the higher income orientation of housing in the Intervention Zone. The issue is not so much that new housing was provided but that it represents a shift in priorities and resources from low income to high-income residents.

Event spaces, such as Expos and stadia, increasingly are challenged by residents and analysts because they take public urban land and funds and redevelop it for private consumption. Hannigan (1998) sees the production of sanitized urban entertainment areas as ways for the affluent to exclude lower income groups from urban space. Segregation occurs through location, with event spaces distant from city centers and low-income areas, and through cost, with entrance charges or meal costs effectively keeping out low income residents. A similar critique could be directed at EXPO98, with a successful middle and upper income district designed in a once poor industrial location. The EXPO98 site is bounded by the Tagus River and major arterial roads that create an isolated enclave of upscale residential and entertainment facilities. Moulaert and Swyngedouw (2000) see the post Expo development as being divorced from the urban fabric, failing to integrate the new development into the functional life of Lisbon.

CONCLUSION

World's fairs are staged because of complex interacting political and economic interests within a defined region or metropolitan area. The event itself, like the Olympics and similar events, offers opportunities for advantage or gain to many actors, who seize upon the event as a vehicle for their actions. World's fairs exemplify the growth machine. Organizations and individuals in a city, region, or country find the world's fair a desirable option for development. The fair is an attractive phenomenon in the eyes of the public, and through government, media, and corporate support, can be made into an icon for local development. Public support can be used to leverage public spending for infrastructure and institution building, and be used for urban marketing and civic boosterism.

One central question to raise today is whether world's fairs have a place in societies with media and Internet saturation. The personal experience of seeing new discoveries and scientific phenomena seem tame in a media rich world. The experience of EXPO2000, with attendance well below half the expected rate and a massive loss predicted, suggests that world's fairs may no longer hold the power to attract and excite. EXPO98 made a dramatic change to Lisbon, turning disused land into new living, recreational and commercial areas, but this redevelopment came at a price. What is clear from the experience of Lisbon and past world's fairs is that the key to understanding the world's fair phenomenon is in the operation of urban growth machines and the political economy of major public investments.

ACKNOWLEDGMENTS

We thank the organizers of EXPO98 for providing materials on the event, and acknowledge the research assistance of Kristin Deridder. Jack Williams provided valuable comments on an earlier draft of this paper that assisted its evolution, although the authors accept full responsibility for the content presented.

REFERENCES

Andersson, A. (1985). Creativity and Regional Development. *Papers of the Regional Science Association, 56,* 5–20.
Associated Press (2000). Despite Gov't Assurances, Taxpayer Gets Hefty Bill for Lisbon World's Fair. *Wire Service,* July 13.
Baptista, L., & Rodrigues, T. (1996). Population and Urban Density: Lisbon in the 19th and 20th Centuries. In: P. T. Pereira & M. E. Mata (Eds), *Urban Dominance and Labour Market Differential of a European Capital City* (pp. 49–74). Boston: Kluwer.
Cabral, J., Rato, B., & Reis, J. (2000). *Lisbon – Portugal: The EXPO'98 Urban Project* http://www.ifresi.univ-lille1.fr/PagesHTML/URSPIC/Raphtml/Lisbonne/Lisbonne.htm
Cagan, J., & deMause, N. (1998). *Field of Schemes.* Monroe, ME: Common Courage Press.
Corkill, D. (1999). *The Development of the Portuguese Economy.* London: Routledge.
EXPO98 (1998) *EXPO98 Official Guide.* Lisbon: EXPO98.
EXPO98 Press Release (1998). EXPO98: Launching of the Book about EXPO92. 8/4/98.
EXPO98 Press Release (1998). We Have Regained the Confidence Within Ourselves. 9/27/98.
EXPO98 Press Release (1998). Mega Ferreira: The Great Show of a People's Freedom was what Moved me Most. 9/29/98.
Gilbert, J. (1991). *Perfect Cities: Chicago's Utopias of 1893.* Chicago: University of Chicago Press.

Greenhalgh, P. (1988). *Ephemeral Vistas: The Expositions Universelles, Great Exhibitions and World's Fairs, 1851–1939* Manchester: Manchester University Press.
Hannigan, J. (1999). *Fantasy City: Pleasure and Profit in the Postmodern City.* London: Routledge.
Heller, A. (1999). *World's Fairs and the End of Progress.* Corte Madera, CA: World's Fair, Inc.
Hill, C. R. (1992). *Olympic Politics.* Manchester: Manchester University Press.
Lucas, J. A. (1992). *Future of the Olympic Games.* Champaign: Human Kinetics.
McGeoch, R., & Korporaal, L. (1995). *The Bid.* Sydney: William Heinemann Australia.
Molotch, H. (1993). The Political Economy of Growth Machines. *Journal of Urban Affairs, 15*(1), 29–54.
Moulaert, F., & Swyngedouw, E. (2000). *UDPs, Socio-Political Polarisation and Urban Governance in Metropolitan Cities.* http://www.ifresi.univ-lille1.fr/PagesHTML/URSPIC/Transve2/Tranvers2.htm
Nunes, A. B. (1996). Portuguese Urban System: 1890–1991. In: P. T. Pereira & M. E. Mata (Eds), *Urban Dominance and Labour Market Differential of a European Capital City* (pp. 7–48). Boston: Kluwer.
Parque Expo98 (1996). *General Information.* Lisbon: Parque Expo98.
Rydell, R. W. (1984). *All the World's a Fair: Visions of Empire at American International Expositions, 1876–1916.* Chicago: University of Chicago Press.
Rydell, R. W. (1993). *World of Fairs: The Century-of-Progress Expositions.* Chicago: University of Chicago Press.
Rydell, R. W., Findling, J. E., & Pelle, K. D. (2000). *Fair America.* Washington D.C.: Smithsonian Institution Press.
Sarmento, M. (1999). *On the impact of World Expositions: The Case of Lisbon Expo98.* Mimeo. Instituto Superior Técnico, Department of Economics and Management.
Scott, A., & Storper, M. (1987). High Technology Industry and Regional Development: A Theoretical Critique and Reconstruction. *International Social Science Journal, 112*, 215–233.
Schneider, M., & Teske, P. (1993). The Antigrowth Entrepreneur: Challenging the Equilibrium of the Growth Machine. *Journal of Politics, 55*(3), 720–737.
Syrett, S. (1995). *Local Development: Restructuring, Locality, and Economic Initiative in Portugal.* Aldershot: Avebury.
The News (Lisbon) (1998). EXPO98 Opens. May 23, Edition 446.

14: PLANNING ISSUES AND THE NEW GENERATION TECHNOLOGY ECONOMY: COMPARATIVE REGIONAL ANALYSIS AND THE CASE OF THE U.S. NATIONAL CAPITAL REGION

Roger R. Stough and Rajendra Kulkarni

ABSTRACT

This chapter examines the recent development history of the U.S. National Capital Region as an example of technology-induced development and the so-called "New Economy". The case is somewhat unique in that over the past 30 years the region's economy has developed one of the largest information technology industrial sectors in the U.S. and that for the first time in the history of the region has created an entrepreneurial commercial industry component. More remarkable it has done so with minimal strategic leadership and planning, processes that are thought to be necessary for sustained economic development. The chapter describes the development history of the region in general and specifically examines the rise of the new commercial economy. An assessment of a range of

International Urban Planning Settings: Lessons of Success, Volume 12, pages 395–429.
Copyright © 2001 by Elsevier Science Ltd.
All rights of reproduction in any form reserved.
ISBN: 0-7623-0695-5

public policy issues follows the analysis of the development process. The final part of the Chapter examines the question of how the region continues to experience sustained development despite the failure to develop strong strategic leadership and planning processes.

INTRODUCTION

Recent publications (e.g. Atkinson, 1999) argue that regional and national economic systems are increasingly of two forms. One, the "old economy", is viewed as an artifact of the former industrial period and typified by vertical or hierarchical organization forms, mass production processes as well as other characteristics (see Table 1). The other, the "new economy", is viewed as the

Table 1.   Attributes of the Old and New Economies.*

Issue	Old Economy (Fordist)	New Economy (Neo-Fordist)
Economy-Wide Characteristics:		
Organizazional form	Vertically integrated	Horizontal networks
Scope of competition	National	Global
Markets	Stable	Volatile
Competition among Sub-national	Medium	High
Geographic mobility of business	Low	High
Role of government	Provider	Steer/row/end
Labor and Workforce Characteristics:		
Labor-Management relations	Adversarial	Collaborative
Skills	Job-specific skills	Global Learning skills and cross-training
Requisite education	Task specialization	Lifelong learning and learning by doing
Policy goal	Jobs	Higher wages and incomes (productivity)
Production Characteristics:		
Resource orientation	Materiai resources	Information and knowledge resources
Relation with other firms	Independent ventures	Alliance and collaboration
Source of competitive advantage	Agglomeration economies	Innovation, quality, time to market and cost
Primary source of productivity	Mechanization	Digitization
Growth driver	Capital/labor/land	Innovation, invention and knowledge
Role of research and innovation in the economy	Low moderate	High
Production methodology	Mass production	Flexible production
Role of government	Infrastructure provider	Privatization
Infrastructure Characteristics:		
Form	Hard (physical)	Soft (information and organizations)
Transport	Miles of highway	Travel time reduction via application of IT
Power	Standard generation plant	Linked power grid (co-generation)
Organizational flow	Highly regulated	Deregulation
Telecommunication	Miles of copper wire	Wireless and fiber
Learning	Taking head	Distance learning

* For a more extended discussion see Jim D. and R. R. Stough (1998)
"Learning and learning capability in the Fordist and Post-Fordist age an integrative framework"
Envirobmental and Planning A, V 30, pp 1255-1278.

basis of success at the turn of the millennium and is typified by a more horizontal organizational form and flexible production process (see Table 1). The purpose of this paper is to examine the rise of the "new economy" in a sub-national regional context, the Greater Washington Region, using both cross-regional comparisons and case study approaches. The paper also illustrates a variety of techniques and methods for planning and policy analysis in a sub-national regional context. Technology and the pace of technological change are viewed as two of the most important distinguishing characteristics of the new economy thus explaining why much of the paper focuses on the role of technology. The first part of the paper examines the issue of technology-led economic growth more generally across regions with the second part stepping the analysis down to the case study level and focusing on the experience of the U.S. National Capital Region. The final part of the paper examines related planning and policy issues, and dilemmas.

Culture, values, institutions and organizations across the U.S. and through-out the world are under great pressure to adapt to the impact of new generic information and computer technology.[1] These technologies are increasingly becoming standard components of most production and service delivery systems (up and down the value delivery chain), including manufacturing, design, finance, marketing, sales and logistics distribution. The same can be said for comparable activities in the public and not-for-profit sectors. Thus, much as transportation and energy technologies drove change during the industrial revolution, information and communications technology is driving change today.

Similarly, economic development is increasingly driven by the technical conversion of the economic base of all regions, states and nations. While this transformation is more visible in California because of the Silicon Valley and in Massachusetts because of the Route 128 technology concentration near Boston, its breadth and depth are not so well perceived. However, it is also occurring in places like South Dakota, Southern Georgia, and Utah. The difference between the more and less visible regions is in start time and pace of change, and the depth to which the transformation has occurred.

The regions that have adopted and incorporated technology more fully in their regional economies have also been viewed as good examples of the "new economy." The new economy concept recognizes that competitiveness and economic success are defined by different attributes than in the industrial economy. Table 1 summarizes a number of attribute differences between the old and new economies ranging from general economy wide characteristics to more specific ones that apply in such areas as labor, production and infrastructure.

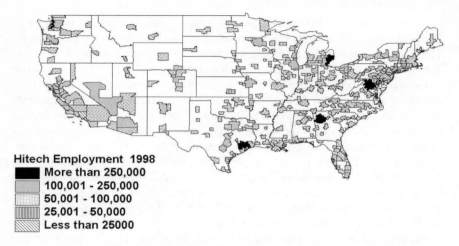

Fig. 1. Technology Employment in U.S. Metropolitan Areas 1998.

Source: U.S. County Business Patterns 1988–1998.

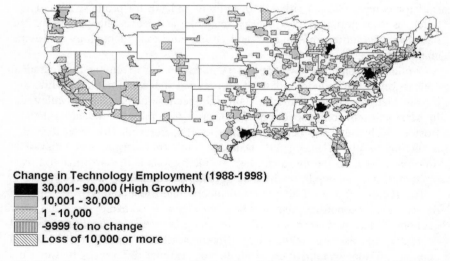

Fig. 2. Technology Employment Change in U.S. Metropolitan Areas between 1988–1998.

Source: U.S. County Business Patterns 1988–1998.

Regions that have a strong technology sector tend to have more of the new economy characteristics than others. Figures 1–2 display the geographic distribution of technology intensive employment for the period 1988–1998 in metropolitan areas. This period was selected because it begins in a year that was at the crest of a business cycle and ends in a year that is part of a strong growth cycle. The analysis is, therefore, end-anchored in years that represent strong growth and define a period that contains a recession, thereby guarding against bias that can arise if measurements are taken from "peak to valley" or "valley to peak" in the business cycle.

GENERAL AND COMPARATIVE ANALYSIS

In this part of the chapter, data describing the geographic distribution of technology employment among U.S. metropolitan areas is presented and described in an effort to illustrate the scale and scope of the technology driven transformation regional economies have experienced over the last decade. This assessment also serves to provide the context for the case study of the National Capital Region that follows.

Technology intensive sectors[2] accounted for 10.1% of the U.S. labor force in 1988. While employment in these sectors increased by more than 3.6 million by 1998, this represented only 9.6% of the 1998 labor force: a 0.5% decrease. This relative decrease may be due to several factors including the classification system used to identify and define technology intensive sectors. Technology sectors used for the 1988 study, as defined by the modified Armington index and modified by Stough (1999), remained constant for the study period despite the fact that technology continued to spread into new sectors up and down the value delivery chain. It may also be due to a net substitution of technology and capital for labor resulting in increased productivity. Thus, a 0.5% relative decrease in technical employment for the study period is not inconsistent with a conclusion that the economy is undergoing rapid technical transformation.

In 1988 the overwhelming majority of technology intensive employment in the U.S. was in metropolitan areas (90.3%). By 1998 this figure decreased slightly to 89.2%. In contrast, the non-metropolitan areas achieved more than a 1% increase. Yet, in 1998 fifty of the 321 U.S. metropolitan areas still accounted for nearly 70% of all technology employment in the U.S. Despite this small relative increase in technology employment in non-metro areas the large majority was in metropolitan areas in 1998. Consequently, the analysis concentrates on metropolitan areas.

Table 1 shows the presence of technology intensive metropolitan employment across the U.S. in 1998. Metropolitan statistical areas (MSAs) with the largest technical employment (more than 200,000) in 1998 from East to West Coasts were Boston, New York City, Philadelphia, Washington D.C., Chicago, Los Angeles, and San Jose (Silicon Valley). Among these, Los Angeles, Chicago and Boston had more than 300,000 technical employees followed closely by the Washington D.C. region with 288,764. The next largest is San Jose with 222,231, which would have had a much larger concentration if the technical employment of other MSAs in the San Francisco Consolidated Metropolitan Statistical Area-CMSA (San Francisco – 93,339 and Oakland – 93,172) were added to this figure but the same argument could be made for other metro areas in the study that belong to a large CMSA (e.g. New York, Los Angeles, and Baltimore-Washington D.C. and Chicago). These data suggest that the absolute amount of technology employment is closely tied to urban agglomeration.

Changes in absolute technology employment between 1988 and 1998 are shown in Fig. 2. From East to West Coasts, the metro areas with the largest

Table 1. Technology Employment Change Between 1988 and 1997 by Region.

Region	1988	1995	1997	% Change 88-97
Austin-San Marcos(TX)*	41,243	78,532	72,693	76.26%
Greater Washington Region***	188,172	281,980	284,724	51.31%
Rt. 128 (MA)**	283,746	285,825	272,098	-4.11%
San Jose(CA)****	306,982	313,953	300,409	-2.14%

*	**	***	****
Bastrop	Arlington	Essex	Alamenda
Caldwell	Fairfax	Middlesex	Santa Clara
Hays	London	Norfolk	
Travis	Pr. Williams	Suffolk	
Williamson	Alexandria		
	Fairfax City		
	Falls Church		
	Manasas Park		
	Manasas		
	Pr. George's		
	Montogomery		
	Wash. DC		

Employment Estimates are derived by aggregating technology intense 3 and 4 digit SIC data for technology intense categories as defined in Appendix A of Technology Region Report CIT, 1998.

absolute technology employment growth were Middlesex-Somerset-Hunterdon, NJ; Washington D.C.; Atlanta, GA; Dallas, TX; Austin San Marcos, TX; Houston, TX.

The largest absolute gains were in Atlanta, GA, Houston, TX and Washington, D.C. Among the seven metro areas with the largest number of technology jobs in 1998, Washington, as one of the ten largest gainers of technology jobs, was unique. The regions with the eighth, ninth and tenth largest number of high technology jobs in 1998 were also among the ten largest gainers for the study period.

The three metro areas with the greatest technology employment losses between 1988 and 1998 were Los Angeles, CA, San Jose, CA and Boston, MA. Despite these large losses, these areas were all among the top five metro areas with the largest absolute number of technology jobs in 1998. It should not be viewed as surprising that some large technology regions experienced large absolute losses: a slight relative decrease to a large base easily translates into a large absolute loss. This is the reason that regions with large percentage increases and decreases are almost all smaller metropolitan regions.

An analysis of the relative importance of technology to the metropolitan economies showed that the only large metro areas that have more than 15% of their employment in technology intensive sectors are San Jose, CA, Seattle, WA and Washington D.C. All other regions with a large concentration of technical employment are small to medium sized metro areas. No major metropolitan area showed large gains or losses in the ratio of technology employment to total employment.

This investigation into the patterns of technology employment at the metro level in the U.S. provides some insight into where recent technology employment is located. Given that this is an exploratory analysis of a large U.S. employment data set it is only possible, for the most part, to suggest patterns and trends. There are, however, a few exceptions. First, the large majority (about 90%) of all technology employment is in metropolitan areas. However, between 1988 and 1998 the proportion of technical employment in non-metropolitan areas increased about 1% while there was a decline of about one% in metro areas. Among metro regions technology employment tends to be highly correlated with the size of the metropolitan area indicating that urban agglomeration economies are important locational determinants. Metropolitan size appears to be a more important factor than geographic location such as east vs. west coast location. However, the larger concentrations of technology employment occur along the two coasts and across the Mid-Western manufacturing belt.

The emphasis in this part of the Chapter has been on identification of the major technology employment centers. It has been shown that the centers and their performance vary with the definition or measure used. For example, when absolute employment is used most of the regions commonly believed to be high tech are named. However, when percentage change or structural change data is used, the mix of regions changes. Nonetheless, some of the regions score strong on all of the measures, i.e. size, structure, and change indicators. One of these is the U.S. National Capital region.

THE U.S. NATIONAL CAPITAL REGION

Background

Washington, D.C. was established several centuries ago at the upper part of the navigable Potomac River on the East Coast of the United States. It, like the numerous other fall line cities, e.g. Boston, Philadelphia, Baltimore, Richmond, Charlotte (N.C.), is located where the coastal plains geological regime transitions into the more rugged Piedmont region of the U.S. Early in its development, Washington, like other fall line cities, exhibited a pattern of wealthier residents locating on the piedmont side of the region and those of less fortune settling in the Upper Coastal Plains to the east where geographic conditions were more demanding. There, drainage problems created marshlands and thus less attractive living conditions. Vestiges of this pattern may still be observed in many of the fall line cities and in the Washington Region. The sector to the west along the Potomac River, as it winds its way up onto the Piedmont, is home to those who have greater wealth and education. It is also the area where the region's recent technically driven commercial development is concentrated.

Today the Greater Washington Metropolitan Region is a three state, federal district region. It is composed of the District of Columbia which forms the historic, geographic core of the region and two major suburban parts: one in the Commonwealth of Virginia and one in the State of Maryland (Fig. 3). The metropolitan region also has two counties located in the state of West Virginia. This multi-state governance context gives the region a special character under the federalist structure of the U.S. political system where states are constitutionally responsible for the health, welfare and education of their constituents. Thus, it is not surprising that institutions with a cross-region integrated perspective and agenda have been slow to form. This coupled with a thirty-year growth rate that surpassed nearly all U.S. metropolitan regions, results in fragmented regional leadership. Rapid growth coupled with fragmented governance mean that leadership for cohesive region wide development and management is a, if not the, fundamental problem the region faces as it moves into the next Millennium.

Washington for most of the 20th Century was a major global policy-making center. This function was increasingly recognized following the First World War and then mushroomed in the Second World War and Cold War eras. As one of the several major centers of global policy influence in the world, Washington became a policy-making gateway. Advisors and those wishing to peddle influence are attracted to the region and those charged with influencing outcomes for the U.S. are sent to other parts of the world. The policy-making function attracts a wide and diverse population to the Washington region from places within the U.S. and from abroad. Policy-making is the historical signature function of the region.

Like most national capitals, Washington attracts a disproportionately large number of young and well-educated people from the U.S. and abroad. Thus, it is not surprising that the region has the 2nd highest average individual and

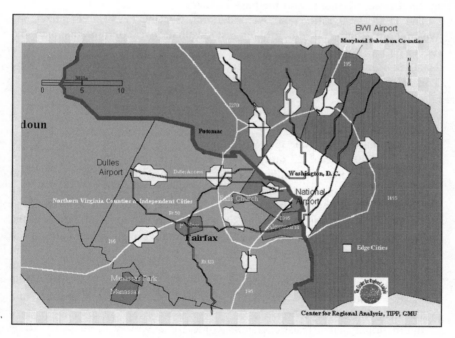

Fig. 3. National Capital Region.

household incomes of all U.S. metropolitan regions and much higher than average education levels (Northern Virginia Economic Development Coalition, 1999; U.S. Bureau of the Census, 1990). It also has the highest proportion of adults with graduate and professional degrees. In short, the region's high income and education levels stem directly and historically from its national policy making-function. Similar patterns persist in many other national capital regions of the world and for similar reasons.

As interesting and important as the Region's domestic attraction for the "best and the brightest" through its policy-making function is, its role as an international migration destination is even more so. Consequently, it has produced an ethnically and culturally diverse population.

Perhaps the greatest source of population diversification (other than the sheer size of the region) stems from the U.S. Amnesty program where foreigners from strife torn situations (military or natural disasters) are allowed to more freely immigrate to the U.S. A large number come to the Washington area because they have direct or indirect ties to U.S. officials or agencies, i.e. to the policy-making function. This has led to the formation of ethnic concentrations in the region, especially over the past 30 years.

The U.S. Immigration and Naturalization Service (1997) recognizes the Washington Region as the fifth largest destination of immigrants over the recent past with 34,327 immigrants in 1996 and between 1990–95 more than 140,000. Regions that attracted larger numbers of immigrants include New York, Los Angeles, Chicago and Miami.

Tourist and Business Attraction

Like most national capitals the Washington Region is a major destination for visitors. In 1997 it had 22 million who generated nearly $6 billion in direct spending in the Region (Fuller, 1998a). More than half of this was in the District of Columbia showing that the primary focus of hospitality expenditures is located in the Region's historic core. However, more than 25% of these expenditures was by business visitors who spent an average of 4.2 days in the region. Business visits are more heavily concentrated in suburban parts of the region, the locus of the large majority of the region's business activity. Ten percent of visitors are from international destinations. More important, the rate of growth of international visitation has been 5% per year since 1994, while domestic visitation grew at 2.5% per annum (U.S. Immigration and Naturalization Service, 1997).

International and domestic visitors come for a variety of reasons. Some arrive merely to sightsee or visit museums, monuments and other historic sites.

Others visit to observe or participate in the public policy-making process. Still others come for the region's performing arts programs which include 19 symphony orchestras including the renowned Washington Philharmonic Symphony, 9 opera companies including such well known ones as the National Lyric Opera, the Washington Opera and the Wolf Trap Opera. The Washington Region had the highest score for the arts among all Metropolitan Areas in the U.S. in 1998 (*Places Rated Almanac*, 1998).

Visitors also come for business as indicated above. Some of the reasons for business visits include influencing the policy process, attending conferences and trade shows, meeting with business suppliers or consultants and accessing the Region's rapidly growing technology services sector. Finally, it offers ready access to amenities such as the Appalachian Mountains to the interior, and the sea (the Chesapeake Bay) to the East and South, all within an hour's drive.

Transport Infrastructure and Network

One of the strongest indicators of a region's global gateway function (Stough, 2000), other than its population size, is its air transport network (O'Connor, 1998) and support operations. The Washington Region has three major airports, two of which have significant international linkages. These are Dulles International and Ronald Reagan National Airports (both located in Virginia) and Baltimore-Washington International Airport (BWI) located on the Maryland side of the region. Of these, Reagan National is located across the Potomac River from the District of Columbia near the Pentagon and serves mostly domestic passengers. Dulles is located about 20 miles to the interior and is the region's primary international airport. In 1997 it had 15.1 million passengers of which 3.2 million were international although Reagan had 207,359 Canadian travelers (Federal Aviation Administration, 1998). In that year Reagan National had nearly 16 million passengers (most were domestic) and BWI, located some 50 miles to the north, had a passenger volume similar to Dulles but with fewer international and business travelers. With these three airports serving the region it has an infrastructure capacity comparable to Atlanta, Chicago, Los Angeles or New York.

About 10% of the region's 22 million annual visitors are international and nearly all of these arrive via air transportation with the large majority coming through Dulles. Dulles currently ranks 8th nationally among airports in terms of the international passenger gateway function and is well positioned to increase its ranking. About 15 years ago Dulles was not ranked as an international passenger gateway. The relative importance of the Region's international passenger gateway activity is illustrated in the following citation from the Washington Airports Task Force Report (1998, p. 2):

> As a transatlantic gateway, the combined Washington/Baltimore region now is behind only the New York/Newark and Chicago areas in terms of weekly flight activity and well ahead of traditional "sea" gateways such as Boston, Philadelphia, Miami, Los Angeles and San Francisco. Atlanta is just ahead of Washington Dulles but behind Dulles and BWI combined. Dulles has 135 weekly flights to 10 European cities. BWI adds 14 weekly flights in two additional markets.

The major international markets served by the region's airports are Europe (with more than half of the traffic), Asia, Canada, Latin America and Oceana in order of importance.

Rise of a Technology Intensive Economy

Unlike most national capital regions, Washington has, until quite recently, been little more than a government policy making and services center. Even today government is responsible for about half of the region's economic activity, with 54% of its gross regional product produced either directly or indirectly by government spending. This is considerably higher than any other U.S. metropolitan area, as 33% alone comes from direct federal spending in the region. Thus, the region's economy is highly dependent on the federal sector (Fuller, 1998b). This dependency includes salary and wages, payments (e.g. social security) and contracts.

Figure 4 shows that the Region has little manufacturing with less than 4% of earnings in that sector. However, government and service sectors are most important both in absolute terms and structurally (i.e. they are relatively more important to the Washington Regional economy than to the nation as a whole). Thus, the Region has and continues to be viewed by many outsiders as little more than a government services center with the federal government providing the economic base and the non-basic services supporting the needs of government workers. This was a generally accurate description of the economy 20 and perhaps even 15 years ago. However, this view fails to recognize that much of the recent growth in the services has been in the technology sector (i.e. export base services) rather than just concentrated in non-basic retail or support services like warehousing. It is largely in the technology services that the region has become a business and entrepreneurial gateway. Much of its new role stems from the concentration of considerable communication and information technology, and Internet related business activity.

An analysis of the region's private sector economy shows that dominant industries, i.e. ones that are more important to the Washington Region than they are nationally, are primarily in the technology sector (Stough, 1999b, 1996). These include systems integration and architecture, information and Internet technology, software engineering, space and aerospace technology, and bio-technology.

Association headquarters, policy related sectors, and tourist and travel related functions are also structurally important (Fig. 5) but secondary to technology. Unlike tourism and associations, technology is a large sector that has more than 300,000 employees in 2000 (the Potomac KnowledgeWay [1998] estimated nearly 400,000) thus making it one of the largest technology regions in the U.S. Its level of technology employment equals or surpasses that of the Silicon Valley, Orange County (Los Angles) and the Boston 128 regions, all of which have more than 300,000 employees in their technology sectors (Table 2). The technology sector has emerged in the Washington Region over the past decade or two and in so doing has created, for the first time in its history, a commercial and industrial economic base. This sector is concentrated in the Maryland and Virginia Suburban parts of the Region (Fig. 6) with a greater concentration on the Virginia side (Stough et al., 1999a; Stough, Kulkarni & Riggle, 1997; Stough et al., 1996).

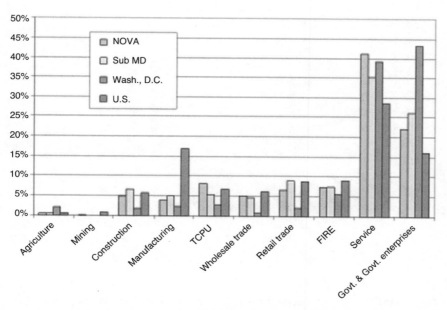

Fig. 4. Main Sector Incomes by Jurisdiction, National Capital Region, 1998.

Figure 7 shows growth in total private sector and technology employment in the Virginia part of the region from 1969. The aggregate private sector and technology sector data generally mirror each other's growth. However, early in the 1980s technology employment growth accelerated slightly relative to total private sector employment. The 1980s, as illustrated in Fig. 7, were years where the technology sector emerged as a foundation component of the region's economic base.

At the start of the Reagan administration in 1980 a defense build-up policy was adopted (Stough, Campbell & Haynes, 1997). Significant growth in federal spending stimulated growth throughout the U.S., which of course included the National Capital Region, as one of the major impact areas. This was also a stimulus to local growth in the technology sector. From that time on, defense spending focused increasingly on the technical and software attributes of arms and arms systems (electronics, design, systems management) rather than on the armaments themselves (e.g. aircraft carriers, airplanes, guns and tanks). Thus, some of the region's 1980s technical growth and related economic acceleration can be attributed to the defense build-up.

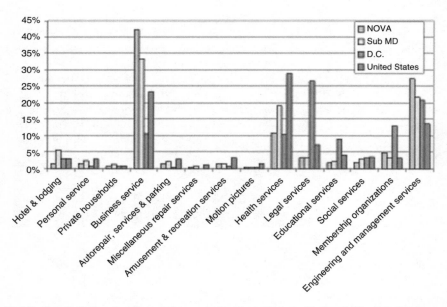

Fig. 5. Detailed Service Sector Incomes by Jurisdiction, National Capital Region, 1998.

Many have forgotten another policy of the Reagan administration that contributed even more to the expansion of the region's technology sector. This was the policy of federal outsourcing adopted early in the Reagan years (Stough Campbell & Haynes, 1997). Federal outsourcing flowed from President Reagan's belief that government had become too pervasive in the lives of Americans. With the formal pronouncement of a policy aimed at increasing the outsourcing of federal goods and services production to the private sector, the growth of the technology services in the region accelerated. While outsourcing impacted all parts of the U.S. economy, the kinds of contracts successfully procured in the Nation's capital focused largely on the design and management of large and complex systems, and projects closely tied to national security (such as the design of new arms and delivery systems). The reason for this was that senior management, e.g. the Joint Chiefs of Staff of the U.S. Department of Defense, did not wish to be geographically separated from the development of these systems for both security and control purposes. Similarly, the procurement of design services for most large, complex non-

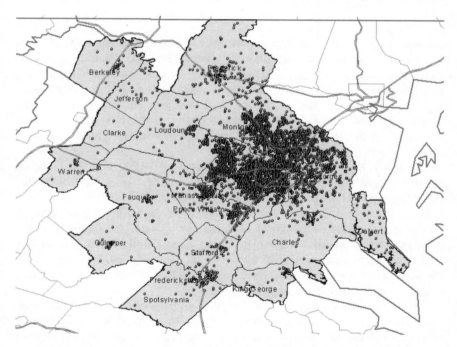

Fig. 6. Greater Washington Region Technology Firms by Location in 2000.

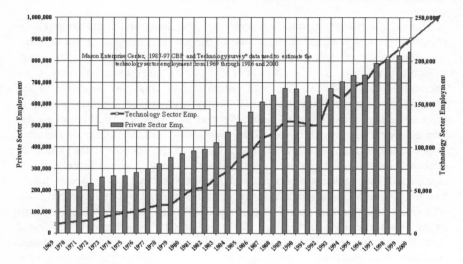

Fig. 7. Technology and Private Sector in Northern Virginia, 1969–2000.

defense government systems, e.g. personnel system reconfiguration, redesign of government payment and distribution systems like Social Security, were also let to contractors in the Capital Region. Thus grew a large technical capacity in systems design, integration and architecture and related capability in software engineering. Much of the growth in the 1980s was focused on the further development and expansion of these industry components. However, this began to change in the late 1980s and 1990s with the rise and concentration of electronic network services in the Region.

The Army Research Programs Administration (ARPA) and the National Science Foundation (NSF) supported the development of several electronic networks (e.g. ARPANET, BITNET and NSFNet) in the late 1960s, 1970s and 1980s (see Zakon, 1999; Leiner et al., 1998; Howe, 1999 for more information on the history of the development of these networks and the Internet). These functioned much as today's Internet but were more limited in scope as they served primarily the needs of military and research groups rather than everyone. These earlier networks and supporting infrastructure may be viewed as the incubators of today's Internet.

The emergence of the Internet with significant parts of the soft infrastructure established in the National Capital Region (e.g. backbone development supported by NSF and its role of creating a registration system for the Internet through a contract provided to Network Solutions, Inc) created a local comparative advantage. This led to the creation of new industries, for example, network products and services and to the transformation and expansion of more traditional ones like telecommunications. Building from this comparative advantage, the region grew a large cluster of Internet and related enterprises of which several have become Fortune 1000 companies, e.g. America on Line and MCI-WorldCom. The emergence of this Internet related sector while stimulated by government action has, unlike the systems integration sector, evolved as a commercially dominated sector, i.e. a large part of the market for Internet related services is commercial. This is, for the first time in the history of the Region, breeding an entrepreneurial culture. The related entrepreneurial and innovative activity has begun to attract investors and create local angel and investor networks (Stough & Kehoe, 2000) that are accelerating the growth of this industry. Today more than half of all of the Internet volume globally is handled or managed by companies in the National Capital Region (Potomac KnowledgeWay, 1998). The 1990s development in the technical sector has accelerated its importance in the regional economy (Fig. 7).

Before concluding this examination it is important to recognize the important role federal government policy played in the development of the technical services industry in the Region, although not an intended one. The decision to expand the defense capabilities of the U.S. and the adoption of an outsourcing policy in the 1980s were driven by much larger macro and ideological forces than those targeted to regional economic and industry development. Likewise the development of the Internet was not a conscious outcome of policies adopted by the U.S. Department of Defense or its National Science Foundation. Thus, the rise of the technology services industry in the Region making it a major national and global player in this industry may be viewed as one consequence of these policies and decisions. This outcome is a good example of how government policy may impact a region, albeit in this case a positive impact.

THE GREATER WASHINGTON REGION IN THE CONTEXT OF THE MID-ATLANTIC REGION

There are a variety of ways that the Mid-Atlantic region has been defined. For this paper it is defined as the states of Delaware, Maryland, New Jersey, Pennsylvania and Virginia and the District of Columbia (Washington, D.C.). The unit of analysis for this part of the chapter is the county or incorporated city (local jurisdiction).

The technology employment and establishments patterns at the state level are described briefly below. In absolute technology employment Pennsylvania is the largest, followed by New Jersey and Virginia. In technology employment relative to population size, Virginia has the largest base. Virginia also has the largest percentage growth after Delaware (Delaware has a small technology employment base so while its growth in absolute numbers has been quite small it registers large percentage growth). The pattern for establishments is very similar to that for technology employment; however, Virginia registered a 10% plus net growth in establishments over the study period, the highest among the five states and indicates that the churn rate is quite high. This is important because churn is a basic measure of competitiveness. The more interesting part of the analysis is, however, at the county level.

Figure 8 shows the distribution of technology employment in 1998 at the county level for the Mid-Atlantic region. Three major regional concentrations stand out: the Greater Washington Region; the Philadelphia Metropolitan region; and the Middlesex-Somerset-Hunterdon region in New Jersey (hereafter called the northern New Jersey region). Another smaller but secondary concentration appears in the Pittsburgh region which is far to the interior. This

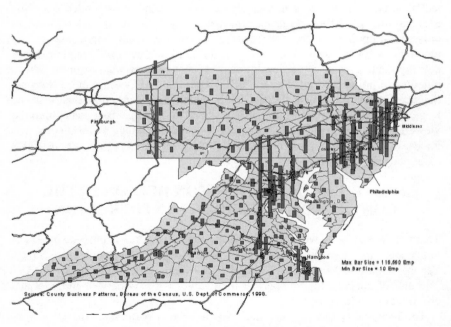

Fig. 8. Technology Employment in the Mid-Atlantic Region, 1998.

pattern reinforces the results of the earlier part of the paper that concluded that technology intensity is closely tied to urban agglomeration economies. The pattern is very similar for technology establishments.

Figure 9 shows technology employment gain from 1988–1998. Only two regions show sizeable increases in technical employment: The Greater Washington and the Northern New Jersey concentrations. Growth in the Philadelphia Region is little more than the background growth that shows up in many other counties throughout the larger region, i.e. growth in Philadelphia is about the same as the background growth in the region. Losses in technology employment also occurred over the study period. One jurisdiction in New Jersey experienced a decline in technology employment that was linked to the heavy manufacturing focus of the economy in that jurisdiction. Baltimore City and the Hampton Roads region in Southern Virginia are the other areas where major declines in technology intensive employment occurred. The Baltimore City decline was likely related to core city decline in general in the U.S. during

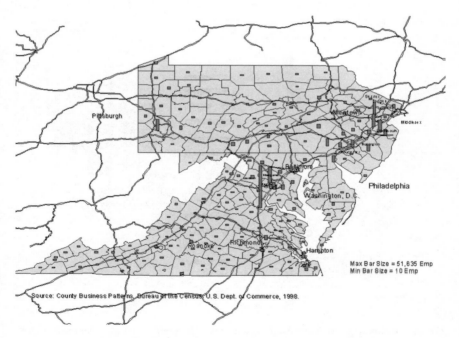

Fig. 9. Technology Employment Growth, 1988–1998.

this period. A decline in Hampton Roads region in southeastern Virginia is linked to the downsizing of the U.S. defense establishment in general and the consequent downsizing of the highly technical shipbuilding industry there over the past decade.

The remainder of the analysis focuses upon the disaggregation of the technology sector in the Mid-Atlantic Region into various sub-technology industries: advanced materials; biotechnology; electronics; energy and environment; technology manufacturing (Fig. 10); management services; information technology and telecommunications; and transportation.

Major concentrations of advanced materials employment are found in the Washington Region with a secondary concentration appearing in the northern New Jersey region. Biotechnology is most heavily concentrated in northern New Jersey and is linked primarily to the pharmaceutical and chemical industries that are located there. A secondary biotechnology cluster is found in

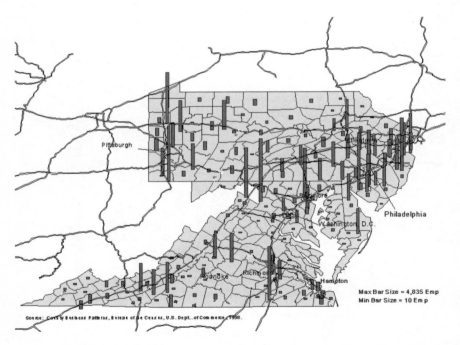

Fig. 10. Technology Intensive Manufacturing Employment in the Mid-Atlantic Region, 1998.

the Philadelphia region. A small but significant concentration of biotechnology employment appears in Baltimore and is linked to spin-offs from the Johns Hopkins University medical complex there. Finally, there are small concentrations of biotechnology employment that show up in Montgomery County in the Greater Washington Region(linked to the location of the National Institutes of Health) and in Richmond Virginia (linked, in part, to the medical complex located at Virginia Commonwealth University).

Electronics industry employment is mostly concentrated in the Philadelphia and northern New Jersey regions. The Washington/Baltimore regional complex offers a secondary concentration. Energy and environment technical employment is concentrated primarily in the Philadelphia region. But, Pittsburgh is heavily represented in this technical area which may be due to its industrial heritage and the need to address the huge environmental problems it created for the region. This is also a reason why the concentration is so strong in Philadelphia.

Figure 10 illustrates the distribution of technology intense manufacturing employment. This is the only distribution that is widely dispersed throughout the whole region. However, this should not come as a surprise as manufacturing was the base of the so-called "old economy" and to the extent that many regions have participated in technology led economic activity it has been through traditional manufacturing firms that have adopted new technology to improve productivity and competitiveness. It is important to note that, other than technology manufacturing, only biotechnology exhibits employment spillovers to the westward interior part of the region.

As noted in the introduction to the paper, information technology and telecommunications (IT&T) technology is viewed as the new generic technology that is transforming regional and national economies. The largest concentration of IT&T employment is in the Washington region with a second concentration appearing in northern New Jersey. When reviewing the distribution of technology employment growth for all technology sectors the IT&T pattern of employment is the same.

The major concentration in technical transportation employment appears in the Hampton Roads region in southeastern Virginia. This concentration exists there because one of the largest shipbuilding complexes in the U.S. is located there along with it being the home base of the U.S. Atlantic Fleet. There would have been a much larger concentration of technical transportation employment in the Philadelphia region if the huge shipbuilding complex located there had not been a casualty of the U.S. Military Base closing initiative a few years ago.

PUBLIC POLICY ISSUES

The purpose in this part of the chapter is to examine a variety of planning and policy issues arising in the context of the "new economy". This discussion is both general and specific to the National Capital Region case study.

The Digital Divide

There is widespread policy discussion about the so-called digital divide. The digital divide is the concept that some are benefiting enormously from the computer and information technology age while a disproportionate many are benefiting much less or are falling behind materially because they do not or no longer have the skills to perform in advanced jobs and/or an organizational niche that provides access. The truth surrounding the debate over this issue is confused because for every new story of a technology entrepreneur making a fortune on an Initial Public Offering (IPO) there are thousands of stories of how individuals have used the Internet to break out of poverty and constrained living situations. For example, on Sunday February 13, 2000 the front page of the *Washington Post* described how villagers in remote parts of China were able to find positions in coastal areas through the Internet that enabled them to dramatically improve their circumstances. Despite such anecdotes, there is significant evidence that many are not participating in the digital age at levels that will improve or even maintain living circumstances. The February 13, 2000 *Washington Post* front page also tells stories of ex-cyber workers in the pre-eminent Silicon Valley Region, who cannot find work and are living with the aid of public and community support.

So at the individual level there are winners and losers and these hinge, for the most part, on education and age differences. However, there is also a sorting out in geographic space with the technology regions the winners. Thus it is no surprise that one of the most fashionable economic development strategies is focused on technology led economic development. All regions want to become the next Silicon Valley!

There is another context in which the geographic digital divide emerges, namely the relationship between a successful technology region and its hinterland such as in the case of the National Capital Region. There, digital benefits are concentrated in one region with minimal geographic spillover effects. The digital divide as it is expressed in this case is illustrated below with an analysis of the Virginia business services sector and the large concentration of technology services that are contained in it. The assessment concludes with the geographical analysis of the distribution of the core components of the business services sector (computer and information technology sub-sectors).

Economic Performance of the Dominant Industry: Business Services

The business services industry has the largest employment of all industry sectors at the 2 digit SIC level in Virginia and it is growing at a rate of 12.3% per year. There are several reasons for this growth, ranging from strong economic conditions over the study period, to economic restructuring and to the development of a more service-oriented economy.

This sector includes activities, and a major task in this highly dynamic sector is to separate out the new economy components from the more traditional ones.

The business services sector is one of the strongest with a large employment base that is increasing rapidly (Fig. 11). The wage level is above the Virginia median and increasing rapidly and is 115% of the national industry average, although this measure of relative strength has been decreasing slowly over the study period. There is considerable firm formation activity, with a net firm formation rate of nearly 10%. Because this is a big industry component in Virginia its contribution to gross state product is large and increasing rapidly.

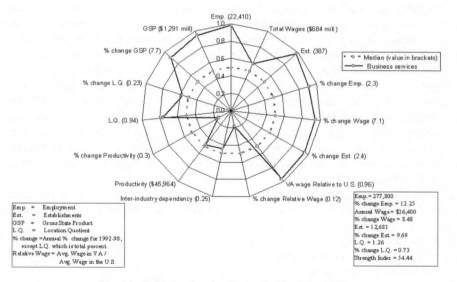

Fig. 11. Business Service Sector in Virginia, 1998.

The relative importance of business services is quite high (the location quotient is 1.26 and growing). Despite these strong indicators the interconnectedness or interdependency of business services with other economic sectors is not quite at the median for all state industries. Productivity levels are at about the median.

As noted above, not all business services are "producer" or intermediate services, i.e. services provided and sold to producers of other goods or services. Many, probably 30–40%, end up as point of sale services that should be classified as retail. The most prominent among the producer services is computer and data processing services, which employs 88,934 and has been growing at nearly 10% per year. The location quotient for this sector is 2.8 and all sub-parts have similarly large location quotients. In order of employment size the sub-sectors are: computer programming services; computer related services not elsewhere classified; computer integrated systems design; data processing and preparation; prepackaged software; information retrieval services, computer maintenance and repair; and, computer facilities management.

The next largest part of the business services sector is personnel supply services, which employs 65,828 and is growing at a rate of more than 16% per year. Sub-parts of this activity are employment agencies and help supply services. This sector is growing because unemployment levels are low and the demand for workers is high. Consequently, there is a premium paid for organizations that can find qualified workers and can help in outsourcing and in hiring temporary workers. While a statewide phenomenon, it is most acute in the Northern Virginia region where unemployment has been below 2% for the past year. Building services employs more than 35,000 and employment is growing at 4.6% per year. Mailing and reproduction services employs more than 10,000 and is growing at nearly 10% per year. Finally, nearly 20,000 are employed in other business services (not elsewhere classified) where growth is nearly 15% per year. Employment and employment growth in this "unable to classify" sector is high because many of the new economy jobs that are being filled do not easily fit into the SIC classes that were developed to suite activities in the old economy.

The business services sector is supported by a variety of other sectors including both manufacturing and services. These are supporting sectors are:

- Real estate
- Professional services
- Industrial machinery
- Communications

- Electronic equipment
- Printing and publishing
- Wholesale trade.

Given that computer services is the largest sub-sector of the business services and growing rapidly, it is no surprise that it is closely linked to professional services (engineering), communications and electronic equipment sectors.

Geographic Distribution

Well over half of the business services jobs are located in Northern Virginia. This is also the case for all information technology sub-sectors and personnel services such as computer integrated systems, data processing, prepackaged software, information retrieval services, computer maintenance, computer facilities management services and computer programming services. A secondary concentration of computer services exists in the Hampton Roads Region. All other parts of the state have minor concentrations in computer services. Finally, all parts of the state have a significant employment presence in personnel services, with Northern Virginia and Hampton Roads having the largest concentrations, although for different reasons. In Northern Virginia the reason is a labor shortage, while in Hampton Roads the unemployment rate is somewhat higher, thus the demand is for finding work there.

This example serves to illustrate the major concentration of technology intensity is located in the Northern Virginia part of the state and even though there are secondary concentrations in other areas in Virginia these are indeed secondary in scale and scope. When data for income levels, employment, growth, relative wages (to national wage levels) are computed across the state, similar distributional patterns emerge. Consequently, it is no surprise that political leadership is concerned with the development of programs that will lead to economic complimentarity between Northern Virginia and the rest of the state's economic regions. In short, there is a need for an emphasis on policies that will promote economic convergence and therefore close the digital divide that has arisen in Virginia.

Entrepreneurial Culture

The development of the information technology and Internet sectors has moved beyond the take-off stage in the Greater Washington Region over the past 4 years. Evidence of this exists in a variety of forms including increased firm formation rates, emergence of a new organizational infrastructure (e.g. the growth in importance of the Northern Virginia Technology Council), and acceleration in the creation of wealth (thousands of millionaires have been created among employees of AOL in the last 3 years according to a recent Washington Post article). Further, the Commonwealth of Virginia was ranked 6th nationally in the amount of venture capital for 1998, up from 13th in 1997 and even higher in 2000, according to PriceWaterhouseCoopers (also, see Fig. 12). Nearly all of this investment was in Northern Virginia. These data show that the region has grown an entrepreneurial culture around the IT and Internet sectors, or as PriceWaterhouseCoopers calls it, the Infocom sector.

While entrepreneurism and innovation characterize the information sectors, most of the rest of the economy remains risk averse and is participating minimally in the transformation. This situation is maintained despite the fact that technology is being embedded in almost all other sectors at an increasing rate. For example, retail, wholesale, transportation, non-basic and non-technical services, construction, finance, real estate and insurance and manufacturing. One of the issues for the Region is how to diffuse and embed a more entrepreneurial culture in these less innovative sectors.

There are several issues that are important to consider in the Region's future development. First, some three years ago the Region viewed capital formation as one of the major bottlenecks to the expansion of the technology sector. Today with the enormous wealth creation that has occurred some argue that

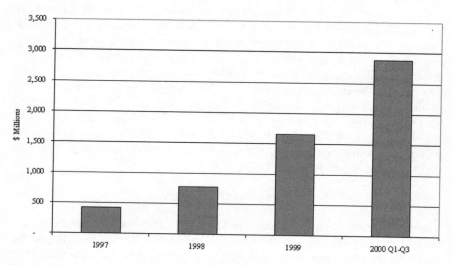

Fig. 12. Venture Capital Funds in Washington D.C. Metropolitan Region by Year (1997–2000).

what is needed is more qualified investment opportunities. This suggests that it will be important to develop the institutional infrastructure to help start-ups learn quickly the necessary business practices to amplify the perceived and real value of their technologies and ideas. This infrastructure is beginning to emerge with increasing growth in incubation programs (with and without walls). At the same time the recent development of private investor clubs suggests that linkage between these clubs and enterprise qualifying organizations will soon emerge.

Second, earlier work by Stough and Trice (1998) indicates that the Region is under-served with business incubation services with only four major business incubators located in the metropolitan region in the fall of 1998. This is far fewer than in most other major technology regions in the U.S. While a significant number of new incubation efforts and programs have been initiated since the fall of 1998, there is a need to link these and earlier efforts into a network of incubators to facilitate greater returns to the region.

One attribute of all regional economic systems is that information and the market for information is imperfect. Consequently, regions that minimize such imperfections will be more competitive because cross-firm and cross-sector transaction costs will be lower. It will be important for the Region to continue to build the institutional and organizational infrastructure necessary to further reduce transaction costs, especially around the uncertainties of starting new businesses and growing them. It will be central to this process to ensure that cooperative behavior characterizes relations between organizations like the Northern Virginia Technology Council, the Center for Innovative Technology, the Chambers of Commerce in the Region and so on. The same conclusion applies to government groups ranging from the Region's economic development authorities to jurisdictional boards of supervisors. While this issue is important in general it is even more important to those sectors that have not yet been major participants in the Region's new economy.

A final initiative is promoting entrepreneurial activity in the non-technical sectors such as construction, retail, wholesale, manufacturing, finance, real estate, insurance, etc. Ensuring stronger cross-industry links between the technical and non-technical sectors could stimulate this. Increasing interlocking board memberships among the organizational infrastructure in the region would be another way. Yet another approach is unfolding at George Mason University where a university-wide entrepreneurship curriculum is being implemented. Seven courses in business, engineering, public administration, liberal arts, nursing and health, and the arts were developed in academic year 1999–2000 and most have now been offered for the first time.

Leadership and Governance

The enormous growth that the region has experienced over the past two to three decades is unprecedented. Further, not only has this growth been large in an absolute sense, it has also been large relative to other U.S. metropolitan areas. The Washington Region has, in a matter of 30 years, grown from a center that was known only for its role as the nation's policy making center to a major multi-function metropolitan region with rapidly evolving commercial and financial sectors. However, it is a region that is still facing considerable institutional turbulence in coming to know its role. All of this reflects on its ability to function in a sustainable way.

The region has had difficulty guiding and managing itself at the region-wide level (Stough, 1994). Consequently, its institutions and organizations which were designed for a metropolitan region with, at best, limited functions and slow or steady growth, have experienced difficulty adjusting to the hard and soft infrastructure demands associated with significant and sustained development. While much of this is due to rapid growth, it is also due to the fragmented multi-state/federal district nature of its local government. This has slowed the formation of effective region-wide organizations that can build agreement on what to do and how to act upon the region's major problems.

The Washington Region is the second most congested (traffic) metropolitan area in the U.S. and has the highest costs associated with congestion (Schrank & Lomax, 1998). A thorough study of the history of surface transportation planning in the region shows that fundamental links in the road infrastructure that were called for in the 1960s were never built. Further, the region, which is divided by the Potomac River, has many fewer bridges linking residents and businesses than other major urban regions in the U.S., i.e. ones divided by a major river (Greater Washington Board of Trade, 1997). In fact, only one new bridge has been constructed in the last 30 years and that was for transit. This problem, while due in part to rapid growth, is also due to the Region's inability to create a region-wide transportation organization to assume responsibility for construction, operations and management of the transport system.

The point of this discussion is to illustrate the difficulty the region has had in forming the region-wide leadership necessary to address the demands of growth and its changing role. Thus, a major issue the region faces at the turn of the Century is how to develop effective leadership to guide its development and to ensure sustainability of its emerging commercial base (DeSantis & Stough, 1999). Maintaining and improving environmental quality and its amenity base, and further developing its emergent economic base in the technology services in general, and its Internet businesses in particular, are also important.

Quality of Life

The quality of life in the Washington Metropolitan Region is exceptional on many dimensions, as described earlier. But quality of life often is increasingly impacted by sustained and rapid growth. Because much of the growth has been fueled by development of so-called "clean industry", air quality impacts and other negative physical environmental effects have been less than anticipated. It is largely in the areas of decentralized land-use impacts that quality of life seems to be most affected.

The region's growth in the technology services sector demanded more campus like commercial space to support the largely human capital intensive nature of this industry. Coupling this to the fact that in the 1970s and the early 1980s most of the more qualified workers lived in bedroom suburban communities, led to the development of so-called Edge Cities (Garreau, 1991). These concentrations, with more than 5 million square feet of commercial floor space and 1 million square feet of retail space, became the new work centers of the region. They were located, as indicated by their name, on the edge of the region. Places such as Tysons Corner, Rockville, Bethesda and Fair Lakes became the new commercial work centers of the region. This changed the character of the geography of the region, which had been a hub and spoke urban region with the central core, the District of Columbia, lying at the geographic heart of the Region.

The Region has become a polynuclear city with several edge city concentrations rivaling and in cases surpassing (e.g. Tysons Corner) the scale and future capacity of the historic geographic core, i.e. the District of Columbia. The Washington Metropolitan Region now has at least 12 Edge Cities by Garreau's definition (1991) and it is composed of 23 counties in three states. The Region has grown in diameter from about 40 miles to more than 100 miles in 30 years (that is, the developed area of the region expanded almost 7 times). It now threatens to expand well beyond this to as much as 130 or 140 miles in the next decade, which is where the highest growth rates are occurring today (Stough, 1995). Despite this spreading out, the Region's congestion level has risen to nearly the highest in the country (Schrank & Lomax, 1998).

Proposals for smart growth and other in-fill concepts are increasingly promoted by growth control interests as a way to turn the clock back to a simpler and less congested time. However, the region continues to be attractive to Internet, E-commerce and information technology companies as it provides one of the best sites for such business in the world (Potomac Knowledgeway, 1998). Smart growth or infill sites are not sufficiently large or numerous for ventures such as MCI WorldCom or AOL which are in need of and, in fact, building large new large campus-like facilities to house their growing global headquarters and production activities. One estimate has that MCI WorldCom needs space to house a workforce of more than 30,000. Such a development can only be located on the edge where space sufficiently large to house such a facility exists. Moreover, application of information technology to support telework, electronic commerce, telebanking and so on make it possible to shrink relatively long commutes when workers need only travel to their workplace two or three days of the week (Stough & Paelinck, forthcoming; Stough, 1995). This in turn creates further demand for residential relocation on the periphery in order to access a more rural residential setting while still capturing urban employment, accessibility, and amenity benefits. As a consequence of these combined forces, continued decentralization is the probable future development trajectory for the region (Stough, 1995). Without enhanced regional leadership this issue will be very difficult to manage. As such it could sow the seeds of decreasing returns that could result, in time, in a failure to sustain growth and development.

Technical Workforce Issues

The Region has recently experienced a large increase in the demand for technical workers, not unlike that which has occurred in other regions. While this demand is outstripping supply nationally and globally (Office of Technology Assessment, 1997) the supply shortfall is particularly acute in regions where technical production is concentrated, like the National Capital Region (Stough & Trice, 1998), and where competition for technical workers is heavy. As a consequence, regions have adopted both attraction and training strategies to better compete for technically skilled personnel. In the National Capital Region efforts to address this issue have expanded considerably. The Greater Washington Initiative of the Greater Washington Board of Trade, Fairfax Chamber of Commerce, various regional economic development agencies and many companies have initiated major attraction efforts. The Northern Virginia Regional Partnership for Economic Development, area universities and community colleges as well as private sector initiatives have taken the lead in training. While the workforce supply problem has and will not go away in the near future, regional leadership through these efforts has been strengthened somewhat. This is an important bi-product of the workforce crisis in the National Capital Region.

Foreign Trade Development

A final issue concerns the National Capital Region's role as a gateway for trade. In 1997 the Region was ranked 17th nationally for of the value of its manufacturing exports and 220th in terms of percentage change in the value of exports (Office of Trade and Economic Analysis, 1999). The Region's role as a gateway for trade thus appears to be quite modest given that it is one of the largest market areas in the U.S. These data are, however, misleading. The Region, as noted above, has a very small manufacturing sector and consequently would not be expected to generate large-scale trade of manufactured goods. Further, it is a technical services economy and anecdotal evidence suggests that exports are increasingly more concentrated in the services, e.g. electronic transmission of computer code and other electronic transactions. Unfortunately there is little reliable data on the volume of tradable services let alone tradable electronic services. At the same time a recent study by DeLoitte and Touche (1998) found a sizeable internationally oriented sector in the National Capital Region with 700 foreign firms employing more than 50,000. Thus, while the trade of manufactured goods is quite modest it is likely that there is considerable trade in the producer and technical service categories.

IMPLICATIONS: STRATEGIC PLANNING AND DEVELOPMENT CHALLENGES IN AN INSTITUTIONAL CONTEXT

DeSantis and Stough (1999) in their investigation of leadership and regional economic development provide empirical evidence of the importance of high level leadership in amplifying the effect of regional resources in the development process. Their work, based on the analysis of a sample of metropolitan areas in the U.S., shows how leadership provides the cohesion needed to bring diverse interests and stakeholders across the region into agreement about strategic development goals and objectives and strategies for solving problems. Given this, it is interesting that the U.S. National Capital Region should perform so well despite highly fragmented regional leadership.

The National Capital Region is a multi-state, federal district metropolitan region. With the federal district at the geographic core and outer jurisdictions in Maryland, Virginia and West Virginia, its different geographic parts have different histories and different cultures. The federal district has evolved as the seat of the national government and the place where national policy is made. Until quite recently it did not participate in any significant economic pursuits other than to provide goods and services for those who served the government function. The Maryland part of the region is in a state that participated fully in the industrial revolution and retains much of the culture that that implies. For example, Maryland has non profit foundations built on fortunes made in the industrial period that provide large potential resources for the development process as, for example, has occurred in Indianapolis from resources provided by the Lilly Foundation.. It also supports unions that grew around the legions of blue-collar workers of the industrial period. Further, it is a strong home rule state. Virginia, by contrast, had a much lower profile in the industrial era when it was dominated by agrarian pursuits. Consequently, it did not participate in the industrial revolution in a significant way, its local government jurisdictions still must seek license from the state legislature to levy taxes or to change significantly any government function. In addition to this, local jurisdictions evolved relatively independently and only recently have they had to try to develop ways to manage cross-jurisdiction issues due to the rapid growth and geographic expansion of the region over the past 30 years. In sum, there are many reasons why this region has failed to develop strategic leadership and a cohesive development strategy.

So why has the region's economy been performing so well given these barriers to strategic leadership and planning? Circumstances arise some times that are so powerful that they support extended development despite a lack of cohesive strategic leadership. This appears to be what has occurred in the National Capital Region. The region benefited from the unanticipated and unintended consequences of federal government policy changes. A policy of outsourcing in the early 1980s coupled with the federal district's historical role as the center of national policy are at base responsible for the region's sustained development. It was during this era that information technology became a core dynamic component of the national and regional economy. In the National Capital Region, the high quality human capital pool placed it as perfectly situated to develop and provide IT services to the federal sector. With the creation of the Internet as a government spin off the region quickly participated in the emergence of Internet related commercial enterprise. The irony is that the region's technology driven development experience was an unintended and unanticipated outcome of several federal government policy and administrative decisions. The consequence of this is that the region has not needed cohesive strategic leadership, a carefully designed strategic plan for economic development and broad based cooperation across the local and state jurisdictions.

So with this we are left with the question of how important is strategic leadership? From this analysis it is clear that in some cases regions can experience extended economic development without significant regional leadership. So we can conclude that there are exceptions to the rule that such institutions are critical parts of the soft infrastructure that region's need for development. At the same time we might explore the counterfactual. The region has a transportation system that is stymied from a lack of strategic cohesive planning, management and construction. It has the second highest congestion level of any metropolitan area in the U.S. and no new bridges across the Potomac River that divides the region have been built in over 40 years except a transit bridge. As discussed in the text, this problem will and is impacting the quality of life in the region. Further, conditions will worsen if the problem is not attended to more strategically in the near future. Regions that have strategic leadership and planning recognize this sort of problem quickly and usually find ways to make improvements.

Another example of some interest revolves around the emergence of entrepreneurism in the region. As commercial ventures began to emerge at increasingly rapid rates in the mid-1990s it was clear that this process would be seriously constrained unless the region increased significantly the availability of capital. Local leadership is not the reason that capital formation became a minor issue. Rather, another unanticipated consequence of the situation was responsible. Namely, the success of some entrepreneurs made it possible for them to cash out their equity much earlier than had been expected. These "cashed out" entrepreneurs achieved rapid and enormous wealth (individually in many cases and in aggregate). This wealth then became a source of venture capital for the region. Only when the region began to generate sizeable amounts of capital itself did it attract venture capitalists from other parts of the country.

The point of these examples is to illustrate how the lack of strategic leadership and planning could improve the region's ability to cope with problems that threaten its sustained development. To date circumstances have favored the region. The future may not be so accommodating.

NOTES

1. In the late 20th century the conversion to flatter organizational forms was a process technology that had similar turbulence producing impact as organizations struggled to convert their operations from a vertical mass production organizational form to a more horizontal flexible production mode (see Piore & Sable, 1984). Information and computer technologies have made it possible for such organizational change to accelerate.

2. Technology employment is defined in terms of 4-digit SIC sectors that have high concentrations of engineering employment, and research and development expenditures (see Stough et al., 1997b).

REFERENCES

Atkinson, R. (1999). *The State New Economy Index: Benchmarking The Economic Transformation in the States*. Washington, D.C.: Democratic Progressive Policy Institute.

Deloitte & Touche LLP and Stephen Fuller (1998). *International business in the Greater Washington region*, The Greater Washington Initiative of the Greater Washington Board of Trade.

DeSantis, M., & Stough, R. R. (1999). Fast Adjusting Urban Regions, Leadership and Regional Economic Development. *Regions et Development*, November 1999.

Federal Aviation Administration (1998). *Passenger traffic in Washington Metropolitan Region Airports:1987–2011*. Airports Council International.

Fuller, S. (1998a). The contribution of nonprofit organizations to economic development in Washington, D.C. Working Paper, Center for Regional Analysis, The Institute of Public Policy, George Mason University, Fairfax, VA.

Fuller, S. (1998b). The Washington, D.C. economy: Its evolution, performance and outlook. Working paper, Center for Regional Analysis, The Institute of Public Policy, George Mason University, Fairfax, VA.

Garreau, J. (1991). *Edge cities: Life on the new frontier*. New York: Doubleday.

Greater Washington Board of Trade (1997). *Board of Trade Transportation Report Series* (Nos. 1–5 and Executive Summary). Washington, D.C.: Greater Washington Board of Trade.

Howe, W. (1999). A brief history of the Internet. [http://www.O.delphi.com/navnet/faq/history.html] (29 December, 2000).

Leiner, B. M. et al. (1998). A brief history of the Internet. [http://www.isoc.org/internet-history/brief.html] (29 December, 2000).

Northern Virginia Economic Development Coalition (1999). *Economic Profile*. Northern Virginia Economic Development Coalition. www.northernvirginia.org. (29 December, 2000).

O'Connor, K. B. (1998). The international air linkages of Australian cities, 1985–1996. *Australian Geographical Studies*, *36*(2), 143–156.

Office of Technology Assessment (1997). *Technology and Metropolitan Development*. Washington, D.C.: Office of Technology Assessment.

Office of Trade and Economic Analysis (1999). Washington, D.C.: U.S. Department of Commerce. [http://www.ita.doc.gov/oetca). (29 December, 2000).

Places Rated Almanac (1998). Comparison of Top 10 Metropolitan Areas in the U.S. New York, NY: Prentice Hall Travel.

Piore, M. J., & Sabel, D. F. (1984). *The Second Industrial Divide: Possibilities for Prosperity*. New York: Basic Books.

Potomac KnowledgeWay (1998). *Toward a new economy: Merging heritage with vision in the Greater Washington region*. The Potomac KnowledgeWay Project.

Schrank, D. L., & Lomax, T. J. (1998). *Urban Roadway Congestion: Annual Report 1998*. College Station, TX: Texas Transportation Institute.

Stough, R. R. (Ed.) (1994). *Proceedings of the 1st annual conference on the future of the Northern Virginia economy*. Fairfax, VA: The Center for Regional Analysis, The Institute of Public Policy, George Mason University.

Stough, R. R. (1995). Technology will spur satellite cities, more sprawl. *The Edge City News*, *3*(4).

Stough, R. (2000). The Greater Washington Region: A Global Gateway Region. In: A. Anderson & D. Anderson (Eds), *Gateway Regions of the World*. London, U.K.: Edgar Elgar.

Stough, R. R., & Kehoe, M. (2000). Initial Round Technology-Intensive Business Finance. Presented at the international workshop: Entrepreneurship, ICT and Local Policy Initiatives: Comparative Analyses and Lessons. Tinbergen Institute, Amsterdam, The Netherlands, May 21–23, 2000.

Stough, R. R., & Paelinck, J. (forthcoming). *Papers in Regional Science.*

Stough, R. R. (1999a). *Technology in Virginia's Regions*. Virginia's Center for Innovative Technology. Herndon, Virginia.

Stough, R. R. (Ed.) (1999b). *Proceedings of the 8th annual conference on the future of the Northern Virginia economy*. Fairfax, VA: The Center for Regional Analysis, The Institute of Public Policy, George Mason University.

Stough, R. R., & Trice, M. (1998). *Regional Information Technology Workforce Survey: 1998 Annual Survey*. Fairfax, VA: Northern Virginia Regional Partnership.

Stough, R. R., Campbell, H., & Haynes, K. E. (1997). Small business entrepreneurship in the high technology services sector: An assessment of edge cities of the U.S. National Capital Region. *Small Business Economics, 9*, 1–14.

Stough, R. R., Campbell, H., & Popino, J. (1996). *Technology in the Greater Washington region*. Washington, D.C.: The Greater Washington Board of Trade.

Stough, R. R., Kulkarni, R., & Riggle, J. (1997). *Technology in Virginia's regions*. Fairfax, VA: Center for Innovative Technology.

U.S. Immigration and Naturalization Service (1997). Immigration by selected metropolitan areas of residence. Washington D.C.: U.S. Immigration and Naturalization Service.

U.S. Bureau of the Census (1990). Washington D.C. Metropolitan Area: Population Distribution by Ethnic Group in 1990. Washington, D.C.: U.S. Bureau of the Census.

Washington Airports Task Force (1998). *1998 Annual Report*. Herndon, VA: Washington Airports Task Force.

Zakon, Robert H'obbes' (1999). Hobbes' Internet Timeline, *4*(1). Washington, D.C.: The Mitre Corporation. [http://isoc.org/guest/zakon/internet/history/HIT.html] (29 December, 2000).

15. ELECTRONIC COMMERCE: PLANNING FOR SUCCESSFUL URBAN AND REGIONAL DEVELOPMENT

Robert G. Fletcher, Brenda J. Moscove and
Kenneth E. Corey

ABSTRACT

The aim of this chapter is to provide local and regional development actors with the background and action framework needed to use electronic commerce (e-commerce) in urban and regional development planning. The magnitude of e-commerce users is described. E-commerce factors are developed, these include information technology (IT) producers and IT-using industries. E-commerce issues are introduced for developing countries, e-commerce markets and distribution networks. An e-commerce primer is explicated for the empowerment of urban area and regional development planners. Ten e-commerce planning elements are developed. This framework includes electronic resources, and it lends itself to transferability and tailoring for application to various localities.

INTRODUCTION

With the beginning of the new millennium a new technological force is rapidly expanding and changing how consumers, businesses, government and nonprofit

International Urban Planning Settings: Lessons of Success, Volume 12, pages 431–467.

organizations conduct their operations. This new force is known as "electronic commerce" (i.e. e-commerce) and it has the potential to radically change many of the common business practices that previously existed. Additionally, the introduction of mobile technology (m-commerce) has vast implications to e-commerce as well. Technological developments along with modern infrastructure have led to the use of the Internet around much of the world. The rapid introduction of the Internet globally has allowed the development of online business transactions, both business-to-consumer and business-to-business, and a vast array of information for consumers and businesses alike.

The purpose of this chapter is to explore the implications of this new technology on how business is conducted, how consumers communicate and purchase goods and services, how governments may utilize and develop Internet sites for their constituents in the future, and how urban areas and regions may utilize e-commerce for successful development. The focal point of this discussion is to highlight the potential impact on urban and regional activities, especially possible changes from the past modes of operation into the new Internet era. After defining and profiling e-commerce, the four principal areas of consideration of the chapter are to discuss the impact of e-commerce upon developing countries, to describe e-commerce markets, to investigate the partial effects of e-commerce on distribution networks, and the use of e-commerce trends and dynamics in the development planning of urban areas and regions. The latter part of the chapter is presented as an e-commerce primer for successful urban and regional development. Its planning elements were derived from international comparative policy analyses.

Throughout this chapter, the reference to "urban and regional" area development means *sub-national* in nature. While such development occurs within a national policy framework, the principal focus here is on localities at the sub-national scale.

E-COMMERCE PROFILE

What is E-Commerce?

"E-commerce" involves online business, or engagement in the digital economy, where firms and consumers buy or sell products and/or services over the Internet. These transactions can be business-to-business, business-to-consumer and consumer-to-consumer. E-commerce involves electronic catalogs, Web site management, electronic marketing research, secure electronic payments, automated negotiations, transaction processing, order fulfillment, customer satisfaction, and data mining and analysis. There are disparities in the *definitions of e-commerce* among groups conducting user surveys for the Internet and/or using the Internet for business purposes. These differences arise generally because individual companies sometimes include online sales transactions that do not include online payments. For example, a customer may establish an account tied to a credit card online, but make the payment for the product by check or money order. Another company may define e-commerce to include only transactions that are conducted totally online. Additionally, someone searching the web for information about a product or service may be defined as an e-commerce user. These different definitions lead to some confusion about the extent and growth of e-commerce on a worldwide basis. However, researchers generally agree that no matter what the definition of e-commerce, there is a significant increase in the use of the Internet for commercial purposes by consumers and businesses, and this trend can be expected to continue into the future.

The digital economy 'has become the driving force of the American Economy,' according to William M. Daley, U.S. Secretary of Commerce. He has said also that the benefits of IT 'are quickly spreading across the board, and eventually will touch every business, from the smallest mom-and-pop shop to the biggest Fortune 100' (Clausing, 2000: 1). In the U.S. in 1999, 2.5 million jobs were in Internet industries; this was a doubling from 1998. Internet industries generated U.S. $322 billion in revenues in 1998, and increased to U.S. $524 billion in 1999 (U.S. Department of Commerce, 2000). This growth is not limited to the United States. 'The number of people in the world with Internet access soared 78% in the last year [1999] to 304 million. That represents a hundred-fold increase since 1994' (Clausing, 2000: 2).

While shoppers on the Internet may choose items online, there are others that use the Internet as an important source of information to allow them to make off-line ordering and purchases; for example, high-cost ticket transactions such as for vehicles, computers, and houses, where the Internet may be used for gathering information rather than the actual purchase. As will be seen throughout this chapter, the Internet and the information technology (IT) industries that make e-commerce possible are providing a platform for business-to-business transactions, consumer-to-consumer communication and the dissemination of information on a global basis. The growing and evolving e-commerce environment is leading to changes in business processes, how consumers and businesses shop and purchase, and an array of other modifications to traditional ways of conducting business.

Who Engages in E-Commerce?

Nua, an Internet strategy firm, estimated in May 1999, that 171 million people around the world had access to the Internet, with over half of them in the United States and Canada. While more than half the people (56.6%) with Internet access live in North America, the U.S. and Canadian share of world Internet users has declined by 5% (62% in 1997 to 57% in May 1999) (Nua Internet Surveys). One of the fastest growing Internet regions is Europe. However, a survey by Booz Allen & Hamilton and the Economist Intelligence Unit (EIU) of 600 chief executives from different industries around the world project that businesses in Asia will jump past Europe in terms of Internet usage over the next few years. Africa and the Middle East, on the other hand, are some of the slowest growing Internet user regions in the world.

Additional data provided by DSA Analytics and International Corporation show the percent of the population with access to the Internet, either at work or at home, by country or country group. Based on relative population, the United States, Canada, the Nordic countries (Denmark, Finland, Iceland, Norway, and Sweden), and Australia have at least twice the level of Internet access in comparison to the United Kingdom, Germany, Japan, and France.

A survey (Commerce Net, 1999) of more than 7,200 participants estimated that 92 million persons over the age of 16 in North America (the United States and Canada) were using the Internet in some form, and that 55 million were shopping online. According to this survey, the number of Internet users in North America increased 16% in just nine months. The 55 million people shopping online in North America, where shopping was defined as researching and comparing the price and features of products and services over the Internet regardless of whether or not the person actually purchased over the Internet, represented a growing body of people who are turning to electronic commerce to transact their business. The April 1999 survey identified males (59%) as the predominant shoppers. Top shopping categories included cars/car parts (18.2 million people), books (12.6 million), computers (12.4 million), clothing (11.6 million), and CD's & Videos (11.4 million).

Twenty-eight million online users of the 55 million people included in the above survey made purchases; nine million of whom purchased online at least once a month. The survey estimated that 27 million people purchased online from work. The majority of these purchasers also were male (62%). Top purchasing categories for these Internet users included books (9.2 million), CDs/Videos (7.2 million), computers (5.4 million), clothing (4.5 million) and software (4.0 million people). In contrast to the United States, about half of online purchases by Japanese consumers in 1999 were for electronic goods while automobile goods accounted for almost 40% of Internet purchases. While about 55% of the Internet sites are English language sites, there is a trend toward non-English-centered e-commerce, especially on a global basis. Some European Web sites offer potential users a choice of languages, for example.

Governments (foreign and domestic) are active participants in e-commerce. For example, the U.S. federal government has numerous Web-sites over which it sells information. In Singapore, government Web-sites sell Geographical Information System (GIS) services, census data, and other information for use by private entrepreneurs actively engaged in real estate. Governments also use the Internet to deliver information and services to the general public. The State of California developed a Web-site where the public can access everything from a single legislative bill to the entire motor vehicle code. The use of the Internet by governments is in its infancy with rapid growth anticipated.

Factors Affecting E-Commerce

There are a variety of factors that influence the use of the Internet to conduct online business. Political and regulatory issues are problems in some countries (Business Week, 1999). Privacy and security of credit card purchases utilized in e-commerce transactions are deterrents for consumers and businesses in many countries. Additionally, the costs of Internet access and use may inhibit increased utilization of the Internet (DSA Analytics, 1999).

In countries such as the United States the flat rate pricing structure of local residential telephone calls facilitates e-commerce growth. Additionally, the flat monthly telephone fee charged to Internet subscribers may entice consumers to browse and purchase without worrying about per minute telephone charges. In contrast, high telephone rates and a shortage of Japanese language Web sites hinder the growth in the Internet in Japan. Many Japanese are beginning to use alternative access devices, such as mobile telephones with Internet capabilities, to circumvent the high telephone charges.

Another factor influencing the growth of e-commerce is the availability and cost of bandwidth access, where bandwidth is defined as the amount of information that can be sent through a connection. As high-speed networks are developed, the distribution of information will increase, especially via bandwidth applications that use graphics and video features. These applications provide the developers of Web sites the opportunity to construct more "real" shopping experiences for Internet users by using 3-D multimedia environments that are immediately available to the Internet user.

The deregulation of telecommunications markets has led to lower prices and increased e-commerce activity. For example, United Kingdom companies are using innovations in pricing and content to counter the advantages of U.S. companies that entered the British market first. Dixons, a large U.K. consumer electronics retailer, took less than five months to become the leader in British consumer Internet subscriptions. This rapid growth was created because subscribers only pay for the cost of a local telephone call; the Internet service is free (Forrester Research, 1999).

A factor that may impede the growth of e-commerce, especially in rural areas and developing nations, is lower educational achievement. While use of the Internet does not take a "rocket scientist" level of knowledge, it does require some level of sophistication with respect to the use of the equipment and sources of information available.

Income levels also play a negative role in the growth of e-commerce in rural areas and developing countries. IT equipment is not inexpensive, especially for households with low-income levels. Businesses in developing countries also may experience difficulties in competing in the rapidly growing global market because of the increased investment in IT equipment that is necessary to compete effectively.

Producers of Information Technology

In the United States, IT-producing industries include producers of computer hardware and software, communications equipment and services, and instruments. Based upon Standard Industrial Classification (SIC) codes, the top five hardware industries include: computers and equipment; wholesale trade of computers and equipment; retail trade of computers and equipment; calculating and office machines; and magnetic and optical recording media. The top five software industries are: computer programming services; prepackaged software; wholesale trade of software; retail trade of software; and computer integrated systems design. The IT-producing industries contributed more than one-third of the total real economic growth in the U.S. between 1995 and 1998. Additionally, price declines in the IT-producing industries led to a decrease in overall inflation (below 2%) in 1996 and 1997 (U.S. Department of Commerce, 1999).

The U.S. Department of Commerce (June 1999) estimates that IT-producing industries' share of the U.S. economy, in current dollars, will increase from 6% in 1993 to more than 8% in 1999. This growth in IT-related production of goods and services mirrors the growth of the Internet since 1995, and includes spending by all industries so as to have been prepared to meet the "Y2K" anticipated computer problems.

IT-Using Industries

The Department of Commerce's Economic and Statistics Administration has used the Bureau of Economic Analysis data of equipment stock to estimate the top fifteen IT-using industries in the United States. The top five IT-using industries are: telecommunications; radio and television broadcasting; security and commodity brokers; health services; and motion pictures. This ranking is based upon industries with the highest share of IT equipment relative to total equipment. The top five IT-using industries in terms of IT investment per worker include: telecommunications; nondepository institutions; pipelines, except natural gas; radio and television broadcasting; and electric, gas, and sanitary services. Several industries in the U.S. rank in the top fifteen by both measures, with the telecommunications industry first in each case.

E-COMMERCE MARKETS

No matter what definition is used for e-commerce there has been a substantial increase in the use of the Internet to conduct business and gather information by both consumers and businesses. This section investigates the impact of e-commerce on economic activity with special reference to the United States. The Internet and e-commerce allow businesses to develop competitive advantages by offering more information, expanding product and service choices, introducing new services, streamlining purchasing processes, and lowering costs. Customers also benefit from access to price and product information from many sources.

E-Commerce and the Retail Sector

When describing retailers on the Internet, distinction should be made between traditional retailers, manufacturers and Web-only retailers. The traditional brick-and-mortar retailers can vary from store chains with numerous outlets (e.g. thousands of stores for giant Wal-Mart) to single store operations. Large retailers have only recently begun to enter the e-commerce market place and, in many instances, their focus has been on using the Internet as an extension of their stores rather than as a completely new retailing concept.

Manufacturers recently have entered into the market place with the advent of the Internet. For example, Levi-Strauss & Co. prohibits J. C. Penney, a traditional retail outlet, from selling its products online and allows Levi merchandise to be sold in stores only. While Levi may have the strength to restrict retailers from marketing its products online, other manufacturers, especially small ones, are finding it difficult to compete with powerful retailers like Home Depot. In a June 1999 letter to its suppliers, Home Depot warned that selling online might result in the removal of goods supplied by these vendors from the giant retailer's stores. In other instances, retailers and suppliers are negotiating to try and resolve the balance of power between them. In any event, the resolution of the relationship between retailers and suppliers is complicated by the global potential of the Internet. In addition, manufacturers can establish a virtual store that is accessible to every online consumer in the world. The advantage to the manufacturer is the ability to avoid the expense of locating and distributing to brick-and-mortar stores and the expense of using middlemen, and so on.

Web-only companies such as Amazon.com and eToys represent a new way of conducting retail business. The storefronts for these types of companies consist of elaborate Web sites that display products, offer information, handle transactions, and ultimately insure that the goods reach the purchaser. The principal advantage of these types of companies is customer convenience, the ease with which to establish the Web site and the potential low cost for conducting business including credit card processing, security and banking facilities. The cost of setting up a Web site varies from high for elaborate and complicated displays to low for smaller and less elaborate sites. However, in terms of powerful retailers and other large organizations, even the costs of sophisticated Web sites may be rather small in comparison to traditional business practices. In addition to cost savings, key advantages of these retail "e-businesses" are the possibilities to expand existing markets and to create new ones without additional investments in brick-and-mortar facilities; the increased information, choice and time savings to consumers; and the possibility of bringing buyers and sellers together in significantly more efficient ways. A boom for smaller businesses, e-commerce is a vehicle for reaching regional, national, and global markets without the expense of brick-and-mortar facilities.

Business-to-Business E-Commerce

Business-to-business (B2B) is forecasted to be the dominant form of e-commerce. B2B e-commerce offers many of the advantages detailed above for retail e-commerce. Small customers, for example, may be able to take advantage of easy-to-use and secure Web sites to select, purchase and receive technical assistance. E-commerce also is influencing business relationships, especially supply chain processes. See the section below on e-commerce and Distribution Networks.

New classes of business intermediaries have formed with the development of e-commerce. Forrester Research has defined these new business activities as follows:

- Aggregators: Aggregators combine supplier content to create a one-stop shopping mall with predetermined prices for buyers within the business community.
- Auctions: Auctions involve buyers to purchase seller surplus. Auctions can occur on the Web without incurring physical-world search and travel costs for the participants.
- Exchanges: Online exchanges provide participants with a trading arena with clear rules, industry-wide pricing, and open market information.

An important common feature of each of these new business activities is the lack of a geographical market area and related costs. Each activity can choose virtually any place on the globe with adequate IT and Internet capabilities to establish operations. Even a home could be a site for conducting online business around the world.

E-Commerce and Target Markets

An emerging issue from the rapid growth of e-commerce concerns the role of marketing and the target customer. Traditionally, marketing's goal is to define the target customer groups and design strategies that will attract these groups. In e-commerce, particularly online sales, the target customer finds the business Web site supplying the goods and services that he/she needs. In other words, the target customer seeks the supplier rather than the supplier seeking the target market. If the target customer does not choose to visit the Web site, the online message will be ignored. Thus, the target customer initiates communication and transactions rather than the business. How to deal with this phenomenon is an essential marketing issue that is vital to the success of any organization engaged in e-commerce.

EFFECTS OF E-COMMERCE ON DISTRIBUTION NETWORKS

Whether dealing in the retail sector or B2B, an important consideration with the development of e-commerce is distribution or order fulfillment as it is referred to in e-commerce circles. Being able to order from a central cyberspace Web site provides convenience to buyers, but also introduces additional concerns for businesses selling the products. For example, many giant retailers are running into problems because they have no central distribution centers to ship products to online buyers across the United States. Expecting suppliers and branch stores to handle distribution for orders generated on the Web has proven expensive, cumbersome, and impractical leading to order fulfillment problems. Even those with a well-conceived distribution network are discovering that the network may not be sufficient to reach online customers. Organizations are discovering that distribution centers may need to be developed and/or relocated in order to serve the additional online customers with on time delivery, efficiency, etc. These organizations are redesigning distribution networks in order to fulfill orders and satisfy their new customers.

As e-commerce competition has increased, fulfillment has become an important separator of e-commerce players. Companies with experience in sending individual packages such as FedEx and United Parcel Service (UPS) have stepped in to accept, warehouse, ship and or track orders for online merchants (Goldman, 1999). This change in business processes has led to new alliances between companies, including companies linking organizations with expertise in distribution with those conducting online business. Not all retailers are handling fulfillment operations with partners. For example, Toys R Us has included its stores in the e-commerce process by allowing Web site customers to avoid shipping charges by picking up their orders and returning merchandise ordered online to its stores. It should be noted that Toys R Us encountered difficulties in order fulfillment during the 1999 holiday season. Wal-Mart hired Fingerhut, a company experienced in logistics and distribution, to handle online orders and ship the goods. Also, it has formed an alliance with Books-A-Million, the third largest bookstore chain, to supply and deliver books ordered over the Internet. This should increase Wal-Mart's ability to compete with the leading online bookseller, Amazon.com (Beck, 1999).

USING E-COMMERCE IN THE DEVELOPMENT PLANNING OF SUCCESSFUL URBAN AREAS AND REGIONS: A PRIMER

Drawing on IT policy planning experience from cases globally, the principal planning elements are presented here for use in e-commerce and in the development of urban areas and regions. Used in combination, these planning elements can function as a primer for e-commerce urban and regional development planning. This primer is directed to and prepared for the use of a range of actors in the urban and regional policy planning and development planning arenas of countries around the world. The roles that these actors play can be in the profit, governmental or non-profit sectors.

E-Commerce and Developing Countries

The global increase in e-commerce is not necessarily going to be uniform. Regions with developing countries may experience slower economic growth and, in some instances, retrenchment in growth. A variety of factors lead to this possible conclusion. Each is discussed below. In addition, the development of new technologies may overcome some of these problems and a discussion of these possibilities is included in this section.

One of the principal problems facing developing countries is their lack of IT infrastructure. An important element in the advent of e-commerce is the availability of electric and telephone infrastructure. For developing countries this represents a problem since electricity and telephones in homes may not exist. Even in places like the United States, there is concern that the IT revolution will lead to gaps between income and demographic groups, and geographic areas, i.e. the digital divide. For example, the growth in access to the Internet has not been as fast (between 1994 and 1997) for both Blacks and Hispanics in the United States in comparison to Whites. Additionally, costs for Internet access have been higher in rural areas than in urban areas and central cities in the U.S. As mentioned above, lower telephone access rates are a minor contributor to the growth of Internet usage and e-commerce. Infrastructure problems probably will be one of the major barriers to developing countries in the future. Without increases in IT capabilities, developing countries may find themselves losing the race to close the gap with more developed economies.

An alternative view to the infrastructure problem (Hudson, 1999) is that technological innovations in telecommunications may overcome the lack of hard wiring in many developing countries. For example, the introduction of wireless communication via satellites affords developing countries the opportunity to enter the digital age without heavy investment in ground wiring. To the extent that this type of technology is made available to these countries, the possibility of growing divergence between developed and developing economies may be mitigated.

IT and e-commerce offer opportunities to developing nations as well as problems. One principal advantage, if infrastructure and educational problems can be overcome, is the chance to bypass certain stages of economic development. There are major changes underway in how business is conducted globally. Developing countries may have the opportunity to omit stages of economic development that developed countries experienced during their evolution. The retail sector and distribution networks discussed above are only two examples where developing countries may be able to take advantage of the new technologies and evolving e-commerce techniques. To accomplish this feat requires additional attention to providing adequate infrastructure, principally IT technology, and increased education in developing regions of the world.

It is recognized that not all actors and nations are willing and or able to embrace e-commerce. For many, e-commerce is seen as a handmaiden of globalization; and many are concerned that economic globalization brings with it cultural hegemony. There are fears that digital divides are occurring and growing. There is concern that, via e-commerce, developed countries will undermine business in developing countries (McNulty, 2000).

The stance taken here is that e-commerce is a phenomenon that is only a few years old and diffusing quickly around the world. For some, it has proven to be beneficial so far; for others, there has not even been exposure to e-commerce. The primer is offered for those who want to engage e-commerce trends and their action implications for urban area and regional development.

E-commerce will not go away. E-commerce for many cities, regions and countries is inevitable. For those from urban areas and regions desiring to be more in control of their future, the following section is offered. The elements of this primer are derived from analyzing recent trends and comments on some likely futures of e-commerce and related IT developments. Since there is little academic and research literature to draw on, the trends and generalizations are drawn largely from a selection of popular electronic and print sources over a time span of about a year in 1999 and 2000. By necessity, the resulting presentation is unabashedly anecdotal, qualitative and descriptive. This approach was adopted, because at this time there is little in the way of research-based empirical and theoretical material to draw on for the use of policy planning and development planners with e-commerce interventions and aspirations for their localities.

Derivation of the Planning Elements

By means of international comparative analysis of the IT public policies planning of four Southeast Asia countries, i.e. Indonesia, Malaysia, Singapore and Thailand, a taxonomy was derived (Corey, 1998; Corey, 2000a, b). From these analyses the following categories are adopted here to organize the primer for e-commerce development planning. These publications explicate empirically the IT planning elements: vision and leadership; modern infrastructure; the regulatory environment; and spatial organization, in particular.

E-Commerce Planning Elements

We may identify 10 elements for planning e-commerce:

(1) Vision and leadership
(2) Modern infrastructure
(3) Regulatory environment
(4) Human resources and training
(5) Organizational dynamics
(6) Culture and political economy
(7) Timing
(8) Spatial organization
(9) Research and evaluation
(10) E-commerce primer electronic resources

The planning element labeled as "spatial organization" is of special interest here. Too often the locational and spatial organization dimensions of e-commerce are dismissed or left implicit in IT and e-commerce analytical and policy discussions (Corey, 2000b).

A number of other important elements and dimensions might have been included here. With more time and space, we might have explicated e-commerce financing. The ups and downs of high-technology stocks and dot-com profitability deserve our attention. This omission may serve as a stimulant to others to explore these e-commerce issues.

Finally, when one recommends how to take advantage of, and plan for IT and e-commerce applications, this often is taken for advocacy of the technology, i.e. "cyberbole." Such advocacy is not intended here. Rather, the intent simply is to have the reader acknowledge that these technologies have the potential to transform, or already are transforming, economies and societies, and their cities and regions around the world. Once this acknowledgment is made, then it is a practical matter of being creative and visionary as to how these technology-driven opportunities might be harnessed and steered to advance the development of one's urban area and region.

Vision and Leadership

From the comparative public policies analyses of Southeast Asian IT policies and planning elements cited above, it was found that the vision of leaders was an early and critical factor in IT innovation (Corey, 1998). Vision and leadership similarly are essential ingredients in e-commerce planning and implementation.

The fundamental question for urban and regional leaders and planners is how should e-commerce be incorporated into the area's development plans? From prior experience in other sectors of IT program planning and implementation, it is known that at least the basic IT policy planning elements need to be in place or factored into the development vision. The overall action goal under this e-commerce planning element should be to create as facilitative an environment as possible to encourage the development of e-business and e-commerce in the urban area and region.

Urban and regional executive and legislative elected officials should not continue to function as if they were still in the pre-ecommerce and pre-Internet era. These new economic and technological forces are stimulating and driving "new local economies," as well as the new global economy. There are many innovative local community efforts in e-commerce planning and implementation; in part, these can be helpful in devising one's own such strategies and positions. Urban and regional areas must reinvent themselves continuously to survive and to prosper. As a consequence, the development implications of e-commerce should be understood and incorporated into the area's and region's development policies and programs. The strategic climate of the locality should be planned to maximize future development opportunities and to anticipate problems. A goal should be to create an environment of local and regional competition for effective innovations in the use and applications of e-commerce to instill (a) the sharing of lessons from projects of excellence from private, public, academic and non-profit organizations, and (b) competition among these organizations, cities and regions.

Part of the visioning and leadership process should include analysis and projection of e-commerce innovations in various economic sectors so as to stimulate e-commerce innovation and synergies throughout the urban and regional economy. Such an example is U.K.'s Tesco. This is a case of an old British grocer that has effectively exploited its assets, e.g. a nationwide network of nearly 650 stores, to become a big and profitable e-tailer (*The Economist*, 2000).

The e-commerce vision must be put into action. Consequently, the urban area, region and its organizations should function from an e-commerce development business plan. The plan should:

- identify the market
- articulate the business goals
- define customers and the audience
- have e-business targets
- devise a marketing campaign
- analyze the competition at the organizational, urban and regional levels
- study the risks and how to mitigate them

- plan a road map for moving from the strategic level to deployment
- integrate local and regional economic systems with national and global business systems.

This business plan template has been adapted and modified from U.S.Web/CKS, 1999: 12.

Modern Infrastructure
One of the key lessons learned to date, in developing IT programs is that modern infrastructure matters. Simply, it is imperative that urban areas and regions anticipate and stay abreast of the latest developments in information and telecommunications technologies. This is true with e-commerce as well. "Modern" here is meant to convey that the latest operational technologies be made available and a system of continuous such investment be planned, updated and maintained. This should occur at the community, organizational, and individual levels.

Beyond the traditional wire, cable, fiber optic, and satellite telecommunications infrastructure, e-commerce can be expected to be changed and advanced by new technological trends. When one scans the near horizon for modern infrastructure trends, at least three emerge and intertwine: (a) wireless technologies and hand-held devices; (b) mobile commerce, or m-commerce (Business Week Asian Edition, 2000); and (c) broadband technologies. These have particular interest here because of their locational and spatial implications. Mobile technologies, at the same time free one from some locational tethers and can provide information about locational constraints, such as where is the nearest parking space to the current location of my automobile? The future portends that wireless Internet services will be interdependent with global positioning satellites (GPS) and therefore will be location-informing, with the result that location assumes even more explicit import in the e-commerce era.

What are some of the infrastructure use forecasts? By 2003, in the U.S., 'the number of people using wireless devices to connect to the Internet will increase 728%. . . . That's an increase from 7.4 million U.S. users in 1999 to 61.5 million users in 2003.' (ISP-Planet Staff, 2000). What are the implications and opportunities for cities and regions when the majority of Internet access is wireless rather than wired? Will wireless technologies be embraced universally and soon, as most forecasts suggest? When the differences and limitations between desktop wired Internet and Web access, and hand-held mobile Internet access devices are experienced more widely by more people, will there, in fact, be the rush to wireless and m-commerce? What will be the nature of this impact?

Another forecast, again for the U.S. in 2003, is that 12 million Internet-enabled hand-held computers will be in use. There were 5.2 million in use in 1999. In 1999, there were 1.1 million browser-enabled mobile phones in use. In 2003, 79.4 million such phones are forecasted to be in use. Presently, Europe is seen to be ahead of the U.S. in the use of wireless technologies, and has begun to adopt Wireless Application Protocol (WAP) – 'a protocol for reformatting Web pages to fit tiny screens." (Rupley, 2000). By 2004, Forrester Research has forecasted "that as many as one-third of all Europeans will use mobile phones to access the Internet.' (Kettmann, 2000).

Europe has a goal, which is based on wireless technology. 'The EC's eEurope strategy is to deliver faster and cheaper access to the Internet for all consumers and businesses.' This goal can be met by using ordinary telephone lines for the movement of fast data traffic. The xDSL family of technologies has been proposed as a means for delivering such services in the short term (Mitchell, 2000).

Smart phones, rather than hand-held devices, or personal digital assistants (PDA) are seen as more mass market and therefore more likely to drive the future market. Consequently, IT and telecommunications companies in Europe are developing smart phones designed to combine telephone, personal organizer functions, e-mail and the Web. There is a mobile television phone currently available in Korea. It offers three and one-half hours of TV. This device will be available elsewhere soon. Portals offering access to newspapers and magazines may be connected by mobile phone or the personal computer (Kettmann, 2000). Richness and diversity of content is the most likely driver of these markets.

Japan has demonstrated some significant leadership in content provision in the cell phone market. Mobilephone Communications International (MTI) offers nearly 200 services. 'It is the world's largest provider of content for the mobile Internet' (Fulford, 2000). MTI founder, 34-year old Toshihiro Maeta, has said that 'within a few years there will be more phones than computers connected to the Web.' Already there are 53 million digital cell phones in Japan. Japan leads the world in mobile e-mail. MTI services were used by 1.4 million people in April 2000. This usage is growing at 330% per year. The company, to date, has been profitable. MTI is tapping into the large youth population in Japan that is willing to embrace new technologies and applications that are attracted to "cellular socializing." MTI currently is developing additional applications in personal services for mobile videophones, including 'music distribution, credit information, games and e-commerce' (Fulford, 2000: 2).

In considering modern infrastructure, and their applications in information, communication, and broadcasting, for urban and regional development planning, it is notable that these applications and content provisions are nearly unlimited. In fact, they and multimedia have been called "unfinished technology," (Williams, 2000). These technologies and their applications may be seen as "inherently experimental," which means that they benefit from interaction with and feedback from users and the local and regional markets. Robin Williams' research has revealed that non-specialist users play important roles in developing *culturally appropriate content*. From these findings, it has been learned that exploiting existing products and building markets may be more effective investments in technologies uses than focusing heavily on the new and the novel; such foci tend to discourage experimentation and stunt the development of relationships with collaborators. The organizational and process learnings dovetail nicely with the effective development of modern technologies.

With the expected dramatic increase in bandwidth, some forecasters see few limitations to online applications in the future. These technologies will become a routine part of daily living. This is referred to as "tele-immersion" (Wright, 2000: 56). This immersion will be driven not only by expanding bandwidth, but also by increased computing power, the expanding applications from global positioning satellites (GPS), remotely-sensed high-resolution satellite images, and virtual reality, among other modern technologies. The more users, the more one can observe "shared enthusiasms," which, in turn, can stimulate more applications and technological innovations. Robert Wright has gone on to write that the increasing penetration of these technologies into our societies can serve either to deepen human and economic rifts, or they can bridge rifts between interest groups and nations (Wright, 2000). To support the latter, he cites the automated language translation of babelfish.altavista.com, as well as "face translation":

> Unveiled last year by the Consortium for Speech Translation Advanced Research, face translation lets you speak into a camera in English and be seen in Russia speaking Russian. And I mean speaking Russian. Your face is morphed so that you seem to be pronouncing the words of the language you don't really speak (Wright, 2000: 58).

Like all technologies, they are double edged. It is up to each of us to engage in the planning and implementation of these modern technologies to insure that our urban areas and regions appropriately exploit the opportunities and deflect the negatives that are produced. Appropriate technological uses are those that are congruent with the locality's culture and political economy. Such uses must accommodate the range of societal diversity of urban areas and regions. Several recently-published technology forecasts may prove useful in preparing the locality for likely or possible futures (Halal, 2000; *Time*, 2000).

Regulatory Environment

The pace of IT development in general, and recently e-commerce in particular, too often has resulted in a lag of regulatory environments and their development. Urban area and regional officials can reduce the negative effects of such lags by early instituting the kinds of legal and law enforcement provisions that have been shown to be helpful elsewhere. For example, the recent infection of the I Love You worm demonstrated the importance of having cyberlaws in the Philippines. In contrast, Singapore and Malaysia have invested a great deal of study and effort into developing systems of cyberlaws (Corey, 2000a).

Anonymity is being squeezed out by the rise of e-commerce. Privacy is at risk because of customer profiling and intrusive marketing techniques such as the use of "cookies" that track user browsing and shopping habits online (Berke, 2000). Of the top 100 most popular online stores:

* 18 did not post a privacy policy; and many of these are "confusing, incomplete and inconsistent"
* 35 have profile-based advertisers operating on their pages
* 87 of the e-commerce sites use cookies
* none of the companies in the survey addressed properly the "Fair Information Practices," that is, guidelines that provide basic privacy protection for consumers. Needed: (1) legally enforceable standards of privacy to ensure compliance with Fair Information Practices, and (2) 'new techniques for anonymity are necessary to protect online privacy' (Olsen, 1999, 2 pp.).

The European Union is seeking to set "the legislative framework for the new economy" at the European level. Additionally, the organizers of the European Internet Foundation seek a trans-Atlantic involvement within the cyberlaw issues framework that is being formed (Norman, 2000).

Facilitative regulatory environments to accommodate and stimulate e-commerce are needed at all scales and contexts. The debate on taxing or not taxing Internet transactions has received a great deal of public attention. This has involved global discussion, via the World Trade Organization, and in the United States the debate has been joined by governmental spokespersons at the federal, state, and local urban levels. Corporate and organizational levels also require regulatory and policy frameworks to guide the new relationships being stimulated by the new opportunities being offered by the Internet. The current three-year moratorium on Internet sales taxes in the United States expires in 2001. Virginia Governor, James Gilmore, Chairman of the federal commission on Internet sales taxation is planning on recommending that congress adopt a five-year ban on Internet sales taxes and encourage states to simplify their tax systems (Murphy, 2000).

An example of needed facilitatory regulatory environment at the organizational level is the university that is engaged in distance learning. Recently, as revenue-generation opportunities in higher education distance learning have begun to expand significantly, universities have realized that they need new conflict of commitment and conflict of interest policies. Without clear regulation, a university's faculty can come into direct conflict with its own institution. As individual faculty offer their lectures and learning exercises to global audiences via the Internet, the stakes get quite high and the intellectual property issues are not as clear as they were in the pre-Web, pre-PC, and pre m-commerce eras. 'More than one-third of all colleges and universities in the United States already offer distance learning, as it is called; by 2002, four of every five are expected to do so' (Steinberg, 2000: 1 week).

Human Resources and Training
After having modern infrastructure in place, one of the most critical planning elements for urban area and regional attention is insuring the supply of IT and e-commerce human resources. Further, given the constantly changing nature of IT and e-business developments, it is imperative that on-going training and education programs for current personnel produce a workforce that is up-to-date, creative and productive. Without the talent to conduct e-commerce, the city and region will be less competitive in the local and global economies.

The human resources and training planning element in the e-commerce context is multi-faceted; it can range from the simple to the complex and systemic. E-commerce enables online employment supports, such as having one's resume' and career objective on the Web, through to having an educational system for young children to secondary and tertiary educational programs to on-job-training and continuing education for experienced personnel. The key is to have the human resources development and training system in place and continuously revised for the availability of the area's needed skills, innovation, and locality-development and culture-enhancing knowledge. In a rapidly-changing, technology-driven local and global environment, an educated populace that is self-sustaining and self-generating of the means to produce and to enjoy the individual and collective fruits of their labors will be happier, and more likely to be productive and competitive.

The Internet, with its Web and email tools, supports such e-commerce conveniences as recruiting and being recruited electronically. For example, elance.com has produced 'a global market for buying and selling freelance services that can be delivered online.' In the global marketplace of technology workers, an electronic service that enables linkages between demand-hungry locations and supply-rich locations, seems to have excellent potential for growth (Piller, 2000). Of course, the Internet enables many of these jobs and work projects to be performed in and from a range of remote, but connected locations, including home (Online. Available WWW: www.ihbn.com).

Little, if any, evidence suggests that the e-commerce era has overturned existing class and economic orders. While new types of actors may be identified, some of the old stratifications patterns prevail. Start-ups are led by entrepreneurs, many of whom have not come from the mythological garage rags to high-tech riches roots. Rather, for example, Britain's top twenty-five startups are led by persons from 'well-to-do middle class families living in London's Notting Hill' (Davison, 2000). What of the employees of the e-commerce companies that develop beyond the startup stage?

In the e-business era, workplace-bound settings at the site of a company have begun to reveal attributes, the understanding of which may assist us in mastering and succeeding in e-commerce development. Some e-commerce employees and new economy production line workers have been referred to as "electronic peasants." In these workplaces, the focus is on output. 'Twelve emails an hour and the sack for anyone who drops below seven and a half' (Halimi, 2000). At such "electronic workplaces," innovation and creativity are not the hallmark of most of the work. Rather, the electronic peasants, Halimi wrote, are characterized often as 'young, unmarried, well educated (working in) tiny, shared cubicles with their eyes glued to the screen they handle millions of email orders a year.' Often under close electronic monitoring, these e-commerce "human resources" require developmental attention and variety in job functioning so as to realize quality performance and productivity. Without such attention, they may well remain the "cyber-damned" of the e-commerce workplace.

Another human resource development issue raised in the era of e-commerce is having in the organization, or having access to, intellectual property knowledge and specialists. They are needed to: (a) create programs to build a company's intellectual property development and commercialization function; (b) develop policies around intellectual property; and (c) maintain initiative in knowledge management.

Organizational Dynamics

A critical element from urban and regional areas in e-commerce development are organizational dynamics. This includes planning and processes such as coordination and business-plan development. See the section above on Vision and Leadership for a generic business-plan template.

Urban and regional governments should have their own professionals (or outsource the function), whose assignment is to research, anticipate and plan for the opportunities and problems presented by e-commerce and the Internet. The lead such position or function might be labeled something like, "Director of IT and Telecom Research and Policy Development, or IT and Telecom Strategic Planning."

In operational terms, what are the components of an e-commerce strategic plan? Building on its pioneering IT planning and accomplishments, Singapore has developed an e-commerce master plan. Its purpose is to enable businesses to exploit the potential and the opportunities of e-commerce. E-commerce may be seen as offering larger markets, reduced business costs and faster turnaround times. E-commerce can assist businesses to be more competitive, by stimulating improved business processes. These are the building blocks of the new ICT 21 master plan (Infocomm Development Authority of Singapore, 2000: 30). The Singapore Electronic Commerce Master Plan's six core thrusts are to: (a) develop an internationally linked e-commerce structure; (b) jump-start Singapore as an e-commerce hub; (c) expedite industry adoption; (d) promote local usage; (e) harmonize cross-border e-commerce laws and policies; and (f) develop and promote e-commerce via research and recognize thought leadership in e-commerce. This means the development of cyberlaw competency, e-commerce measurement and business models.

Organizational dynamics in e-commerce development experience suggest that the following issues be considered. In the continuous implementation of e-commerce plans and strategies, it is important to attend to: the early provision of content; constant innovation; and the deepening of services and continuous content provision and enhancement. Close attention to customer relationship management (CRM) is imperative. Such attention can produce customer-driven organizations. Such organizations are more likely to be profitable. In order to measure an organization's potential for engaging in the Internet economy; take the Cisco Internet Quotient Test (Cisco, 2000).

Both in the planning and implementation of e-commerce, it is important to pay systematic attention to learnings from other e-commerce activities. This should include studying best practices and devising benchmarks, against which to measure, monitor and evaluate progress on e-commerce goals and objectives.

Best practices analysis and benchmarking might be aided by using the Internet to communicate and network with other similar urban areas and regions regarding their lessons and results in e-commerce (Online. Available HTTP: http://www.bestpractices.org). There might be great usefulness in twining with comparable counterpart organizations elsewhere. Such networking may enable "delphi-like" studies and information clearing with sister cities and regions. The Internet enables the bridging of knowledge as well as distance.

Given the recency of e-commerce, it is important to learn from one's own organizational experiments and implementation. Such lessons can be critical in improving e-commerce development and effectiveness. As a consequence, local and regional e-commerce requires organization-based research. It must be early and continuous. E-commerce organizational research must include the monitoring and evaluation function. It is critical to track the local e-commerce efforts and the larger e-commerce trends elsewhere. See the section below on Research and Evaluation. Such research may be conducted within the organization, or it may be delegated, in whole or in part, outside the organization. The local or regional research university may be a useful source for such delegation.

As part of accountability within the public policy context, it is important to disseminate an annual report card for the urban area and or region on progress toward the e-commerce goals and according to the area's strategic plan.

The organizational aspects of planning for e-commerce development are critical. This element is one of the most important. It should reflect and accommodate the locality's macro level institutional requirements, and the individual organization's need to operationalize the micro-level and pro-grammatic dimensions of planning and implementing e-commerce initiatives.

Culture and Political Economy
In a February 21 issue of *Time* magazine, Robert Wright wrote that the question is 'what activities will still be off-line in 2025?' Like the telephone earlier in human history, one may agree with Wright that "cyberspace will have re-shaped life" by 2025 (Wright, 2000: 57). Wright calls this "tele-immersion," i.e. cyberspace 'will just become a part of life' (p. 56). It is understandable that we might be enthusiastic about the potential of IT and related technologies for the conduct of e-business and e-government. However, we do not want such enthusiasm to blur our sense of proportion.

There is a strong tendency for observers of the development of the Internet and e-commerce to function and think as if the U.S. and relatively wealthy English-speaking IT users are nearly the only people on earth. The World Bank has a public service announcement running in Asia that says half the world's population has not made a telephone call. In such a contrasting world, great caution must be exercised to avoid drawing conclusions and making plans that are too sweeping and full of hype. This admonition applies both domestically and internationally. The blending of culture and political economy, therefore, is a planning element that must be embraced and taken into account fully in planning and applying e-commerce strategies for urban areas and regions.

The following observations are offered to illustrate the kinds of issues that characterize the culture and political economy e-commerce planning element. 'There is information on Africa on the Internet, but much of it is not by Africans' (Society for International Development, 1999: 6). Comparisons across countries of differing approaches to e-commerce can be revealing of variations in culture and political economy. For example, in contemporary political campaigns. U.S. presidential candidate Senator John McCain raised about U.S. $7.5 million in online contributions in just three weeks time in late February and early March 2000. This was accomplished by overt direct and "aggressive pop-up pitches" for political donations, i.e. a kind of e-commerce transaction for influence, support and the sale of campaign artifacts. In Spain, by contrast, public funding finances campaigns. Spanish party Web sites are characterized by exciting graphics, broad political statements, and "European style pandering" such as promise of a reduced work week and 'a tree for every city resident' (Thomas, 2000: 2). In contrast, U.S. campaign Web sites seek volunteers, post endorsements and sell bumper stickers, in addition to requesting contributions. The lower-impact "duller and less inventive" Spanish sites also may reflect later entry into Web applications to politics; see the section below on Timing.

There is a hunger site at the United Nations. It includes a button that, when clicked, gets some hungry person somewhere in the world a meal paid for by a corporate sponsor. One gets one click per day. On the surface, this seemingly well-intentioned tactic generates a feel-good emotion for some button clickers, for others, however, they see this as a form of corporate sleaze with the UN aiding and abetting in the process. One objector wrote, 'If I don't press the button tomorrow will someone starve? . . . I hate it when companies stoop to this level to sell a product, "look at our commercial or we'll let this kid die." ' The point is that e-commerce, even when a form of e-philanthropy, can be taken quite differently, depending on one's political philosophy and sensitivity (Lowenhaupt, 1999).

The distribution of e-commerce acceptance and usage is anything but uniform globally. Recently, e-commerce in Japan has shown evidence of growth. A November 1999 survey of 2,645 respondents demonstrated that 56% made at least one online purchase in the last twelve months. That was up 38% from February 1999 and 25% in February 1997. Increased spending was in the clothing and travel sectors. Because of high local telephone rates and the "relative unpopularity of personal computers," the growth of Internet usage in Japan has been slower than in the U.S. In 1998,

* there were eight million Internet users in Japan.
* there were 62.8 million online users in the U.S. (Nandotimes, 2000).

In order to help shape public policies responsive to the unique potential and character of Europe's Internet revolution, the European Internet Foundation, via the foundation's Website, has solicited policy views. However, the relatively high cost involved in making such policy suggestions, via associate membership in the foundation, limited participation principally to wealthy individuals and corporations. Such costs serve to widen the digital divide and skew participation in the policy formulation process.

There also is the problem of a political culture of little or no vision and leadership about e-commerce and the Internet. This may be a function of generational lag as well. In early 2000, the U.S. presidential candidates demonstrated nearly no such positions, with the exception of calling for filtering out electronic pornography and advocating the continuation, for now, of no taxes on e-commerce. The candidates and their parties are silent on the huge technology company mergers, such as the America Online and Time Warner merger announcement (Sanger, 2000). What are the foreign policy implications of U.S. domination of the Internet? The same for English-language hegemony of e-commerce and the Internet? What are the competing visions for closing the digital divide at home and abroad? What public policies should be planned for such issues as: privacy of personal electronic records, encryption of electronic messages, electronic terrorism, and electronic economic policies for national, regional and urban development?

Political Web sites have been categorized into three types: (a) for-profit for watchers and for information; (b) not-for-profit political sites to enlighten and to get viewers to contribute and to vote; and (c) activist for-profit Web sites that promote non-partisan democracy in general and participation in government. The latter type was seen by Chris Suellentrop as well-intentioned, but because of its "activism in the abstract," it has not demonstrated effectiveness at encouraging actual political activism. This is in contrast to the demonstrated use of the Internet as a powerful political action tool as in the cases of raising millions in campaign contributions and enabling politically like-minded people to communicate their support across distance and physical space (Suellentrop, February 23).

One of the more powerful Internet tools in addressing cultural and political economy factors is foreign language translation service. There are Web sites that perform increasingly effectively in simple translations between English and most European languages. Also, see the Modern Infrastructure section above that includes the reference to "face translation."

The Internet has been dominated by the English language, to the point where it has been labeled the "Anglo-Net." That is beginning to change, and may result in an early opening up of huge markets in Asia and other non-English speaking regions of the world. The conversion of non-English languages to code that enables the registration of Internet domain names in such languages as Chinese, Thai, Tamil and so on, is changing the language and cultural landscapes of electronic space. This innovation also may be leading to a new, a global standard that will hasten the use of the Internet for e-commerce and other applications across international borders (Dolven, 2000).

In a litigious political economy and society such as the United States, e-commerce growth and diffusion raises issues and concerns that might be less or more accepting in other cultures. The monitoring of e-mail inside companies and organizations is a case in point. Techrepublic.com, for example, advertises its e-mail surveillance service by asking what about 'your company's liability for what goes into those e-mails?' Techrepublic then stated that 'e-mail surveillance might be your answer.' This kind of an issue also intersects with the Regulatory Environment planning element discussed above (Whitener, 2000).

From these general snippets, one may construct analogous cultural and political economy issues for understanding and applying at specific urban and regional levels. Simply, e-commerce initiatives are more likely to be successful and effective when they are congruent with the area's population in all of its cultural variation and economic spatial distributions. This planning element further explicates the importance of planning e-commerce and e-business initiatives as sub-elements of a much more comprehensive whole, that is, a whole that goes beyond IT, and that encompasses and addresses the needs of the area's people whether or not they are tele-immersed.

Timing
In this era of accelerating technological and organizational complexity timing is everything. The issue of timing in e-commerce development for urban and regional areas is a multifaceted issue. Currently, it is not too late to plan e-commerce area-development strategies. Indeed, there may be some value in implementing e-commerce strategies some time after other areas have pioneered e-commerce programs. By learning what has worked and what has worked less well, it may be possible to leap frog a bit. Thus, the importance of analyzing the strategies and results of others can be invaluable.

From an area-development perspective, the often touted early bellwether Silicon Valley area of the southern San Francisco Bay area demonstrates many of the problems that a relatively unplanned urban technology center and multicentric area can produce. These problems there have included: traffic congestion, environmental degradation, excessive commuting distances, homelessness, low housing inventories, and high-priced housing.

In contrast, an early bellwether for planned urban technology center development is Singapore. As early as 1981, the government of Singapore had put in place a program for computerization of its civil service. This represented the initiation of a formal policy of embracing IT as a major pillar of its national development. This policy direction has been sustained and deepened from that time until the present. Building on the early and proven foundation of IT-driven community development, Singapore recently embraced e-commerce planning. IT has been included as part of the country's new InfoComm objectives. The Singapore e-commerce blueprint master plan may be examined at www. ida.gov.sg. Given all of the infrastructural investment and IT organizational and planning experience that has formed a solid foundation, Singapore can be expected to be relatively successful in its e-commerce innovations and applications. Most recently, Singapore leadership has turned its vision for the new digital economy to better serve its citizens and businesses by outlining the strategic thrusts of e-government.

Spatial Organization
Empirically, cyberspace has changed our collective perception of earth space. Geographer David Newman has written,

> The McDonaldization of the world's landscapes allows my Bedouin neighborhoods to order a burger and fries and take them back to a shanty town encampment which is still fighting to get a paved road. The globalization thesis is both discipline and culture specific.

Professor Newman sees borders as changing and flexible. 'But we should not be naïve or deterministic in automatically assuming that a globalized world is a world without borders' (The Chronicle of Higher Education, 2000).

There are few spatial organizational models for localities to follow in planning for e-commerce as an important part of an urban area's and region's development strategy. Singapore, for example, is planning for the delivery of most public services online by 2001. Singapore ONE's master plan is a model for incorporating the entire country's set of households and firms into a fiber optic and cabled network system. This kind of full spatial and areal technological coverage is the ultimate in geographic delivery of Internet, video and multimedia services. This strategy is laid out in a master plan (Online.

Available HTTP: http://www.s-one.gov.sg/mainmenu.html). This approach can serve as a model for spatial planning and for the comprehensive multi-thematic planning that is required for contemporary IT and e-commerce planning (Tan & Subramaniam, 2000).

Singapore's action plan in support of e-commerce has a four-pronged approach. Two of these are spatial and geographical in nature: (a) developing e-commerce leadership in Singapore and the Southeast Asian region; and (b) e-commerce leadership in international policy development. The e-commerce master plan for Singapore includes several additional core thrusts that are spatial in nature. Also, the city-state has the goals to: become internationally linked; develop into an e-commerce hub; and harmonize cross-border e-commerce laws and policies (Infocomm Development Authority of Singapore, 2000).

Conceptually, the recency of e-commerce, to date, has produced spotty attention from the research and policy communities. In particular, in the first generation of e-commerce scholarship and news coverage, the locational and spatial organizational aspects of this emergent social and economic dimension barely have been mentioned. The exception, often heard, is the statement that real space and distance are nearly irrelevant factors of doing IT-based business nowadays.

Regional scientists, geographers, urban and regional planners, and some regional economists probably are best positioned to make research contributions to the collective understanding of the spatial aspects of e-commerce. By drawing on theories and concepts from the past and by inventing new conceptualizations, e-commerce spatial organization research path-breaking can begin; the results of which can be a fuller expansion of knowledge of the principal dimensions of e-commerce and related IT and communication technologies-influenced activities.

Some spatial organization and spatial synergies, in fact, have been identified from empirical analyses as critical elements in the planning and implementation of IT policies and programs. Recently, one form of spatial organization research was conducted in the context of IT communities development planning (Corey, 2000b). That paper included an analysis of the role of intelligent hubs, clusters, technology corridors and economic triangles as evolving forms of IT-based spatial organization.

Extending current IT spatial organizational forms into the future, a hierarchy of digital development has been identified. From micro-scale to global-scale, the hierarchy includes: cyber communities; intelligent corridors; cyber conurbations; intelligent megalopolitan development; national-scale information infrastructures; regional-scale information infrastructures; and the global-scale intelligent "ecumenopolis" (Doxiadis & Papaioannou, 1974). This initial attempt at identifying spatial organization in local-to-global IT development is merely one simple example of analyzing and forecasting spatial patterns driven by information and communication technologies. Similar or analogous spatial organizational analyses are needed for a more robust understanding of e-commerce.

The spatial aspects of e-commerce include spatial variations and disparities. Comparisons, in this context, might be made between boundaries identifying technological "have" from "have not" areas in virtual space and in real space. One might see this as a geography of inequity, and at various scales ranging from such patterns inside cities at neighborhood scales to large regional variations across the globe producing "information colonies". Such disparities exist, and they need measurement and mapping for full understanding. As e-trading and related e-commerce activities might become more geographically centralized in particular cities and within districts of cities, i.e. Silicon Alley in New York City, what patterns of hubs and hub hierarchies emerge among these e-commerce geographies? The networks connecting these hubs are conduits of information flows that also represent different levels and hierarchies. To what extent do bandwidth and response time play a role in e-commerce spatial organization?

What is the role of boundaries and borders in e-commerce? Some perceive cyberspace as without boundaries, yet jurisdictional borders do, in fact, play a role in political space, and therefore in real space. The current debate in the United States on how to tax the sale of goods bought over the Internet has raised these issues to high-profile discussions among inter-governmental officials and business leaders. The spatial organization of regulation, taxation, and enforcement of law in e-commerce needs the research attention of regional scientists and political geographers.

Each of these spatial organizational examples may lend themselves to the *geometric approach* of seeking patterns among e-commerce activities as they are analyzed to conform to points, areas, lines, flows, shapes, distance, direction, agglomeration and so on. These variations over space – as well as over time – probably are the fundamental conceptual building blocks for beginning the systematic identification of the spatial organization of e-commerce. This challenge needs attention from the community of regional science researchers and urban and regional planners. Such attention will serve to advance the state of knowledge of geography and regional science; but more importantly, such attention should serve to make a contribution to a better operational understanding of the new society and the new economy of the information age and the knowledge age.

Research and Evaluation

It is important for the planners of e-commerce development at the urban area and regional levels to construct an external-environment scanning system for research and intelligence gathering. The taxonomy to be used for such monitoring should be derived from the realities and needs of the locality, and the regional and nation of which it is a part.

In addition to the planning elements used and developed above for our purposes here, we have found it useful also to collect and organize trend information according to other dimensions. These might include: demographics as in the use and users of e-commerce; examples and cases of local applications i.e. sub-national in scale; and by the various major thematic sectors of society, e.g. retailing, travel, broadcasting, digital divide, etc. National geographic areas, e.g. Japan, India, Brazil, New Zealand, etc., is yet another useful category to track so as to be able to make systematic international comparisons across political economies and policy approaches and to derive benchmarks and best practices for contextual e-commerce development.

Given the dynamism and rapid pace of e-business it is essential that such tracking be conducted and sustained. There are numerous ways to organize to do this. One of the lower-cost and immediate ways to begin the exogenous ecommerce research, monitoring and evaluation function is to subscribe – selectively – to relevant listservs. In the section on Electronic Resources that follows, such a selection is offered as an aide in initiating the tracking and local- tailoring process. A selection of Web sites also is offered; these should be bookmarked and routinely monitored and supplemented. A particularly valuable Web site for tracking e-commerce trends is the "Intelligence Store," which is operated by The Standard. See http://www.thestandard.com/research/store.

Research partnerships with other organizations with comparable needs and complementary interests should be considered. For instance, local research collaborations might be formed with a combination of local research and educational institutions from government, the for-profit sector and its associations, e.g. chamber of commerce, non-governmental organizations, and tertiary education institutions and universities. In the latter case, for example, the locality needs the research and evaluation to be done, and students and faculty need to learn and to teach such skills and designs; the basis for a reciprocal and beneficial relationship therefore may exist.

Research partnerships that are extra-local also should be explored and considered. By use of the Web, even global, as well as regional networks can be tapped. The Electronic Space Project is an example of a global network of researchers, policy planners, and private sector representatives who are devoted to understanding the dynamics of IT in society, economy, policy and spatial organization, among other themes. The Electronic Space Project is sponsored by Michigan State University, and since 1994 it has hosted an annual workshop at various locations around the world. See the Electronic Space Web site at http://www.ssc.msu.edu/ ~ espace for follow up.

Another means of staying abreast of e-commerce developments and planning based on future trends, is to attend some of the now-numerous e-commerce, e-business and cybersociety conferences and meetings that are being offered. These are being held all over the world at local and regional levels; e.g. "Virtual Society? Get Real?" Conference, May 4–5, 2000, Hertfordshire, England, and The Realities of E-commerce Symposium, November 11, 1999, London. Such conferences can enable the tracking of contemporary issues and topics, and they permit the identification of some of the leading thinkers and doers in e-commerce and related IT and socio-economic-policy-spatial interactions. Such exposure can lead to networking and consultative relationships for the locality.

The relative ease of access and the availability of the Internet enables the use of survey methods and futures analysis techniques with greater speed and less cost than ever before. For example, InsightExpress.com conducts most Web-based surveys at modest cost (Online: Available HTTP: http://InsightExpress.com). Or, an e-mail design can be used to network with the appropriate contact in e-commerce-successful cities and regions and use a modified delphi approach, i.e. a one-to-many and many-to-many approach, to identify innovative and feasible solutions to e-business issues and problems. See askme.com for a one-to-one approach to solutions.

E-Commerce Primer Electronic Resources

Research and evaluation are core to the effective evolution of e-commerce in the planning and development of urban areas and regions. This allows for both the monitoring of e-commerce initiatives and the futures-scanning of the macro and exogenous e-commerce forces, so as to be contemporary and able to reformat and calibrate plans to maximize development potential.

One way to stay abreast, and even ahead, of e-commerce developments, is to monitor and systematically research technology and business trends and forecasts. A relatively inexpensive and rapid means of exploiting e-commerce lessons and innovation potential is to regularly scan, learn from elsewhere, and to tailor selected findings to the local urban area and region, the most appropriate uses of e-commerce. Such findings should be used for context and to assess progress on the locality's e-commerce initiatives.

Table 1 lists a selection of Web sites, e-mail services and listservs that should be useful in devising e-commerce strategies for one's urban area and region. This list of resources is merely a sampling. It is exemplary only. It is not intended to be comprehensive or exhaustive. The list is organized by the principal planning elements that were derived from international comparative IT-policy analyses (Corey, 1998). The list may be useful to policy planners and development planners as they grapple with the relative unknowns and ambiguities of e-commerce.

The selection of electronic information resources is overlapping and often multifaceted. For example, the resources under the Vision and Leadership planning element are useful for monitoring and understanding several of the other planning elements. The same is true for most of the other planning elements.

Other dimensions may be added to complement the basic e-commerce planning elements. The table lists "demographics," that can include genera- tional and life-span statistics and trends. For example, Japan's aging population is an important variable for understanding that nation's use of e-commerce; for purposes of leaving no one behind, it is critical to track IT accessibility and e- commerce use so as to be able to identify the "haves" and the "have nots," or the severity of the technological "digital divide," both internationally and within countries. The divide between the developing world and the developed world is of particular concern globally.

A "must" component of the Research and Evaluation planning element is the conduct of forecasts and futures analyses. It is important that trends and anticipated developments be factored into urban area and regional e-commerce leadership, visioning and planning. Several of the electronic resources in the following table are suggestive of ways that "futuring" and "futures scanning" might be implemented and routinized as part of a locality's strategic planning for e-commerce development.

CONCLUSION

One of the cornerstones of IT and e-commerce is the rapid and transformational change that has taken place over such a short period of recent history. The use of e-commerce can be expected to become more popular in the future. The real questions are how many, what kind, and where e-commerce transactions will occur. Another factor influencing the growth of e-commerce is the type of legislation that will evolve governing e-trading in each part of the world. A

Table 1.   Electronic Resources for Researching and Evaluating Ecommerce.

Planning Elements

Vision and leadership
- Online: Available e-mail listserv: townsnda@yahoo.com
- Online: Available HTTP and e-mail listserv: http://www.unn.ac.uk/cybersociety
- Online: Available HTTP: http://www.brunel.ac.uk/research/virtsoc/intro.htm
- Online: Available HTTP: http://www.thestandard.com
- Online. Available HTTP: http://www.internet.com
- Online: Available WWW: www.benton.org/News

Modern infrastructure
- Online: Available WWW: www.wired.com
- Online: Available HTTP: http://www.nandotimes.com
- Online: Available WWW: http://www.techweb.com
- Online: Available WWW: http://news.cnet.com
- Online: Available HTTP: http://www.wow-com.com

Regulatory environment
- Online: Available email listserv: filter-editor@cyber.law.harvard.edu
- Online: Available HTTP: http://www.epic.org

Human resources and training
- Online: Available HTTP: http://chronicle.com
- Online: Available HTTP: http://www.fathom.com
- Online: Available email listserv: notices@eto.org.uk

Organizational dynamics
- Online: Available HTTP: http://www.bestpractices.org
- Online: Available HTTP: http://www.unesco.org
- Online: Available HTTP: http://www.planmaker.com/about-btp.html
- Online: Available e-mail listserv: subsigno@orion.cpwebmedia.com
- Online: Available HTTP and e-mail listserv: http://www.kmworld.com
- Online: Available HTTP: http://www.govexec.com
- Online: Available WWW: www.cisco.com/warp/public/750/indicator/quiz.html

Cultural and political economy
- Online: Available HTTP: http://babelfish.altavista.digital.com/cgi-bin/translate?
- Online: Available HTTP: http://www.go.com
- Online: Available HTTP: http://slate.msn.com
- Online: Available HTTP: http://otal.umd.edu/ ~ rccs/newplate.html

Timing
- Online: Available e-mail listserv: cyber-society-live@mailbase@unn.ac.uk
- Online: Available e-mail listserv: IWNews@iwnews.iw.com

Table 1. Continued.

Planning Elements

Spatial organization
- Online: Available HTTP: http://cyberatlas.internet.com
- Online: Available e-mail listserv: listsupport@internet.com
- Online: Available HTTP: http://geography.about.com
- Online: Available HTTP: http://www.informationcity.org/telecom-cities
- Online: Available HTTP: http://www.cybergeography.org
- Online: Available HTTP: http://www.ssc.msu.edu/ ~ espace
- Online: Available WWW: www.geoplace.com
- Online: Available HTTP: http://novica.com

Research and evaluation
- Online: Available HTTP: http://www.thestandard.com/research/store
- Online: Available HTTP: http://firstmonday.org
- Online: Available HTTP: http://www.zdnet.com/e. . . /resources
- Online: Available HTTP: http://InsightExpress.com
- Online: Available HTTP: http://www.nsol.com/statistics
- Online: Available HTTP: http://www.askme.com
- Online: Available e-mail listserv: futurist-update@wfs.org
- Online: Available WWW: www.gwforecast.gwu.edu
- Online: Available e-mail: megaphone@zdemail.zdlists.com
- Online: Available HTTP: http://cyberatlas.internet.com

Other Dimensions

Demographics
- Online: Available HTTP: http://www.nua.ie/surveys
- Online: Available WWW: www.snowball.com
- Online: Available HTTP: http://www.aarp.org
- Online: Available HTTP: http://www.isoc.org

Local applications
- Online: Available HTTP: http://www.ci.san-carlos.ca.us
- Online: Available HTTP: http://www.fairfaxcountyeda.org

Sectors
- Online: Available WWW: www.ebusinessforum.com
- Online: Available HTTP: http://www.fedsources.com
- Online. Available HTTP: http://worldbank.org

third factor is the rate of e-commerce growth that will occur in the developing nations – will there be a rapid transition between the infancy and maturity stages or will the change occur more slowly? Also, how profitable will e-commerce enterprises be?

In the future it is expected that e-commerce will expand beyond the current heavy retail activity into other sectors of the global economy such as manufacturing and wholesaling. Clearly there should be cost savings in doing business over the Internet if distribution and service networks can be designed effectively. The impact of e-commerce will change the role of the retailer dramatically; the retailers who are unwilling to adapt to e-commerce will find it more difficult to compete in the marketplace. Government also is active in e-commerce, especially at the information level. With e-commerce, the role of marketing could be reversed; instead of sellers taking the initiative to locate target customers, the potential buyers assume the initiative to contact target sellers. The full impact of this phenomenon has yet to be examined.

The spatial implications of e-commerce are enormous. Research in this area is needed. E-commerce may demand different models and different ways of thinking about location, distance, and agglomeration. E-commerce poses the challenge of becoming a new frontier in the way business is conducted, where it is conducted, and when it is conducted. The topic offers opportunities to pioneer new strategies and theories by economists, geographers, business persons, academics, and others.

In the Internet age, urban areas and regions around the globe have a unique advantage; they are local. Their leaders know their people, and the local society and local economy. So, in an era of globalization and concerns over homogenization of local cultures through music, movies and television, local area and regional leaders and opinion setters need to know what they want by way of e-commerce, and to pursue it. Strategic planning and the development of business plans, to enable the implementation of e-commerce initiatives locally, are imperative so as to be able to control their own futures as much as possible. Seeking to stay ahead of these powerful external global forces will require a great deal of local vision, focus and effort. From some of the local applications of e-commerce development planning cited above, e.g. Singapore and others, it is clear that visionary leadership, combined with intelligence-based effective planning at multiple levels can produce a difference, that is, a supportive e-commerce-development environment. The primer outlined above is suggestive of some of the key planning elements that can be helpful in realizing a locality's e-commerce goals. Tailoring the primer to the unique development requirements of the organizations and institutions of the urban area's and region's e-commerce vision is the challenge to realizing more successful development in the future.

REFERENCES

Ba, S., Whinston, A., & Zhang, H. (1999). Small Business in the Digital Economy: Digital Company of the Future. For Conference 'Understanding the Digital Economy: Data, Tools and Research'. Washington, D.C.: U.S. Department of Commerce.

Beck, R. (1999). Competition for Cybershoppers on Rise. *Bakersfield Californian*, E1.

Beck, R. (2000). E-tailers Attempt to Put a Wrap on Missed, Late Delivery Dilemma. *Bakersfield Californian*.

Berke, R. (2000). What Are You Afraid Of? A Hidden Issue Emerges. *The New York Times*. 1 and 20 week.

Business Week (1999). Asia's Net Snoops are Wasting Their Time. *Business Week*, 64.

Business Week (2000). Wireless in Cyberspace. *Business Week*, Asian Edition.

Choi, S., Stahl, D., & Whinston, A. (1997). *The Economics of Electronic Commerce*. New York: Macmillan Technical Publishing.

Cisco (2000). *Cisco Internet Quotient Test*.
Online: Available WWW: www.cisco.com/warp/public/750/indicator/quiz.html

Clausing, J. (2000). Digital Economy Has Arrived, Commerce Department Says. *The New York Times*.
Online: Available HTTP: http://www.nytimes.co. . . 00/06/cyber/capital/06capital.html

Clemente, P. (1998). *The State of the Net*. New York: McGraw-Hill, Inc.

Commerce Net/Nielsen Media Research Internet Demographic Survey (1999). Complete survey results are
Online: Available HTTP: http://www.commerce.net/research via GIDEON, the Web-based program that allows users to analyze demographic data.

Corey, K. (1998). Information Technology and Telecommunications Policies in Southeast Asian Development: Cases in Vision and Leadership. In: V. Savage, L. Kong & W. Neville (Eds), *The Naga Awakens: Growth and Change in Southeast Asia* (pp. 145–200). Singapore: Times Academic Press.

Corey, K. (2000a). Electronic Space: Creating Cyber Communities in Southeast Asia and the U.S. In: M. Wilson & K. Corey (Eds), *Information Tectonics: Space, Place and Technology in an Electronic Age* (pp. 135–164). Chichester: John Wiley & Sons.

Corey, K. E. (2000b). Intelligent Corridors: Outcomes of Electronic Space Policies. *Journal of Urban Technology* (Forthcoming).

David, P. (1999). Digital Technology and the Productivity Paradox: After Ten Years, What Has Been Learned? For Conference 'Understanding the Digital Economy: Data, Tools and Research'. Washington, D.C.: U.S. Department of Commerce.

Davison, J. (2000). Internet Whizz Kids Backed by Rich Parents. *The Independent*.
Online: Available E-mail: j.armitage@technologica.demon.co.uk

Dolven, B. (2000). What's in a Name? *Far Eastern Economic Review, 163*(7), 53.

Doxiadis, C. A., & Papaioannou, J. (1974). *Ecumenopolis: The Inevitable City of the Future*. New York: W. W. Norton & Company.

DSA Analytics (1999). The Internet User and Online Commerce in Japan, 1999. Executive Summary. DSA Analytics.
Online: Available HTTP: http://www.dsasiagroup.com

Forrester Research (1999). European Retail Set to Spiral. *The Forrester Brief.*
      Online: Available HTTP: http://www.forrester.com
Fulford, B. (2000). Upwardly Mobile. *Forbes.com.*
      Online: Available HTTP: http://www.forbes.com/forbesglobal/00/0207/0303059a.htm
Goldman, A. (1999). E-Commerce Gets an F Without the 'D' Word. *Los Angeles Times*, C1.
Goldman, A. (1999). Battle for Web Customers Pits Retailer Against Manufacturer. *Los Angeles Times.*
Greenstein, S. (1999). Framing Empirical Research on the Evolving Structure of Commercial Internet Markets. Conference for 'Understanding the Digital Economy: Data, Tools, and Research'. Washington, D.C.: U.S. Department of Commerce.
Gurmukh G., Pastore, D., & LaPorte, S. (1999). *The Emerging Digital Economy II.* Washington, D.C.: U.S. Department of Commerce.
Halal, W. (2000). The Top 10 Emerging Technologies. *The Futurist* Special Report, *34*(4), 1–10.
Halimi, S. (2000). The Cyberdamned.
      Online: Available E-mail: j.armitage@technologica.demon.co.uk
Haltiwanger, J., & Jarmin, R. (1999). *Measuring the Digital Economy.* Washington, D.C.: Center for Economic Studies, U.S. Bureau of the Census.
Hoffman, D., & Novak, T. (1999). The Evolution of the Digital Divide: Examining the Relationship of Race to Internet Access and Usage Over Time. Conference for 'Understanding the Digital Economy: Data, Tools and Research'. Washington, D.C.: U.S. Department of Commerce.
Hudson, H. (1999). Access to the Digital Economy: Issues in Rural and Developing Regions. Conference for "Understanding the Digital Economy: Data, Tools and Research". Washington, D.C.: U.S. Department of Commerce.
Infocomm Development Authority of Singapore (2000). The Ecommerce Blueprint. *Ideas, 1,* 29–34.
ISP-Planet Staff (2000). Wireless to Outstrip Wired Net Access.
      Online: E-mail: townsnda@yahoo.com
Kettmann, S. (2000). Wireless Sparks Euros at CeBIT. *Wired News.*
      Online: Available HTTP: http://www.wired.com/news/print/0,1294,34475,00.html
Kling, R., & Lamb, R. (1999). IT and Organizational Change in Digital Economies: A Socio-Technical Approach. Conference for 'Understanding the Digital Economy: Data, Tools and Research'. Washington, D.C.: U.S. Department of Commerce.
Kobrin, S., & Johnson, E. (1999). *We Know All About You: Personal Privacy in the Information Age.* Philadelphia: The Wharton School, University of Pennsylvania.
Lowenhaupt, T. (1999). Watch the Commercial or I'll Let the Kid Die!
      Online: Available E-mail: tom@ix.netcom.com
Lyons, M. (1999). Wake up to Ecommerce Opportunity. *The Irish Times*, City Edition, 58.
Margherio, L. (1999). *The Emerging Digital Economy.* Washington, D.C.: U.S. Department of Commerce.
McNulty, S. (2000). Mahathir Finds New Demon in E-Business. *Financial Times, 3.*
Melnicoff, R. (1999). The eEconomy: It's later than you think. *Outlook 1999, 21.* Andersen Consulting.
Mitchell, H. (2000). *Unbundling the Local Loop.*
      Online: Available E-mail: notices@eto.org.uk
Moulton, B. (1999). *GDP and the Digital Economy: Keeping Up With the Changes.* Washington, D.C.: Bureau of Economic Analysis, U.S. Department of Commerce.

Murphy, K. (2000). Compromise on Net Taxes Would Lift Ban in 2006. *Internet World News*, 2(36), 4–5.
Nandotimes (2000). *Web Woos Japanese Shoppers, Survey Shows*.
    Online: Available HTTP: http://www.nandotimes.com/technolo . . .
    2554–500222849–501063962–0,00.html
Norman, P. (2000). EU E-Economy Forum Aims to Speed Laws. *Financial Times, 8*.
Nua Internet Surveys. Online: Available HTTP: http://www.nua.ie
Olsen, S. (1999). Top Web Sites Compromise Privacy. *CNET News.com*.
    Online: Available HTTP: http://cnet.com/news/o-1007–2 . . . 0309.html?
Orlikowski, W. (1999). *The Truth is Not Out There: An Enacted View of the 'Digital Economy'*.
    Cambridge, Massachusetts: Sloan School of Management, Massachusetts Institute of Technology.
Piller, C. (2000). Truly a Worldwide Web. *Nandotimes*.
    Online: Available HTTP: http://www.nandotimes.com/technolo . . .
    2565–500222865–501063856–0,00.html
Rupley, S. (2000). Get Ready for Mobile E-Commerce. *E-Business*.
    Online: Available HTTP: http://www.zdnet.com/e . . . ess/stories/0,5918,2429575,00.html
Sanger, D. (2000). On the Campaign Trail, Whistling Past the New Economy. *The New York Times*, 1 and 4 week.
Society for International Development (1999). *SID Newsletter, 6*.
Steinberg, J. (2000). Boola, Boola: E-Commerce Comes to The Quad. *The New York Times*, 1 and 4 week.
Suellentrop, C. (2000). Passive Activism. *Slate.com*.
    Online: Available HTTP: http://slate.msn.com/netelection/entries/00–02–23–75737.asp
Tan, L., & Subramaniam, R. (2000). Wiring Up the Island State. *Science, 288*, 621–623.
The Chronicle of Higher Education (2000). Why Disciplines Split on Globalization. *The Chronicle of Higher Education*.
    Online: Available E-mail: daily@chronicle.com
The Economist (2000). Tearaway Tesco. *The Economist, 354*(8156), 62.
The Straits Times (1999). Watch Out for Five E-Commerce Trends. *The Straits Times, 51*.
Thomas, J. (2000). The Campaign. *Slate.com*.
    Online: Available HTTP: http://slate.msn.com/netelection/entries/00–02015074973.asp
Time (2000). The Future of Technology. *Time, 155*(25), 62–116.
U.S. Department of Commerce (2000). *Digital Economy 2000*. Washington, D.C.: U.S. Department of Commerce.
U.S. Department of Commerce (1999). *The Emerging Digital Economy II*. Washington, D.C.: U.S. Department of Commerce: 15–16.
U.S.Web/CKS (1999). *Strategies for Growing Your Business Through E-commerce: Proven Techniques for Expanding Your Business with a Successful E-commerce Initiative*. San Francisco: U.S.Web/CKS.
Varian, H. (1999). *Market Structure in the Network Age*. Berkeley, California: University of California.
Whitener, R. (2000). *Monitoring E-mail and Formulation of Policy*.
    Online: Available E-mail: rwhitener@louky.org
Williams R. (2000). Social Learning in Multimedia (SLIM). *Final Report*.
    Online: Available HTTP: http://www.rcss.ed.ac.uk/research/slim.html
Wright, R. (2000). Will We Ever Log Off? *Time, 155*(7), 56–58.